TRANSACTIONS OF THE
ROYAL HISTORICAL SOCIETY

FIFTH SERIES
VOLUME 27

LONDON
OFFICES OF THE ROYAL HISTORICAL SOCIETY
UNIVERSITY COLLEGE LONDON, GOWER ST., WC1E 6BT
1977

ISBN 0 901050 38 5

Made and Printed in Great Britain by Butler & Tanner Ltd, Frome and London

CONTENTS

TRANSACTIONS OF THE
ROYAL HISTORICAL SOCIETY

URBAN DECLINE IN LATE MEDIEVAL ENGLAND

By Professor R. B. Dobson, M.A., D.Phil., F.R.Hist.S.

READ 6 FEBRUARY 1976

> 'For so moche as dyvers and many Howses Mesuages and Tenementis of Habitacions in the Townys of Notingham, Shrewesbury, Ludlowe, Brydgenorth, Quynborowe, Northampton and Gloucester nowe are and of long tyme have been in greate ruyne and decaye . . . specially in the chief stretes . . . desolate and void groundys, with pittys, sellers and vaultes lying open and uncovereyd, very peryllous for people to go by in the nyght without jeopardy of lyfe'.[1]

MORE than four centuries have passed since the famous preambles to the various Tudor acts for the re-edifying of English towns generalized with such unnerving confidence about the lamentable state of provincial urban communities in the early sixteenth century; but no historian today who has the temerity to walk through those still perilous streets can be under any illusion as to the continued hazards of such an expedition. Yet that this journey, despite its dangers and frustrations, deserves to be undertaken more frequently and more urgently than ever before seems very clear. Even the most optimistic historian must occasionally suffer some qualms at a situation in which the single most important issue in pre-industrial English urban history—the exact contribution of the late medieval and early modern town to the society and economy of the nation as a whole—seems to be becoming more rather than less mysterious with every detailed monograph and every new methodological problem. For here of course, much more in 1976 than in 1894, we are in the presence of one of those 'burning questions in which impetuous economists have outrun the historians, and have not found it premature to set in order by the help of accepted theories the obscure chaos of social history in the Middle Ages'.[2]

[1] *Statutes of the Realm* (London, 1810–28), iii, 531–32; cf. *ibid.*, pp. 127, 176–77, 768–69, 875, and the recent discussion of these statutes in G. R. Elton, *Reform and Renewal: Thomas Cromwell and the Common Weal* (Cambridge, 1973), pp. 106–09.

[2] A. S. Green, *Town Life in the Fifteenth Century* (London, 1894), i, p. xii. For the

It could, and indeed has, nevertheless been argued that the question of late medieval urban decline is in the last resort unanswerable. Characteristically wise in his time, F. W. Maitland was long ago 'far from thinking that any one history should be told of all our boroughs'; while as recently as last year it has been argued that 'the town as such, and possibly even the type of town, is not, beyond the most preliminary stage, a useful or appropriate object of social analysis'.[3] It is certainly already clear that the analytical problem which has tended to obsess the medieval historian more than any other, the definition and the categorization of the urban communities of provincial England, is never likely to lead to any positively illuminating general conclusion. Even the admirably pragmatic solution of 'three tiers of urban society' recently suggested for the early modern period rests so heavily on the criterion of numerical size that it can rarely be applied with confidence to a medieval England so notoriously devoid of reliable population statistics.[4] That said, it ought to be pointed out that the primary concern of this paper is the economic fortunes of those forty or so English towns, not including London, known to have had a tax-paying population of 1,000 or more at the time of the 1377 Poll Tax.[5] Such concentration on the major urban centres has its obvious dangers; and naturally 'not even the strictest stagnationist denies the growth of craft industry in the countryside'.[6] What remains profoundly uncertain is whether the development of that rural industry and such spectacular consequential successes as those of Totnes and Tiverton, Lavenham and Lewes should be interpreted as symptoms of general urban strength rather than of weakness. In the case of England's largest and oldest towns the problem can be posed at least a little

first, and still one of the best, attempts to reconcile what were already 'strangely conflicting opinions' on the fortunes of the later medieval English town, see W. Cunningham, *The Growth of English Industry and Commerce during the Early and Middle Ages* (Cambridge, 4th edn., 1905), pp. 369–80, 452–56, 506–21.

[3] F. W. Maitland, *Township and Borough* (Cambridge, 1898), p. 36; P. Abrams, 'Towns and economic growth: some theories and problems', *Towns and Economic Growth* (Proceedings of Past and Present Society, Annual Conference, 1975), p. 4.

[4] *Crisis and Order in English Towns, 1500–1700*, ed. P. Clark and P. Slack (London, 1972), pp. 4–5.

[5] J. C. Russell, *British Medieval Population* (Albuquerque, 1948), pp. 140–43. All but seven of these towns figure among the forty wealthiest urban contributors to the Lay Subsidy of 1334; and similarly all but seven (not the same seven) occur among the forty English towns most heavily assessed in the Tudor subsidies of the 1520s: see *The Lay Subsidy of 1334*, ed. R. E. Glasscock (London, 1975), *passim*; W. G. Hoskins, *Local History in England* (London, 1959), pp. 176–77; *A New Historical Geography of England*, ed. H. C. Darby (Cambridge, 1973), pp. 179–85, 241–43.

[6] R. H. Hilton, *The English Peasantry in the Later Middle Ages* (Oxford, 1975), pp. 37–38.

more simply. 'Sethen the makyng of which statute and ordinaunce', declared a statute of 1512 referring to a period almost two centuries earlier, 'many and the most partie of all the cities, bouroughes and townes corporate wythin this realme of Englonde be fallen in ruyne and decaye and not inhabited with marchauntes and men of such substaunce as they were at the tyme of makyng of the foreseid statute and ordinaunce'.[7] Is that melancholy judgement likely to be more right than wrong?

On Maitland's own familiar principle that all students of the medieval town must be prepared to think themselves 'back into a twilight',[8] it would in any case seem proper to preface any investigation of late medieval urban decline with the comments of those Tudor observers who first posed the problem for posterity. Familiar though so many of these lamentations are, their cumulative effect can leave one in no doubt of contemporary bewilderment at a society which had allegedly 'let fal into ruyn and dekey al theyr cytes, castelys, and townys'.[9] Undoubtedly a safer guide to social thinking than to social realities in the sixteenth century, such jeremiads themselves need to be placed as firmly in a historical context as the conditions they purport to describe. What they do not deserve is the fate of casual dismissal out of hand. Even polemical literature reveals its unintended secrets; and perhaps the most remarkable feature of the great Tudor debate on the nature of the Commonweal is the way in which 'the great plentie of povertie in all the cities great townes and other inferior market townes in England and Wales' is so rarely regarded as anything but self-evident.[10] Less dramatic but certainly unenthusiastic were the comments on provincial English towns made by the first Italians to leave on record théir impressions of this country. For experienced and no doubt blase travellers like these, not only was Canterbury, its cathedral apart, a town 'about which there seems to be nothing to be said'; but it could even be broadly asserted, in a particularly famous dismissal of 1496–97, that 'there are scarcely any towns of importance in the kingdom' except for London, Bristol and York.[11] Although so sweeping a judgement

[7] *Statutes of the Realm*, iii, 30.

[8] Maitland, *Township and Borough*, p. 11.

[9] *England in Henry VIII's Time: A Dialogue between Cardinal Pole and Lupset by Thomas Starkey*, ed. J. M. Cowper (Early English Text Society, Extra Series, xii, 1871), p. 93.

[10] Bodleian Library, Oxford, Jones MS. 17 (Thomas Lupton's proposals to ameliorate the conditions of the poor in London, York, Canterbury and Lincoln), fo 6; cf. W. R. D. Jones, *The Tudor Commonwealth, 1529–1559* (London, 1970), pp. 108–32.

[11] *A Relation, or rather a True Account, of the Island of England . . . about the Year 1500*, ed. C. A. Sneyd (Camden Society, xxxvii, 1847), p. 41; *cf. English Historical Documents*, iv, *1485–1558*, ed. C. H. Williams (London, 1967), pp. 188, 200.

was perhaps the product of a carefully cultivated ignorance, even Polydore Vergil, that Italian who must have known early sixteenth-century England better than most of its natives, combined conventional tributes to the more famous English cities with the rhetorical but probably considered view that the English 'do not so greatlie affecte citties as the commodious neareness of dales and brookes'.[12]

Needless to say, Polydore Vergil's elementary generalization pales into complete insignificance by comparison with the voluminous results of 'the Laboriouse Journey and Serche of Johan Leylande for Englandes Antiquitees'.[13] Naturally Leland was neither an impartial nor indeed an unemotional guide; and it may not be too fanciful to suggest that for him, as for Dr Johnson in the university city of St Andrews in 1773, the sight of a town 'pining in decay and struggling for life, fills the mind with mournful images and ineffectual wishes'.[14] However, Leland certainly did have an appreciative eye for a 'praty market' like Leeds, for 'the fair streates' of Exeter and even for the remarkable new 'bewty' of Birmingham; and it is precisely because he was such an observant as well as 'totally enflamed' traveller that one can never ignore his melancholy verdicts on those once prosperous towns, like Boston, Carlisle and Coventry, where 'the old glory and riches' had departed.[15] For Leland, and for those who came after him, it was within the smaller urban communities that physical decay was most immediately apparent. What the reader of the *Itinerary* is likely to remember most vividly are the sorrowful images of places which were no longer towns at all: Reculver in Kent, which 'at this time is but village like'; Hedon in the East Riding, with 'but a few botes'; and Brougham in Westmorland, 'now very bare, and very yll buylded: yet yt hathe bene some very notable thinge'.[16] No doubt, as befits the bible of the English local historian, Leland's *Itinerary* provides innumerable different texts to support a variety of different interpretations. What certainly needs no urging is that Leland not only encountered nu-

[12] *Polydore Vergil's English History from an Early Translation . . . containing the first eight books*, ed. H. Ellis (Camden Society, xxxvi, 1846), p. 4; *cf.* D. Hay, *Polydore Vergil* (Oxford, 1952), pp. 116, 121. Similarly, John Major paid due respects to the distinction of Coventry, Norwich and Bristol but seems to have been well aware of the decline of Lincoln ('of renown in old days') and of York ('In circuit it is great but not in population or in wealth'): *A History of Greater Britain . . . by John Major*, trans. and ed. by A. Constable (Scottish History Society, x, 1892), p. 22.

[13] *The Itinerary of John Leland in or about the years 1535–43*, ed. L. Toulmin Smith (London, 1907–10), i, p. xxxvii.

[14] *Johnson's Journey to the Western Islands of Scotland and Boswell's Journal of a Tour to the Hebrides*, ed. R. W. Chapman (Oxford, 1924), p. 8.

[15] *Itinerary of Ireland*, v, 39; i, 227–28; ii, 96–97; iv, 114, 181–82; v, 52–53; ii, 106–08.

[16] *Ibid.*, iv, 59; i, 61–62; v, 147.

merous examples of urban decay but was often prepared to explain that decay—usually as a consequence of the decline of cloth-making in the case of the larger towns, and of the reduction or abolition of markets in the case of their smaller counterparts—in terms still acceptable to the modern local historian.[17]

From the pages of Leland's *Itinerary* even more specific themes unmistakably emerge. Most obvious and familiar of these is the decay of the urban castle, a phenomenon for which there is also copious documentary evidence from most parts of the country. All allowances made for Leland's obsessive interest in the ruined castle and also for the obvious exceptions, like Carlisle, Durham and Pontefract, which prove the rule, there can be no reasonable doubt that from Richmond to Leicester and from Hereford to Southampton most of the great urban fortresses of medieval England now 'tendith towards ruine'.[18] At Gloucester the king's castle had been positively 'thrown down' by 1489; at Bristol 'the great hall and other elegant buildings designed for the reception of royalty were crumbling into ruin'; and even at York what had once been the most important centre of royal authority in the north never recovered from the 'takyng doune of youre Castell thar by King Richard [III]', a monarch who had originally intended to undertake its reconstruction.[19] Better interpreted as a symptom of governmental financial stringency than of increased royal confidence in either gunpowder or the prospects for internal peace, the gradual dilapidation of the urban castle towards the end of the middle ages must naturally be interpreted within the context of the decay of late medieval English fortifications as a whole. Nevertheless it is unlikely to have been a matter of complete indifference to the citizens of the adjacent town: at the least it was often alleged to have helped to promote that much lamented development, perhaps only partly reversed during the course of the sixteenth century, whereby 'Every gentylman flyth into the cuntrey. Few that inhabyt cytes or townys'.[20] A much more

[17] 'What we do know is that, by about 1640, the 1,500 or 2,000 medieval markets of England had shrunk to fewer than 800': A. Everitt, *New Avenues in English Local History* (Leicester, 1970) p. 10. For an especially illuminating regional study of this decline see D. M. Palliser and A. C. Pinnock, 'The markets of medieval Staffordshire', *North Staffordshire Journal of Field Studies*, 11 (1971), pp. 49–59.

[18] *Itinerary of Leland*, i, 7, 15; ii, 64, 105; iv, 25; v, 19.

[19] *Calendar of Patent Rolls, 1485–94* (London, 1914), p. 298; M. D. Lobel and E. M. Carus-Wilson, 'Bristol' (*Atlas of Historic Towns*, ed. M. D. Lobel, ii, London, 1975), p. 13; York City Archives, House Book 6, fo 83; *An Inventory of the Historical Monuments in the City of York*, ii: *The Defences* (Royal Commission on Historical Monuments, 1972), pp. 19, 67.

[20] *Dialogue between Pole and Lupset*, p. 93. It needs no urging that a high proportion of successful sixteenth-century merchants were, like their medieval predecessors, of gentry origin; but the direct evidence for the alleged 'return to the towns'

direct index of an urban corporation's economic fortunes and financial priorities was however likely to be afforded by the state of its own defences, its walls and gates.

Now that medieval historians have at last been forcibly reminded that few English towns 'of importance were without walls by the end of the fifteenth century', they can be under no doubt that capital expenditure on the maintenance and repair of those walls was one of the most common and most burdensome financial commitments undertaken by the burgesses of the later middle ages. Quite how voluntary and sustained a commitment that was remains a much more open question: perhaps the greatest single revelation to emerge from Dr Hilary Turner's preliminary exploration of the subject is the extent to which the initiatives in this field derived from the royal government rather than from within the cities and towns themselves.[21] More generally, it is now clear that the golden age for the building of stone walls around medieval towns lay in the late thirteenth and early fourteenth centuries. Of the hundred or so walled towns of medieval England, apparently only the defences of Alnwick can be confidently dated, in their entirety, to the period after 1400.[22] How many towns would have been able to preserve substantial sections of their walls into the early Tudor period without the national government's willingness to supplement its local murage grants with remissions of the fee-farm and assignments on the national customs revenues is bound to be a debatable matter; but, as it was, several smaller towns, like Richmond and Warwick, gradually lost their defences altogether and even more substantial urban communities found the financial strains of maintaining their walls almost insupportable.[23] In 1460 the walls on the landward side of Southampton

---

of the Tudor gentry themselves still seems much less than conclusive: see, for example, W. T. MacCaffrey, *Exeter, 1540–1640, The Growth of an English County Town* (Cambridge, Mass., 1958), pp. 247–63; A. D. Dyer, *The City of Worcester in the Sixteenth Century* (Leicester, 1973), pp. 181–88; C. Platt, *The English Medieval Town* (London, 1976), pp. 188–90.

[21] H. L. Turner, *Town Defences in England and Wales* (London, 1971), pp. 13–16, 25, 30–44, 90–91; M. W. Barley, 'Town defences in England and Wales after 1066', *The Plans and Topography of Medieval Towns in England and Wales*, ed. M. W. Barley (Council for British Archaeology, Research Report No. 14, 1976) pp. 57–71.

[22] G. Tate, *The History of the Borough, Castle and Barony of Alnwick* (Alnwick, 1866–69), pp. 238–41. The stone wall of Coventry is perhaps the major exception to prove the rule: built at erratic intervals during the long period from 1356 to 1534, 'it is perhaps remarkable that the campaign was eventually completed' (Barley, 'Town Defences', p. 68; E. Gooder, *Coventry's Town Wall* (Coventry and North Warwickshire History Pamphlet, No. 4), 1971, pp. 3–37).

[23] *E.g. Calendar of Patent Rolls 1377–81* (London, 1895), p. 76; *Itinerary of Leland*, i, 79; v, 147; M. W. Barley and I. F. Straw, 'Nottingham' (*Atlas of Historic Towns*, i, 1969), p. 5; *Victoria History of the County of Warwick*, viii (London, 1969), p. 420.

were 'so feble that they may not resiste ayenst any gonnes shotte, and so thynne that no man may well stond upon them to make eny resistance or defence'; by 1486 the walls of Chester were also alleged to have fallen into ruin and decay; while for the modern visitor to York a comparison between the handsome limestone ashlar Walmgate Bar and barbican of the fourteenth century and the prosaically humble brick 'Red Tower' built three hundred yards away in the early 1490s conveys its own dispiriting message.[24] On the increasingly popular assumption that medieval town walls should be interpreted as conscious symbols of municipal independence and civic pride, the condition of those walls in the late fifteenth century is often bound to raise disquieting questions about the state of that independence and of that pride at the end of the middle ages.

A much simpler and less complicated physical manifestation of these qualities in the medieval urban community is likely to be afforded by municipal buildings proper, and above all by a borough's Common or Guild Hall. It may well be that the history of the town halls of medieval England can never be written, partly because so few of them survive intact and partly because the medieval archives of individual towns, in this case even those of London, usually preserve such fragmentary and inadequate references to their very existence before the late fourteenth century. Nevertheless it seems worth emphasizing that most of the evidence at present available points to the first fifty or sixty years of the fifteenth century as a time of a veritable boom in the building or rebuilding of town halls within the largest England boroughs, a boom which was apparently over by the 1470s.[25] The correct interpretation of this fashionable phenomenon, especially as so little is usually known about the sources of revenue from which these guildhalls were financed, is once again an exceptionally delicate matter; but it seems impossible not to see the new town halls of the early fifteenth century as the material expression of that late medieval transition from urban community to urban corporation which caused Maitland to characterize the

[24] C. Platt, *Medieval Southampton* (London, 1973), p. 172; K. P. Wilson, 'The port of Chester in the fifteenth century', *Transactions of the Historic Society of Lancashire and Cheshire,* cxvii (1966), p. 2; T. P. Cooper, *York: The Story of its Walls, Bars and Castles* (London, 1904), pp. 291–304, 328–30; *Inventory of Historical Monuments in York, The Defences*, pp. 19–20, 139–40, 142–49.

[25] *E.g.* at Cambridge, Canterbury, Coventry, Hull, Ipswich, King's Lynn and Norwich as well as York and London: see J. Harvey, *English Medieval Architects* (London, 1954), pp. 260, 299; M. D. Lobel, 'Cambridge' (*Atlas of Historic Towns*, ii), pp. 15–16; *V.C.H., Warwickshire,* viii (1969), pp. 141–42; *V.C.H., Yorkshire, East Riding*, i (1969), p. 398; V. Parker, *The Making of King's Lynn* (London, 1971), pp. 140–48; J. Campbell, 'Norwich' (*Atlas of Historic Towns,* ii), p. 15.

fourteenth century as 'the golden age of the boroughs'.[26] Such a judgement can still afford to stand, provided that the achievement of corporate or (for a select dozen late medieval towns) county status is not automatically interpreted as a consequence of economic confidence on the part of mayors, bailiffs and aldermen. At Lincoln, for example, the royal creation of a 'county of the city' in 1409 was evidently desired as a political cure for economic ills. Not surprisingly the cure in this and several other cases proved inefficacious. As the Lincoln citizens' inability to rebuild the Guildhall they had pulled down in the late fourteenth century demonstrates, corporate ambitions could easily outstrip economic resources.[27] By definition the building of a municipal common hall was an enterprise likely to be restricted to those larger towns with the financial means to convert their corporate ambitions into stone and mortar; and after the completion of the stone fabric of York's Guildhall in the late 1450s it becomes increasingly difficult to find many examples of urban communities which decided that heavy expenditure on such a cause was either justifiable or indeed economically practicable.[28]

But 'What do the perpendicular churches prove?' Nearly forty years since that familiar problem was posed it is not a little remarkable that the historian's response remains so tentative. Professor Postan's own reply to his own question, that 'their architectural excellence has nothing to do with either the growth or the decline of English industry, agriculture or trade' has never commended itself to all; and despite the additional and often unconvincing complications more recently introduced by the advocates of a coincidence between 'hard times' and periods of heavy investment in art and architecture, there still remains room for William Cunningham's simpler view: 'there is hardly any token of general prosperity on which we may rely with more confidence than the fact that many people are able and willing to expend money in building'.[29] It might be suggested that the real problem now facing the late medieval urban historian is less the general validity of that principle than the

[26] Maitland, *Township and Borough*, p. 85; *cf.* M. Weinbaum, *The Incorporation of Boroughs* (Manchester, 1937), pp. 45–96.

[27] *Calendar of Close Rolls 1389–92* (London, 1922), p. 135; J. W. F. Hill, *Medieval Lincoln* (Cambridge, 1948), pp. 254, 270–71.

[28] Of the various exceptions, perhaps the most significant is the Guildhall at Exeter which was substantially rebuilt from a ruinous state in 1468, on the eve (as Professor Joyce Youings kindly informs me) of that late fifteenth-century period of expansion 'which made Exeter one of the wealthiest and most populous cities in the land': E. M. Carus-Wilson, *The Expansion of Exeter at the Close of the Middle Ages* (University of Exeter, 1963), p. 31.

[29] M. M. Postan, *Essays on Medieval Agriculture and General Problems of the Medieval Economy* (Cambridge, 1973), p. 46; Cunningham, *Growth of English Industry and Commerce*, p. 294.

practical difficulties of applying it. Most of those difficulties are obvious enough: it is, for instance, dangerously easy to generalize on the basis of the fifteenth-century churches which survive, at the expense not only of those earlier medieval churches which preceded them but of those which were dismantled or reconstructed in a later age. At a more practical level, the perpendicular churches of medieval England are often notoriously difficult to date at all precisely. More serious still is our ignorance of who actually paid for the rebuilding and refurbishing of most late medieval parish churches. Failure to at least consider that question has often led to the making of many unjustified assumptions about the wealth of particular provincial towns: it apparently still needs to be pointed out—to take a very special case—that the multiplication of academic colleges in fourteenth- and fifteenth-century Oxford and Cambridge is so far from supporting a thesis of urban prosperity that it could be seen by the burgesses of both those two university towns as an objectionable symptom of their own decay.[30]

For these and many other reasons, the time has certainly not yet come to generalize with confidence as to the economic and social implications of late medieval ecclesiastical building in the English town. However, the recent intensive if highly localized researches of the Royal Commission on Historical Monuments have done little as yet to rebut the traditional view that the third quarter of the fifteenth century was a period of comparative building inactivity.[31] By the 1450s the fabric of the four largest urban parish churches of medieval England, Boston, Yarmouth, Hull and St Michael's Coventry, seems to have been substantially complete; and it is of course to Lavenham and Long Melford, to Cullompton and Cirencester rather than to the older corporate English towns that one must turn to see the best urban or quasi-urban examples of the great *floraison* of late Perpendicular Gothic. So crude and perhaps over-familiar a contrast certainly admits of several exceptions, most obviously at Norwich, and tends to ignore the gradual processes of piecemeal accretion which characterize the architectural history of

[30] 'Parliamentary Petitions relating to Oxford', ed. L. Toulmin Smith, *Collectanea* iii (Oxford Historical Society, xxxii, 1896), pp. 139–59; H. E. Salter, *Medieval Oxford* (Oxford Historical Society, 1936), pp. 87–89; R. H. C. Davis, 'The Ford, the River and the City', *Oxoniensia*, xxxviii (1973), pp. 258–68; *Rotuli Parliamentorum* (Record Commission, 1783), iii, 185, 254, 260, 515; v, 432; vi, 436; M. D. Lobel, 'Cambridge' (*Atlas of Historic Towns*, ii), p. 13.

[31] P. Kidson, P. Murray and P. Thompson, *A History of English Architecture* (revised edition, London, 1965), pp. 128–32; *An Inventory of the Historical Monuments in the City of Oxford* (R.C.H.M., 1939), pp. 125–47; *An Inventory of the Historical Monuments in the City of York*, iii: *South-West of the Ouse* (R.C.H.M., 1972), pp. xlii–xlv, 3–5, 10–11, 16–17, 20–22, 26–27.

most English parish churches. But those who believe that the foundation and construction of chantry chapels may be a safer guide to the wealth of a city's richest inhabitants than the general architectural history of the parish churches to which they were annexed, can give but little comfort to the advocates of urban prosperity. In several of the largest English towns—quite how many future research has yet to reveal—the foundation of new perpetual chantries by laymen in urban parish churches seems after 1450 to be in full decline, a decline most readily explicable in terms of economic rather than 'liturgical bankruptcy'.[32] Nor can the copious evidence for the increasing poverty of existing late fifteenth-century perpetual chantries and urban parish churches be readily discounted. As the notorious petition of the mayor, bailiffs and commonalty of Winchester to the government of Henry VI bears witness, a petition which conveyed the alarming information that by 1450 no fewer than seventeen named parish churches in the city 'ben fallen downe', the inhabitants of late medieval English towns undoubtedly did see a close connection between the prosperity of their community and the welfare of its churches.[33] Without taking this type of evidence further than it is at present legitimate for it to go, it remains necessary to consider not only why more town churches disappeared in the century between 1450 and 1550 than ever before or since but also why the modern visitor to England's oldest towns will find so comparatively few physical memorials to the achievements of that particular hundred years.

If, after all, the perpendicular churches may in time produce revelations of interest to the urban historian, what about that most notorious evidence of all—petitions to the crown for remission of a borough's fee-farm or its exemption from parliamentary subsidies? So numerous are these plaintive documents that they can certainly never be ignored; but here again the late medieval urban historian is faced with one of those antiquated controversies whose final resolution must nevertheless still be delayed until the exchequer records of the fifteenth century have been made to disclose the detailed consequences of such petitions on governmental principles and practice. No medievalist in his senses would wish to take these lamentations, usually presented within the comparatively conventional format of a parliamentary petition, entirely at their face

[32] R. B. Dobson, 'The Foundation of Perpetual Chantries by the Citizens of Medieval York', *Studies in Church History*, iv, ed. G. J. Cuming (Leiden, 1967), pp. 22–38; *cf.* A. G. Dickens, 'A Municipal Dissolution of Chantries, 1536', *Yorkshire Archaeological Journal*, xxxvi (1944–47), pp. 164–73.

[33] 'A petition of the City of Winchester to Henry VI, 1450', *Archaeologia*, i (1770), p. 94; *cf. Calendar of Patent Rolls, 1436–41*, p. 400; *ibid., 1441–46*, p. 84.

value. Indeed the very fact that so many of these petitions were presented in parliament clearly encouraged borough representatives there to emulate each other in the art of producing a convincing plea of poverty: as it happens, perhaps the single most eloquent petition to survive, the articles of 'the causez of the ruyne of youre Cite of Lincoln' presented to Richard III is to be found in the municipal archives not of Lincoln but of Grimsby.[34] Nevertheless, as Professor Postan was the first to emphasize, what is at stake here is less the veracity of the petitioners than the vigilance of the English government. Occasionally perhaps, and most notably in the short and chequered reign of Richard III, a king may have been unusually generous in his response to such petitions, less because he was moved to commiseration by the woes of his burgesses than because he was prepared to sacrifice long-term financial resources for immediate political and military assistance. But throughout most of the fifteenth century the readiness of a financially embarrassed monarchy to make such substantial fiscal concessions (amounting to over £60,000 in the case of remissions on tenths and fifteenths alone between 1433 and 1472)[35] is best interpreted as a reluctant recognition of reality, an acknowledgement that any attempt to enforce payment would produce 'no profit to yor gode grace'.[36]

Towards the lowest end of the economic spectrum there can, in any case, be no doubt of genuine civic destitution. At Wallingford, where only forty-four householders (*lares foventes*) survived by 1439, the only possible solution to the problem of the fee-farm was the taking of the borough into the king's hands.[37] A few years later the city of Winchester, 'which in ancient times was chosen out for the coronations and burials of kings' was similarly in such decay 'that, withoute gracious conforte of the Kyng our soverayn lord, the mair and bailiffs must of necessitee cesse and deliver uppe the citee and the kayes into the Kynges hands'.[38] Moreover, when such petitions contain specific corroborative detail, the information provided (whether the 'scarce two hundred citizens' still resident at Lincoln in 1447, or the decay of '300 and more dwelling places' at Gloucester in 1487–88, or even the '987 messuages in ruin' at Winchester in

[34] Grimsby Borough Archives, Petition of Citizens of Lincoln; *Historical Manuscripts Commission, 14th Report*, Appendix viii (1895), pp. 263–65.

[35] *Rotuli Parliamentorum*, iv, 425; v, 5, 37, 68–69, 142, 228, 497; vi, 40 (usefully calendared in Cunningham, *Growth of English Industry*, pp. 454–55).

[36] *Historical Manuscripts Commission, 14th Report*, p. 264, and *cf.* pp. 10–12; Hill, *Medieval Lincoln*, pp. 285–88.

[37] Public Record Office, Patent Roll 17 Henry VI, ii (C.66/444), memb. 11d; *Calendar of Patent Rolls, 1436–41*, pp. 317–18.

[38] 'Petition of the City of Winchester, 1450', *op. cit.*, pp. 94–95.

the 1440s)[39] rarely seems to be beyond the bounds of possibility. Similarly, the allegation of the burgesses of Great Yarmouth in 1471 that their previous fleet of '80 ships with *fore castellis* and 140 others' had shrunk to only 24 '*naves vocati ffishers*' is by no means out of line with the results of modern research.[40] Somewhat ironically, a recent attempt to apply critical scrutiny to a genuinely suspect series of petitions for relief of fee-farm ends by conceding that the citizens of Chester between 1445 and 1486 do in fact 'appear to have had some justification'.[41] Nor for the fortunate historian who is able to test the veracity of a borough's representations to the crown by the evidence of the matters discussed at its council meetings can the conclusion be very different. No one who pursues the tortuous course of the campaign for tax remission waged by the mayor and aldermen of York from 1482 onwards through the folios of the contemporary civic 'house books' can seriously doubt the gravity of a crisis evident even to 'the blessed Trinite'. When on 17 September 1483, the new king Richard III summoned before him in the chapter-house of the Minster 'the said Mair, hys brethyr the Aldermen, and many othir of the comuns of the said Cite' to rehearse 'the dikey and the great poverte of the said Cite', he may have been anxious to reward a group of exceptionally loyal adherents for their services during an unprecedently tumultuous summer; but it is inconceivable that such poverty and decay did not exist.[42]

Nor need even the most sceptical historian be unduly perturbed by the revelation that many and perhaps most towns assigned the payment of their fee-farms to a particular category of their total revenues.[43] Given the antiquity of the *firma burgi* and the almost universal rigid separation between its constituent resources and

[39] *Calendar of Patent Rolls, 1436–41*, p. 400; *1446–52*, p. 80; *Calendar of Records of the Corporation of Gloucester*, ed. W. H. Stevenson (Gloucester, 1893), nos. 58–59.

[40] P.R.O., Patent Roll 49 Henry VI (C.66/491), memb. 17d; *Calendar of Patent Rolls, 1467–77*, pp. 250, 393; *cf. Materials for the Reign of Henry VII*, i (Rolls Series, 1873), pp. 326–27, 330; G. V. Scammell, 'English Merchant Shipping at the end of the Middle Ages: some east coast evidence', *Economic History Review*, 2nd series xiii (1961), pp. 327–41.

[41] Wilson, 'The Port of Chester', *op. cit.*, p. 10.

[42] York City Archives, MS. A/Y, appendix fo 14; *cf. York Civic Records*, ed. A. Raine (Yorkshire Archaeological Society, Record Series, 1939–53), i, 65–66, 71, 73, 82, 135–37, 165–67; ii, 36–37, 70, 81, 83; and *cf.* British Library, Harley MS 433, fos 38, 81.

[43] Green, *Town Life in the Fifteenth Century*, ii, 216–17, 332, 406, 410–11; A. R. Bridbury, *Economic Growth: England in the later Middle Ages* (London, 1962), pp. 75–76. By contrast, the discussion of these issues in A. P. M. Wright, 'The Relations between the King's Government and the English Cities and Boroughs in the Fifteenth Century' (University of Oxford, D.Phil. thesis, 1965), pp. 173–230, suggests that even when urban claims for tax exemption on grounds of insufficiency were specious in detail they were often well founded in substance.

those of the separately administered civic chamber, it would be surprising if such were not the case. In practice most of the larger English towns seem to have paid their fee-farms from what the citizens of Lincoln called their sheriffs' 'tollez, courtes, finez and amerciaments', forms of revenue which—like property rents themselves—often did tend to dwindle and atrophy during the course of the fifteenth century.[44] Not for nothing, after all, did the inhabitants of late medieval English towns apply to their general economic plight a word most familiar to them, as to us, in the context of '*Decasus Redditum*' within an annual civic account roll. But to what other sources of income could the financially embarrassed municipal corporations of the late fifteenth century have turned? At the risk of making yet one more premature generalization, it seems clear enough that the supposed 'immense wealth' of late medieval urban corporations is largely chimerical: what is remarkable, especially by continental standards, is how few English cities—at any period of the middle ages—enjoyed annual net incomes comparable to those, of, say, the major religious houses in their vicinity. The real problem, and an exceptionally difficult one, is the extent to which the poverty of a civic chamber could co-exist with the presence in the urban community of individually wealthy citizens. On grounds of psychological probability alone, is it likely that the comparatively small and introspective urban community of the later middle ages would tolerate great wealth without great responsibility?

To that particular question the records of a very large number of fifteenth-century English towns do indeed seem to offer a partial answer by their revelation of an often obsessive preoccupation with the notorious problem of the withdrawal of labour from civic office-holding. As distraint of knighthood will always remind us, ambivalence of attitude towards the heavy burdens that went with the high status of administrative office was a familiar feature of medieval society at every level. Certainly a disinclination to undertake these burdens was not a novel development in the fifteenth-century town. Nevertheless, and all due allowances made for the extent to which individual cases of exemption from office-holding are much better documented in late medieval rather than earlier civic records, it is during the period after 1450 that the evidence for massive evasion of civic office becomes almost universally conspicuous. To a problem that was continuously discussed in the council meetings of every late fifteenth and early sixteenth-century town where records

[44] *E.g.*, York City Archives, Chamberlains' Accounts, 1397–1502 (C.1–C.5); *V.C.H.*, *Yorkshire, City of York* (1961), pp. 72–73; *V.C.H.*, *Yorkshire, East Riding*, i, 40–42; E. Gillett, *A History of Grimsby* (London, 1970), pp. 55–56, 66–67; M. D. Lobel and J. Tann, 'Gloucester' (*Atlas of Historic Towns*, i), pp. 10–11.

survive there was clearly no easy solution. A gradual increase in the number of civic chamberlains 'to bere such great charges' was one of the more common responses; and so too was the imposition of increasingly stringent financial and other penalties on the recalcitrant citizens who refused to serve. At York, the especially copious evidence for widescale attempts to evade office suggests a remarkably close chronological correlation with the process of general urban decline.[45] Similarly, at Bristol in 1518, in a particularly informative *cause célèbre*, William Dale responded to his election as sheriff by an appeal to the Star Chamber against the mayor and aldermen of that city, men who had themselves allegedly only 'passed the daungeour of the said office by the great substance that they hadd before gottyn'.[46] Other examples, derived from published town records alone, could be multiplied *ad nauseam*; and it is for each historian to decide at what point the accumulation of isolated instances of evasion from office signifies for him a general crisis. For the citizens of Lincoln in the 1480s there could be little doubt: their analysis of their own plight ended with the claim that it was the expenses of office-holding which 'causeth many men that hath beene brought upp in thys Cite by prentishode, service, or oder wyse, to avoyed and goo forth thereof, and to inhabett theime in oder placez; and there ys nedere craft man ne soiourner that wille come too a bide or dwelle here, for fere of the seyd office; and thus this Cite dissolatez and fallith in grete decaye'.[47]

Evidence for the reluctance or inability of late fifteenth-century burgesses to take up office has moreover long been familiar to English medievalists in a very different and especially intriguing field. The invasion of the borough constituencies of the English parliament by members of the county gentry is usually interpreted in terms of the increasing aggressiveness of the fifteenth-century magnate and his affinity.[48] Yet the implications of that 'revolution in the personnel of parliament' for the victims of this process are surely quite as thought-

[45] *Statutes of the Realm*, ii, 359; *York Civic Records*, i, 135–37; *V.C.H., Yorkshire, City of York*, pp. 74–75, 139. The refusal of civic office in early sixteenth-century York is to be discussed at length in Dr David Palliser's forthcoming history of the Tudor city: I am most grateful to him for his generous assistance on these and other issues.

[46] *Select cases before the King's Council in the Star Chamber*, ii, ed. I. S. Leadam (Selden Society, xxv, 1911), pp. cii–cxviii, 142–65.

[47] *Historical Manuscripts Commission, 14th Report*, Appendix viii, p. 264.

[48] *The Paston Letters*, ed. J. Gairdner (London, 1904), i. 152; iii, 53–55; M. McKisack, *The Parliamentary Representation of English Boroughs during the Midde Ages* (Oxford, 1932), pp. 60–64, 100–18; *cf.* P. Jalland, 'The Revolution in Northern Borough Representation in Mid-Fifteenth-Century England', *Northern History*, xi (1976 for 1975), pp. 27–51.

provoking. The revelations of the Paston Letters and other sources have made it abundantly clear that by the 1450s the landed aristocracy and gentry were highly interested in the possibilities of influencing the results of parliamentary elections at Norwich and Exeter, let alone Yarmouth and Maldon. It has recently been suggested that 'representation by a respectable gentleman might well increase the effective volume of the urban voice', an argument which concedes the main point and was in fact anticipated by Ralph Neville, second Earl of Westmorland, in the famous letter whereby he asked the mayor and burgesses of Grimsby to return 'ii of my counsale to be Burgessis for youre seid towne'.[49] By the later fifteenth century, as Dr Alan Rogers has amply demonstrated in the case of Stamford, there is no doubt that many of the smaller boroughs elected country gentlemen and royal officials on their own initiative.[50] Can one seriously interpret such a ubiquitous and important phenomenon except in terms of a comparative lack of power or of confidence, or of both, on the part of the burgesses themselves? The truth is that the incursus of the county gentry into the borough seats may be seen as merely one of the many manifestations of the obsessive search for 'good lords' which characterized the policies of most late fifteenth-century towns. This is obviously not the place to enlarge upon the various ways in which civic politics of the late fifteenth century became embroiled in the national factionalism of the period; but it may still need to be said that a study of any reasonably informative civic archive to survive rapidly dispels the curiously persistent myth that English towns found it easy to remain uninvolved and unaffected by the civil wars of the period. Such admittedly exceptional catastrophes as the 1461 siege of Carlisle and sack of Stamford apart, there is much evidence to suggest that, as one would expect, the major protagonists of the Wars of the Roses were no respecters of urban persons. Reading, Coventry, Leicester, Nottingham and Salisbury, to mention only five examples at random, were all compelled to make substantial contributions to Edward IV's war effort; and Professor Storey has recently shown how easy it was for Lord Egremont to recruit men in the streets of York itself during the 1450s.[51] Indeed in a not too incredible piece

[49] Grimsby Borough Archives, HMC. OL 2/21; *Historical Manuscripts Commission, 14th Report*, Appendix viii, p. 252; *cf.* A. Rogers, 'Parliamentary Elections in Grimsby in the Fifteenth Century', *Bulletin of Institute of Historical Research*, xlii (1969), pp. 212–20: Clark and Slack, *Crisis and Order in English Towns*, pp. 9–10.

[50] A. Rogers, 'Late Medieval Stamford: A Study of the Town Council, 1465–92', *Perspectives in English Urban History*, ed. A. Everitt (London, 1973), pp. 28–29.

[51] *Reading Records: Diary of the Corporation, 1431–1654*, ed. J. M. Guilding (London, 1892–96), i, 52; *Coventry Leet Book, 1420–1555*, ed. M. D. Harris (Early English

of special pleading to Henry VII in December 1485, the York corporation attributed the origins of their 'povertie, decay and ruyn' to Edward IV's indignation that so many men of the city had fought on the Lancastrian side at the battles of Wakefield, St Albans and Towton.[52] Nor can the single most famous example of urban involvement in fifteenth-century national politics, the 'special relationship' between Richard of Gloucester and the aldermen of York, be made to seem intelligible unless one supposes that the civic oligarchy saw that particular *dominus specialissimus* as the saviour who might lead them out of their current economic wilderness.

No doubt such emotive language, though considerably less melodramatic than that often used by the inhabitants of English towns themselves, should be out of place in any investigation of late medieval urban decline; and it must certainly be conceded that most of the evidence so far adduced in this paper has been highly impressionistic. Are there any alternatives? To the urban historian brave enough to wrestle with statistical material there are indeed, most obviously in the form of figures arising from the annual admission of freemen into a city's liberty; from the fluctuations of overseas trade in the Enrolled and Particular accounts of the national customs; from the rise and fall of rent values within particular towns; and finally from comparisons between a highly heterogeneous collection of surviving taxation assessments. Perhaps there will always be a division between those historians who, to adapt a phrase of Professor Postan, approach these sources 'in the hope of finding general causes, and others who do the same in the hope of losing them.'[53] As it is, research in these increasingly technical spheres is still genuinely in its infancy; and one can only hope that the present state of confusion, whereby the two most forceful and influential historians of the subject have at times used exactly the same statistical evidence to come to opposite conclusions, may not be indefinitely prolonged.[54] In the case of surviving freemen's registers, some reservations have already been expressed about their limitations as an absolutely reliable guide to both total demographic trends and to

---

Text Society, 1907–13), pp. 313–19, 353–58; *Records of the Borough of Leicester, 1103–1603*, ed. M. Bateson (Cambridge, 1899–1905), ii, 279, 315–16; *Records of the Borough of Nottingham*, ed. W. H. Stevenson (London, 1882–1900), ii, 257; *English Historical Documents, 1327–1485*, ed. A. R. Myers (London, 1969), pp. 507–508; R. L. Storey, *The End of the House of Lancaster* (London, 1966) pp. 125–32, 142.

[52] *York Civic Records*, i, 135–37.

[53] Postan, *Medieval Agriculture and General Problems*, p. 274.

[54] *Ibid.*, pp. 44–46; M. M. Postan, 'Medieval Agrarian Society in its Prime: England', *Cambridge Economic History*, i (1966 edn), p. 568; Bridbury, *Economic Growth*, pp. 56–64.

occupational distribution within the late medieval town.[55] Nevertheless, and at the risk of seeming to want to leave the cake and yet to eat it, one may still suspect that whereas the high rates of freemen admission so often encountered in the years immediately after the first outbreak of bubonic plague in 1348–49 are largely attributable to heavy mortality within the existing citizenry, the comparatively low rates of recruitment characteristic of the years around 1500 may sometimes reflect a provincial town's genuine inability to attract an adequate supply of new freemen at that time.[56]

Analogous problems of interpretation lie in wait for those who would wish to utilize statistical material from other sources. Precisely because the evidence of the national customs accounts has so often, and so skilfully, been exploited to support the case for economic growth in certain areas of late medieval England, it was salutary to be reminded a few years ago by one of the editors of *England's Export Trade, 1275–1547* that at least in Southampton flourishing commercial activity could co-exist with a 'miserably poor' civic body.[57] Sometimes, no doubt, conclusions based on too simple an interpretation of the customs accounts may err in the opposite direction; in addition to the familiar problems created by royal licences to export free of subsidy and by an unascertainable amount of smuggling, Mr James Campbell has recently suggested that economic historians hitherto may have seriously under-estimated the value of the late fourteenth-century export trade in worsteds from Norwich and Great Yarmouth.[58] And whereas the 'unprecedented boom' in cloth exports from Exeter must be directly related to the commercial 'vitality' of much of south-western England at the end of the fifteenth century, even a sympathetic observer of the progress of English merchant shipping on the east coast has concluded that 'it was not until about 1550 . . . that the numbers, and probably the tonnage of c. 1340–1440 were re-attained and surpassed'.[59]

[55] R. B. Dobson, 'Admissions to the Freedom of the City of York in the Later Middle Ages', *Economic History Review*, 2nd series, xxvi (1973), pp. 1–22; *cf.* D. M. Woodward, 'Freemen's Rolls', *The Local Historian*, ix (1970), pp. 89–95.

[56] *The Records of the City of Norwich*, ed. W. Hudson and J. C. Tingey (Norwich, 1906–10), ii, pp. xxx–xxxii, cxviii–cxxii; *A Calendar of the Freemen of Lynn, 1292–1836* (Norfolk and Norwich Archaeological Society, 1913), pp. 1–42; *V.C.H., Yorkshire, East Riding*, i, 56; *Register of the Freemen of the City of York*, i (Surtees Society, xcvi, 1897), pp. 213–52; Bridbury, *Economic Growth*, pp. 65–69; *Exeter Freemen, 1266–1967*, ed. M. M. Rowe and A. M. Jackson (Devon and Cornwall Record Society, Extra Series i, 1973), pp. xiv, 54–69.

[57] O. Coleman, 'Trade and Prosperity in the Fifteenth Century: Some Aspects of the Trade of Southampton', *Economic History Review*, 2nd series, xvi (1963), p. 21; *cf.* the less melancholy verdict of Platt, *Medieval Southampton*, pp. 141–63.

[58] J. Campbell, 'Norwich' (*Atlas of Historic Towns*, ii), p. 16.

[59] Scammell, *op. cit.*, p. 339.

However, the difficulties of coming to a balanced view in that long cultivated field pale into insignificance when compared with those which will one day confront the analyst of urban rent values. At this early stage of investigation on so important a topic it would be dangerously facile to offer any general verdict on the basis of the declining rent-rolls of so many fifteenth-century urban corporations and religious bodies. For the greater landlords themselves, some compensation may have been forthcoming during a period when 'the main trend after the building expansion of the thirteenth century seems to have been towards institutional ownership of the bigger blocks of urban property'; but for that reason among many others it still seems unlikely that historians will ever be able to interpret the acquisition and management of real property in the fifteenth-century English town as a genuinely dynamic feature of its economy.[60]

In the case of taxation records, whether those of the early fourteenth-century Lay Subsidies, the poll taxes of 1377–81 or the sixteenth-century Tudor subsidies, their limitations as an index of either the population or the absolute wealth of individual English towns are currently under such heavily critical scrutiny that one might hesitate to do more than suggest that they can sometimes be a guide to the more dramatic rises and falls of particular urban fortunes. Unfortunately demographic historians have not yet been able to consider the general implications of Dr Neville Bartlett's startling discovery that at least 'part of the 1381 York Poll Tax Returns was a deliberate fraud based on the Lay Subsidy Rolls of twenty-three years earlier'.[61] Nor, perhaps, does an especially learned and influential attempt to utilize a comparison between the Lay Subsidy of 1334 and the Tudor Subsidy of 1515 to suggest that at the latter date 'urban wealth constituted a far larger proportion of total lay wealth' than previously emancipate us from similar problems. Not only does extensive suburban development complicate the already difficult task of distinguishing between town and country but the use of different categories of wealth as the basis for the taxes in question introduces the possibility of almost unpredictable distor-

[60] R. H. Hilton, 'Some Problems of Urban Real Property in the Middle Ages', *Socialism, Capitalism and Economic Growth*, ed. C. H. Feinstein (Cambridge, 1967), p. 337; *cf.* Platt, *English Medieval Town*, pp. 181–82.

[61] N. Bartlett, 'The Lay Poll Tax Returns for the city of York in 1381', *Transactions of the East Riding of Yorkshire Antiquarian Society*, xxx, p. 7. Dr Bartlett's edition of these returns remains, most regrettably, unpublished; but an offprint is included in his 'Some Aspects of the Economy of York in the Later Middle Ages, 1300–1550' (University of London, Ph.D. thesis, 1958). *Cf.* J. I. Leggett's 'The 1377 Poll Tax Return for the City of York', *Yorkshire Archaeological Journal*, xliii (1971), pp. 128–46.

tion.[62] There are also some grounds for believing that in the early fourteenth and early sixteenth centuries alike the assessment of taxation in towns could differ quite markedly in practice from that in the country. The extraordinary variation in the number of tax-payers recorded on the several surviving subsidy returns for the early sixteenth-century city of York is hardly likely to enhance one's confidence in any one urban assessment.[63] More alarming still is the possibility that the early fourteenth-century wealth of the English towns was consistently under-valued by the taxers of the lay subsidies, themselves usually leading citizens of the communities they were assessing. Professor Beresford has already pointed out that the decision, first taken in 1294, to levy the subsidy at a higher rate in the towns than the country 'is an interesting comment on economic development' at the time.[64] Indeed it is, but (when one considers all the complications of classifying taxation boroughs that ensued) may it not also be a decision prompted by the Edwardian government's awareness that there was no more subtle method available of trying to correct the imbalance of the comparative under-assessment of the real wealth of the English towns?

The extent to which such reservations may or may not be justified only much current research is likely to reveal. It would, in any case, be folly to imagine that the economic development of all English urban communities can be easily 'fitted into any pre-conceived pattern'.[65] Some towns, like Grimsby and Dunwich, Northampton and Winchester, manifest symptoms of decline long before the end of the thirteenth century; others, like Salisbury and Reading, Exeter and Ipswich, may well have been positively prospering at the end of the fifteenth century; and in the case of many cities and boroughs, most obviously Newcastle-upon-Tyne, the most mysterious as well as the most successful of all the 'new towns' of post-conquest England, the sparsity of the evidence makes it almost pointless to put the question. Nevertheless, all due allowances made for important chronological and regional vicissitudes, that there is a common if not universal story to be told seems undeniable. What that story was

[62] R. S. Schofield, 'The geographical distribution of wealth in England, 1334–1649', *Economic History Review*, 2nd series, xviii (1965), pp. 483–510; Bridbury, *Economic Growth*, pp. 78–82; and *cf.* D. J. Keene, 'Suburban Growth', *Plans and Topography of Medieval Towns* (1976), pp. 71–82.

[63] *V.C.H.*, *Yorkshire*, *City of York*, p. 121.

[64] M. W. Beresford, *The Lay Subsidies and the Poll Taxes* (Canterbury, 1963), p. 3; *cf.* the differentiated lists of items exempted from taxation as summarized in J. F. Willard, 'The Taxes upon Movables of the Reign of Edward I', *Eng. Hist. Rev.*, xxviii (1913), pp. 517–18.

[65] E. M. Carus-Wilson, *The Expansion of Exeter at the Close of the Middle Ages*, p. 5.

the abundant records of late fifteenth-century York, a city whose economic fortunes were much more representative of those of other major English towns than has usually been recognized, tell only too clearly. By the 1460s and 1470s signs of York's economic distress are visible in every conceivable quarter. As always, it is the merchant and aldermanic classes who have left the most abundant evidence of their own reduction from a previously proud state to that of self-styled 'hevie creatours'. From the mid-century onwards they moved into an increasingly desolate era of contracting personal fortunes; an era when an ever-growing proportion of those fortunes appear to have been invested in rural rather than urban property or trade; when several of their members are known to have migrated to London and elsewhere; when one mayor (John Tonge, 1477–78) could be defamed as 'bot a beggar' by a local parish priest, and another distinguished ex-mayor (Thomas Gray, 1497–98) eventually had to resign his aldermanic gown because of his great 'decay and poverty'; and when the dominant figures in York politics and society, like Sir Richard York and Sir George Lawson, owed much of their ascendancy to their connections with the Yorkist and the Tudor courts.[66] To the aldermen of York the nature of their disaster was clear enough: in the words of a petition to Henry VII on St George's Day 1487, a petition to whose premises the king himself explicitly assented, 'ther is not half the nombre of good men within your said citie as ther hath beene in tymes past'.[67]

To that particular problem not even a modern government can provide an easy solution; and that it was the fundamental problem for the town councils of the vast majority of all late medieval corporate towns their own words testify. Too often the manifestations of severe population decline within and indeed without the fifteenth-century provincial town—the supposed 'restrictive practices' forced on so many urban craft guilds by the decline of consumer demand for their products, the drift of the textile industry into rural areas, the gradual usurpation of regional trading functions by the merchants of London—have been interpreted as the primary causes of urban decay. But only the existence of prolonged and remorseless demographic attrition in England as a whole, an attrition emphatically not generally reversed at some unascertainable point in the fifteenth century, seems capable of explaining the ubiquity of the

[66] *York Civic Records*, i, 32; J. C. Wedgwood, *History of Parliament: Biographies of Members of the Commons House, 1439–1509* (London, 1936), p. 389; *Testamenta Eboracensia* (Surtees Society, 1836–1902), iv, 134–37; D. M. Palliser, *The Reformation in York, 1534–1553* (Borthwick Paper No. 40, York, 1971), pp. 1–2, 5; *V.C.H., Yorkshire, City of York*, pp. 89–91, 105–06, 110–13, 117, 122–26.

[67] *York Civic Records*, ii, 9.

urban malaise. This was a process which, by very definition, was likely to cripple the smaller cities, like Lincoln and Winchester, at an early stage of its course; whereas the largest English towns might, like York, be presented with the temporary consolation of an Indian summer of remarkable affluence before they too succumbed. That in time almost every large English city did succumb, dependent as they all were on regularly sustained immigration for their very survival, there can be no reasonable doubt. Perhaps the single most dramatic and well-attested example of decline and fall is that provided by the so-called Coventry 'censuses' of 1520 and 1523.[68] But it can certainly be regarded as no coincidence that of the three leading English provincial towns, York and Bristol both welcomed the person of the first Tudor king in 1486 with pageants which bemoaned their desolation and decay; while a few years later the third, Norwich, secured statutory relief on the grounds that 'an auncient Citie is greatly decaied'.[69] Until such decay began to be arrested, at various dates in different centres but usually at a comparatively late point in the sixteenth century, English provincial towns are most notable for how little and not for how much they contributed to the cultural and social life of their age, an age whose most meaningful dichotomy long remained one of court and country rather than of town and country. Nor is the failure of its towns to act, in Braudel's words, as the 'transformers' and 'accelerators' of early modern English society necessarily quite as inexplicable as it has sometimes seemed to the present generation of economic theorists. Whether or not the concept of an 'autonomous death-rate' should be seen as an admission of defeat on the part of modern economic historians, to the late medieval historian it can only prove a liberating influence, emancipating him from the sterile and indeed ultimately impossible task of attempting to construct hypothetical population trends from scattered references to plague and disease. Quite when the process of demographic regeneration began is fortunately not the concern of this paper; but perhaps it is still worth listening to the advice offered to Cardinal Pole by Master Lupset as late as the 1530s: 'Sir, indede, when I loke to the cytes and townys and vyllagys in the cuntrey, I can not deny but ther hath byn more pepul here in our cuntrey than there ys now. Wherfor, wythout

[68] See C. Phythian-Adams's forthcoming *Coventry in Crisis, 1518–25*; *cf. V.C.H., Warwickshire*, viii, 4–5; J. C. Lancaster, 'Coventry' (*Atlas of Historic Towns*, ii), p. 9. I am most grateful to Mr Phythian-Adams for permission to consult two unpublished papers which argue the case for the persistence of general urban decline in early sixteenth-century England at considerable length.

[69] *Statutes of the Realm*, ii, 577; *York Civic Records*, i, 158; S. Seyer, *Memoirs, historical and topographical, of Bristol and its Neighbourhood* (Bristol, 1821–23), ii, 206.

ferther cauyllatyon, agreying apon thys, let us go forward.'[70] Neither the medieval nor the Tudor historian is likely to want to go forward anything like so quickly in the company of so committed a controversialist as Thomas Starkey; but it could be both interesting and illuminating to consider what might happen if they did.[71]

[70] *Dialogue between Pole and Lupset*, *op. cit.*, p. 76; *cf.* I. Blanchard, 'Population change, enclosure, and the Early Tudor economy', *Econ. Hist. Rev.*, 2nd series, xxiii (1970), p. 435.

[71] I am heavily indebted to Professor Joyce Youings, Dr David Palliser and Dr Paul Slack for their invaluable criticisms and comments on an earlier version of this paper.

THE TREATMENT OF THE NEWS IN MID-VICTORIAN NEWSPAPERS

By Lucy Brown, M.A., Ph.D., F.R.Hist.S.

READ 5 MARCH 1976

THIS paper is concerned with the way in which news was handled by the four main London dailies, *The Times*, the *Daily News*, the *Daily Telegraph* and the *Standard* which, by the late 1870s, enjoyed the largest circulations. They differed from each other considerably in character and history, and in the kind of historical record which they have left behind. Much more is known about *The Times* than about any of the others. In the 1860s it was a 16-page paper, costing 3*d*, with a circulation declining slowly from 65,000 to 60,000.[1] The fact that it could maintain this circulation, when it was three times as expensive as its main rivals, is by itself evidence of the value that contemporaries placed upon it. It had far greater assets than any of its rivals, and the Walter family were willing to invest heavily in the paper as and when funds were needed. Its greater resources were shown, partly in its technical equipment, and partly in the range and quality of writing in the paper itself. *The Times* had more correspondents reporting more frequently and fully from more European capitals than its rivals, and much of its prestige had been derived from that fact. It also employed in London a staff of educated writers such as George Brodrick and Robert Lowe. Unlike its rivals it could afford to pay salaries which enabled it to impose on its writers the condition that they wrote for it exclusively. (The lives of a number of notable late nineteenth-century journalists show that they tried to make up income by writing too much simultaneously, for too many different publications.[2]) All the same, in the 1860s and 1870s, *The Times* was beginning to show symptoms of sclerosis.

[1] *The History of the Times*, ii, *The Tradition Established, 1841–1884* (London, 1939), pp. 345–57.

[2] These working conditions are made clear in the correspondence of Thomas Chenery, editor of *The Times* 1877–84, and of William Mudford with T. H. S. Escott, Escott papers B.L. Add. MS 58,777, letter dated 3 Nov. 1882, and 58,787, fos 66–69. For the volume of work undertaken by journalists, see for example Henry Lucy, *Sixty Years in the Wilderness* (London, 1909), pp. 111 ff., or *The life and adventures of George Augustus Sala, written by himself* (London, 1896), pp. 346 ff. The Escott papers, taken as a whole, tell much the same story: Escott, a journalist who was writing for the *Standard* and the *World* at the same time as he was editing the *Fortnightly Review*, appears to have collapsed from overwork.

Delane had been editor since 1841: he did not adapt to the political changes after the death of Palmerston, and the paper was slow to learn the technical possibilities which were opening up, mainly through the use of telegraphy.

The second paper was the liberal *Daily News*. This was an 8-page paper, reduced from 2*d* to 1*d* in 1868. Compared with *The Times* it was poor and struggling: the reduction in price was a gamble which would certainly mean an immediate reduction of 50% in the yield from sales, though it was hoped that a subsequent rise in circulation would more than compensate. It was so short of funds that in 1869 John Robinson, the manager, is reported to have taken a share in the proprietorship in lieu of salary, a decision which in the end rewarded him handsomely. The proprietorship is not clear. It was owned by a syndicate of Liberals of whom Samuel Morley was the best known. In 1869 its future character and prospects were radically changed when Henry Labouchère bought a share in it, possibly 25 per cent. The significance of the purchase was that Samuel Morley was a Liberal patriarch with his own industrial interests and with strong views on particular subjects, notably on temperance. The new proprietor was a much younger man who had no particular occupation, but had general political ambitions. He was also extremely rich, having inherited his uncle's fortune, estimated at a quarter of a million, in the same year.[3] He seems to have been someone rather like the young Disraeli in temperament, but with massive funds at his disposal. The full extent, or persistence, of his involvement in the running of the paper is not known, but it is clear that he was active. Of the four papers under discussion, the *Daily News* is the only one which can be shown to have been in regular informal association with party political figures.[4]

The histories of the other two newspapers are much more obscure. The *Daily Telegraph* was the great success story of the 1860s. It had been acquired in 1855 by its printer, J. M. Levy, when it was running into debt. With his son Edward as editor, he made a conspicuous success of it as a penny paper. There is very little reference either to father or to son in the main relevant manuscript sources and memoirs of the period. The paper described itself as 'independent Liberal'; it seems probable that the Levy-Lawson family, who had acquired it, so to speak, by accident, looked on it primarily as a commercial venture which should be run for profit.

[3] Hesketh Pearson, *Labby: the life and character of Henry Labouchère* (London, 1936), pp. 68–69.

[4] This can be seen in the correspondence of the editor, Frank Harrison Hill, with Dilke, B.L. Add. MS. 43,898 *passim*, and in the letters of Labouchère to Herbert Gladstone, *ibid.*, 46,015–16, *passim*.

The outline of the fourth paper, the *Standard*, is very hazy indeed. It was an old-established Conservative newspaper which had been bought, together with the *Morning Herald*, by an accountant, James Johnstone, in the general rush towards penny morning dailies which had followed the abolition of the stamp duties. He brought it out as a morning as well as an evening paper and reduced the price to a penny, and in 1858 it had a circulation of about 30,000.[5] In the 1860s it was run in close association with the Conservative parliamentary leaders.[6] It was edited by a Captain Hamber and was regarded as the reading matter of the country gentry. In the early seventies it is recorded that John Gorst was working for it at exactly the time when he was also employed in the reorganization of the Conservative Central Office.[7] At the end of 1874 William Mudford, an unknown professional journalist working in the *Standard* office, became editor. The sources, scanty as they are, agree that the fortunes of the paper were at a low ebb when Mudford took it over, and that he was a conspicuous success. It is certain that by 1882 its circulation had risen to 232,000, closely rivalling the *Daily Telegraph* at 241,000.[8] After the departure of Gorst the nature of its association with the Conservatives is hard to assess. Mudford's obituary in *The Times* in 1916 describes him as a recluse, 'He was not to be seen at a dinner party, or a reception, or any other social entertainment.' It suggests that this was partly to resist political pressure, 'Whatever the faults of the *Standard* under his regime . . . nobody could impugn its honesty and courage.' Mudford himself explained his success by saying that 'he represented the thought of the villa resident order of Englishmen'.[9] Whatever the explanation, the *Standard*, in the period under review, was enlarging its range of support closely in step with the revival of the Conservative party, particularly in the London area.

The technical changes which were transforming newspaper production in the late 1860s are well known. The rotary press, printing from continuous rolls of newsprint, was being developed in France and the United States. As well as saving labour, the new machines enabled a paper to produce a large number of copies very quickly—a paper with a large circulation could go to press that much later.

[5] *History of the Times*, ii, p. 298.

[6] See the Disraeli papers at Hughenden, Box 88, for the correspondence of Hamber and Disraeli in the 1860s.

[7] The history of the *Standard* is given by Joseph Hatton, *Journalistic London* (London, 1882), pp. 143 ff. and by T. H. S. Escott, *Masters of English Journalism* (London, 1911), pp. 201 ff. Both authors had worked for the paper.

[8] Escott papers, B.L. Add. MS. 58,795, Robert Wilson to T. H. S. Escott, 26 September 1882.

[9] *The Times*, 20 October 1916.

Two of the papers under discussion were installing rotary presses in the late 1860s: *The Times* had its own version, the Walter press, from 1868, while the *Daily Telegraph* was printed by the American Bullock machine from 1870. In the 1870s the other two papers had to equip themselves similarly. The new machines were very expensive: in 1875 it was reported that the *Daily Telegraph* was spending £80,000 on a second generation of Hoe machines, the Bullock machine having proved unsatisfactory.[10] The rotary press was tending to make newspaper production more expensive and more of a gamble. For a Sunday paper in which late news was not a major element, which might be printed, in whole or in part, during the second half of the week, the new machines might not be relevant, but for the big London morning dailies, competing with each other in offering the latest news, they were essential. On the other hand, if circulations did not rise to the expected level, the capital cost could prove an incubus. They posed the familiar problems of advanced technology: the certainty of great initial cost, the possibility of great rewards, and the risk of disaster.

The second major technical change was the telegraph. The network had been growing, as an effective channel of communication, over western Europe since the 1840s; but two dramatic extensions were completed in the sixties; the Atlantic cable in 1865, and the links to India in 1869. Perhaps we do not stress the momentousness of this development sufficiently: for once the overworked word 'revolutionary' is appropriate. News could now come in a matter of minutes rather than weeks: the greater the distance the more dramatic the saving.[11] By 1870 the basic technical conditions which underlie modern newspaper production had come into existence and probably did not change much until the general use of air transport in our own day.

No doubt, whatever the technical circumstances, it has always been a main objective of a paper to be first with the news, though this might be an objective which could only be attained with great expense and effort: in the late 1830s there had been the notable effort of *The Times*, through the agency of Lieutenant Thomas Waghorn, to find the fastest possible route from India.[12] But in the late 1860s there were several papers in competition, and there was a belief that greatly expanded circulations were possible, if only the

[10] Ellic Howe, *Newspaper Printing in the Nineteenth Century* (London, 1943), pp. 25 ff. The *Printer's Register*, a London trade paper, contains a great deal of detailed information on newspaper production.

[11] The telegraph plays a central part in the plot of Jules Verne's *Round the World in Eighty Days*, first published in 1874.

[12] This is described in the *History of the Times*, ii, ch. IV.

right formula could be found, and the objective began to be more insistently felt. Exceptional news could bring vastly inflated sales. When the evening edition of the *Standard* printed the news of the victory of Tel-el-Kebir in September 1882, it sold half a million copies—compared with the usual 230,000 for the morning and evening editions combined.[13]

In this period the services of the news agencies were available. Reuters had been established in 1851, and all the papers under discussion used its service of telegrams. These covered as full a range of events as any paper, but in brief telegraphic fashion. They offered summaries of the kind of news that was public property, as it were, in the country of origin: the ministers who had been appointed and resigned, the provisions of new laws, some business news, general information about the weather or the harvest, or outstanding disasters. They provided enough to keep the informed person up to date, but needed plenty of interpretation and embellishment to be intelligible to the general reader. Reuters was no substitute at all for the correspondent on the spot. The same may be said of the Press Association, founded in 1868 as a cooperative venture by the Provincial Newspaper Association to strengthen their competitive position against the London papers. The Press Association provided a similar infrastructure of home news, together with such things as the racing results, but it did not do the work of a London correspondent. The news agencies in fact, while they appeared to strengthen the smaller paper in relation to the larger, and the provincial in relation to the metropolitan, had a very limited effect on their relative positions.

The present paper is concerned with the impact of these events on news reporting, and concentrates discussion on three limited periods. The first is the first fortnight of March 1863. At that time there were four main news stories going on: two of them in continental Europe. There was a revolution in Greece: on 2 March, *The Times* printed two columns on the subject from their special correspondent: none of the other papers noticed this revolution at all during this fortnight. The second event was the Polish rising of 1863. All the papers had something to say about it: *The Times* published a daily report of one or two columns from their special correspondent stationed in Cracow. The other papers all gave some news, sometimes derived from *The*

[13] Escott papers, B.L. Add. MS. 58,795, Robert Wilson to T. H. S. Escott, 26 September 1882. This is not out of line with some other sales figures: it was reported that the *Manchester Examiner and Times* sold over 192,000 copies on 23 September 1867, the day after the execution of three Fenians at Manchester—its normal circulation must have been about 30–40,000 (*Printer's Register*, March 1869).

Times, or in the case of the *Daily News*, from the French papers as well. Apart from this *The Times* had long reports from Berlin, St Petersburg, Paris, Constantinople and Naples: the other papers had something from France and Italy, but not from elsewhere. As for European news, this sample period reveals what would be expected: the immensely greater range and professionalism of *The Times*.

The third main news story was the American Civil War. Here the limitations of the pre-telegraphic age are seen. *The Times* could give a daily account of events in Poland, but in this fortnight only one ship arrived with American news, and on 5 March all the papers appeared with substantial accounts, either from their own correspondents, or taken from the New York and Boston papers.

The remaining event, and the reason for choosing this fortnight, was the marriage of the Prince of Wales. It provides a striking contrast in its press reporting to similar events a decade later, and the arrangements had been in progress since at least the end of the previous year. It is clear from the advertisement columns that there was a great deal of public excitement about it: there were rooms to be hired from which to watch the procession through London, books of songs, or dances, and souvenirs to celebrate the event, and plans for illuminations. The papers made very little attempt to exploit this interest. *The Times* had a report from its correspondent in Copenhagen, but none of the other papers sent a man there to describe Princess Alexandra's departure, or to interview the man in the street about it, by asking, for example, his opinions on the effect it would all have on the Schleswig-Holstein question. The only paper with a sense of the commercial possibilities of the occasion was the *Daily Telegraph*, which sent a correspondent to Flushing to see the Princess embark for England: he datelined his despatch 'off Margate'. It showed a further touch of the same 'penny paper' quality a few days later when it reported the princess' drive through London. All gave a great deal of space to the occasion: the *Daily Telegraph* had the imagination to collect all its wedding news into a four-page supplement marked 'Gratis'.[14] Nobody provided a map of the processional route. The wedding itself was very fully reported on 11 March by all the papers: the *History of the Times*, in its list of exceptional sales achieved on important occasions in the 1850s and 1860s, shows that on these two days they had their highest of all sales: 98,000 on the day of the procession and 108,000 on the day of the wedding.[15] The reporting of the wedding was a sober description of what was in any case a great public event: the press was not engaged in creating a spurious enthusiasm.

[14] *Daily Telegraph*, 9 March 1863.

[15] *History of the Times*, ii, p. 358.

The second period under discussion is much longer and includes events of a totally different order of magnitude, namely the Franco-Prussian war, from its outbreak in July 1870 until the suppression of the Commune in May 1871. Too much happened in that year for reporting to be analysed in any detail, yet, as it is this article's thesis that this war transformed the behaviour of the British press, something must be attempted. It needs no effort of imagination to see the effects of the war on the news: apart from its intrinsic importance it was so near at hand, so long drawn out, and with so many unexpected turns of events. It dominated the newspapers (except perhaps *The Times* which was much larger than the others), to the exclusion of most other foreign, and a good deal of home news. War reporting itself was no novelty: leaving more remote examples aside, there had been in recent years the American Civil War, the Austro-Prussian war, and Napier's expedition to Ethiopia in 1868. The papers tended to employ the same correspondents in successive campaigns, and as they usually moved about and worked together they had developed a fair amount of collective experience.[16] The practice had been, if a telegraph system existed, for a brief summary of events to be telegraphed, which would be followed by a long letter, sent by whatever post was available, and this would be printed a few days later. This system was in use during the first six weeks of the war, that is down to the surrender of the Emperor at Sedan. It became clear, especially towards the end of the period, that it could not provide a coherent picture of events. These events themselves unrolled extremely fast: there is less than a fortnight between Bazaine's investment in Metz and the declaration of the Third Republic. The Prussian armies were divided in two, and the newspapers tried to have a correspondent with each. These were small resources with which to keep abreast of a very complicated situation: the despatches, laboriously written out in the evenings, could take a long time to arrive, or go astray altogether.[17] Thus, by the beginning of September 1870, the London papers were publishing (in addition to short telegrams describing the events of the previous forty-eight hours) news that was very stale indeed: on 5 September, the day after the declaration of the republic, *The Times* published despatches

[16] A good general description of the life and working conditions of a war correspondent is given in by G. Manville Fenn, *George Alfred Henty, the Story of an Active Life* (London, 1907). Henty was employed as a special correspondent by the *Standard* between 1866 and 1878. He used his experiences as the basis for many of his boys' stories.

[17] Archibald Forbes, *Memories and Studies of War and Peace* (London, 1895), gives many examples of the practical difficulties experienced by correspondents in despatching their reports, both in 1870–71 and after.

from William Howard Russell dated 25, 27 and 28 August, all dealing with events before the final series of battles that had defeated the French armies: they were valuable perhaps as history, but they were no longer news.

The business of assembling and presenting a coherent account of the probable state of affairs rested with the newspapers' London offices. They used information coming from Belgium, but relied chiefly on the official communiqués issued in Berlin. It was at this point that the *Daily News* began to show the consistent skill and intelligence in its handling of the news which made the paper's reputation. The person whose name appears again and again in the memoirs of those concerned was the manager, John Robinson, whose name is hardly known today. The greater effectiveness of the *Daily News* can be demonstrated in the minor matter of war-maps. Both *The Times* and the *Daily News* had published maps of north-west Europe at the outbreak of war. The *Daily News* in late August produced a fresh map, considerably further west than the original one, and on 25 August produced one of Paris and its surroundings. On 2 September the *Daily Telegraph* produced one also. *The Times* on the other hand had a single map stretching from Carlsbad in the east and just including Paris on the west. It printed this map on a number of occasions, the last being on 3 September, two days after Sedan. It was not till ten more days had passed that it too printed a map of the Paris region.[18]

Robinson also was responsible for the engagement of Archibald Forbes, who for the next fourteen years was the paper's star war correspondent. He had been reporting the war for a small paper, the *Morning Advertiser*, whose editor decided that after the fall of the Empire there was no longer any need for his services. Forbes approached *The Times* and was rebuffed, and then went to the *Daily News*. Robinson, according to his own account, offered him £20 a week and his expenses: '"By George", he said, "I'll start tonight." . . . he agreed to meet me in the evening at the Reform Club, and I was to have ready for him £100 in French five-franc pieces.'[19]

Thirdly, memoirs agree that Robinson urged his correspondents to stop sending their main despatches by the uncertain postal system, but to telegraph direct. Telegraphy, as has been shown, had been made little use of in the opening stages of the war. Both these developments have one thing in common: they show a willingness to spend money liberally. The £20 a week offered to the then unknown Forbes was substantial pay: it was not much less than the salary of

[18] *The Times*, 14 September 1870.

[19] John Robinson, *Fifty Years of Fleet Street*, compiled and edited by Frederick Moy Thomas (London, 1904), p. 169.

the editor of the *Pall Mall Gazette* in the eighties, at the height of its fame.[20] How a paper which, the year before, had been in financial difficulties could afford to do this is not known: but it must be suspected that Labouchère, who could spend money very freely when he chose, was in some way responsible.

Labouchère can be shown to have been personally involved with reporting from this time. On Sunday, 4 September, he was in Paris on the day of the revolution. He went round, seeing, and as a good republican approving, what was going on, and in the evening adopted the new system in an ecstatic telegram which was printed the following morning.

> 'Paris is in a state of indescribable and intense enthusiasm. The whole city is, as it were, *en fête*. On every side, in almost every street I have passed through, I have heard cries of "Vive la République". . . . Upon the quay I saw busts of the Emperor pitched out of the houses and thrown into the Seine amidst tremendous shouts of applause. . . . Soldiers in every direction turn their muskets upside down and fraternise with the people. . . . Everybody is laughing and weeping with joy. Everybody is shaking hands and embracing his neighbour.'

These are extracts from a telegram exactly 250 words long: its effect, when the reader has been going through a paper where telegrams have been restricted to the baldest statements of fact, is still electric at the present day. Only a proprietor, perhaps, could have dared to telegraph in this abandoned way. On the same page were also printed telegraphed reports of popular reactions from the paper's correspondents in Karlsruhe, Brussels and Berlin. It seems that the paper had tried successfully to produce what the B.B.C. today describes as a 'round-up of reactions'.

After that occasion the same level of organization and excitement in the presentation of the news appeared on exceptional occasions such as the fall of Metz in October, or the Russian agreement to come to a conference in London in December on the question of the Black Sea Clauses.[21] Telegraphy also began to be used for the routine transmission of news from the siege of Paris: Archibald Forbes has left a description of the elaborate arrangements he made with a telegraph master in Saarbrücken which ensured that his reports were in the *Daily News* twenty-four hours after their despatch.[22] The *Daily Telegraph* also began printing long telegraphed personal assessments by their reporters outside Paris. Telegraphy,

[20] J. Saxon Mills, *Sir Edward Cook, K.B.E.* (London, 1921), p. 121.

[21] *Daily News*, 28 October and 2 December, 1870.

[22] *Op. cit.*, p. 225.

which had been accepted as the normal channel of communication by the American press well before this time, was becoming accepted in England.

During the winter of 1870–71 events in France did not pose the difficulties of interpretation and collection that the six weeks' war had done: the news from the Prussian side came regularly, and the news from Paris, arriving by balloon or otherwise, had so much novelty and character as to make up for its irregularity. The events were unprecedented, and gripped the attention of the public. How sharp was the effect of the news is illustrated by an anecdote of Joseph Wright, who later became the compiler of the *English Dialect Dictionary*. In 1870 he was a fifteen-year-old illiterate, working as a wool-sorter in Bradford. According to the biography by his widow, he used to listen during the Franco-Prussian war 'to the men who worked with him reading aloud from newspapers in their dinner-hour vivid accounts of battles and sieges and discussing with one another the things they read. He was intensely interested. Why should he be debarred from getting all this first-hand? He determined to acquire the art of reading.'[23] The same sort of thing is suggested in the daily lists of donations to a French relief fund published by the *Daily Telegraph* in January 1871:

> 'a waiter, 2*s*, an engine driver, G.E.R., 2*s*, a trifle from sympathisers at Widford, 5*s*, collected in St. Mary's and St. Michael's, Commercial Road East, £6, a few engineers, Lambeth, £2, collected from the servants and workmen on the Woolhampton estate, £2 6*s*, collection by a junior clerk £5 5*s* . . . a few working men near Enfield Highway 6*s*.'

These all come from a single issue of the paper.[24] They show not only the impact of the news but also the range of the *Daily Telegraph*'s public. The hold which the news from France exerted is shown also by the spate of war correspondence re-published in book form in the spring of 1871. The *War Correspondence of the Daily News* was published by Macmillan in January 1871: by March it was into its third edition, and a second series, covering events down to the end of February, was out. By 1 April it too was into its second edition and Labouchère's *Diary of a Besieged Resident*, and *The Fall of Metz*, by G. T. Robinson, the special correspondent of the *Manchester Guardian*, were also out.[25]

[23] E. M. Wright, *The life of Joseph Wright* (London, 1932), i, pp. 36–37. It is fair to add that the author goes on to say that after this Wright never took in a paper until he was 40.

[24] 19 January 1871.

[25] See advertisements in *Daily News*, 31 January, 21 March and 31 March 1871.

What was the effect of the war on circulations? Sales of *The Times* increased, but to no very marked extent.[26] There is no information about the *Telegraph* or the *Standard*, though it would be reasonable to assume that they increased to some extent also. The effects on the *Daily News* were spectacular: it is supposed to have raised its circulation threefold, from 50,000 to 150,000, though it dropped back after the war to about 90,000.[27] It moved, during the war, from the second to the first rank of London papers, and its financial troubles were over. In 1872 and 1873, it could advertise that, thanks to the increased circulation brought about by its war reporting, 'There is no better medium for advertising wants of all kinds.'[28]

The lessons to be learned from the Franco-Prussian war seemed pretty clear. Long personal despatches, by a competent writer, even if he were anonymous, would attract a following of readers, and the expense of telegraphing them was worth while. It also became usual to place greater emphasis on a main news page, supplied partly by Reuters, and partly by the paper's own correspondents: that is a conspectus, as far as possible, of what had happened the day before. The long, personal despatches were not necessarily sensational, though they opened a door to florid writing. It is noticeable that quite different literary conventions governed the writing of the special correspondents. Most of the contents of a mid-Victorian newspaper consist of straightforward reporting of business transacted: in this sense, perhaps, facts were sacred. The special correspondent, however, was free to record his own feelings and reactions, and to record them in the vocabulary of popular fiction. Much of the news sent during the siege of Paris was not strictly war correspondence at all: much of it was simply descriptive of daily life—about food, drink and winter fuel, what the Prussian soldiers were doing, and what life was like in the occupied territories. It could be argued that, in giving their correspondents space to develop and qualify their themes without interruption, Victorian editors succeeded in giving a more intelligible picture of events than television, with all its resources, succeeds in giving today.

In the years immediately after 1871 there are hints that, with declining or at best static post-war circulations, the papers were trying to repeat the successes of the Franco-Prussian war. The correspondent could also be used at home. For about a week in April 1872, the *Daily News* gave a great deal of space to highly

[26] *History of the Times*, ii, pp. 357–58.

[27] Information on circulations is summarized by A. P. Wadsworth, *Transactions of the Manchester Statistical Society* (1954–55), pp. 18 ff.

[28] *Mitchell's Newspaper Press Directory*, edns. of 1872 and 1873.

emotive reports by Archibald Forbes of Joseph Arch's movement.[29] Another reporter, Henry Lucy, was sent at the end of the year 1872–73 to South Wales to cover a coal strike: he describes how he spent every day telegraphing a long letter to his paper, and how the principal London and provincial newspapers followed the *Daily News*' lead, the reporters including G. A. Henty of the *Standard*, who was another veteran of the siege of Paris. The *Daily News* organized a relief fund for the coal-miners, as it had done for the French in 1870–71 and is stated to have raised £30,000 in three weeks.[30] This interest in industrial relations may have been an attempt to interest working-class readers, but it does not seem fanciful to see in it also a re-enactment of the situations of the siege of Paris: there were confrontations at the centre and the hardships of non-combatants to describe. It was the *Daily News*, again, with its eye for a story, which sent McGahan to Bulgaria in July 1876 to investigate the reports of atrocities.[31] The same sort of desire to keep up the level of public interest, indeed to create objects for it, may lie behind the *Daily Telegraph*'s decision to finance an expedition to Nineveh: in December 1872 George Smith of the British Museum had deciphered cuneiform inscriptions giving an independent account of the Deluge: the *Daily Telegraph* offered £1,000 towards sending out an archaeological expedition provided that Smith led it.[32]

The third period should demonstrate the way in which things were changing. It covers the second and third weeks of January 1874, when a large number of topics were competing for attention. In Europe the Carlist war was reported infrequently by special correspondents of all the papers. There were also the relations of Church and State in both France and Germany: this, which was not a subject of immediate popular interest, was hardly noticed except by *The Times*,[33] which still maintained its tradition of relying more on the judgement of its able correspondents resident abroad and less on the work of special correspondents, sent out to cover events which promised to be exciting. There was also an important long-running news story in the trial of the Tichborne claimant for perjury. This, which reached its 170th day on 31 January, had pride of place over all other news: every day each paper devoted about a page to a verbatim report of the hearing. Labouchère is supposed to have said that circulations were higher during those hearings than

[29] 27 March to 8 April 1872. See also Disraeli's comments, *ibid.*, 5 April 1872.

[30] Lucy, *op. cit.*, p. 102.

[31] R. T. Shannon, *Gladstone and the Bulgarian Agitation, 1876* (London, 1963), pp. 38 ff.

[32] See the entry for Smith in *D.N.B.*

[33] *The Times*, 29 January 1874.

during the Franco-Prussian war.[34] There were also reports, dating from the previous December, of a famine in Bengal: by mid-February the *Daily News* was printing reports from Archibald Forbes who was their 'special commissioner' there.[35]

There remain two news stories which can be compared directly with examples which have already been discussed. One was the Ashanti war. The expedition, led by Wolseley, had set out at the end of the previous year, and there had been plenty of time for the papers to prepare for it. They sent out their special correspondents. The telegraph did not reach West Africa, so the despatches came by sea to Lisbon and were telegraphed from there. Except that it was a war involving British troops, the Ashanti war was a small affair, and, it might be thought, one where the result could be easily predicted. The papers published, as they received them, long telegraphed reports, two or three columns in extent, describing the state of the expedition, the climate, the manners and customs of the natives—whereas a few years before the telegraph had been restricted to brief news summaries.

The remaining news story, the wedding of Queen Victoria's second son, the Duke of Edinburgh, was in striking contrast with earlier practice. He had become engaged in the previous autumn to the Grand Duchess Marie Alexandrovna, the only daughter of the Tsar Alexander II. The occasion, unlike the wedding of 1863, was exploited to the full. According to the *Standard*'s special correspondent in St Petersburg there was

> 'hardly a newspaper in London that is not represented by a special correspondent. The pictorials, not to be behindhand, have sent out talented artists, some of whom are really doing wonders in circumstances of no little difficulty. The great officials, seeing such a crowd of intelligent men all directing their energies to one point, are beginning to understand that the press is a power in England, if it is not in Russia, and are disposed to grant facilities for obtaining information which they never dreamt of affording to the representatives of the native press.'[36]

These 'facilities' included a noticeably greater ease of access to the ceremonies than the British press had enjoyed at home in 1863: they were taken on a tour of the Winter Palace about a week before the wedding: this was reported at length by the *Standard* and the *Daily Telegraph*, in the latter case by telegraph. On the day of the ceremony, 23 January, the British press was present at the two

[34] Algar Thorold, *The Life of Henry Labouchère* (London, 1913), p. 106, quoting *Truth* of 23 October 1884.

[35] 13 February 1874.

[36] *Standard*, 23 January 1874.

marriage rites, one Anglican, the other Orthodox, at a wedding dinner, and at a ball in the evening. All this was reported at length the following morning in England; the length of the reports varying from six columns (*Daily Telegraph*) to one and a half columns (*Daily News*). The coverage of the wedding was massive: Berlin correspondents telegraphed to say that the Prince and Princess of Wales had passed through Berlin,[37] special correspondents telegraphed to say when they arrived in St Petersburg.[38] Taken altogether, and allowing for any padding out of these despatches in Fleet Street, the total number of words telegraphed on this subject must have been very large indeed.

On 23 January, the very day of the wedding, Gladstone announced his unexpected dissolution of Parliament. The sudden and unforeseen irruption of this major issue, which was very fully reported throughout, provides a way of testing the newspapers' attachment to the existing popular topics. There was no perceptible reduction of the attention given to the Tichborne case by any paper, and the news from Ashanti continued to be printed as it arrived. The wedding was over, and there was nothing much more to record until the bride and bridegroom arrived in London three weeks later. Nevertheless the papers continued to print anything which arrived by the mails: *The Times*, learning the technique of popular reporting, printed three-quarters of a column on the bride's wedding trousseau on 28 January, and another similar amount, on 2 February, describing, in unctuous detail, how '*The Times*' special correspondent has visited the apartments of the newly married pair . . . the dressing room is in gray satin and leads to a small bathroom, dainty and beautiful with Moorish pillars and enamelled decoration, and where is sunk a white marble bath.'

The probability is that, if anything was pushed aside through pressure on space in the days before the election, it was the general run of unsensational home and foreign news.

It remains to suggest, briefly, some of the implications of these tendencies in news reporting. The first, and least controversial, must be concerned with the economics of newspaper production. There had been a marked switch to telegraphy, and this represented an increase in costs. For once, in this poorly documented subject, there is some firm evidence: the Post Office produced figures for a select committee in 1876, showing that, since its taking over of the telegraph system in 1870, there had been no increase in revenue from the Press Association, but a threefold increase in the expendi-

[37] *The Times*, 13 and 14 January 1874.
[38] *Daily Telegraph*, *Daily News*, 16 January 1874.

ture by newspapers on telegrams from their own reporters.[39] This refers to inland telegrams. Newspapers were using their own staff more and more, in comparison with their use of the agencies and of casual contributions from the public. Where overseas telegrams were concerned, the trend must have been more marked. In particular the telegrams from the back of beyond were very expensive indeed. In the Russo-Turkish war of 1878 the Press rate charged by the Eastern Telegraph Company was two shillings a word, and it was estimated that the *Daily Telegraph* and the *Daily News* were spending £70 to £80 a day on telegrams.[40] It was expected that costs would be higher in the Afghan war of 1879: it was later claimed that the *Standard* had spent £800 on a single despatch from Afghanistan.[41] In the Transvaal war of 1879, the *Daily News* was reported to have spent over £400 on a single despatch.[42] The magnitude of these sums is shown when they are compared with the gross revenue from sales of a paper with a daily circulation of about 200,000—that is just under £1,000 a day.

The London papers in competing with each other had added significantly to their costs and were caught in a vicious circle. It was necessary to adopt each advance in technology in order to maintain or increase circulations: yet each of these advances added to costs and made the competition for circulation still sharper. By moving into this situation they prevented themselves from reducing the price from a penny: they aimed at a more elaborate product in preference to a cheaper one, and by so doing restricted their chances of an increased circulation. In the last quarter of the nineteenth century prices of consumer goods were to fall, but the price of the morning dailies did not. When, in 1896 to 1900, the *Daily Mail* broke through to far higher circulations than any of these papers, one of the ways in which it was done was by a reduction in price: it was advertised as 'the penny paper for a halfpenny'. Nor did the dailies of the 1870s compete with one another by the free gifts and gimmickry which were employed by the national dailies between the wars, in somewhat similar economic circumstances.

There are also implications for the quality of the news which the British public, with its rapidly expanding electorate, was getting—a matter of some importance. The four main London dailies were the only ones which could afford to provide a news service of this kind: the lavish style of foreign news reporting which was coming in separated them sharply from the important provincial dailies

[39] Select Committee on the Post Office (Telegraph Department) H.C. 1876 XIII, qn. 3372.

[40] *Printer's Register*, December 1878.

[41] Joseph Hatton, *op cit.*, p. 144.

[42] *Printer's Register*, July 1879.

and from the lesser London dailies. Even so, their resources were small; the examples already quoted show that each paper had only a handful of correspondents in the field at any one time. This imposed on editors and managers the need for rigid selection of the stories to be covered, and the criteria they used were probably of great importance during the next twenty or thirty years. Limited resources were probably also responsible for the somewhat erratic handling of particular subjects: a correspondent could not be in two places at the same sime. The result might be that, once a man had been sent to Ashanti or St Petersburg, every word that he wrote would be printed, regardless of its importance. Alternatively, if he were sent on elsewhere, the subject would be dropped altogether; thus in the summer of 1876 the *Illustrated London News* interrupted its reporting of the Turkish campaign in Bulgaria in order to give news of Schliemann's excavations in Mycenae. The general effect, however, was to expose a few foreign or imperial questions to a bombardment of vivid reporting: Gladstone's denunciation of 'Beaconsfieldism' as his election cry to the public in 1879–80 must be seen in this context.

A further question concerns the extent to which a popular press, with its wide-eyed interest in foreign events, could have been a vehicle for favourable publicity for particular causes. At the St Petersburg wedding it seems at least possible that the newsmen were given easy access to the ceremonies, not because they were powerful, but because a favourable press in Britain was desirable. It is also possible that the Duke of Edinburgh, or his advisers, thought that the publicity (none of which was hostile) might do something to mitigate the current unpopularity of Queen Victoria. In Ashanti, and in his later campaign in the Transvaal, Wolseley, at that time in conflict with the Duke of Cambridge at the War Office, may have encouraged the work of the war correspondents who could show the success of his methods. His private papers certainly show that he had friends and supporters among the special correspondents.[43]

The same sort of thing may lie behind the reporting of the Franco-Prussian war. All war correspondents stressed that the Prussians gave much greater facilities to them than did the French. The extreme case was William Howard Russell. By 1870 he was a figure of international repute, and he was the representative of *The Times*. He was accredited to the headquarters of the Crown Prince of Prussia, and seems to have become psychologically absorbed into it. His diary shows him constantly in the company of the Crown Prince,

[43] Wolseley papers, Hove Public Library, especially letters from G. A. Henty (*Standard*) and the Hon. F. C. Lawley (*Daily Telegraph*).

not actually offering advice, but totally committed to the Prussian side. On the evening after Sedan he dined with him and his entourage, and afterwards his description of the battle was taken off by a royal courier for despatch. (The courier was captured and the despatch never arrived.) Russell describes all this without any suggestion that his judgement might have been influenced by so much friendliness.[44] There was much reference in contemporary writing to the intrusiveness of the press, and interviewing was regarded as the curse of the age, but it often seems possible that the persons interviewed stood to gain: social intimacy with the great and powerful, while less crude than the bribery and intimidation of an earlier generation, might be equally effective.

The final question must be concerned with the reading public: how far did the influence of these papers spread? We do not know what papers were being read by Joseph Wright and his workmates in Bradford in the dinner-hour in 1870, but since only a few years later the newspaper train arrived there at 10.10 a.m., they could probably have had a London paper by the dinner-hour on the day of publication. Or, a little later in the day, they could have had the halfpenny *Leeds Express*: this evening paper was almost entirely composed of the morning's war news copied directly from the London papers. Or, they could have had a more critical account the following morning in the *Bradford Observer*, the *Leeds Mercury* or the *Yorkshire Post*: these were all dailies in 1870. In all of these they would have found somewhat abbreviated versions of the London correspondents' writings: Labouchère's telegram appears again and again. London newspapers in the 1870s complained bitterly of the fact that news which they had collected at great cost could so easily be copied by the provincial papers, but they were unprotected by copyright and could find no effective remedy.[45] On the other hand, this situation meant that the special correspondents' writings, which were the most interesting and easily read parts of the London papers, were reaching a very wide public indeed. Their effect can only be guessed, but at a time when travel was rare, and state education was rudimentary, it is hard to see how people's mental picture of the remoter parts of the world could fail to be influenced by them: the special correspondents, in their expeditions to forbidden cities in Turkestan or to the deserts of Khartoum, provided late Victorian England with the equivalent of *Mandeville's Travels*.

[44] William Howard Russell, *My Diary During the Last Great War* (London, 1874), p. 211.

[45] Select Committee on the Post Office (Telegraph Department) H.C. 1876 XIII, evidence of John C. Macdonald, manager of *The Times*.

GREGORY KING AND THE SOCIAL STRUCTURE OF PRE-INDUSTRIAL ENGLAND[1]

By Professor G. S. Holmes, M.A. B.Litt., F.R.Hist.S.

READ 14 MAY 1976

DESPITE the rich and exciting work of recent years, the social history of England between the Restoration and the Industrial Revolution still bears something of a hangdog look, scarcely warranting, as yet, the cosmic conclusions and ferocious controversies to which students of early Stuart and early nineteenth-century society have grown accustomed. Yet, thanks to the work of one remarkable Englishman, who was born in 1648 and died in 1712, there is one aspect of this pre-industrial period—its social structure—on which we are all happy to pontificate. Gregory King's table of ranks and degrees, on which in the last resort so much of this confidence rests, has now acquired a unique cachet. The continual reproduction in post-war textbooks of this famous document,[2] which we think of as King's 'social table' but which he described as his 'Scheme of the Income and Expense of the Several Famillies of England', is just the most obvious symptom of its dominant historiographical influence.

It is my belief, however, that this trust has been misplaced; that King has been responsible for much complacency and confusion about the pre-industrial social structure; indeed that, historiographically speaking, one of the worst things that could have happened for the study of that society was that in 1696 one of the cleverest, most original men of his day should have chosen to write down, on one page of a celebrated manuscript work, what *seems* to be a cameo of the social structure of his day.

A few amber lights, admittedly, have flashed on the table from

[1] A preliminary version of this paper was delivered to the Cambridge Social and Economic History seminar in February 1976. I am grateful for the suggestions made on that occasion by Professor D. C. Coleman and Mr Peter Laslett. I am also indebted to Professors C. D. Chandaman and Henry Horwitz, Mr Clyve Jones, Mr Alan Downie and Drs J. V. Beckett, M. B. Rowlands and W. A. Speck for helping in various ways to further my understanding of King and his work.

[2] In whole or in part. The sequence runs to at least a dozen, beginning with G. M. Trevelyan, *English Social History* (2nd edn., London, 1946) and G. N. Clark, *The Wealth of England* (London, 1946), and ending with P. Mathias, *The First Industrial Nation* (London, 1970) and J. D. Chambers, *Population, Economy and Society in pre-Industrial England* (Oxford, 1972).

time to time: Mingay's against the incomes of the aristocracy, for instance, and Mathias's against the concealment of important occupational groups within King's 'families' and blanket categories.[3] In 1967, J. P. Cooper iconoclastically suggested that the 'evident uncertainty' in King's mind, revealed by his working papers, about the numbers of paupers, farmers and freeholders raised some queries against his methods as a social analyst.[4] But we have been reluctant to take these hints: inhibited, no doubt, by the manifest admiration for King's achievement which even his cautious scrutineers display. Mathias, for instance, can still describe the table as 'the most precise picture of the British economy and social structure just before the industrial revolution'.[5] And more recently Mr Laslett has paid glowing tribute to 'the first man to study the structure of a pre-industrial society . . . on lines at all similar to the social scientific procedures of our own day', compelling respect by the official status of his sources as well as the solidity of his methods, and producing findings of 'the highest authority'.[6]

Why should dependence on King have remained so total? It is true that his work as a social analyst towers over an extended plain mid-way between two peaks: Thomas Wilson's *State of England*, written in 1600, and Patrick Colquhoun's *A State of Indigence*, in 1806.[7] Scattered over this plain are occasional small hills,[8] but only one mountain. But a more insidious cause of the veneration bestowed on King's table is that he speaks the language of our own

[3] G. E. Mingay, *English Landed Society in the Eighteenth Century* (London, 1963), pp. 20–22; P. Mathias, *op. cit.*, pp. 25, 29, pointing especially to the concealment of servants and manufacturers (*cf. idem*, 'The Social Structure in the Eighteenth Century: a Calculation by Joseph Massie', *Econ. Hist. Rev.*, 2nd ser., x, 1957). See also P. Laslett, *The World we have Lost* (2nd edn., London, 1971), p. 270, n. 38—an aside which expresses some uneasiness at the danger that 'our view of pre-industrial social structure as a whole', being too King-centred, may prove to 'be true of the 1690s only'; and the general caution against 'the frankly uncertain statistical foundations' of much of King's political arithmetic in Colin Brooks, 'Taxation, Finance and Public Opinion, 1688–1714' (Cambridge Univ. Ph.D. thesis, 1971), p. 276, n. 1.

[4] J. P. Cooper, 'The Social Distribution of Land and Men in England, 1436–1700', *Econ. Hist. Rev.* 2nd ser., xx, 1967, pp. 432–34.

[5] *First Industrial Nation*, p. 23 (my italics).

[6] Introduction to *The Earliest Classics: John Graunt and Gregory King* (Pioneers of Demography series, London, 1973), pp. [2], [6]–[8]. Mr Laslett adds: 'He seems to have been commissioned by the Government, and, within certain limits, he was undoubtedly believed by the Government'.

[7] For Wilson's work see Camden Society, 3rd ser., lii, 1936, ed. F. J. Fisher. Colquhoun's treatise (1806) provided for the year 1803 a structural and statistical breakdown of the society of his day as ambitious as King's and evidently influenced by the latter's approach.

[8] Notably those of Edward Chamberlayne (social estimates included in the numerous edns. of *Angliae Notitia*, 1669–1702), and Joseph Massie (see above, n. 3).

generation. He speaks not with the tongues of men but with the symbols of mathematicians. Is it not this that makes us so peculiarly receptive today to King: that he chose to adopt in the 1690s the quantitative approach to social analysis? On to that one celebrated page of manuscript King crammed no fewer than 285 lovely, hard figures, comprising *in toto* 1,015 digits. In an age which deifies the statistic and grovels before the graph, King can hardly miss.

To reinforce our confidence, his credentials as a demographer have now been most impressively endorsed;[9] and the consequent temptation to attach the same weight to his skeletal picture of society as we do to his painstaking calculations of population size and trends is bound to be a hard one to resist. And so, we permit ourselves the usual token laughs at his leverets and his medieval history; we may even admit that the frailty of his commercial and comparative statistics has been exposed;[10] yet we take it as read that when Gregory King told posterity about the social structure of late seventeenth-century England, he knew what he was talking about.

But did he? What were his sources of information? And how scientifically did he use them? Can we be sure that he even intended his 'ranks, degrees, titles and qualifications' to be a realistic representation of the framework of his own society? And if not this, then what was the table's purpose, in the context of the whole work—the *Natural and Political Observations*—of which it is such a small part? Would it not have alarmed King deeply (adamant as he was against personally publishing anything of his major work in his own lifetime)[11] to know that these columns of figures, with their cryptic categories, would serve a generation eleven times removed from his own as a model? And can we conceivably justify any King-based models of today which are applied not simply to a once-for-all situation but to an essentially static pre-industrial social pattern?

[9] Notably by D. V. Glass, 'Two papers on Gregory King', in D. V. Glass and D. E. C. Eversley, *Population in History* (London, 1965). See T. H. Hollingsworth, *Historical Demography* (London, 1969), pp. 81–88, esp. 85–87 for the only serious recent attempt to blacken King's demographic reputation; Anne Whiteman, 'The Census that Never Was', in A. Whiteman, J. S. Bromley and P. G. M. Dickson (eds.), *Statesmen, Scholars and Merchants* (Oxford, 1973), for a refined but devastating scholarly demolition of Hollingsworth's case.

[10] See R. Davis, 'English Foreign Trade, 1660–1700', *Econ. Hist. Rev.* 2nd ser., vii, 1954, p. 155, n. 6; E. Le Roy Ladurie, 'Les comptes fantastiques de Gregory King', *Annales E.S.C.* 23, 1968, pp. 1086–1102 (Professor D. C. Coleman kindly drew my attention to the latter article).

[11] Charles Davenant, *An Essay upon the Probable Methods of making the People Gainers in the Balance of Trade*, 1st edn. (London, 1699), pp. 23–24; British Library, (B.L.), Harl. MS. 6944, fo 117: Leibniz to Samuel Stebbing, Hanover, 4 September 1708 (postscript: 'je vous prie Monsieur de faire mes complimens... à Mons. King qui obligeroit le public s'il publiois ses calculs politiques').

These are some of the questions to be considered in this paper. An indispensable key to virtually all of them is the problem of King's intentions: of what were the general impulses which drove him to the study of political arithmetic, his specific objectives in writing the *Observations*, and above all his reason for including in it a 'social table'. Our *point d'appui* throughout, in fact, will be the man himself. Although biographical material is patchy[12] there are four things of particular relevance to our questions which his papers do disclose: his frustrated ambition; his deep conservatism; his obsessive, ensnaring passion for figures; and yet with all this, a certain underlying humility. These personal facets will provide the framework of much of my argument.

In the first place, why in 1695 did King quite suddenly develop, at the age of 46, an absorbing interest in 'political arithmetic'?[13] The clue lies in his frustrated professional ambitions. Although late in life he became a public servant,[14] his principal professional career was centred from 1677 on the College of Heralds,[15] where in 1688 he became Lancaster Herald. Dugdale apart, Gregory King was arguably the most accomplished and authoritative herald of the seventeenth century. Yet twice in his career he had to suffer the most bruising setbacks to his just professional aspirations and pride. It is the first of these occasions which is crucial for us. During 1694 and in the winter of 1694–95 King twice fell foul of the Earl Marshall.

[12] Brief sketches of his life and professional career have been written in this century by Thompson Cooper (*D.N.B.*) and G. E. Barnett (introduction to *Two Tracts by Gregory King*, Baltimore, 1936). More illuminating and very carefully researched is the account by D. V. Glass (see 'Two papers', n. 9 above). All owe a good deal to King's first and still fullest biographer, Sir George Chalmers (1802). The greater part of King's surviving correspondence is in B.L. Harl. MS. 6815, 6821, 6837, 6944 and 7525. There are also some items of biographical interest in P.R.O., T.64/302 (King Papers) and T.1/130; in the unpublished papers of Robert Harley (B.L. Loan 29); in one of King's business letter books for the years 1704–07 (B.L. Loan 57/73, Bathurst Papers); and in his 'Staffordshire Notebook', 1679–80 (*Collections for a History of Staffordshire*, ed. by G. P. Mander for William Salt Arch. Soc., 1919, London, 1920). King's autobiography (Bodleian Library, MS. Rawlinson C.514, printed in J. Dallaway, *Inquiries into the Origin and Progress of the Science of Heraldry*, Gloucester, 1793) unfortunately stops in 1694.

[13] There is not a hint of such an interest in his autobiography, down to 1694; though his 'Staffordshire Notebook' (see n. 12 above) reveals an early awareness of the size and social composition of communities.

[14] He was by then 54. See p. 50 below.

[15] Having earlier spent five years in the 1660s as clerk-assistant to Sir William Dugdale, he was appointed Rouge Dragon Poursuivant in 1677 and Registrar of the College in 1684. King was also a man of many other parts, as his epitaph properly records: an expert map-maker and surveyor; something of a property developer; a most polished etcher and engraver; and a mathematician (his father's occupation).

As a result, he found himself not merely anchored to the position of Lancaster Herald, but removed from the Registrarship of the College; and when, shortly afterwards, a charge of embezzlement was brought against him in connection with royal funeral fees, King's disillusionment with the heraldic career reached an extremity.[16] It is no coincidence that it was in that year, 1695, that he sat down and wrote his autobiographical essay.[17] It was a watershed in his life: a time for stocktaking, then for forging boldly ahead to deploy, in a completely fresh field, those remarkable talents he well knew he possessed.

But if the personal impulse was powerful, the intellectual and political climate of 1695 was singularly appropriate for its accommodation. In Britain 'the art of reasoning by figures, upon things relating to government', as a contemporary described political arithmetic,[18] was a novel science. Its founding father was generally held at the time to be Sir William Petty,[19] and as late as 1688 its distinguished practitioners had been few. However, over the next six or seven years what had started as a largely academic study received the stamp of deadly earnestness from the War of the League of Augsburg. And in 1695, exactly at the time when King was ripe for a new intellectual challenge, this war had reached its climax. The cost in blood, taxation and commerce had already far surpassed that of any war in living memory. A national bank had been created, and a funded National Debt inaugurated. And amid all the prevailing fever and uncertainty, an increasingly Whiggish ministry was besieged by platoons of optimistic 'projectors', hatching and peddling a variety of new money-raising schemes.

What government fiscal policy needed at this juncture, above all else, was a rational foundation of reliable information. Thus far William III's ministers had been heavily dependent on Petty's work for their estimates of the size of the population and the total wealth of the nation, and the results had not been reassuring.[20] In any case,

[16] Dallaway, App. p. xlvi *et seq.*; G. P. Mander, intro. to 'Staffs Notebook', *loc. cit.*, p. 193.

[17] See n. 12 above. The essay parades past achievements as a backcloth for present discontents.

[18] *The Political and Commercial Works of . . . Charles D'Avenant, LL.D.*, ed. Sir C. Whitworth (London, 1771), i, 127 [hereafter Davenant, *Works*].

[19] King himself would not have agreed. He looked to John Graunt as his mentor. See Glass, 'Two papers', *loc. cit.*, pp. 162–63.

[20] Petty's *Verbum Sapienti*, in which his original population estimate for England and Wales of 6 mns appeared, was written in 1666 but not published until 1691. Meanwhile he had produced in the 1680s at least three revised estimates, based on Hearth Tax returns, ranging from 7.0 mn to around 7.4 mn. The figure of 7 mn was most widely entertained. Greater London Council Library, the 'Burns Journal' of Gregory King, hereafter cited as B.J., pp. 120, 121(3), 275. (The Burns Journal

a current tendency for the Commons to resort regularly to graduated poll taxes and to excises made it desirable that the government should also have clearer insight into how numbers and wealth were distributed between different sectors of society.[21] In this social territory, however, just as in the demographic field, the working politicians were still groping around in a fog of uncertainty and confusion.[22]

The advance signal of relief came during 1695 when a former Excise official, Dr Charles Davenant, lifted the whole debate on fiscal policy on to a new plane by publishing his *Essay on Ways and Means of Supplying the War*. This marked the beginning of a spate of constructive writing, and not least of a further stream from Davenant's own fluent pen. His 'Memoriall concerning the Coyn of England' and 'Memoriall concerning Creditt', for instance, followed rapidly in November 1695 and July 1696, and were privately submitted to leading ministers.[23] But the most crucial significance of the *Essays on Ways and Means* lay in its effect on Gregory King. Quite probably he was already friendly with Davenant; and they certainly remained on the closest terms from now until King's death.[24] Over the next few years the two men were to exchange ideas and information freely, and during that time Davenant frequently picked King's brains without much shame.[25] Yet at the outset it was King who

---

is photographically reproduced in *The Earliest Classics*—see n. 6 above); C. Brooks, *op. cit.*, pp. 312–13. In the early 1690s two members of the Royal Society, John Houghton and Thomas Neale, had supplied Parliament with fresh data, but in the latter's population calculations, at least, little confidence could be reposed. See H. Horwitz (ed.), *Parliamentary Diary of Narcissus Luttrell* (Oxford, 1972), pp. 112, 123, 141; W. Cobbett, *The Parliamentary History of England*, v, App. x, for Houghton's *Account of the Acres and Houses* (London, 1693).

[21] 'In these sort of speculations not only the quantity but the quality of the inhabitants must be duly pondered. They must be divided into their several ranks and classes'. Davenant, *Works*, ii, 173.

[22] See *Luttrell's Parl. Diary*, pp. 144, 160, for the Commons' finance debates of January 1692 during which Paul Foley and Sir Edward Seymour differed by an incredible 100,000 in their estimates of the number of gentlemen in England.

[23] The first was addressed to Godolphin, First Lord of the Treasury, 'in obedience to your Lordshipp's commands', and the second to the Treasury Commissioners in general. There are copies in London Univ. Library, MS. 60, Davenant's MS. tracts, 1695–96; also in B.L. Harl. MS. 1223, fos 71–95, 115–56, which suggests they either came into Robert Harley's possession directly, in the 1690s, or were acquired by him later, *via* Gregory King (Harley acquired many of King's papers after the latter's death in 1712).

[24] See, e.g., a letter from Davenant to King, dated 'Nov. 17th, 1710. My birthday', and signed 'Your most affectionate servant', in P.R.O. T.64/302.

[25] The full extent of Davenant's indebtedness is revealed by comparing his unpublished tracts—for example, the two cited above (n. 23) and the 'Essay on Publick Virtue' (London, 1696: submitted to Godolphin and Shrewsbury)—with

was the chief debtor. Quite apart from the general stimulus it afforded him in directing his pent-up energies and frustrations into the exciting channel of political arithmetic, the Lancaster Herald owed specifically to the *Essay on Ways and Means* the base figure, culled by Davenant from the very last set of Hearth Tax records, of the number of houses in England and Wales in the year 1690. This figure, of just over 1,300,000 houses, was to be the point of departure for all King's own subsequent researches, even into social structure.[26]

As he worked away with consuming energy at the groundwork for his masterpiece, for much of 1695 and on into 1696, he did so with two overriding objectives in mind. He lays them down in the very first sentence of the *Observations*: 'to be well appriz'd of the true state and condition' of England, '*in the two main articles, of its people, and wealth*'. These he considered the twin foundations of sound government at any time; but as imperative necessities 'at a time when a long and very expensive war against a potent Monarch . . . seems to be at its crisis'. On these foundations—an accurate calculation of the population and as close an estimate as he could reach of the national wealth and expenditure over the first seven years of the war—he proposed to build all else: his forecasts of future trends, if the war continued; his fiscal recommendations, the chief *raison d'être* of his work; his careful comparisons between England's position and that of France and Holland.

What is more, King approached his main objectives with a very clear order of priorities in mind. Top priority went to cracking the toughest nut of all, the population nut. Next, he probed towards various general conclusions about the national income and wealth, in peace and war.[27] Only then did he attempt an anatomy of the

---

King's notebooks and *Observations*. In the 'Essay on Publick Virtue' wholesale borrowings which had started out purportedly as a common endeavour, or as what 'upon a nice & strict inquiry *wee* find very strong reason to believe' (see London Univ. MS. 60, pp. 113, 114) ended, rather disgracefully, as 'these observations [which] *I* have gathered by long enquiry and study in these matters . . .' *Ibid.*, p. 270.

[26] King began the first chapter of his *Natural and Political Observations* with the statement, taken directly from Davenant, that 'the number of houses in the kingdom, as charged in the books of the hearth office, at Lady-day, 1690, were . . . 1,319,215'. G. Chalmers, *An Estimate of the Comparative Strength of Great Britain* (London, 1804), App., p. 33. (All references to the *Observations* hereafter are to the Chalmers version, 1804 edn., cited: Chalmers, App.) That King never checked this figure personally (see p. 58 and n. 81 below) is a truly extraordinary fact in view of John Houghton's conflicting evidence on the same point, published in 1693 (see n. 20 above).

[27] Under three heads: (a) the rental and capital value of its lands and property (calculated at 18 years' purchase), (b) the annual produce of its trade, (c) the

nation's income and expenditure, in details that could be roughly related to various points of the social scale and set alongside a corresponding social breakdown of his population total. His analysis of the social structure was at no time envisaged as an end in itself. Rather he saw this 'scheme' of income and expenditure as an ambitious top crust to be superimposed on the foundations already laid: something that might enable a more sophisticated superstructure of proposals to be erected above them. That this was the way King thought, and worked, is beyond doubt. The evidence contained in Davenant's 'Memoriall concerning Creditt', submitted to the Treasury lords in July 1696,[28] is in itself convincing; and it is supported to the hilt by the two major survivals from King's own working notebooks of the years 1695 to 1700.

From the 'Memoriall' it is obvious that, while King had completed his demographic calculations long before the midsummer of 1696 and had communicated much of their detail to his friend (as he had to others),[29] Davenant had only had the benefit of the herald's unfinished work and very tentative conclusions in dealing with the annual income and outgoings of the nation—even in general terms.[30] In view of this it is no surprise to discover that the notebook embodying some of King's first explorations into political arithmetic, early in 1695, contains only two oblique and speculative ventures into the social structure: to call them ranging shots would be complimentary.[31] Much more revealing is that the same experimental pattern, and the very same order of priorities, is repeated in King's later and far more compendious journal, now known as the Burns Journal, in which the first entries were made in the summer of 1695.[32]

This journal must have been the immediate predecessor of another (now, alas, lost) in which the very last weeks of preparation for the writing of the *Observations* were recorded. Even so, the Journal's 295 pages[33] cover almost every inch of the ground brought within the

'stock of the Kingdom' in a variety of commodities, from coin and plate to livestock and industrial products.

28 Though much of it was probably drafted a month or two earlier. See B.J., p. 221 *et seq.*

29 *E.g.* to George Stepney in April 1696, and (in an earlier and somewhat different version) to a prominent peer in the government, probably Lord Godolphin, late in 1695. B.J., pp. 171, 269, 271, 275.

30 *Cf.* London Univ. MS. 60, pp. 113–19 *passim* with Chalmers, App., pp. 47, 49, 61 and B.J., pp. 247, 261, 270–71.

31 P.R.O., T.64/302: '[Com]putations of the Numbe[r] of People, etc. by Greg^y. King 1695', pp. 14, 18v. (hereafter P.R.O., T.64/302: notebook).

32 See n. 20 above. The journal continues into 1696, with some entries added as late as 1700.

33 The pagination runs from 1 to 291, but the unnumbered page opposite p. 1

compass of the end-product; and only 15 bear in any way on the social structure.[34] In some of them the social material is fragmentary and incidental; even the most extended piece of social analysis in the journal was plainly regarded by its author as no more than a preparatory exercise.[35] In the latter part of the journal there is, significantly, a batch of truly definitive material which, having passed through at least a year of refining fires, was communicated by King to Davenant in July 1696[36]—just too late to be incorporated into the 'Memoriall'. It supplemented at great length the demographic data which Davenant had received long before, with what was, in effect, the substance of at least six further chapters of the *Observations*. But it included no social table, nor anything remotely resembling one. Indeed the Burns Journal must leave any careful student convinced that it was only after the midsummer of 1696 that Gregory King (almost as an afterthought?) decided to put the icing on the otherwise almost-finished cake of his great creation, by drawing up the full 'Scheme of the Income and Expense of the Several Families', as we now know it; and having made the decision, proceeded to re-order these calculations, by taking them back from the year 1695, to which (up to now) he had invariably made them relevant, *to the year 1688*.

Something which has attracted only spasmodic notice is that although the bulk of the factual and statistical data contained in the *Observations* is related in one way or another to the mid 1690s, the famous social table itself is, as we are explicitly told, 'calculated for the Year 1688'. Why was this? The answer has the closest bearing on the value of King's table to us as a social document; for it is intimately connected with the second major facet of the man himself which I suggested deserves our attention, namely, his conservatism.

Gregory King was a deeply conservative man, in two senses. In the first place, he was politically conservative. Bluntly, he was a thorough, divine right Tory; and it is really very odd that this point has never appeared to be of much significance to historians. As his

---

is utilized and three sets of 'pages 120–21' are included, only one of the four supernumerary pages being a blank.

[34] B.J., pp. 65–67, 70–75, 209, 246, 265, 270, 280–81.

[35] B.J., pp. 280–81. It occurs among a long series of 'Conclusions or Aphorisms' drawn up in the last 2–3 months of 1695 (the statistical conclusions concerning England relate explicitly to Michaelmas 1695). Although in many respects fuller in information than the 'social table' of the *Observations* it omits such crucial occupational groups as freeholders and farmers, army and navy officers, soldiers and seamen.

[36] Or perhaps in June—King does not seem quite certain which month, on recollection. See B.J., pp. 221–30, inclusive: indexed on p. 285 'Observations upon the People of England in a kind of Treatise as given to Dr. Davt.'.

autobiography shows, King was a warm admirer of Charles II in that monarch's closing years, and was distressed by his death; and although, as a good professional, he was to conform to the post-Revolution regime in 1689 and officiate at the coronation of William and Mary, he admitted to having had some sympathy with James II.[37] It was not entirely coincidental that both the major setbacks of his heraldic career occurred at periods of Whig ascendancy;[38] still less was it coincidence that, despite his obvious inclination in the mid-nineties to serve the government,[39] he had to wait until the Tory resurgence following Queen Anne's accession for his first mark of official favour, the secretaryship of the Commission of Public Accounts.[40] Almost certainly he owed it to the rising star of Robert Harley, who had shown distinct interest in King's major work in 1696–97, after its completion.[41] Thus King's career shows marked parallels with that of his friend Davenant, another unabashed Tory.[42]

[37] Dallaway, xxxvi, xxxviii–ix; *cf.* Chalmers, *op. cit.*, App. 'Notices of the Life of Gregory King', pp. 16, 18.

[38] Especially striking was the second, in 1709–10, when his claims to the plum vacancy of Clarenceux King of Arms were rejected in favour of Sir John Vanbrugh, the Marlboroughs' architect at Blenheim and the darling of the politically-influential Kit-Cat Club. See Chalmers, App., pp. 25–26; B.L. Harl. MS. 7525, fos 40–41: King to Harley, 2 January 1710[–11]; 'Staffs Notebook', *loc. cit.*, p. 197, for King's 1679 estimate of Clarenceux's total emoluments as second only to those of Garter King, viz. at £230 p.a. 'clear', plus lodgings and visitation fees, and a Herald's income, 'clear', at only £50 p.a., plus lodgings valued at £20 p.a.

[39] See his draft letter to Sir Stephen Fox, 19 December 1695, in B.J. p. 241.

[40] The Commission's first Secretary in the 1690s was George Tollet. King's appointment, worth £100 p.a., was made in April 1702. (See J. A. Downie, 'The Commission of Public Accounts and the formation of the Country Party', *Eng. Hist. Rev.*, xci, 1976, p. 38, n. 3; N. Luttrell, *A Brief Historical Relation of State Affairs*, Oxford, 1857, v, 160; B.L. Add. MS. 29568, fo. 89: King to Hatton, 18 August 1702.) He held the post in both periods of this Tory-dominated body's operation in Anne's reign, 1702–04 and 1711–12. In between times he served in a £300-a-year job as Secretary to the Commissioners of Army Accounts, and in 1708 was appointed one of three commissioners to state the debts of King William III. (Bodl. MS. Rawlinson A.289, for his official correspondence 1705–06; Luttrell, *Brief Hist. Rel.* vi, 314.)

[41] See letters from King to Harley, 1697 and 1711, in B.L. Loan 29/298M, especially that of 8 December 1697; B.L. Harl. MS. 7575: King to Harley (copy), 2 January 1711; National Lib. of Australia, Kashnor MSS: copy of the *Natural and Political Observations*, 1697, bearing Harley's 'Queries and Observations' and King's replies to them. This latter document has been consulted on microfilm, hereafter cited, Kashnor MSS., *N.P.O.*

[42] For all his furious activity with the pen in the 1690s, Davenant did not re-enter government service, as Inspector General of Imports, until 1705. He had, however, refused Godolphin's offer of a post in the Excise in November 1702. H.M.C. *Portland MSS.* iv, 52: Godolphin to Harley, 21 November, 24 November 1702. In general see D. A. G. Waddell's biographical essay in *Econ. Hist. Rev.* 2nd ser., xi, 1958–59, pp. 279–88.

However, he and Davenant shared something more than the ups and downs of the political see-saw. They nursed a mutual suspicion of Continental entanglements. Above all, they shared an instinctive conviction that no protracted war could possibly have other than ill effects for England: ill effects on her wealth, on her economy, on her social well-being and even on her population growth. In chapter 10 of the *Natural and Political Observations*—the great statistical *tour de force* entitled 'The State of the Nation, Anno 1695'—King charted year by year what he implicitly believed had been England's descent down the slippery slope towards penury since 1688. His conclusion was stark: 'That, after the year 1695, the taxes actually raised will fall short every year, more and more, to that degree, that *the war cannot well be sustained beyond the year 1698 upon the foot it now stands*...'[43] Davenant, in his 1696 'Memoriall', had made precisely the same prediction as to when the point of utter exhaustion would be reached. Their words echo like some funereal duet. And since William III, by making peace at Ryswick, deprived the country this time round of the chance to disprove their case, Davenant had not changed his tune by 1699, as the mournful dirge on 'the wounds of the late war' in his *Balance of Trade* essay bears witness.[44]

Such an outlook, admittedly, was not freakish in the 1690s; and in 1695 there was still *prima facie* evidence—heavy shipping losses and trade dislocation, especially—which seemed to many to justify it. What is truly instructive, however, is that this fundamentally pessimistic, Tory-'Country' view of England's incapacity to bear for long the burdens of large-scale warfare was so ingrained in Gregory King that right at the end of his life, despite all the triumphs of the Spanish Succession War, he was quite unconverted. In an eloquent memorandum which he sent to Davenant in December 1710, he argued that in fighting for seventeen years 'so potent an enemy as the French King', with his unparalleled resources, it had been folly 'in the beginning of the last warr, *when the kingdom was at the heighest pitch of wealth*', to embark on a policy of accumulating a great funded debt.[45] And in the maestro's final, fascinating exercise in political arithmetic, a detailed draft letter endorsed 'Upon Mr. Scobel's proposition for raysing a considerable sum by a Tax on Traders and

[43] Chalmers, App., pp. 61–62 (my italics). King firmly believed that the war had caused a decline in population to set in. See *ibid.*, pp. 42–43; Kashnor MSS. *N.P.O.*, in which King elaborates his reasons for this conviction, for Harley's benefit.

[44] See n. 11 above and *Works*, i, 135.

[45] By 'long mortgages and anticipations of the flower of the revenue'. P.R.O. T.1/130/15E, endorsed 'Observations on the Two Lotteries of 1694 and 1710—Sent to Dr Davenant circ. 8 Dec. 1710'.

Retailers, aº 1710–11',[46] he contended that the nation was decidedly poorer now than it had been even in 1695, let alone in 1688; and, as ever, he was prepared to get down to figures to drive home his point.[47] He had calculated in the *Observations* that at the time of the Revolution 511,586 families were 'increasing the wealth of the Kingdom' and 849,000 families 'decreasing' it. But he now attested, early in 1711, that 'in all probability the increasers are not at this time above 400,000 families and the decreasers, and not increasers, 900,000 families.'[48]

Here, then, is our clue to why King determined some time in the summer of 1696 to relate all his calculations about the nation's wealth and taxable capacity—and therefore his social table too—to the year 1688. For him 1688 marked the line between normality and grave aberration; and such it remained until the day of his death.[49] If I seem to have somewhat laboured this point, it is because it has something of fundamental importance to tell us about King's limitations as a social analyst. It indicates why, even in his own day, his famous table was never a strictly contemporary social document. And it heavily underlines the dangers of using a 'Scheme of the Income and Expense of the several Families' for the year 1688 as a model for interpreting the social structure of England during much, or all, of the subsequent pre-industrial period. For not only was King's resort to social categorization entirely subordinate to a deeper purpose—a fiscal purpose; his whole thinking about society was retrospective. Despite the veneer of modernity which overlays his work King's attitudes were, up to a point, the anachronistic social attitudes of a herald who had made his last provincial visitation in 1684:[50] at a time when visitations themselves had become a hopeless anachronism.

The fact is, the English society of 1695–96 was already in a state of flux: it was already beginning to witness important changes in

[46] P.R.O., T.64/302. Francis Scobell, the experienced High Tory M.P. for Launceston, had made his proposal to the Commons' Committee of Ways and Means.

[47] *E.g.* he claimed the general national income was in 1711 only 39 mns, 4½ mns less than he had believed it to be at the Revolution. Such evidence as that in 1709 it had taken a mere four hours to attract £2 mn in subscriptions to a new Bank loan to the government—more than Charles II's ministers could normally expect from the produce of two years' ordinary revenue—apparently left him unimpressed.

[48] He appears to have calculated that the population had fallen by 1711 close to 5,300,000.

[49] Davenant's attitude was much the same: see *Works*, i, 132 (written October 1697).

[50] Of Cambridge and Huntingdon. He later attended Clarenceux on the final London Visitation of 1687. Chalmers, App., pp. 16–17.

the landowning sector, the rise of a new 'monied interest' in the City, the rapid expansion of the civil service and of the armed forces, vital new stimuli to certain branches of industry and distributing trades, and the inauguration of a period of steady urban growth in some parts of the provinces; not to mention many subtler transmutations. King was in a position to have recorded the first phase of these changes, had he had any desire to do so; for, like many of his contemporaries, he cannot have been entirely unaware that something was stirring. But for him the only true society, the only firm base to which all must return if there was to be any future health for England, was the *societas ante bellum.*

By itself this is a misfortune for historians. What makes it a dangerous snare into the bargain is that the fossilizing effects of his socio-political outlook were magnified by a second aspect of Gregory King's intense conservatism. So far from having any vision of England's potential greatness—though he wrote at the very moment of time when she was taking the first strides along the road to first-class European status—he was on the contrary obsessed by her vulnerability, by the fragility of the foundations on which even her pre-war prosperity had rested. By the end of 1695 his demographic work had convinced him that all previous political arithmeticians had seriously exaggerated the size of the country's population.[51] This, he thought (and with justice) had had in turn a damaging effect on fiscal policy: '. . . the calculations of Sr. Wm. Petty, & others, of the number of People obtaining too much credit with the House of Commons, makes all our Poll Bills and other Taxes which depend upon that Article, to fall so very short'.[52] And these convictions led him to the far more sweeping conclusion that Petty, through misplaced national pride, had inflated almost all his reckonings, notably those concerning the wealth of the nation relative to its neighbours. In an early draft of his manuscript King roundly deplored 'the vanity of over-valuing our own strength [which] is so natural to our Nation . . .'[53]

It was his stern determination not to fall in the same trap as Petty, linked with his resolve to provide the Treasury and the Commons with more realistic data from which to estimate tax yields, which has posed the gravest problems for the social historian. For King's highly conservative over-reaction against the more euphoric assumptions of recent years frequently led him into contrary error whenever he left firm demographic ground. To be more specific: it produced in his social table serious distortions of two vital sets of statistics, in a

[51] See especially B.J., p. 275.
[52] *Ibid.*, p. 241: draft to Sir Stephen Fox, 19 December 1695.
[53] *Ibid.*, pp. 1, 240.

downward direction. It beguiled him (1) into underestimating the number of families in some of the wealthiest, and fiscally most productive classes; and (2) into underestimating (sometimes quite grossly) income levels at many rungs above the poverty line.

In the brief time available I can offer but a handful of examples from each of these two broad tracks of error. I will begin with incomes; since I am convinced that King took as one of his two salient points of reference in the table a total income figure for the whole nation which was unquestionably too low and that this critically affected his judgment of both incomes and numbers at many individual social levels: *because the way he worked made it imperative that both columns should add up in the end to his pre-calculated totals.*[54]

The case of the peers' incomes has attracted attention: and it is important enough to deserve re-emphasizing. Lawrence Stone has estimated the mean gross income, from all sources, of 121 peers in 1641 at £6,060.[55] Since then, the English peerage had acquired a net increase of roughly forty new members, many of whom were, to put it mildly, plump in the pocket. King's £2,800 for the peers' gross income in 1688 is as ludicrous as the somewhat earlier figure in his notebook of £2,000 for their annual rental income.[56] No doubt the peerage was a wealthier body a generation after 1688 than at the time of the Revolution: by 1710 three giants were topping £30,000 a year,[57] at least four other peers were amassing between £20,000 and £30,000;[58] over £10,000 a year had become perfectly commonplace above baron's rank. But the change inside a mere twenty years can hardly have been a massive one. In the significantly revised version of his table which Gregory King supplied to Davenant in 1698[59] he cautiously pushed up the average gross income of his peers

[54] For my hypothesis about King's methods, and further comments on his total income figure, see below pp. 61–62 and n. 90.

[55] *The Crisis of Aristocracy* (1st edn., Oxford, 1965), p. 762.

[56] P.R.O., T.64/302: notebook, p. 14. Office-holding alone was a major element in aristocratic wealth. In 1714 at least 42 English peers held office (civil or military) or pension: the emoluments were very rarely less than £1,000 p.a. (the minimum pension for a nobleman). In many cases the rewards amounted to £3,000–4,000 p.a. G. Holmes, *British Politics in the Age of Anne* (London, 1967), pp. 436–39.

[57] Dukes of Newcastle, Bedford and Beaufort.

[58] Dukes of Ormonde, Somerset and Devonshire (the latter with the aid of the Lord Steward's office) and Lord Brooke.

[59] This was the version printed as 'Scheme D' in Davenant's *Essay on the Probable Methods of making the People Gainers in the Balance of Trade* (London, 1699). The table is omitted from the Whitworth edition of Davenant's works. The differences between this revised version and the original version (in the form reproduced by G. E. Barnett, from B.L. Harl. MS. 1898 in *Two Tracts by Gregory King*, Baltimore, 1936) are laid out below in an appendix to this paper.

at the time of the Revolution from £2,800 to £3,200. If he had doubled that sum he would still have been too conservative.

King had no second thoughts in 1698 about the baronets' income. Yet at £880 a year it was almost as unrealistic as his figure for the peers. His contemporary, Chamberlayne, confidently declared that the baronets were 'possest, one with another, of about 1200*l* a year', and further specified that this was '*in lands*'.[60] But even this may have been decidedly too low an average for 1688. Professor Aylmer has suggested that the mean income of all English baronets in the early 1630s was roughly £1,500;[61] and among those promoted to the rank between the Restoration and the Revolution not many lean kine can be identified. Recent work[62] has shown that even in the notoriously poor counties of Cumberland and Westmorland £1,000 a year was a low income for a baronet by the first half of the eighteenth century. Moving down the ladder, King's figures for landed esquires[63] could well be a 25 per cent underestimate; and the implications for the total landed wealth of the esquires of an error of even £100 per family are manifest.[64] As for the income of the knights, King's figure of £650 a year will scarcely bear examination: quite apart from what is known of the position in the early seventeenth century,[65] one must take account here of the great accretions of wealth to the dozens of 'City knights' during the commercial boom of the 1670s and 1680s.[66] King's view of the knighthood in 1688 was detached from late seventeenth-century reality.

60 Edward Chamberlayne, *Angliae Notitia* (18th edn., London 1694), p. 442.

61 G. E. Aylmer, *The King's Servants* (1st edn., London, 1961), p. 331. This estimate is for 1633. It is amply borne out by local studies: *e.g.* the 31 baronets of Kent, *c.* 1640, had average incomes of £1,405 p.a. and the 28 baronets of Yorkshire £1,536 p.a. A. Everitt, *Change in the Provinces: The Seventeenth Century* (Leicester, 1969), p. 55, drawing on his own work on Kent and that of J. T. Cliffe on Yorkshire. *Cf.* J. T. Cliffe, *The Yorkshire Gentry* (London, 1969), chs. 2, 5, *passim.*

62 J. V. Beckett, 'Landownership in Cumbria, *c.* 1680 – *c.* 1750' (Lancaster Univ. Ph.D. thesis, 1975).

63 £450 p.a.

64 This margin may be conservative. It is based partly on early seventeenth-century evidence (*e.g.* Aylmer's estimate for 1633, *op. cit.*, p. 331, is £500 p.a.), partly on my own awareness of the sizeable flock of esquires in the 'great commoner' class of the county *élites* (£2,000–£15,000 p.a.) by *c.* 1700. I hope to develop this point in a forthcoming essay on the early eighteenth-century gentry.

65 *Cf.* Aylmer and Everitt, *loc. cit.*

66 Among the tycoons of the 1690s who had been knighted before the Revolution were Henry Johnson, William Ashurst, John Eyles, John Parsons, Benjamin Newland, John Bludworth, John Lethieullier, Robert Clayton, Patience Ward and Basil Firebrace. Even for the *landed* knights Chamberlayne estimated an average of £800 p.a. (*Angliae Notitia*, London, 1694, p. 442). A Norwich brewer was thought to have earned a knighthood in 1711 when he had achieved £2,000 p.a. H.M.C. *Portland MSS.* v, 29.

But elsewhere, too, he seems to be in an income world of his own. The case of the lawyers is not the most aggravated; but even so the incomes of several thousand provincial attorneys and court officials would have had to be microscopic to explain a mean of £140 a year, considering the princely incomes of the judicial *élite* of late seventeenth-century England, in which annual pickings of £2,000 were modest for a successful barrister. In many cases, those humbler incomes were not microscopic.[67] As for his 'shopkeepers and tradesmen'—surely the craziest of all King's categories—we need only reflect that it included many innkeepers who we now know could vie in wealth and standard of living with the lesser gentry;[68] literally thousands of master manufacturers who have no other home in the table;[69] and not least astonishing, all the great wholesalers and factors in England. We then get the £45 a year for this 'class' in something like its true perspective.

When it comes to enumeration of families, it is more difficult to corner King, if only because many of his categories are so ill-defined, or outmoded, or both. If Massie,[70] who aped King in numerous respects, found it necessary to include in his calculations in 1760 four income groups of master manufacturers and five of tradesmen, what was so radically different about the situation seventy years earlier? King's inclusion of scriveners among the lawyers,[71] instead of in the business sector, is another instance of smudgy, antiquated thinking. But the smokescreen is nowhere thick enough to obscure the fact that guesswork abounds in King's enumeration; or that there are in columns 1 and 2 the strangest anomalies and confusions, even where one might least expect them. Harley criticized King for underestimating the numbers of clergy, and King's defence is unconvincing.[72] In 1698 he himself conceded that he had put too low a number, by 10,000, on the shopkeepers and tradesmen. His 1711 estimate,

[67] *Cf.* the life-style of the attorneys, notaries, proctors and other officials who served the duchy court at Preston, of the local lawyers who handled most of the business of the assize towns, such as Leicester, and 'the rich attorneys in great practice' who clustered round the Cornish Stannary towns. On the other hand King presumably omitted *knighted* lawyers—most of them, by definition, successful—from this category.

[68] A. Everitt, 'The English Urban Inn, 1560–1760', in A. Everitt (ed.), *Perspectives in English Urban History* (London, 1973).

[69] The category of 'merchants and traders by land' which occurs in the frequently-quoted version of the table printed by Chalmers, App., pp. 48–49, is a copyist's freak peculiar to the manuscript version of the *Observations* which Chalmers used.

[70] See note 3 above.

[71] B.J., p. 280.

[72] Especially as he admitted including householding dissenting ministers in his 10,000 clergymen. See Kashnor MSS., *N.P.O.*, ch. 6, reply to Harley's 'Clergymen 10,000. These too few . . .'

in response to Scobell, reveals that by then he recognized the gross inadequacy even of his revised figure of 50,000.[73]

With the 'freeholders' and 'farmers' King was for a long time utterly at sea, his estimates for their combined total oscillating wildly, in a series of entries from the spring of 1695 to the summer of 1696, between 240,000 and 780,000.[74] It is with the table's 12,000 'Gentlemen', however, that the problem of definition, and therefore of enumeration, takes on its most baffling form. Did King have in mind only armigerous gentlemen at this point of his table? Almost certainly not. The Burns Journal establishes that in some of his early social explorations he was happily accepting the pragmatic approach of recent Poll Taxes, which imposed the lowest gentry rate on those 'owning themselves gentlemen' and recognized as such by their neighbours—'reputed gentlemen', King calls them.[75] With them in mind he played around at one time with figures as high as 20,000 or even 23,000. Why he settled for 12,000 is, on the face of it, inexplicable. That he was perfectly aware of the phenomenon of the urban gentry, as well as taking account of non-armigerous country gentry, some of his notes again make clear.[76] If he left them out of the final scheme, where did he put them? Urban gentlemen alone were to be numbered in many thousands by 1700. Only a fraction were government office-holders, and the proportion actively engaged in a profession at any one time cannot have been large. Two statistics help to put this problem of the gentry in context and underline its gravity. Professor Aylmer suggests a figure for the esquires and 'gents' together in the 1630s, before the most startling proliferation of pseudo-gentry had begun, of between 17,000 and 23,000.[77] In the Land Tax Act of 1702 there were roughly 32,000 commissioners named, and only a tiny proportion were below the rank of gentle-

[73] P.R.O., T.64/302: 'Upon Mr. Scobel's Proposition . . .' In this paper he postulates for fiscal purposes no fewer than 151,000 'traders' (including overseas merchants), vintners, brewers and public-house keepers, and it is inconceivable that only a third of them were deemed heads of households. About a year earlier King had calculated that there were then some 24,500 merchants, tradesmen and artificers in London, who were householders and who also kept apprentices. P.R.O. T.1/130/15F: paper endorsed '1709/10. Computation of the amount of the money taken with apprentices'.

[74] P.R.O., T.64/302: notebook, pp. 14, 18v.; B.J., pp. 65, 209; *ibid.*, p. 270, where the figures eradicated and the alternatives inserted are equally revealing. It seems highly likely that King's final choice of 330,000 (amended in 1698 to 310,000) was reached by a process of elimination, working downwards from a total number of solvent householders; though his figure of 40,000 for the 'freeholders of the better sort' was fixed at an earlier stage.

[75] The 'pseudo-gentry' of modern historians' usage. See B.J., pp. 67, 70.

[76] *E.g.* B.J., pp. 59, 64, 91.

[77] G. E. Aylmer, *The King's Servants*, p. 331.

man. Yet King's combined total for the whole 'mere' gentry in 1688 is but 15,000.

Why was such opacity and confusion possible? Why was so much guesswork seemingly unavoidable? Why was King so error-prone that he even contrived to underenumerate the peers by almost a sixth?[78] These questions direct attention inexorably to the sources and the methods to which he resorted in compiling the 'social table'. Most critically, we need to know whence he derived the first four columns—the most important for the student of the social structure—and also the cardinal dividing line, that grimly fascinating horizontal line between those 'increasing' and those 'decreasing' 'the wealth of the kingdom'.

A common illusion is that King's social statistics were based, in the main, on a study of the Hearth Tax returns. This statement appears to originate with Dorothy George in 1931.[79] Though often repeated, it is wholly erroneous, stemming from Mrs George's misunderstanding of a passage of Davenant's.[80] Indeed it is virtually certain that King never went back *in person*, in the 1690s, to the general records of the Hearth Office, not even to check his population figures.[81] On the other hand, plausible contemporary support can be mustered for the theory that King used Poll Tax material in constructing his table. Four Poll Taxes had been imposed between 1689 and 1694;[82] and when the revised version of Gregory King's table was printed in 1699, by Davenant, the Doctor made impressive claims on his friend's behalf:

> This skilful and laborious gentleman has taken the right course to form his several schemes about the numbers of the people; for besides many different ways of working, he has very carefully inspected the poll books, and the distinctions made by those acts,

[78] There were in 1688 approximately 30 holders of Scottish and Irish peerages whose main estates and normal residences were in England. Their numbers, and wealth, increased during William III's reign. In one of his early tables, dating from autumn 1695, King rightly included these peers, bringing his total for the lay nobility to a realistic 200. (B.J., pp. 280.) Subsequently, however, they slip out of the reckoning into some undiscoverable limbo.

[79] D. George, *England in Transition* (Pelican edn., London, 1953), pp. 10, 16.

[80] *Cf. ibid.*, p. 16, with Davenant, *Works*, ii, 203–04.

[81] No other deduction seems possible from King's replies to two of Harley's queries and objections in 1697: viz. 'Are these [King's figures for inhabited houses in provincial towns] estimated or numbred from the Hearth Books?', and 'It is to be doubted these Assessments [on Births, Marriages and Burials] are of no very g[ood] foundation'. Kashnor MSS., *N.P.O.*, ch. 1.

[82] These were the Single Polls of 1689 and 1690 and the Quarterly Polls of 1692 and 1694.

and the produce in money of the respective polls, going everywhere by reasonable and discreet mediums; besides which pains, he has made observations of the very facts in particular towns and places, from which he has been able to judge and conclude more safely of others. So that he seems to have looked further into this mystery than any other person.[83]

Does this mean that King had at his disposal for social analysis official material as susceptible to scientific 'sampling' techniques as that which underpinned his demographic work? Although it is a fallacy to suppose he was employed by the government in the 1690s, it is hard to escape the deduction that he did have some friends in official places,[84] in view of the limited access he managed to acquire, while working on the *Observations*, to certain government records. What could be more natural, one might think, than that King should use these contacts to 'carefully inspect the poll books'? Unfortunately, a careful combing both of King's papers and the Exchequer records compels a very different, and quite unexpected conclusion. We now know from his notebooks that he probably had the first inklings of the importance of the poll tax returns as social documents as early as September 1695. Once aware of this, it becomes terribly hard to credit that only at the eleventh hour—at the point, in fact, where the preparatory work in the Burns Journal stops, almost a year later—did he suddenly secure access to a marvellous seam of this material, which is nowhere revealed in those voluminous notes. In that case it must surely have taken something like a further year to complete his labours, instead of a few weeks.

Strong suspicion turns to certainty on examining King's meticulous replies, in April 1697, to the comments of Robert Harley on his conclusions and his methods. Nowhere in these answers did King claim to have seen the original poll tax records, central or local. On the contrary, he confirms that even for the bare total yield of those two Polls which he did make some use of, he had relied on the figures printed in Davenant's *Ways and Means* essay and not on any civil servant's goodwill.[85] His transparent eagerness elsewhere in his

[83] *Essay upon . . . the Balance of Trade*. See Davenant, *Works*, ii, 175.

[84] One or two contacts in the Exchequer can surely be assumed; one 'good friend' we know of (Sansom) in the Customs, and another (George Stepney) in the diplomatic service. Also King himself was named a commissioner for London (one of over 300) in the 1694 Act for levying new duties on births, marriages and burials. B.L. Loan 57/73, fo 83; B.J., p. 171; Chalmers, App., pp. 23–24; *London Inhabitants within the Walls* (London Record Society, 1966), intro. (by D. V. Glass), p. xvii.

[85] This was more than strongly hinted in the earlier Burns Journal. *Cf.* J. Thirsk and J. P. Cooper (eds.), *Seventeenth-Century Economic Documents* (Oxford, 1972),

'Reply' to reveal his sources of information, and (in merciless detail) his methods of deduction from them, make it inconceivable he would not have displayed a first-hand acquaintance with 'the poll books', if only he had been in a position to do so. He was not; and the truth is that, even if he had been so remarkably favoured as to be allowed a free run of the Exchequer's poll tax returns, he would have found there precious few, if any, *assessments* (the key social documents) for William's reign, and not many even dating from Charles II's time.[86]

Assuming, therefore, as we must, that Davenant misunderstood the devious intricacy of his friend's methods, and in consequence deceived himself about the *bona fides* of the social table's foundations, what hypothesis is it reasonable to advance about King's sources and methods on the evidence that survives?

In the first place it can be either demonstrated or deduced that he was able to draw on four sources of some official standing. They were: (1) The actual provisions of the first three Poll Acts, those of 1689, 1690 and 1692;[87] (2), as already noted, the total yields of the 1689 and 1692 Polls (these totals he culled from Davenant and they were inaccurate, though not seriously so); (3) some of the assessments (mostly London assessments) for the 1695 duties on Births, Marriages and Burials—those same duties which proved such a boon to King's demographic studies;[88] and (4) the total number of houses

---

pp. 770 n. 1, 785–86, 798, 802–03. Harley proceeded to make corrections in King's (*i.e.* Davenant's) figures, adding for good measure the yield of the two remaining Polls; and King significantly began his reply: 'In the consideration of the Poll bills (the true produce whereof you having favour'd me with, requires my particular acknowledgments) those two which I examined [i.e. the statutes themselves] were the first Twelve penny Poll and the first Quarterly Poll'. Kashnor MSS., *N.P.O.*, ch. 9.

[86] The pattern for William's reign was established by the first Poll Act of 1689 (1 Gul. and Mar., sess. 1, c. 13) which required the Exchequer to receive, in addition to the proceeds of the Poll, and the Receivers' accounts, (a) (from the Commissioners) 'a true duplicate of the whole summe charged within every hundred, lath, wapentake, parish [or] ward . . . *without naming the persons*', and (b) (from the Receivers-General) full schedules of defaulters, drawn up by the Collectors. The accounts are now in P.R.O., E.181, the duplicates and defaulters' schedules mostly in E.182. It is clear that the detailed assessments of individuals and families were intended to remain in the counties, and almost invariably did so. Under the vast umbrella of P.R.O., E.179 there are a fair number of detailed assessments relating to the first post-Restoration Poll Tax, 12 Chas. II (*e.g.* for parts of Devon, Cornwall, Lancs. Glos. etc.) and distinctly fewer relating to the levies of 18 and 29 Chas. II (*e.g.* for Hunts.); but by the 1690s the cupboard is almost totally bare.

[87] For 1689 and 1692, see King to Harley in n. 85 above. For 1690, B.J., pp. 71–72.

[88] B.J., pp. 59, 64 and *passim*: *cf.* Chalmers, App., p. 59; Glass, 'Two papers', *loc. cit.* King saw the assessments for 18 London parishes and 7 'outparishes'; some of them listed occupations, one (for St. Mary Le Bow) being a superb social document. *London Inhabitants within the Walls 1695*, pp. xvii–xix.

officially excused from paying the window tax in 1696.[89] These, I believe, were the only solid official bricks which Gregory King used in the creation of that amazing framework on to which historians have hung so many conclusions and hypotheses about pre-industrial society. And, cleverly as he manipulated them, these bricks made up a very, very small pile. In the second place—and of more importance to him—he made use of two pre-cast pillars to hold up the whole construction. These were the two vital totals which King had arrived at quite independently of any Poll Tax material: namely, the total number of households in the land, clearly derived from his base figure for inhabited houses of close to 1,300,000; and the total annual income of the whole population, calculated at £43·5 millions, a figure he arrived at by the most convoluted and questionable means, which he later explained, in mind-boggling detail, to Harley. And I would argue that it was because King was too conservative in arriving at this *national* income figure, and not least because he badly undervalued the total for landed rents (misled by the yield of the Land Tax) that he got so many of his specific income figures, later, seriously wrong.[90]

For the rest, King drew to some extent (though a great deal less than has sometimes been assumed) on his heraldic experience; he drew on smatterings of literary evidence, which happened to lie conveniently to hand.[91] But above all, he drew on his own resources of mind—those mathematical gymnastics which mark almost all his work, but which were nowhere more severely stretched than in compiling his 'Scheme of the Income and Expense of the several Families of England'.

How much help did he get altogether from his fiscal sources?

[89] See Chalmers, App., pp. 59–60; Kashnor MSS., *N.P.O.*: King's replies to Harley's queries on ch. 9, 'A Calculation of the Poll-Bills and some other taxes . . .'. *Cf.* B.J., pp. 156–57.

[90] For King's curious calculations on national wealth, see Kashnor MSS., *N.P.O.*, ch. 6. Much of this long passage is conveniently reprinted, with some textual corruptions, in Thirsk and Cooper, pp. 791–95, but a key section on the land tax yield, including King's euphoric, unwarrantable deduction that 'the omissions, the fraud, the favours and the great underrating complaind of in the North West is nothing so considerable as we are apt to believe', is omitted.

Modern economic historians would do well to look again at King's £43·5 mns, bearing in mind not only the dubiety of his methods but later figures for *c.* 1800 (both contemporary and otherwise), *e.g.* Deane and Cole's estimate for the total national income in 1801 at £232 mn. Even an error in the region of 3 mns was crucial for King's purposes, since it would be reflected overwhelmingly in his estimates for the *higher* income groups in his table.

[91] *E.g.* he told Harley that he had based the number of 'common seamen' [50,000] on Sir Francis Brewster's estimate of merchant seamen in 1687. King's notes on Brewster's *Essay on Trade* (London, 1696), pp. 75–80, are in B.J., p. 209.

Relatively little, it seems; and only in one area that was fundamental. It was what he could glean about tax exemptions, in conjunction with a national Poor Rate figure of £665,000 per annum for 1685 (borrowed from Davenant, again)[92] which led him to a fairly certain belief that the number of insolvent persons in England in 1690 had been about 2.8 millions. By translating this figure into households,[93] and by keeping as the basis of all his social calculations thereafter—since it was his firmest ground—the *heads of households*,[94] he established the limits of his two major construction sites, the numbers of solvent and insolvent families. Thereafter, those samples of the 1695 assessments for the births, marriages and burial duties which King managed to see, and analyse, yielded him solidly-based information about household size at different social levels;[95] and this clearly played its part in the drawing up of the valuable 'heads per family' column. Yet so too did his personal surveys, such as the scrupulously detailed one he made of Sevenoaks parish, Kent, in June 1695,[96] bearing out Davenant's claim that, for sampling purposes, he had 'made observations of the very facts in particular towns and places'. In the end, one can only conclude that the direct harvest of the Poll Tax, garnered into the final table, was in statistical terms a meagre one.

On the other hand, it was in the Poll Acts themselves that he distinguished both those social groups which Parliament deemed particularly suitable for fiscal milking and those groups which were officially considered too poor to pay; and these gleanings helped to determine the social categories which King eventually chose to include in column 2 of his table. Thus an earlier list of social groupings, compiled about Michaelmas 1695, is headed 'According to their Degrees, Titles & qualities, as they are generally distinguisht in Poll Bills & other Taxes'.[97] And frustratingly for the historian, King

[92] 'That the Poors rate exhibited by the Author of Wayes and Means p. 77 and 79 being at the latter end of K. Cha. 2d reign abt. £665,000, we may estimate the same anno 88 at £680,000 and anno 95 at £740,000 . . .' King to Harley, comments on ch. 9, Kashnor MSS., *N.P.O.*

[93] By applying a ratio appropriate to 'poorer houses'. *Ibid.*

[94] This was a point he was at great pains to emphasize to Harley: *e.g.*, on the clergy, 'I state them only with respect to "Heads of Families"'; on the common seamen, 'so as to denominate them Masters of Families, in w[ch] respect only they are here inserted'.

[95] See. *e.g.*, P.R.O., T.64/302, notebook, p. 17v: 21, 24 June 1695. The same sources, the Burns Journal suggests, may also have led him to make suppositions about the relative proportions of knights and baronets to esquires and of both to 'gentlemen'.

[96] *Ibid.*, pp. 15v–17. He surveyed 395 households, including 206 in Sevenoaks town on 10–11 June.

[97] B.J., pp. 280–81.

demonstrates in the Burns Journal that, working within these guidelines, he was well able to attempt a far more sophisticated breakdown of some of the general professional and business groups than actually appears at the end of the line. No-one interested primarily in conveying as full a picture as possible of the social structure could have resisted the inclusion of such precise data as that, for example, there were among the lawyers 500 clerks in Chancery and Exchequer, among the clergy 200 pluralists in parish livings worth at least £120 a year, or among the tradesmen 5,000 substantial innkeepers. But, as I have stressed, detailed social analysis was not King's purpose. With his overriding fiscal interest he concentrated austerely on just those basic divisions which, he believed, helped to illuminate in bold outlines his scheme of incomes and expenses.[98] He even excluded his intriguing estimate, made at a late stage of his work in 1696, that of the 364,000 'Day Labourers & Outservants' inserted in the final table some 300,000 were in rural employment.[99]

Yet this last figure, which does not appear in the table, typifies so many that do. For it is patently far more the product of strained deduction, of mathematical juggling, or even plain guesswork, than of firmly-grounded information. Words such as 'I compute', 'I estimate', occur again and again in King's notes, with no source given or hinted at. That he was uncomfortably aware that chapter 6 of his work, of which the 'Scheme' forms the centrepiece, was one of the most vulnerable parts of the whole exercise is all too evident from the distinctly frenetic tone of his defences against Harley's thrusts at this Achilles heel in 1697, as compared with the absolute conviction of some of his earlier replies to that rigorous examiner. And when, in 1698, he supplied Davenant with the second version of the table, we may assume he took as much account as *amour propre* allowed of reactions to the first;[100] for numerous manuscript copies of the *Observations* had been circulated in the past two years.

Gregory King was enormously proud of his *Observations*, taken by and large. But he was realist enough, and in the end had enough basic humility, to appreciate that in some areas of knowledge there were severe limits to what any political arithmetician, even the most brilliant and resourceful, could achieve with the evidence currently available to him. The social structure was one such area. Even

[98] Among the detail jettisoned as superfluous or subsumed elsewhere in the table were such titbits as that King believed there to be 500 dissenting preachers in England, 800 goldsmiths (300 in London) and 200 London doctors. For these estimates, those cited in the text above, and others, see B.J., pp. 70–73, 265, 280–81.

[99] B.J., p. 209.

[100] On this point *cf.* David Cressy, 'Describing the Social Order of Elizabethan and Stuart England', *Literature and History*, no. 3 (March 1976), p. 32.

supposing most government financial records to be accurate—and King was not ingenuous enough to make such a supposition—no-one could reasonably expect unrestricted access to them, certainly no-one concerned to advance basic premises critical of current government policy. Davenant later voiced bitter resentment at the many rubs which he, a former member of the bureaucratic brotherhood, had been forced to endure from officialdom in the course of his own research and writing.[101] As for King himself, he made his common-sense pragmatism perfectly plain in the preface to the *Observations*. To know the 'true state' of a nation—this was the highest ideal: 'but since the attaining thereof (how necessary and desirable soever) is next to impossible, we must content ourselves with such near approaches to it, as the grounds we have to go upon will enable us to make'.[102] And inscribed philosophically on the second leaf of the Burns Journal, standing alone on an otherwise blank page, is this aphorism:

> Pour bien savoir les choses, il en faut savoir le détail: et comme il est presque infiny, nos connoissances sont toujours superficielles et imparfaites.

This could well have served as King's own epitaph on his 'social table'. But what should be ours? Whatever our reservations, it would be rank injustice to regard it as anything less than an extraordinary pioneering feat, a creation of awesome scale and of the boldest originality. Even when stripped of many of its dubious statistical embellishments, its ravaged grandeur will always retain features of lasting value to the historian. Sparse as King's official sources were, they were enough to allow him a more penetrating and dramatic insight into the frightening extent of the problem of poverty in late Stuart England than any previous economist or political arithmetician had achieved.[103] As for his social categories, and the seemingly deliberate status-order in which they are arranged: although we ought to recognize them for what they are—a monument to a static, and in some ways anachronistic view of a pre-war society, an *ancien régime*—they remain a legacy of permanent value, in the sense that they reflect how the pre-industrial Englishman of a traditionalist cast of mind preferred to think his social order was constituted. Seen in this light, Gregory King's table is in direct line of descent from

[101] See Davenant, *Works*, i, 149; ii, 168—two very important, and largely unnoticed passages written in 1697 and 1699, in the second of which he speaks for his fellow political arithmeticians as well as for himself.

[102] Chalmers, App., p. 31.

[103] As Davenant recognized at the time, this was the table's most important message for contemporaries. *Works*, ii, 198.

the sumptuary laws of the late fifteenth century, through Sir Thomas Smith, Wilson and Chamberlayne, to Massie, and perhaps even to Colquhoun.[104]

Far more vital to the historian, however, is to keep in mind at all times that King's great 'Scheme' was the work of flesh and blood and not the creation of some wholly objective and impersonal genius. In it we should recognize the brainchild of a brilliant yet uneasy man: a man who had been cruelly frustrated in his profession and who was almost too anxious to prove himself in a novel sphere of activity; a man who knew his way to truth but could not rest content when he found it barred; a man who at times allowed his hyperactive mind to fall victim to his greatest obsession, bemused and entrapped by the web of figures he had spun for himself. Not least, we must never impose upon his scheme far greater strains than he himself meant it to bear. So it need not surprise us that what had never been designed as an exact mirror of England's social structure even in 1688 was producing grave distortions already by the time of King's own death in 1712.

The social structure of pre-industrial England was a thing of infinite subtlety. It deserves to be studied intensively, not least at local level,[105] and in its own right; and studied as the structure of a society which was never static and was capable, certainly during periods of prolonged warfare, of positive dynamism. There is so much yet to be done; and such a wealth of material still to be fully worked.[106] However great our admiration for the work of 'G. K. Esq$^{r.}$ Lancaster Herald', Davenant's 'wonderful genius, and master of the art of computing', is it not time that as students of a past society we determined no longer to be suffocated by his pervasive presence?

[104] Professor Donald Coleman first drew my attention to the significance of this continuity. Cressy argues, however (see n. 100 above), that 'King's is the first ranking of the social order which combines reference to economic circumstances with a system of esteem'.

[105] For example, we need many more social anatomies of provincial communities, following the admirable models of G. H. Kenyon's work on Petworth and J. D. Marshall's on Kendal. See *Sussex Arch. Collections*, xcvi (1958), xcviii (1960); *Trans. Cumberland and Westmorland Antiq. and Arch. Soc.*, lxxv, New Series (1975).

[106] The surviving poll tax assessments of 1661–98 warrant a sustained assault. So do the lists of Land Tax commissioners incorporated in successive Aids and Land Tax bills from 1689: by 1700 they represent a nearly complete roll-call of the upper and middling gentry of every shire. Freemen's registers; jurors' lists; poll books for some of the large boroughs (e.g. Norwich, Bristol, Liverpool, Newcastle) which supply voters' occupations as well as names; poor rate books; the militia muster rolls of the Seven Years' War—all await the systematic scrutiny of the social historian.

APPENDIX

Gregory King's 'Scheme of the Income and Expense of the several Families of England, . . . for the Year 1688'

(The 'Barnett version', 1936, from B.L. Harleian MS. 1898; amendments in square brackets from the revised, 'Davenant version', 1698[9])
N.B. The first five columns of figures and the last (9th) column only are reproduced below.
Column 7, 'Annual expenditure per family', has been reconstituted from King's *per capita* figures.

Number of Families	*Ranks, Degrees, Titles, and Qualifications*	*Heads per Family*	*Number of Persons*	*Yearly Income per Family* £	*Total Yearly Income* £	*Annual Expenditure per Family* £	*Total Increase of Wealth Yearly* £
160	Temporal Lords	40	6,400	2,800 [3,200]	448,000 [512,000]	2,400 [2,800]	64,000
26	Spiritual Lords	20	520	1,300	33,800	1,100 [900]	5,200 [10,400]
800	Baronets	16	12,800	880	704,000	816 [784]	51,200 [76,800]
600	Knights	13	13,800	650	390,000	598 [585]	31,200 [39,000]
3,000	Esquires	10	30,000	450	1,200,000	420 [410]	90,000 [120,000]
12,000	Gentlemen	8	96,000	280	2,880,000	260 [256]	240,000 [288,000]
5,000	Persons in [greater] offices [and places]	8	40,000	240	1,200,000	216 [208]	120,000 [160,000]
5,000	Persons in [lesser] offices [and places]	6	30,000	120	600,000	108 [102]	60,000 [90,000]

10,000	Persons in the Law	7	70,000	140 [154]	1,400,000 [1,540,000]	119 [91]	210,000 [280,000]
2,000	[Eminent] Clergymen	6	12,000	60 [72]	120,000 [144,000]	54 [60]	12,000 [24,000]
8,000	[Lesser] Clergymen	5	40,000	45 [50]	360,000 [400,000]	40 [47]	40,000 [32,000]
40,000	Freeholders [of the better sort]	7	280,000	84 [91]	3,360,000 [3,640,000]	77 [82–5]	280,000 [350,000]
140,000 [120,000]	Freeholders [of the lesser sort]	5 [5½]	700,000 [660,000]	50 [55]	7,000,000 [6,600,000]	47–10	350,000 [330,000]
150,000	Farmers	5	750,000	44 [42–10]	6,600,000 6,375,000	42–10 [41–5]	187,000 [187,500]
16,000 [15,000]	Persons in Sciences and Liberal Arts	5	80,000 [75,000]	60	960,000 [900,000]	57–10 [55]	40,000 [75,000]
40,000 [50,000]	Shopkeepers and Tradesmen	4½	180,000 [225,000]	45	1,800,000 [2,250,000]	42–15 [40–10]	90,000 [225,000]
60,000	Artisans and Handicrafts	4	240,000	40 [38]	2,400,000 [2,280,000]	38 [36]	120,000
5,000	Naval Officers	4	20,000	80	400,000	72	40,000
4,000	Military Officers	4	16,000	60	240,000	56	16,000
511,586 [500,586]		5¼ [5⅓]	2,675,520 [2,675,520]	67 [68–18]	34,495,800 [34,488,800]	63 [62–15]	2,447,100 [3,023,700]

*This *should* be the revised figure. In fact it stays as 1,600,000

Number of Families	Ranks, Degrees, Titles, and Qualifications	Heads per Family	Number of Persons	Yearly Income per Family £	Total Yearly Income £	Annual Expenditure per Family £	Total Increase of Wealth Yearly £
							Decrease
50,000	Common Seamen	3	150,000	20	1,000,000	22–10	75,000
364,000	Labouring People and Outservants	3½	1,275,000	15	5,460,000	16–2	127,500
400,000	Cottagers and Paupers	3¼	1,300,000	6–10	2,000,000	7–6–3	325,000
35,000	Common Soldiers	2	70,000	14	490,000	15	35,000
849,000		3¼	2,795,000	10–10	8,950,000	11–4–3	562,500
	Vagrants as Gipsies, Thieves, Beggars. etc.		30,000	2	60,000	3	60,000
	So the General Account is				—	—	
511,586 [500,586]	Increasing the Wealth of the Kingdom	5¼ [5⅓]	2,675,520	67 [68–18]	34,495,800 [34,488,800]	63 [62–15]	2,447,100 [3,023,700]
849,000	Decreasing the Wealth of the Kingdom	3¼	2,825,000	10–10	9,101,000	10–19–4	622,500
1,360,586 [1,349,586]	NEAT TOTALS	$4\frac{1}{20}$ [$4\frac{1}{13}$]	5,500,520	32–0 [32–5]	43,505,800 [43,491,800]	30–12–7 [30–8–6]	1,825,100 [2,401,200]

CROMWELLIAN REFORM AND THE ORIGINS OF THE KILDARE REBELLION, 1533–34

The Alexander Prize Essay

By B. Bradshaw, B.A., Ph.D.

READ 11 JUNE 1976

AMONG the major political events in a century of momentous political change in Ireland the Kildare rebellion of 1534–35 has been accorded a special significance by contemporaries and historians alike. The downfall of the most renowned Anglo-Irish noble family and the personal tragedies of the doughty old earl and his dashing young heir, gave the story an aura of romance that caught the fancy of the Elizabethans—it inspired an Elizabethan drama—and partly accounts for its prominence in popular histories. More scholarly commentators have emphasized its significance as a watershed in the history of English government in Ireland. The subsequent course of events reveal it as a point of transition from the medieval to the early modern phase of Irish political history, the juncture at which the hold of Anglo-Irish feudal magnates on crown government was broken and at which the period of uninterrupted supervision from England began.

Surprisingly, in view of all this, the event itself attracted little serious scholarship until recently.[1] Its historiography was more a product of hindsight than of insight and analysis. This is true equally of the study of its origins as of its sequel. From the forward vantage point the ingredients that produced the rebellion seemed easily identifiable: a power struggle within government—yet another attempt to break the political hegemony of the Fitzgeralds; dynastic rivalry between the house of Kildare and the Butlers of Ormond and Ossory; and the royal divorce, bringing in its wake a religious Reformation unpopular in Ireland and complications in England's

[1] After years of neglect the rebellion recently attracted the attention simultaneously of two able research students. The resultant theses make very substantial progress towards a fullscale revision of the received historiography, S. G. Ellis, 'The Kildare Rebellion', unpublished M.A. thesis, Manchester, 1974; Lawrence Corristine, 'The Kildare Rebellion', unpublished M.A. thesis, University College, Dublin, 1975. I have to thank Professor G. R. Elton for helpful advice in the preparation of this paper. It has also benefited from discussions with Mr Ellis.

foreign relations. These, it seemed, were the ingredients, but little attempt was made to describe how precisely they combined to make up a recipe for rebellion in 1534.

It is little wonder, therefore, that Richard Stanihurst's account of the circumstances immediately surrounding the outbreak of the rebellion, written some forty years after the event, has stood the test of time. It was never subjected to critical analysis. Stanihurst explained the eruption by reference to two factors. One was factional politics. He traced the source of the rebellion to a plot to oust Kildare hatched by an alliance comprised of an anti-aristocratic English element connected with the Dublin administration—the former lord chancellor, Archbishop Alen, his aide, John Alen, the former lord deputy, Sir William Skeffington, and his secretary, Thomas Cannon—these combined with the local rivals of the Fitzgeralds, the Butlers, and their henchmen, the Cowleys. According to Stanihurst, the charges of treason pressed by his enemies were responsible for Kildare's summons to London and, once there, for his imprisonment in the Tower. The way was thus prepared for the dramatic events in Dublin where the second factor came into play, the personality of Silken Thomas. Every Irish schoolboy knows the story of how the young gallant whom Kildare left in charge of government in his absence was gulled by a false report of his father's execution in London and rushed into rebellion. The gist of Stanihurst's account was assimilated into the historiography, though more recently his conspiracy thesis was expanded to allow for the interaction of factional politics between the two administrations. Cromwell and the anti-Geraldine alliance are presented battling it out against Norfolk, Wiltshire and the Fitzgeralds.[2] Stanihurst has obvious claims on the historian's attention. He was close enough to the event to avail himself of the testimony of eye witnesses. As a member of a leading Dublin patrician family, much involved in politics throughout the sixteenth century, he was familiar with the story as it was handed down by members of the political establishment of the Pale who had themselves played a part in it.[3] Furthermore, the factual basis of his narrative is beyond dispute since many of its important details can be corroborated from documentary sources. Despite all of this it will be argued here that Stanihurst's account radically distorts what

[2] N. Stanihurst, 'The chronicles of Ireland' in *Holinshed's Chronicles*, vi (London, 1808 edn), 285–93. For examples of the later historiography see especially P. Wilson, *The beginnings of modern Ireland* (Dublin, 1912), pp. 87–94. *Cf.* R. Bagwell, *Ireland under the Tudors* (London, 1885) i, pp. 158–63. A. Gwynn, *The medieval province of Armagh* (Dundalk, 1946), pp. 68–69.

[3] A lengthy entry on Richard Stanihurst in the *D.N.B.* deals with the history of the family in the sixteenth century.

actually took place and that in consequence a fundamental misconception about the origins of the rebellion persists in modern accounts.

The first step in bringing the distortion to light is to note the way in which Stanihurst's account was moulded by the purpose of his work as a whole. This was political rather than historical. He chronicled Ireland's history since the conquest as a tract for his own times. One of the major concerns of the work was to vindicate the old Anglo-Irish nobility as the leaders of the loyal community in reaction to the chauvinism and growing assertiveness of the new English colonists of the early Elizabethan period. In particular he wished to vindicate the political respectability of the Fitzgeralds of Kildare following their restoration under Queen Mary. The Kildare rebellion was, therefore, a considerable embarrassment which Stanihurst tried to get round by treating it as an isolated aberration in the history of the family's loyal service and by pleading special mitigating circumstances. The strategy of his defence was to exculpate the old earl by placing full responsibility for the rebellion on Silken Thomas and then to diminish Thomas's culpability by presenting him as an inexperienced young man, tricked into rebellion by the mischief of others and by the reckless, if noble, impulses of youth. In highlighting the distortion which this involved, the task is to distinguish between the facts and the gloss in Stanihurst's narrative. This can be done simply by checking his account against the documentary sources and noting the discrepancies.

As well as taking issue with Stanihurst this study tests the views expressed by a distinguished modern historian. Some fifteen years ago Professor D. B. Quinn had occasion to consider the rebellion in the course of a review of Henrician government in Ireland in the period 1509–34. Apart from surveying the evidence with a professional thoroughness lacking in previous accounts, his major contribution was to raise the question of the relationship between the origins of the rebellion and Tudor political reform.[4] Quinn's reassessment produced an odd result. On the one hand his interpretation of the situation that precipitated the rebellion was surprising for its very lack of surprise. On the other hand he offered a challenging view about the role of political reform in the episode. According to his analysis the rebellion resulted from a concatenation of active and passive factors. The active elements were those known to the received historiography already rehearsed. The passive element was Tudor political reform. Here Quinn argued an interesting thesis about the initial affect of Thomas Cromwell's preeminence in

[4] D. B. Quinn, 'Henry VIII and Ireland, 1509–34' in *Irish Historical Studies*, xii (1961), pp. 340–43.

government. He suggested that this event brought an end to a phase of experimentation in the government of the outlying regions —the north of England, Wales, Calais, Ireland—which began with Wolsey's fall. Cromwell seemed 'still too ignorant or too unfamiliar with the problems of the outlying parts to have any policy before 1534 but laissez faire'. Quinn took Ireland as a particular illustration of the general situation. There, he asserted, the years 1533–34 were characterized by the 'apparent absence of an effective policy' in contrast to the preceeding three years which were 'interesting and active'. This, according to Quinn, is the wider political context in which the origins of the Kildare rebellion is set. Cromwell's failure to provide effective government 'left the way open for the rising'.[5]

Professor Quinn, therefore, adds his caveat to the many entered—some by Professor Elton himself—against the assessment of Cromwell which appeared in the original edition of *England under the Tudors*. No doubt it is imperative in the interests of historical truth to reveal Cromwell 'warts and all' like his later namesake. At the same time and for the same reason it is imperative to reveal him only with those warts that were there. This might be sufficient to justify the rather extended refutation of Quinn's interpretation in what follows. However, Cromwell's stature as an administrator is not the only issue nor, indeed, the most important one. It will be argued in this study that Quinn's interpretation involves a serious misunderstanding of the circumstances which precipitated the first major rebellion in Ireland in the modern period and that it perpetuates, in consequence, the false assumptions of the traditional historiography concerning the issues that were involved. It is proposed to look more closely than Quinn had scope to do at the genesis of Cromwell's first scheme for reform in the Lordship and to re-examine the influence of political reform on the outbreak of the Kildare rebellion. It is hoped to show that Quinn's impression of Cromwell as 'ignorant or unfamiliar' with Irish conditions in the initial period of his administration was mistaken; that, in fact, his Irish education was in progress for quite some time before he grasped the reins of government. Building on this it is hoped to show that Quinn was mistaken also in presenting Cromwell in a passive role in relation to the Kildare rebellion. It was not that Cromwell by neglecting Irish government, allowed the rebellion to happen. It was rather that his application to Irish reform brought the rebellion about. It should emerge from all of this that the factors to which the outbreak of the rebellion are traditionally attributed—internal faction, religious resentment and

[5] D. B. Quinn, 'Henry VIII and Ireland, 1509–34' in *Irish Historical Studies*, xii (1961), p. 343.

international politics—were incidental to the main issue which was Cromwellian political reform.

The tendency to envisage Tudor political reform in terms of a London-based movement has caused the important fact to be overlooked that in the case of Ireland at least the movement had local roots also. These were located in the Pale, Dublin's fertile hinterland, stretching north and west over an area of some twenty square miles. Here political reform was associated with a special professional class, preconditioned to respond favourably to the notion. It was a class composed of lesser nobility and gentry who in addition to being substantial landowners customarily received legal training also and thus equipped themselves for service in the central administration in Dublin which they traditionally staffed. The concerns of this group and their approach to political reform are reflected in the political treatises which emanated from the reforming *milieu*. The earliest surviving examples of these can be traced to the second decade of the sixteenth century.[6] Here the malady of crown government in Ireland is diagnosed in terms of the centrifugal pressures of bastard feudalism and the anarchic consequences of magnate power politics.

For the purposes of the present discussion it is particularly instructive to note the interaction between the local reform movement and the movement from the centre on the occasion of Henry VIII's first attempt to launch a programme of political reform in Ireland through the expedition of the earl of Surrey in 1520–22. It is clear that local reformers were responsible in part at least for persuading the king to launch the attempt and were subsequently closely associated with the venture. Among Surrey's most enthusiastic local assistants were Sir William Darcy and Sir Patrick Finglas, both members of the Dublin administration and authors of two of the earliest surviving examples of the *genre* of political treatise just mentioned.[7] Although Surrey's expedition was a failure it provided the

[6] Two can be traced to this period. One is a series of articles submitted by Sir William Darcy to the English privy council in 1515, Lambeth, Carew MS. 635, pp. 188–89 (*Cal. Carew MSS.*, i, no. 2). The other is a more elaborate anonymous treatise, copies of which survive in two slightly different versions, P.R.O., S.P. 60/1, no. 9. (S[tate] P[apers] *Henry VIII*, ii, p. 1), British Library, Add. MS. 4792, fo 96 ff. On the Anglo-Irish movement of political reform see B. Bradshaw 'The Irish Constitutional Revolution, 1515–57', unpublished Ph.D. thesis, Cambridge, 1975.

[7] On Darcy's treatise, see above, n. 6. A contemporary copy of Finglas's 'Brevyate of the conqueste of Ireland and of the decay of the same', written in the hand of his son, Thomas, is in P.R.O., S.P. 60/2, no. 7. Later copies are in Lambeth, Carew MS. 600, p. 204, 621, p. 92 (*Cal. Car. MSS.*, i, no. 1). An extended version of Finglas is found in copy in Trinity College Dublin MS. 842, fos 25–36. This version was published at Dublin by Walter Harris in *Hibernica* in 1747. For the

local movement with an *entrée* to the corridors of power in England, and it is clear that the advantage was taken. For instance, Thomas Bathe, a member of a prominent Pale family who had assisted Surrey in 1520–22, is found in 1528 visiting the former lord lieutenant, now Duke of Norfolk, to discuss Irish affairs with him. Norfolk provided him with a letter of introduction to Wolsey, commending him as a man who 'doth more love the welth of that lande, than any of the parties of the Garentynis [Fitzgeralds] or Butlers'.[8]

The relevance of this background will become more apparent as the discussion proceeds. Immediately, however, it may be pointed out that *a priori* it raises doubts about the validity of the suggestion that Cromwell was too ignorant of Irish problems to take them in hand in the early years of his administration. For almost two decades previously these problems had been formulated and discussed in written treatises, precisely with a view to dispelling the ignorance of English politicians. Secondly, it is not as plausible as it may seem to suggest that Cromwell was too taken up with the great ecclesiastical changes in England to devote time to the Irish question until after 1534. The foregoing review suggests that Cromwell's education is unlikely to have awaited his own initiative. Once he emerged as a politically influential figure Anglo-Irish reformers would have been as keen to lobby him as they were to lobby Norfolk and Wolsey. As we shall see, the hard evidence indicates that this is precisely what happened.

Cromwell's own background also points in the direction of antecedent knowledge rather than ignorance. After all, he had been closely associated with the king's previous chief minister for at least a decade. It is true that his function in Wolsey's household was to act as a legal and business agent in the cardinal's affairs, not to involve himself in matters of state. Nevertheless, in view of the capacity for politics and public administration that he later displayed, it is hardly conceivable that he could have spent so long a period in such close contact with the man who was at the hub of government without becoming familiar with the great problems of state including the problem of Ireland.

In any case, there is a more cogent consideration. Prominent with Cromwell in Wolsey's household was the ecclesiastic, John Alen, for whom the cardinal obtained the archbishopric of Dublin and the office of Irish lord chancellor in 1528. The work of these two men

---

association of Darcy and Finglas with Surrey's expedition see *S.P. Henry VIII*, ii, 61, 63. Quinn, 'Henry VIII and Ireland' in *Irish Historical Studies*, xii, p. 324, also Bradshaw, unpublished Ph.D. thesis.

[8] *S.P. Henry VIII*, ii, p. 135 (*L*[*etters and*] *P*[*apers*], [*Henry VIII*], iv (ii), no. 4459).

brought them into close contact, especially when they collaborated on the project of dissolving the rundown monasteries that endowed the cardinal's college at Oxford. Their contact was renewed in 1530, after Wolsey's fall, when Cromwell had entered government service. Like Wolsey himself, Alen appealed to the rising king's servant for assistance in extricating himself from the penalties of praemunire and, like the cardinal also, was treated with the sympathy due to an old and esteemed acquaintance. Although the only letter from Alen to Cromwell dating from that episode is confined to recounting the archbishop's personal plight, the renewal of the contact could not have failed to deepen Cromwell's knowledge of Irish conditions, especially since Alen was now prominently associated with the cause of political reform in Ireland and with opposition to Fitzgerald hegemony in government.[9]

By this means Cromwell was brought into direct contact with the personnel of government in Ireland almost as soon as he entered the king's service. His contacts became more extended as his political influence grew between 1531 and 1533. Two of his early petitioners are of special interest in this discussion. One was the clerk of the council, also named John Alen, who came to Ireland as the archbishop's secretary, a circumstance which no doubt explains how he was put in touch with Cromwell. To that connection can be attributed Alen's promotion to the office of master of the rolls in July, 1533, following a visit to court.[10] The other petitioner provides the first evidence linking Cromwell with the Anglo-Irish movement for political reform. He was Thomas Cusack, the landowner and lawyer from Cosingston in Co. Meath. Sometime before the autumn of 1531 Cromwell is found arranging to obtain the royal signature on a bill on behalf of Cusack.[11] Cromwell's early association with Alen and Cusack has a particular significance. Not only were they closely involved in launching his first reform programme but they proved to be dominant figures in the history of political reform in Ireland through three succeeding decades.

One other contact dating from Cromwell's earliest years as a royal servant calls for comment. This one is usually emphasized to the exclusion of all others and loaded with misleading implications. In a letter

[9] *S.P. Henry VIII*, ii, p. 158 (*L.P.*, v, no. 878). A. Gwynn, *The Medieval Province of Armagh* (Dundalk, 1946), pp. 63–66. On all of this see the note on Alen in the *D.N.B.*

[10] *L.P.*, vi, nos. 929 (26), 1051.

[11] P.R.O., E.36/139, p. 17, *L.P.*, vii, no. 923 (iv). Cromwell's Anglo-Irish contacts at this time included at least two others who were associated with reform, viz. Thomas Luttrell from the Pale, *L.P.*, vi, no. 727, and William Wise of Waterford, *L.P.*, vi, no. 815.

to Cromwell at the beginning of January 1532 Piers Butler, earl of Ossory, referred to the friendship newly established between them.[12] The alacrity with which Ossory attached himself to the emerging administrator indicates his need for a friend at court to counterbalance the influential contacts among the court nobility of his rival, the earl of Kildare. The latter had acquired an English nobleman as a father-in-law, the Marquis of Dorset. More recently the dispute between the Butlers and the Boleyns over the Ormond inheritance enabled Kildare to win the goodwill of a more important person, Wiltshire, the father of the future queen, and by Wiltshire's good offices to secure the favourable disposition of the Duke of Norfolk. Since Wiltshire and Norfolk were Cromwell's competitors for royal influence Ossory's intention was, of course, to establish a Butler–Cromwell nexus to counteract the Fitzgerald–Boleyn–Howard one.

The interaction of the factional struggles within the two administrations seriously complicated the preparations for launching the programme of Cromwellian reform and, indeed, contributed something to the situation in which these preparations precipitated a rebellion. At the same time it would be a great mistake to suppose that Cromwell identified himself with the Butler faction and that his intrusions into Irish affairs at this time can be explained on that basis. If his policy had an anti-Kildare bias it was neither inspired by nor directed towards Butler interests. The dominant local influence upon him was not the Butler faction but the local movement for political reform. As we shall see, the objective he pursued was more comprehensive and more constructive than simply the overthrow of the Fitzgeralds. Meanwhile Ossory's letter of January 1532 has a more immediate interest. It provides an example of the way in which Cromwell's Irish suitors at this early stage provided him with a flow of information on the local situation. If the earl's account was strongly influenced by his prejudices Cromwell may be credited with the necessary acumen to extract its useful content.

A final document must be noted in assessing the state of Cromwell's knowledge about Irish affairs in the earliest years of his administration. Late in 1534 one of his clerks listed the papers then held by him, placing them in broad chronological categories. Those retained from the two year period beginning at Michaelmas 1531 included a set of articles put in by William Fagan, an Anglo-Irish intermediary with O'Neill, documents and reports relating to the shortlived experiment of installing an Englishman, Sir William Skeffington, as lord deputy in 1531–32, a deposition against Kildare's liberty jurisdiction, two 'books of the description of Ireland', and a

[12] *S.P. Henry VIII*, ii, p. 153 (*L.P.*, v, no. 688).

device on Irish affairs by John Alen.[13] The list is not unimpressive since it takes account only of the papers from the earlier period still held by Cromwell late in 1534.

In the light of all of this the view of Cromwell as unfamiliar with Irish affairs in the opening years of his administration will hardly stand. The process of familiarization must have begun in the course of his service in Wolsey's household. From 1530, the beginning of his period as a royal servant, the evidence suggests a steady accumulation of information and contacts.

This clears the way for an examination of the central question. At what point did Cromwell formulate and begin to implement an Irish policy? Did preoccupation with the ecclesiastical revolution in England push Irish problems beyond the range of his practical concerns until their urgent need for attention was brought home to him by the rebellion in the summer of 1534? Did it take the Irish crisis, therefore, to produce an Irish policy? The thesis argued in the following pages is that Cromwell embarked upon a policy of Irish reform in the summer of 1533 and applied himself to it steadily thereafter, despite the gravity and urgency of other business claiming his attention. Cromwell's Irish policy was launched, therefore, no more than six months after he had attained the status of chief minister and almost a year before the Fitzgeralds went into rebellion.[14]

Characteristically Cromwell's reform began with the personnel of the Irish administration. The appointment of John Alen as master of the rolls early in July 1533 was the first major step towards refurbishing that body.[15] This event assumes a special significance in retrospect since Alen appeared in the second half of 1533 as the chief link between the reforming element in the Irish executive and the London government. In view of his activities in the second half of the year a special significance attaches also to the promotion of Thomas Cusack around the same time to a minor post in the exchequer.[16] Further proof of the direction in which Cromwell was moving—steadily towards reform—was provided after the death of Sir Bartholomew Dillon, the chief justice of the king's bench, late in the summer. Cromwell proposed to utilize the vacancy to effect an administrative reshuffle which would bring in Sir Patrick Finglas, the pioneering reformer, as chief justice and would enable two Co. Dublin administrators, Gerald Aylmer and Thomas Luttrell, to

[13] P.R.O., E.36/139, pp. 83, 95, 114 (*L.P.*, vii, no. 923 (xix, xxi, xxxi)).

[14] On Cromwell's rise to power, see Elton, *The Tudor Revolution in Government* (Cambridge, 1969), pp. 71–98.

[15] *L.P.*, vi, no. 929 (26).

[16] *L.P.*, vi, no. 105 (16), 1250.

follow Finglas up the ladder.[17] Time was to reveal the close association of these last two also with Cromwellian reform.

The projected reshuffle in the administration did not take place immediately. It may have been blocked by factional interests in circumstances that will soon appear. Alternatively, Cromwell, realizing the sensitivity of the issue, may have held it over in order not to prejudice the outcome of his next move. This was a summons to Kildare to come to court which issued early in the autumn of 1533.[18] The enormity of the complication this caused is illustrated by the fact that the promotions proposed in the autumn did not take place until the following summer.

In examining Kildare's reaction to the royal summons the first significant discrepancy between Stanihurst's account and the documentary evidence is brought to light. According to Stanihurst the earl answered with prompt obedience, deputing his heir, Silken Thomas, to substitute as head of government and exhorting him to moderation and to docility to the Irish Council. Kildare was thus exonerated from blame for the later upheaval and the unpremeditated nature of the event was subtly emphasized.[19] The documentary sources in contrast provide evidence that already at this stage the family foresaw and planned for the possibility of rebellion and that the earl himself was the prime mover in the proceedings.

By the time Kildare received the call to court the scent of battle was already in the air. Cusack's minor appointment produced an early sniff of resentment. Kildare, acting within the terms of his patent as lord deputy, had himself disposed of the office as a perquisite to one of his supporters, Richard Delahide, the chief justice of the common pleas. Delahide refused to give way to Cusack without sight of a royal patent, despite a supporting letter from Cromwell.[20] Inkling of the proposed Finglas promotion roused Kildare into mobilizing his English alliance. A letter to Wiltshire for support played on the Boleyn–Butler dispute, alleging Finglas's attachment to the Butler interest.[21] When, on top of this, the summons to London came, enough had happened to convince the earl that the tide was running against him at court once more, scarcely twelve months after he had regained office. Accordingly he stalled and sent his English wife to plead his inability to attend on grounds of illness.

[17] B.L., Titus B, i, fos 453–57 (*L.P.*, vi, no. 1381).

[18] The date cannot be fixed precisely, but Kildare's wife had appeared at court in answer to the call by 3 October, *L.P.*, vi, no. 1249.

[19] Stanihurst, *cit.*, pp. 286–87.

[20] *L.P.*, vi, nos. 105 (16), 841 (i), 1250. *Calendar of patent rolls Ireland, Henry VIII–Eliz.*, p. 4.

[21] *L.P.*, vi, no. 944.

He was, in fact, suffering from the effects of a gunshot wound sustained some months earlier.[22] Nevertheless, he was well enough to undertake business of ominous implications. In September 1533 an agent informed Cromwell from Dublin that Kildare had begun to transfer the royal ordnance from Dublin Castle to his own strongholds. The ostensible purpose was to fortify the borders of the Pale against Gaelic inroads. But Cromwell's informant was convinced that it was a reaction to a recent letter from the king.[23] The chronology would suggest that the royal letter in question was the summons to court and though this cannot be verified from the context it is at least clear that Kildare's action was prompted by a new sense of danger from England.

Despite the risk of appearing to carp it is necessary to refer here again to Quinn's thesis since it suggests that Cromwell was guilty of fatal negligence at this point. He argues that 'there is ample evidence that the Geraldine rising ought never have been allowed, by Henry and Cromwell to take place'. Had an English lord deputy been installed in the autumn of 1533 dissent would have been nipped in the bud. But nothing was done. Fitzgerald suspicion and resentment built up and eventually erupted in rebellion.[24] The criticism does not seem to take adequate account of the delicacy of the political situation in the autumn of 1533 or of the objective towards which Cromwell was working.

The suggestion of a bloodless *coup* which would have effected a swift change of lord deputy before the Fitzgeralds had gathered their wits is not realistic. The dynasty had enough experience of tussling for office by the 1530s to have standardized their method of coping when ousted. It was, in short, to fight their way back in, though the strategy was slightly more sophisticated than it sounds. The idea was to demonstrate their indispensability in government by reducing the colony to political chaos when relieved of it, either indirectly by manipulating their Gaelic allies or, if necessary, directly by going into open rebellion. In any case, it would have been impossible to catch Kildare by surprise. He was bound to have advance warning either through his own agents in London—Thomas Howth was acting on his behalf in the autumn of 1533—or through his court connections.[25] It can be taken for certain, therefore, that

[22] *L.P.*, vi, no. 1249. J. O'Donovan (ed.), *Annals of Ireland* (Dublin, 1846), v, pp. 1410–11.

[23] *L.P.*, vi, no. 1072. *Cf. Statutes at Large* (*Ire.*), i, p. 66 ('For the attainder of the earl of Kildare and others').

[24] Quinn, 'Henry VIII and Ireland, 1509–34' in *Irish Historical Studies*, xii, p. 342.

[25] For a contemporary explanation of the Geraldine tactic see *S.P. Henry VIII*, ii, p. 169, *L.P.*, vi, no. 1582 (2). *Cf. Statutes at large* (*Ire*), i, p. 66. On Howth see *L.P.*, vi, nos. 944, 1170.

the effect of a peremptory change of deputy in the autumn of 1533 would have been to precipitate a political upheaval at that time rather than in the following summer.

Apart from the poor prospects of success, a take-over of government in the autumn of 1533 would have been premature in view of the full dimensions of Cromwell's policy. It is customarily assumed that his only thought at this stage was to break the power of the Fitzgeralds. On the contrary, the evidence indicates that Cromwell did not envisage the dire fate that overtook the family until after they went into rebellion. In fact, as we shall see, the evidence indicates that at this stage he was preparing the way for launching a full scale programme of political reform in the Lordship in which his plan for the Fitzgeralds was reform not damnation. His anxiety to bring Kildare to London before launching the reform programme can be understood. In London the earl could be exposed to persuasion from the highest possible sources to accept the disagreeable reforms. At the same time, his presence there would minimise his opportunities for making trouble locally at the crucial initial stages of the reform campaign and would provide the government with a hostage, in effect, for the good behaviour of his kinsmen.[26]

The manœuvres that occupied the autumn and winter of 1533–34 must be set against this background. From Cromwell's point of view the situation called for patient diplomacy rather than precipitate action. Kildare's ploy of evasion on grounds of illness met with a firm reiteration of the summons to court. But he was authorized to nominate his own substitute and the royal command was entrusted to Lady Kildare to deliver, both gestures of reassurance and goodwill. This provided further opportunity for procrastination. Skeffington, holding a watching brief for Cromwell in the west country, reported in November, a month after Lady Kildare presented her husband's excuses at court, that her messengers had at last reached the coast after a leisurely journey from London and now were further delayed by contrary winds.[27]

When eventually it was delivered, the second summons placed Kildare on the horns of a dilemma. Bitter experience warned him of the dangers of the call. On the other hand he could not be sure of the king's mind and he hesitated to forfeit the possibility of a political

[26] Thus the imperial ambassador advised Charles V in April 1534 that the likelihood of Kildare's son engaging in subversion could be discounted so long as his father was in London, *L.P.*, vii, no. 530. For this reason also the earl had been detained in London in the course of the Surrey expedition and again in 1529–30. The same thinking prompted Robert Cowley to blame the outbreak of rebellion on the decision to allow Silken Thomas to return to Ireland from his period of attendance at court, *S.P. Henry VIII*, ii, p. 197.

[27] *S.P. Henry VIII*, ii, p. 182 (*L.P.*, vi, no. 1397).

victory by downright disobedience. Accordingly he made preparations to go to court. These included the council meeting at Drogheda to which Stanihurst refers where he formally deputed Silken Thomas to take charge of government in his absence. There is no reason to doubt that the exhortation to docility and moderation which Stanihurst puts in the earl's mouth on that occasion was in fact delivered. However, the meeting with the Irish council had been preceded by an intensive round of consultations within the kin itself. Before young Thomas was entrusted to the wisdom and experience of the Irish council a senior group of family councillors had already been appointed for his guidance in his father's absence. In the light of the earlier history of attempts to oust the Fitzgeralds from government it can hardly be doubted that the possibility of rebellion entered the calculations of the dynasty at this point though, no doubt, only as a contingency that it was hoped to avoid.[28]

When precisely Kildare reached court is uncertain. Chapuys, the imperial ambassador in London who had a special interest and was well-informed, did not mention the earl's presence when he covered Irish affairs in a dispatch on 4 February 1534. The next occasion he dealt with the Irish situation was on 22 April at which point he reported Kildare's appearance but gave no indication of when he arrived. Probably he turned up in the second half of February because a memorandum that can be placed in the first half of March shows Cromwell engaged in negotiations with him.[29]

Meanwhile the game had entered a new and grimmer phase. The political pressure against the earl in London had been mounting throughout the second half of 1533. Robert Cowley pressed the attack on behalf of the Butlers.[30] Skeffington, whose brief experimental period of office had ended with the reinstallation of Kildare in 1532, submitted his own indictment.[31] The political reform movement of the Pale was active through Thomas Cusack and Thomas Finglas, the son of the reforming chief baron of the exchequer. These left for court in the late autumn of 1533, and a surviving copy of Patrick Finglas's treatise on political reform, the 'Brevyate', written in the hand of his son may well belong to this episode.[32]

[28] Lambeth, Carew MS. 602, fo 138 (*Cal. Carew MSS.*, i, no. 84). P.R.O., S.P. 60/2, no. 63 (*L.P.*, ix, no. 514).

[29] *L.P.*, vii, nos. 152, 530. P.R.O., S.P. 1/83, p. 46 (*L.P.*, vii, no. 44 (ii)). The memorandum can be dated to a period after the issue of the *congé d'élire* for the election of a prior for Thugarton (3 March 1534) and before the issue of a *congé d'élire* for the election at Tewkesbury, *L.P.*, vii, no. 419 (2), (23).

[30] P.R.O., S.P. 60/6, no. 33 (*L.P.*, xiii (i), no. 883). *Cal. Carew MSS.*, i, no. 126.

[31] *S.P. Henry VIII*, ii, p. 181 (*L.P.*, vi, no. 1347).

[32] P.R.O., S.P. 60/2, no. 7. For a holograph in the hand of Thomas Finglas see

However, the most authoritative indictment was that brought across by John Alen. It took the form of a report on the state of the Lordship supported by an impressive array of signatories, eight high-ranking ecclesiastics, two of the Pale nobility, and three of the Pale's administrators. It vented no personal spites and had no axe to grind except political reform. In this case it was critical of Anglo-Irish magnates in general, and of Kildare and Ossory in particular, and pleaded for the rescue of government from their control. The message of this report was spelt out in greater detail in two anonymous treatises submitted during the same period.[33] The weight given by Cromwell to these three documents is clear from subsequent events. To a considerable extent his strategy in the ensuing months and the content of his first programme of political reform followed their prescriptions.

Despite the scanty documentation Cromwell can be seen, throughout the spring and early summer of 1534, applying himself to three major projects preparatory to launching the general programme. These indicate how comprehensive and well thought out was his design in contrast to the ill-considered and shifting attempts between 1529 and 1532. One was, of course, the installation of an English lord deputy. However, there was no naïve expectation that a new head of the administration with the assistance of a small military retinue could accomplish all. As we have seen, the executive was to be thoroughly refurbished by the appointment of suitable personnel to outstanding vacancies. The most novel aspect of the preparations was the determined attempt to come to grips with the problem posed for government by the overmighty earls of Kildare and Ossory. The latter as well as the former was brought to court. The aim was twofold, to pacify the feud between the two which had been the cause of so much political instability in the Lordship, and to secure a formal indenture from both binding them to cooperate with the revival of crown government, including its extension into their territories.

A later report by Chapuys indicates that in January 1534—before

---

S.P. 60/2, no. 18 (*L.P.*, viii, no. 1081). Cusack's departure for court in the autumn of 1533 is referred to in *L.P.*, vi, no. 1250.

[33] Alen's 'Instructions' claimed the authority of the Irish Council, but this can hardly be accepted. It lacked the support not only of the acting lord deputy, Kildare's son, but of the Geraldine chief justice of the common pleas, and the lord of Howth, *S.P. Henry VIII*, ii, p. 162 (*L.P.*, vi, no. 1586). The two anonymous treatises are not dated but internal evidence places them in the winter of 1533–34, *e.g.* both were written while Kildare and Ossory were on their way to court, P.R.O., S.P. 60/2, pp. 4–13, 30–37. *S.P. Henry VIII*, ii, pp. 166, 182 (*L.P.*, vi, no. 1587, vii, no. 264).

Kildare reached court—an alternative to his government was under active consideration. Cromwell floated the idea of sending the Duke of Richmond, the king's illegitimate son, with the title of lord lieutenant. But it was sunk by Norfolk who, if Chapuys is correct, was less disturbed by the threat to Kildare than to his own political influence, since Richmond was his son-in-law, and, therefore, a valuable asset at court.[34] By February, as another indirect source indicates, the final solution had already emerged. Maguire, the ruler of the Gaelic lordship of Fermanagh, replying to a letter from Henry VIII on 20 February, made reference to a statement of intent by the king to appoint a new lord deputy. The news was particularly welcome to him as a loyal underlord of O'Donnell and, therefore, an opponent of the Fitzgerald–O'Neill alliance. Very likely primed by John Alen who brought the letter, Maguire pleaded for the appointment of an Englishman and put forward the name of Skeffington with whom he had previously concluded an indenture of peace.[35]

Before the appointment of the lord deputy could proceed other aspects of the programme had to receive attention and Cromwell is found pushing ahead with these throughout March, despite the massive weight of English business, including the great corpus of ecclesiastical legislation. Indeed, by early March matters had been brought to a point where he felt the need for consultation with the king with a view to finalizing arrangements. In a series of Cromwellian memoranda dating from this period an item that regularly crops up is 'to know the king's pleasure for my lords of Kildare and Ossory and for the determination of the matters of Ireland'. Consultation of the originals shows that Cromwell himself was responsible for giving Ireland priority, writing in the item as an addition to the original draft and then whittling down the second draft to a final short list of twelve on which it was included.[36] When the discussions took place and with what results cannot be stated precisely but a sequel may be seen in another Cromwellian memorandum, also dateable to the first half of March. Here Cromwell reminded himself 'to send my lord of Kyldare the copye of the artycles'.[37] It may be surmised that these were intended to provide the basis for a formal indenture regulating the relationship between the earl and crown government along the same lines as the indenture formally ratified by the king

[34] *L.P.*, vii, no. 1141 (*cf. L.P.*, vi, no. 1069).

[35] *Cal. Carew MSS.*, i, no. 41 (*L.P.*, vii, no. 211).

[36] The memoranda are placed in incorrect sequence in *L.P.*, vii. The correct sequence is B.L., Titus B, i, fo 459 (*L.P.*, vii, no. 108), P.R.O., E.36/143, p. 43 (*L.P.* vii, no. 50), S.P. 1/82, p. 130 (*L.P.*, vii, no. 107).

[37] P.R.O., S.P. 1/83, p. 46 (*L.P.*, vii, no. 414 (ii)). For the dating see above n. 29.

and Ossory at the end of May. Another aspect of the programme figures on an agenda in the second half of March 'to remind the king of the appointment of judges and other officers in Ireland'.[38] Then in the first half of April Cromwell returned to the appointment of the lord deputy, reminding himself, as he nervously reviewed the defence situation in the aftermath of the spring session of parliament, that the matter called for urgent attention.[39]

Despite this Ireland recedes from view in the documentation for the rest of April. It may very well be that pressure of other business did indeed cause Irish affairs to be set aside for this brief period. This was the month when the national campaign for the administration of the oaths of supremacy and succession was launched in England, when the first national visitation of the religious orders was undertaken, and when the government was generally much concerned with overcoming internal opposition and preparing to resist foreign attack. On the other hand it may be that the reason for the delay was connected with the project itself. Perhaps a last effort was made on Kildare's behalf by his powerful sympathizers at court, or perhaps Cromwell himself paused to make a bid to bring negotiations with the earl to a successful conclusion.

In any case the die was cast in May. The issue of a patent on behalf of Sir Patrick Finglas on 8 May for the post of chief justice of the king's bench—the proposal against which Kildare had protested so vehemently to Wiltshire the previous August—signalized that the process of finalization had begun. Finglas's appointment was followed by the reshuffle projected the previous autumn. Aylmer got Finglas's old post as chief baron of the exchequer but, deviating from the original plan, Cusack was put in to fill Aylmer's vacancy instead of Thomas Luttrell. It seems that the latter was held in reserve with a view to higher things for he got the post of chief justice of the king's bench when the Geraldine, Richard Delahide, was ousted in October. Finally, Thomas Finglas was given a start as protonotary of the common bench.[40] Meanwhile the appointment of Skeffington as lord deputy was also put in train as letters from him to Cromwell on 24 May indicate.[41] On the last day of the month the king and Ossory formally subscribed an indenture by which the earl bound himself and his heirs to act 'in all and every thinge, as apperteyneth to their

[38] *L.P.*, vii, no. 48. This memorandum belongs to the same period as that of *L.P.*, vii, no. 257, viz. between the election and consecration of the bishops of Ely and of Coventry and Lichfield, *L.P.*, vii, no. 587 (28), 761 (17).

[39] *L.P.*, vii, no. 420.

[40] *Calendar of patent rolls, Ireland, Henry VIII–Eliz.*, p. 12. *Fiants, Ireland, Henry VIII*, p. 36.

[41] *S.P. Henry VIII*, ii, p. 193 (*L.P.*, vii, nos. 704–05).

duties of allegiaunce of an Inglishe subjecte'.[42] The various clauses which spelt out in detail what this implied will be discussed later. Here it need only be noted that Ossory's indenture provided for a particular application of a general programme of reform outlined in a set of 'Ordinances for the government of Ireland' which were intended as a blueprint for the new government. These were conceived as part of the strategy of constitutional and administrative engineering by which Cromwell sought to consolidate the outlying areas of the king's dominions. In effect they passed sentence of death on bastard feudalism in the colonial area of the Lordship and decreed the resuscitation of crown government. John Alen later reminded Cromwell that the 'Ordinances' 'wer made ther by the king and his counsaile . . . and gret paynes your mastership ded take in the divising and debating of them'. But they owed much of their detail to the proposals brought by Alen himself late the previous year and to the related anonymous treatises.[43]

Thus final arrangements for launching a full scale programme of Cromwellian reform in the Lordship were put in train in May 1534. Sir William Skeffington was nominated to replace Kildare as lord deputy and a shake-up of the administration was undertaken. A detailed blueprint for the overhaul of government was provided and Ossory was bound by indenture to cooperate in its implementation. Early in the second half of the month the first steps were taken to prepare the way in Ireland. Thomas Cusack and Thomas Finglas were dispatched at that time with instructions from the king which were to be delivered to the Irish Council assembled with their acting head, Kildare's son, Silken Thomas.[44] Then the whole plan went awry. Silken Thomas rejected the king's instruction to assemble in council and went into rebellion.[45]

The concentration of effort necessary to meet this new situation resulted in the postponement of the programme of reform until the spring of 1535. It was then taken up and pursued relentlessly during

[42] *S.P. Henry VIII*, ii, p. 194 (*L.P.*, vii, no. 740).

[43] *S.P. Henry VIII*, ii, 207. The 'Ordinances' are not dated so that it cannot be said precisely at what date prior to Skeffington's departure for Ireland, at the beginning of August 1534, they were devised and put into print, *L.P.*, vii, no. 105. However, a delay of some months must be allowed for printing. The complementary nature of the indenture concluded with Ossory on 31 May suggests that the two documents were prepared in conjunction. For Alen's comment see *S.P. Henry VIII*, ii, p. 226. On the reform of the outlying areas see Elton, *England under the Tudors* (2nd edn, London, 1974), pp. 175–76, D. M. Loades, *Politics and the nation, 1450–1660* (Brighton, 1974), pp. 175–79.

[44] P.R.O., S.P. 60/2, no. 63 (*L.P. Addenda*, i (i), no. 889), S.P. 60/2, no. 63 (*L.P.*, ix, no. 514), *L.P.*, vii, no. 736.

[45] P.R.O., S.P. 60/2, no. 63 (*L.P.*, ix, no. 514). Lambeth, Carew MS. 602, fo 139 (*Cal. Carew MSS.*, i, no. 84). *S.P. Henry VIII*, ii, p. 197 (*L.P.*, vii, no. 915).

the remaining five years of Cromwell's administration.[46] However, it should be clear from the foregoing that the work begun in the spring of 1535 was not a response to the Kildare rebellion but the culmination of a project that the rebellion interrupted. The Kildare rebellion did not elicit Cromwellian reform, the relationship was exactly the reverse. Conversely, to make the point again, Cromwell's original concept of reform in the colony, paralleling his strategy in the North and west, did not envisage the destruction of Kildare. The rebellion was not deliberately fomented in order to crush this major rival for hegemony in the colony. The intention was rather to reformulate the jurisdictional relationship between the crown and the local magnates in such a way as to transform the latter into true agents of the former within the framework of a properly centralized government.

The outstanding question is why was this new deal rejected by the Fitzgeralds? Was it a case of old fashioned bastard feudalism with overtones of traditional Anglo-Irish separatism? Or did the crisis discover in the Fitzgeralds a full blown nationalism in which feudal magnate autonomy was no more than a residual element? Was the embroilment of religion a crucial issue. The evidence is fragmentary and does not allow of an absolutely clear cut answer. But an examination of the immediate circumstances in which the rebellion was precipitated indicates the priorities.

What happened to Kildare when he reached London in the spring of 1534 is obscure. According to Stanihurst the anti-Geraldine alliance pressed charges of treason and Kildare, too sick to defend himself properly, was committed to the Tower. The story contains no more than a grain of truth. It is true that the earl's call to court released a barrage of complaints against his administration. But the documentary evidence shows that he remained at large, despite the accusations made against him, until news of his son's rebellion reached London at the end of June.[47] Stanihurst's emphasis on factional vendetta has been followed in subsequent accounts to the exclusion of the crucial factor in the situation. This was Cromwellian reform.

Kildare's place in the story of the preparation to launch the programme of reform, from his arrival in London in the spring of 1534 to his dispatch to the Tower in the summer, can be pieced together from a number of documents. A pointer to the nature of his initial contact with Cromwell is provided in one of the anonymous treatises referred to earlier which heavily influenced the formulation of the

[46] See my unpublished Ph.D. thesis, 'The Irish constitutional revolution', Cambridge, 1975.

[47] Stanihurst, *cit.*, p. 287. *L.P.*, vii, nos. 957, 1015.

reform programme. At the time it was written Ossory as well as Kildare had been called to court. The author urged that both earls be tackled about the inordinate jurisdiction they exercised, political, financial and judicial and that both be required to give a formal undertaking to submit to reform. It is certain that Cromwell proceeded with Ossory on this basis. The indenture concluded on 31 May 1534 was the outcome.[48] There is no reason to think that Kildare was dealt with differently. Cromwell's memoranda from the middle of 1533 onwards normally couple the two earls together, giving the impression that to him, as to Anglo-Irish reformers, they were both guilty of the same perversion—bastard feudalism—and required to be recalled to virtue by the same means.[49] When, therefore, the chief minister reminded himself in the first half of March 'to send my lord of Kyldare the copye of the artycles' he may well have been referring to the initiation of negotiations with Kildare with a view to the conclusion of an indenture on the same basis as with Ossory.[50]

Even though no copy of such articles survives the implications of the reform programme for the Fitzgeralds can be gathered from the conditions enjoined upon Ossory and from the 'Ordinances for the government of Ireland'.[51] What was envisaged was considerably more than the removal of Kildare from office though substantially less than the destruction of the dynasty. As well as the loss of hegemony in central government, a redefinition of the earl's local status was entailed in order to eliminate the elements of sovereignty attaching to it. This extended both to the exercise of external jurisdiction over neighbouring Gaelic or disobedient Anglo-Irish lords—which was now reserved explicitly to crown government—and to the exercise of internal autonomy—which was to be superseded by a reintroduction of the machinery of the central administration. The 'Ordinances' provided for one other substantial derogation in the case of Kildare. Whereas no move was proposed against the ancient Ormond liberty of Tipperary the recently revived and legally dubious liberty of Kildare was to be abolished.

The earl's reaction to all of this may be inferred from the absence of a formal undertaking on his part to submit to the conditions of the programme of reform, paralleling the indenture concluded between the king and Ossory. Ironically, the vulnerability of Ossory was his salvation. Lacking allies at court—at variance with Norfolk and Wiltshire—or a watertight title to the Ormond earldom—at this point claimed by Wiltshire as heir general—the hope of gaining both

48 *S.P. Henry VIII*, ii, p. 182, above p. 85.
49 *L.P.*, vi, nos. 551, 1056, vii, nos. 50, 107, 108.
50 P.R.O., S.P. 1/83, p. 46. *L.P.*, vii, no. 414 (ii).
51 *S.P. Henry VIII*, ii, pp. 194, 207.

through Cromwell disposed Ossory to accept the limitations of the Cromwellian reform. By contrast, the strength of the Fitzgeralds, based on a secure title to the earldom, local hegemony, and court alliances, served to embolden Kildare to stand in the way of Cromwell's policy, and to be crushed in consequence.

The sequence of events in May and early June 1534 that translated Geraldine determination to resist into violent rebellion focuses attention on the rôle of Silken Thomas, on his place in Cromwell's plans for launching the reform programme, and on the interaction between him and his father in London. It will be recalled that, as part of the final preparations for launching the programme in the second half of May, Thomas Cusack and Thomas Finglas were dispatched with a letter from the king to the Geraldine heir summoning him to attend the Irish council where the royal pleasure was to be fully declared. The precise purpose of this move is unclear but it was obviously intended to pave the way for the impending programme by neutralising resistance in advance.

Unfortunately for the success of the mission Silken Thomas's response was conditioned by prior intelligences from England. One message is certainly known to have come directly from his father. It was brought to him by a Co. Dublin farmer who had been on a trip to London. It told of a scheme to carry Thomas off to England where he was to be put to death and it warned especially of the evil designs of the Irish council should he fall into their power. The second message, the source of which is not stated, was even nearer the mark. It relayed reports of a supposed mission by Cusack and Gerald Aylmer who were said to have received rewards from the king for undertaking to capture Thomas and his five uncles.[52]

How are these reports to be assessed? They are credible to the extent that they indicate a desire on the part of the government to secure the presence of Silken Thomas in London. Chapuys also mentions such a scheme, and it makes good sense.[53] The danger of sabotage to the reform programme would have been much the less if the heir as well as his father were deprived of the opportunity to interfere. However, the crucial consideration here may well have been the state of Kildare's health which, according to three different sources, had become critical by the end of April.[54] This rendered

[52] The evidence for these is a deposition taken from a retainer who went to England with Kildare and returned in May 1534 to join Silken Thomas, Lambeth, Carew MS. 602, fo 138 (*Cal. Carew MSS.*, i, no. 84). The account there provided is implicitly corroborated by an interrogatory prepared for Silken Thomas in 1535, P.R.O., S.P. 60/2, no. 63 (*L.P.*, ix, no. 514).

[53] *L.P.*, vii, no. 957.

[54] Lambeth, Carew MS. 602, fo 138 (*Cal. Carew MSS.*, i, no. 84). P.R.O., S.P. 3/4, p. 111 (*L.P.*, vii, no. 614). *L.P.*, vii, no. 530.

the presence of Silken Thomas in Ireland especially menacing. The death of the father would have deprived the government of their hostage while leaving the son the undisputed leader of the dynasty. It may well be, therefore, that Cusack and Finglas had secret instructions to inveigle Thomas into going to England. The insinuations about the government's intention to undertake a wholesale purge of the family may be discounted. However, they are significant in reflecting the extent to which the attitude of the Geraldine circle towards government had come to be dominated by pessimism and mistrust.

The deepening mood of desperation in the Fitzgerald camp is reflected in another development linking Kildare and his son in the course of May. At the beginning of the month three highly placed members of the earl's retinue in London returned to Silken Thomas in Ireland. They were followed a few weeks later by members of Kildare's most intimate circle, two of the family, Katherine Fitzgerald and Rose Eustace, a priest, Dr Hickey, and a layman, Edmund Nele.[55] A later deposition explained that the decision to return was taken in view of the earl's critical state of health; it was felt that in the circumstances Silken Thomas in Ireland offered a better opportunity for service.[56] Such reasoning may seem callous. But Kildare himself probably instigated the return. The instinct for the survival of the dynasty allowed little scope to spurious sentiment. It was a time to look to the living rather than to the dying and so the focus of familial piety shifted from the earl in England to the heir in Ireland. To the heir, therefore, the family rallied as the day of reckoning seemed to draw nearer in May.

As a result of all the traffic from father to son there was no chance of a successful outcome to the mission of Cusack and Finglas by the time they reached Ireland early in June. Henry VIII's letter directing Thomas to assemble with the Irish council met with flat refusal.[57] The crown and the dynasty were now in direct confrontation. The signal for battle was provided a few days later by the famous incident of Cannon's letter.

That story has been recounted a thousand times since Stanihurst first put it in his chronicle: Thomas Cannon, Skeffington's secretary, wrote to a priest friend in Dublin boasting that 'the earle of Kildare . . . was alreadie cut shorter, as his issue presentlie should be' and that his own master was to regain the office from which Kildare had ousted him four years earlier. Whether by accident or by

[55] Lambeth, *ibid.* P.R.O., S.P. 60/2, no. 63 (*L.P.*, ix, no. 514).
[56] *Loc. cit.*
[57] *Loc. cit.*

design, as Stanihurst suspected, the letter fell into the hands of Silken Thomas. Goaded partly by anger at his father's fate, and partly by fear that it might foreshadow his own, Thomas galloped with his retinue on St Barnaby's Day, 11 June, 1534, to St Mary's Abbey in Dublin where the Irish council was assembled. There he threw back the sword of state declaring 'I am none of Henrie his deputie, I am his fo'.[58]

The story of Silken Thomas, 'youthfull, rash and headlong' rushing into rebellion to avenge his father's death and to defend himself from a like fate provided not only the climax of Stanihurst's account but the clinching argument in his interpretation of the origins of the Kildare rebellion. He would have been gratified by its ready accepttance by historians. While it is true that the basic elements of the episode—Cannon's letter and its sequel, the renunciation of loyalty before the Irish council—are authenticated by documentary evidence,[59] the story built upon them is another matter. The outbreak of the Kildare rebellion cannot be explained as the responsc of an impulsive youth to news of his father's death. In parenthesis it should be pointed out that the text of Cannon's letter does not survive and that it is not clear whether in fact it contained a false report of Kildare's death or simply referred to the imminent launching of the reform programme. In either case the effect would have been the same. The deciding factor for Silken Thomas and his advisers was the knowledge that Kildare had lost the political battle in London. They correctly took Cannon's letter as final confirmation of this and, consequently, as a sign that the moment had come for the traditional Geraldine last word—a practical demonstration of what the extrusion of the dynasty from government meant, political chaos. Whatever the mood of the young heir as he galloped towards Dublin on St Barnaby's Day, his action was a premeditated response to a contingency that had been anticipated as far back as the previous autumn.[60]

A final discrepancy between Stanihurst's account and the contemporary evidence serves conveniently to round off the thesis about the origins of the Kildare rebellion presented here. It relates to the

[58] Stanihurst, 'The chronicles of Ireland' in *Holinshed's Chronicles*, vi, 290.

[59] The deposition already referred to mentions both. It was provided by a member of the retinue who accompanied Silken Thomas to the meeting of the Irish Council, Lambeth, Carew MS. 602, fo 139 (*Cal. Carew MSS.*, i, no. 84). *Cf.* P.R.O., S.P. 60/2, no. 63 (*L.P.*, ix, no. 514). See also below, n. 63.

[60] In this matter I share the view of crown government at the time. *Statutes at Large* (*Ire.*), i, 66. Despite differences of emphasis and of interpretation the two theses mentioned in n. 1 reach a similar conclusion about the premeditated nature of the revolt.

attitude of the earl himself to his son's action. Stanihurst concludes his exculpation of Kildare by presenting us with the pathetic picture of him dying of a broken heart in the Tower 'for thought of the young man his follie'.[61] The imperial ambassador had quite a different story for Charles V shortly after news of the rebellion reached London. Despite Kildare's extreme illness and the consequences for himself, imprisonment in the Tower, he was heartened by news of the rebellion and regretted nothing so much as his son's lack of age and experience for such a weighty enterprise. Chapuys mentioned a government proposal to send Kildare back to Ireland to persuade his son to surrender and commented that it would be as the dispatch of Regulus to Rome by the Carthaginians.[62] This report may have been coloured by the anxiety of Chapuys to emphasize resistance to the government generally at this time—he urged that a Spanish invasion would meet with popular local support. Nevertheless, it is clear that he had contact with the earl's entourage and the reaction he portrays fits much better than Stanihurst's the character of the old lion-heart whose career showed markedly more evidence of loyalty to his own dynasty than to the crown.

The response of government to the outbreak of rebellion brings the discussion back finally to its major theme, Cromwellian reform. If, as Stanihurst alleged, Cannon acted as part of an anti-Geraldine faction, the treatment meted out to him by government indicates that Cromwell was not part of the alliance. He was lodged in the Tower as soon as news of his provocative letter reached London.[63] It is worth remembering also that Kildare himself was not sent to the Tower until news of the rebellion broke. Evidently Cromwell had continued to hope in the meantime for a settlement with the family by means of negotiation. The rebellion brought a complete change of attitude on his part. Mercifully, Kildare died in September 1534 while the rebels were still in the flush of initial success.[64] The outbreak was eventually crushed with unprecedented ruthlessness. Silken Thomas and his five uncles were rounded up and allowed to languish for a year in the Tower before being executed early in February 1537. The conduct of the government throughout showed scant regard for mercy, honour or even justice.

Yet it will be clear from the foregoing study that the man who supervised the destruction of the Fitzgeralds with such thoroughness would have preferred to reform them. The exigencies of reform, not

[61] Stanihurst, 'The chronicles of Ireland in Holinshed's *Chronicles*, vi, 304.

[62] *L.P.*, vii, no. 1141. Chapuys noted the earl's death late in September, *L.P.*, vii, no. 1193.

[63] *L.P.*, vii, no. 957.

[64] *L.P.*, vii, no. 1193.

factional vendetta, decreed their fate. What brought down the implacable wrath of Cromwell upon them was not their alliance with his political rivals but their decision to challenge in arms the forces of reform. The Fitzgeralds were victims, therefore, not of their enemies, but of their own refusal to adapt to a new political era.

The place of the religious Reformation and of international politics in the origins of the Kildare rebellion can be dealt with by way of postscript. Discounting arguments of the *post hoc propter hoc* variety, evidence of the influence of these factors is exceedingly flimsy. The diplomatic contact of Silken Thomas with the emperor did not begin until after he went into rebellion. He may have had previous fleeting contact with an imperial agent who visited the earl of Desmond in the second half of 1533, but there is no hard evidence to support the view that international politics exercised a decisive influence in precipitating the rebellion.[65] So far as religion is concerned, the hard evidence, such as it is, runs counter to the notion of the Fitzgeralds as champions of papal supremacy. As late as 1525 Kildare denounced Ossory to London for his attachment to papal jurisdiction, claiming that the churches in Kilkenny and Tipperary were falling into decay and pastoral care was neglected as a result of Butler predilection for papal provisions.[66] Were it not for subsequent developments historians might well discern in this the cry of the nascent Reformation. It should also be borne in mind that when the Fitzgeralds went into revolt no practical steps had yet been taken to implement the Reformation in Ireland. The situation was hardly ripe, therefore, for popular religious protest. What the evidence suggests is the existence of a pro-papal lobby among the clergy of the Pale who encouraged Thomas to give his rebellion a religious dimension.[67] But there is nothing to suggest that the religious factor exercised a significant influence in the period before the rebellion. In short, if the royal divorce can be considered the remote cause of the Kildare rebellion that is not because of the religious changes and the international complications that resulted from it, but solely because it placed Thomas Cromwell in a position to launch a programme of political

[65] On the operations of the imperial agent in Ireland in the second half of 1533 see *L.P.*, vi, no. 815, vii, nos. 122, 152, 229, 945, 980, 1057, 1095, 1297, also Ellis, 'The Kildare rebellion, 1534' unpublished M.A. thesis, Manchester, 1974, and *idem* 'The Kildare rebellion and the early Henrician Reformation' in the *Historical Journal*, xix (1976), pp. 807–30, Ellis takes a different view to the one expressed here.

[66] *S.P. Henry VIII*, ii, p. 120.

[67] This is implied by the interrogatory devised for Silken Thomas in 1535, P.R.O., S.P. 60/2 no. 63 (*L.P.*, ix, no. 514). Ellis, 'The Kildare rebellion and the early Henrician Reformation' in the *Historical Journal*, *op. cit.*

reform in Ireland. The influence of the religious Reformation and of international politics on the course of the rebellion and the relationship of all three in the context of later sixteenth century-history do not come within the compass of the present study.[68]

[68] They are discussed from rather different angles by Ellis, n. 1. above, and Bradshaw, 'The Irish constitutional revolution 1515–57, unpublished Ph.D. thesis, Cambridge, 1975.

THE USES OF LITERACY IN ANGLO-SAXON ENGLAND AND ITS NEIGHBOURS

By C. P. Wormald, M.A.

READ AT THE SOCIETY'S CONFERENCE 16 SEPTEMBER 1976

AS the recent lament over falling standards by the Secretary-General of the United Nations reminds us, universal literacy is today considered a necessary feature of civilized society. This may be one reason why the problem of medieval literacy, of a society where the ability to read and write was apparently confined to a clerical *élite* has so intrigued modern historians. In this paper, I wish to reconsider the extent of lay literacy in England before the Conquest.[1] But first we must be clear what we mean by literacy. The ability to read does not necessarily imply the ability to write. To take only the most famous medieval example, Charlemagne could speak Latin, and enjoy the *City of God*, but he never learnt to write.[2] What Parkes calls 'pragmatic literacy' may extend from the capacity to recognize, if not sign, one's own name, to the ability to write a formal document in Latin. What might be called 'cultured literacy' could range from reading free prose in the vernacular to composing Latin in the classical tradition.[3] The more advanced types of pragmatic literacy might well overlap with the more basic cultured levels. But it is obvious that we cannot deduce a widespread ability to read anything from the fact that the names of owners or makers were sometimes engraved upon Anglo-Saxon coins, weapons or memorials; or a generally high standard of lay culture from the fact that there were documents in the vernacular. If we are to describe early English society as literate in a sense that would satisfy the ancient, or later medieval, historian, we must show that the proportion of laymen able to read at least a vernacular writ or poem was socially, if not statistically, significant.

[1] I am profoundly grateful to the various friends who have helped me with aspects of this paper; especially to Dr C. J. Wickham, Mr D. Ganz, Dr T. M. Charles-Edwards and Dr M. T. Clanchy; needless to say, they are not responsible for any errors of fact or interpretation which follow.

[2] Einhard, *Vita Karoli*, xxiv, xxv, ed. O. Holder-Egger, M.G.H., S.R.G. in us. schol., pp. 29–30.

[3] M. B. Parkes, 'The literacy of the laity', *Literature and Western civilization: the Medieval World*, ed. D. Daiches and A. Thorlby (London, 1973), p. 555.

A further source of possible confusion is the 'Fallacy of the Anticipated Audience'. Inscriptions in sufficient quantity and quality *may* be symptoms of a literate society, as in the ancient world, but they do not themselves establish its existence. Even so extended and impressive a text as the *Dream of the Rood* on the Ruthwell Cross only might have been designed to expound the Redemption to a secular public; it might just as well have been addressed to the Redeemer himself. Apparently more persuasive are the cases when we are told that a book was directed at a prominent layman. When the book is in Latin, this does indeed create a presumption of learning, and thus literacy, in its recipient, but the case of Charlemagne shows what its limits might be, and men might be flattered by such works, even when they could not read them.[4] Books for laymen in the vernacular offer some evidence for secular interest in literature, but even less justification for supposing that the dedicatee was literate; as late as the second half of the twelfth century, Baldwin II of Guines had books collected and translated, but they must have been read aloud to him, since he could no more read French than Latin.[5] It is not sufficiently appreciated that vernacular translations, in the first instance, merely allow works to be read to illiterates. Other things being equal, a written vernacular could permit the development of lay literacy, and its literary status must be discussed in any investigation of the education of the medieval layman. But vernacular literature does not in itself imply a wide reading public.

Finally, it is not possible to prove widespread literacy by citing a series of individual cases. Even so impressive a catalogue of learned laymen as that of Thompson does not seriously dent the case for an effective clerical monopoly, because, in the total absence of statistics, there is no way of establishing that his examples are representative.

Instead, we must seek for *all* the symptoms of a *civilization de l'écrit*: not just inscriptions and a written vernacular, but also schools catering for laymen, books owned and written by laymen, and a significant role for writing in government.[6] We should further examine not only the Anglo-Saxon evidence, but also its European context; early English society was exposed to most of the same pressures as the rest of barbarian Europe, and a preliminary consideration of the continental and insular background, as it has been laid bare in several notable recent studies, should give us some in-

[4] *Cf.* P. Riché, *Education et Culture dans l'Occident barbare* (Paris, 1962), pp. 92–93, 461–62.

[5] J. W. Thompson, *The Literacy of the Laity in the Middle Ages* (New York repr., 1963), pp. 141–42.

[6] Riché, *op. cit.*, pp. 220 ff.

dication of what to expect in England.[7] Above all, we must consider attitudes to literacy within and without the Church, following the example of the exciting collection of anthropological Essays edited by Dr Goody on *Literacy in Traditional Societies* where attention is given to the social and cultural forces which determine the distribution of literacy in society.[8]

Among the explanations offered by Goody and his colleagues for 'restricted literacy' in societies comparable with early medieval Europe are the vested interests of learned classes like the Brahmans, who sought to monopolize literacy as they had more traditional forms of learning; and such technical problems as the complexities of non-phonetic alphabets, or the domination of education by the (to sub-Saharan peoples) foreign language of Arabic.[9] This last point obviously offers an attractive parallel with the position of Latin in the medieval West. But difficulties with alphabets scarcely arise in the medieval context, and one cannot easily represent the early medieval clergy as a closed *élite*; unlike the Brahmans they were not (at least in theory) a hereditary caste, and were far from seeking to restrict all forms of learning to themselves. In the early Middle Ages, it seems more useful to cite a factor for which anthropological parallels are also available: indifference or even hostility to literacy within classes of society which cherished other values.[10]

The most vivid illustration of this attitude on the part of the Germanic warrior-class concerns Theodoric the Ostrogoth. That this 'barbarian champion of civilization' could have been illiterate has seemed so much at variance with what else we know about him that the possibility has given rise to controversy.[11] Yet this is what we are explicitly told by one source, and it is strongly supported by the judicious and knowledgeable Byzantine historian Procopius.[12] Theo-

[7] Besides the works of Riché and Thompson already cited, see: R. R. Bezzola, *Les Origines et la Formation de la Littérature courtoise en Occident* (Paris, Bibl. de l'école des hautes études, cclxxxvi, 1944, cccxiii, 1960); E. Auerbach, *Literary Language and its Public in Late Latin Antiquity and the Middle Ages* (New York, 1965), pp. 237–338; Riché, 'L'instruction des laics en Gaule merovingienne', *Settimane di Spoleto*, v (1958), pp. 873–88; 'L'enseignement et la culture des laics dans l'Occident precarolingien', *ibid.*, xix (1972), pp. 231–53; 'Recherches sur l'instruction des laics du IXe au XIIe siècle', *Cahiers de Civilization médiévale*, v (1962), pp. 175–82; above all, H. Grundmann, 'Litteratus-illiteratus', *Archiv für Kulturgeschichte*, xl (1958), pp. 1–65.

[8] J. Goody, *Literacy in Traditional Societies* (Cambridge, 1968).

[9] *Op. cit.*, pp. 11–24, 34–42, 165–71, 189–93, 221–41.

[10] *E.g.* the reaction of the Six Nations Indians to the invitation to send boys to William and Mary College, cited by T. C. McLuhan, *Touch the Earth* (London, 1972), p. 57.

[11] Grundmann, *op. ct.*, pp. 25–31.

[12] *Anonymous Valesianus*, ii, 61, 79, ed. and trans. J. C. Rolfe (Loeb series, 1939),

doric's daughter, the regent Amalasuntha, wished to give her son a Roman education, but the Goths protested:

> 'Letters,' they said, 'are far removed from manliness . . . The man who is to show daring . . . and be great in renown ought to be freed from the timidity which teachers inspire, and take his training in arms . . . Even Theodoric would never allow any of the Goths to send their children to school; for he used to say . . . that, if the fear of the strap once came over them, they would never withstand sword and spear.'

This story shows that, whatever the level of Theodoric's pragmatic literacy, and whatever the impression he sought to make upon Romans, he did not wish to seem educated to his warriors and it shows why. It may stand as symptomatic of a consistently powerful alternative educational tradition throughout the early Middle Ages. In his commentary on the Rule of St Benedict, written during the second quarter of the ninth century, Hildemar of Corbie contrasted Benedict's *schola divini servitii* with the *schola humani servitii*, 'in which men serve the king, and learn the methods of war and the hunt, and everything to do with honourable conduct in this world.'[13] Letters were not always despised, but the priorities of an upper-class education were quite different until well on in the Middle Ages.

But this assertion needs one important qualification. As Grundmann has demonstrated, and as the case of Amalasuntha has already indicated, there is reason to suppose that, throughout much of the period, women were often better educated than men. Laywomen are surprisingly prominent as the owners, dedicatees, even authors, of books, and as the decisive influence upon the education of their families.[14] It would seem that the gentler skills in which women were trained were not so antipathetic to the pursuit of letters as the warfare and hunting that dominated male adolescence. This curious cultural anomaly, at least by the standards of most pre-industrial societies, thus sets off the role of the warrior-ethic in curbing the spread of secular literacy among men. But it also highlights the survival of traditions in the early medieval West that could counterbalance the robust instincts of Theodoric and his followers, and tend, in some circumstances, to foster the growth of lay literacy.

---

pp. 544–47, 556–59; Procopius, *History of the Wars*, V, ii, 11–17 ed. and trans. H. B. Dewing (Loeb, 1919), iii, pp. 16–19.

[13] *Vita et Regula S. Patris Benedicti una cum Expositione Regulae a Hildemaro tradita*, iii (Regensburg, 1880), p. 66; *cf.* V. H. Galbraith, 'The literacy of the medieval English Kings', *Proc. Brit. Acad.*, xxi (1935), pp. 202–05.

[14] Grundmann, 'Die Frauen und die Literatur im Mittelalter', *Archiv für Kulturgeschichte*, xxvi (1936), pp. 129–61.

The most important of these traditions was of course that of the Church. Christianity is a religion of the Book; and not just of the Bible, but also of the works of the Church Fathers, and of Canon Law. That clergy should be adequately literate was axiomatic, in theory, from the very earliest days of Christian discipline. As churchmen came to demand from kings some of the same qualities as they expected in bishops and monks, royal literacy seemed increasingly important. Writing to Charlemagne in 775, Cathwulf instructed him to establish the *Lex Dei* over all his people, 'and read it all the days of your life, that you might be imbued with divine wisdom and secular letters, as David and Solomon and other kings were'; the king's *sapientia* was to be founded, like that of Old Testament kings, on knowledge of the Divine Law, which could not but involve some literate learning.[15] The effect of this advice tended to be reinforced, especially in southern Europe, by the memory of Roman literary standards. It is possible that lay literacy survived in Italy throughout the early Middle Ages, while, in Spain and southern Gaul, a few Roman families preserved their educational values until the Arab conquest. In the ninth century, the wills of two great Carolingian noblemen, domiciled respectively in northern Italy and Burgundy, bequeathed spectacular collections of books, some to laymen.[16] On the pragmatic level, southern France remained, at least residually, a *Pays du Droit écrit*, and not only the Romanized Visigoths, but also the resolutely barbarian Lombards spawned comprehensive codes of law which conformed much more closely than northern legislation to the standards that the Romans had expected in their lawmakers.[17]

The most revealing illustration of the impact of these traditions is the fate of the Germanic vernacular. One of the most remarkable facts of European history is the failure of the conquering barbarians on the continent to develop and impose their own linguistic heritage. The Byzantine and Orthodox tradition encouraged, even organized, the development of written vernaculars among the peoples they converted, including the Goths, the Slavs and eventually even the Eskimoes; but the western Church was uncompromisingly Latin, and here the barbarians accepted, even defended the domination of

[15] Ed. E. Dümmler, M.G.H., Ep. Kar. Aev., ii, p. 503.

[16] Riché, 'Recherches', pp. 179–80; *Education*, pp. 227–54; 'Les bibliothèques de trois aristocrates laics Carolingiens', *Le Moyen Age*, lxix (1963), pp. 87–104.

[17] The Visigothic Code (ed. K. Zeumer, M.G.H., Leg. Sect. I, i) was arranged in twelve books, like the Code of Justinian and the Twelve Tables, and specified that it, and no other law, was to be used in court (II, i, 4, 10, 11, 13, 14, pp. 47, 58–61); the Lombard edict, and all subsequent legislation, (ed. F. Beyerle, Germanenrechte, 1962) were securely dated: on the whole, these are unusual features of barbarian legislation.

literate communication by the language of their Roman victims.[18] Throughout most of Europe, Latin remained the only language in which other than an elementary literary education was possible. It was the Romano-Christian cultural tradition that did most to inspire the development of literacy in Germanic society; but, paradoxically, its prestige was such that it squeezed out the native languages in favour of Latin, and thus, like Arabic in Africa, actually contributed towards the restriction of literacy.

The Germanic barbarians of the early Middle Ages therefore illustrate some of the same contradictions and ambiguities that are familiar in the Third World today. They had a sense of being heirs to a more sophisticated civilization, whose more striking features they wished to imitate; but they were reluctant, in certain respects, to jettison their traditional culture. The dialectic between these contradictory forces was never wholly resolved in the early Middle Ages. Charlemagne was primarily interested in the education of the clergy, but his court school and *Hofbibliothek*, and the local schools which he and bishops like Theodulf tried to set up, should have had some effect upon the literacy of the secular aristocracy, and handbooks were indeed written for some of its members.[19] Yet literacy was probably less well established among Carolingian kings and nobles than their Merovingian predecessors.[20] Similarly, Carolingian capitularies, considerably more copious than the Merovingian, betray a serious and consistent attempt to encourage the use of writing in government and legal business; yet the early capitularies at least are so lacking in formal structure that Ganshof has argued that what gave them legal force was not their written form but the *verbum regis*, the oral pronouncements of the king, and that what we have are more or less *ad hoc* minutes of what was decreed, preserved not in royal archives but in the libraries of clerical *missi*.[21] Later Carolingian legislation represents a significant improvement in these

[18] H. I. Marrou, 'L'école de l'Antiquité tardive', *Settimane di Spoleto*, xix (1972), p. 137.

[19] *Capitularia regum Francorum*, 22:72; 29; 116: 11, 12; 150:6; 196:24, 39; ed. A. Boretius, M.G.H., Leg. Sect. II, i, pp. 59–60, 79, 235, 304, ii, pp. 37, 40; *Concilia*, 37:3, ed. A. Werminghoff, M.G.H., Leg. Sect. III, ii, pp. 274–75; *Capitula of Theodulf*, i, 20, P.L., cv, col. 196. For the Manuals, *cf.* H. H. Anton, *Fürstenspiegel und Herrscherethos in der Karolingerzeit* (Bonn, 1968), pp. 83–85, 213.

[20] Bezzola, *op. cit.*, i, pp. 48–54, 98–119, ii, p. 5; Riché, 'L'Instruction', p. 887; Merovingian kings signed diplomata personally, and their referendaries were usually laymen, but neither was the case in France for many centuries afterwards: G. Tessier, *Diplomatique royale francaise* (Paris, 1962), pp. 26–30, 91–97.

[21] F. L. Ganshof, 'The use of the written word in Charlemagne's administration', *The Carolingians and the Frankish monarchy* (London, 1971); 'Recherches sur les capitulaires', *Revue historique de Droit francais et etranger*, IV, xxv (1957), pp. 50–61, 69–85, 196–212.

respects, but its output fell away dramatically after the death of Charles the Bald (877).[22] Carolingian government must temporarily have raised the level of pragmatic literacy in its dominions, but written law did not take root in ninth-century Francia, whether we blame Viking birds of the air, or the tares of aristocratic secularity. Again, Charlemagne encouraged the use of the vernacular, and, later in the century, east Frankish scholars discussed the history of translation and inspired vernacular versifications of the Gospels.[23] But there was usually a note of apology about the use of native speech. European vernacular literature remained, for the time being, fragmentary and marginal.[24]

Before turning to the English evidence, we may glance briefly at Ireland. Despite the existence of the pre-Christian Ogham script the development of Irish literacy was closely bound up with the impact of the Church,[25] but we must here make two important modifications to any impression that the clergy alone were literate. The first is that the sons of kings and nobles were apparently entrusted to monastic schools, as they had once been to the fosterage of the Druids, even when designated for a secular life.[26] Secondly, and more important, Ireland already had wholly secular learned professions, guardians of its legal, historical and poetic lore. This is undoubtedly why the writing of the native language developed so precociously alongside Latin: as early as the seventh century, law-tracts and epics like the *Tain Bo Cuailnge* were being written down, and, by the ninth, the vernacular was used even for annals and biblical commentaries.[27] Some scholars have argued from the exclusively monastic provenance of the early manuscripts of indigenous learning that the *filid* and *brehons* contented themselves with their traditional oral methods, and that their works were written down by converted members of the class, who combined the

[22] The criticisms of Ganshof in R. Schneider, 'Zur rechtlichen Bedeutung der Kapitularientexte', *Deutsches Archiv*, xxiii (1967), pp. 273–94, are more valid for the later, than for the earlier, Carolingian period.

[23] W. Betz, 'Karl der Grosse und die Lingua Theodisca', *Karl der Grosse*, ii, *das geistige Leben*, ed. B. Bischoff (Düsseldorf, 1965), pp. 300–06; M. L. W. Laistner, *Thought and Letters in Western Europe* (Ithaca, 1957), pp. 375–77.

[24] B. Bischoff, 'Paläographische Fragen deutscher Denkmäler der Karolingerzeit', *Frühmittelalterliche Studien*, v (1971), pp. 101–33.

[25] D. A. Binchy, 'The background of early Irish literature', *Studia Hibernica*, i (1961), pp. 7–9.

[26] A. Lorcin, 'La vie scolaire dans les monastères d'Irlande', *Revue du Moyen Age Latin*, i (1945), pp. 221–36.

[27] F. J. Byrne, 'Seventh century documents', *Proceedings of the Irish Catholic Historical Committee*, iii, 1965–67, pp. 5–23; J. Kenney, *Sources for the Early History of Ireland* (New York, 1929), p. 11.

professions of monk and poet or judge.[28] On the other hand, the early literature and laws were clearly influenced by Latin grammar, but scarcely at all by Christianity; their authors were educated, yet tolerant of pagan traditions to an extent which must have been beyond even the most secularized Irish cleric.[29] It does, therefore, seem likely that the *filid* preserved an independent literary tradition. But if so, they offer a much better example than Christian clergy of the sort of jealous restriction of literacy described by Goody. Their learned language was systematically obscure, and their status could be acquired only by birth, or training in their own schools.[30] In Ireland, then, the same social factor that was responsible for the existence of non-clerical literacy, and for the much wider and more confident use of their vernacular than by other barbarians, was also, by another paradox, responsible for the failure of these developments to bear fruit in a more general ability to read and write.

When we turn to the Anglo-Saxons themselves, there is one figure who must stand at the centre of the argument. Quite apart from what he had to say, and tried to do, about Anglo-Saxon literacy, the character and career of King Alfred crystallize nearly all the important issues. In his epistolary preface to his translation of the *Pastoral Care*, he wrote that, whereas there had formerly been many wise men in England, 'both of spiritual and lay orders', and 'kings prospered both in warfare and in wisdom', learning had now decayed so completely that there were, 'very few men on this side of the Humber who could apprehend their services in English, or even translate a letter from Latin . . .' Alfred was surprised that learned men had produced no translations before; 'but then I answered myself . . . : "They did not think that men would ever become so careless and learning so decayed; they abstained intentionally, wishing that here in the land there should be the greater wisdom the more languages we knew." Then,' he continued, 'I remembered how the divine law was first composed in the Hebrew language, and afterwards . . . the Greeks . . . turned it into their own language, and also all other books. And the Romans likewise . . . And also all other Christian peoples turned some part of them into their own language.' So the king had decided to translate the books, 'which may be most necessary for all men to know'; as he said further on, though knowledge of Latin had declined, 'many could read things written in English'. It was his hope that, 'if we have the peace, all the youth

[28] R. Flower, *The Irish Tradition* (Oxford, 1947), pp. 72–75; P. MacCana, 'Mongan mac Fiachna and Immram Brain', *Eriu*, xxiii (1972), p. 103, n. 1.

[29] J. Carney, *Studies in Irish Literature and History* (Dublin, 1955), pp. 277–78; the point is demonstrated for the laws by Dr Charles-Edwards in a forthcoming edition of *Bechbretha*.

[30] Binchy, *op. cit.*, pp. 10–13.

now in England born of free men . . . may be devoted to learning as long as they cannot be of use in any other employment, until such time as they can read . . . English. One may then teach further in . . . Latin . . . those whom one wishes to . . . bring to holy orders.'[31] The implications of this famous letter for the literacy of the Anglo-Saxon layman may be considered under three headings: the situation Alfred inherited; his policy; and its results over the last century and a half of the Old English kingdom.

Alfred's account of the early history of Anglo-Saxon literacy raises two issues, which it is as well to keep separate: the use of the vernacular, and the literacy of the laity. The written vernacular was of course well established before Alfred's time, in legislation, in documents and in poetry.[32] In this respect, England resembled Ireland rather than Europe. In England, as in Ireland, Latin was a completely 'dead' language; on the other hand it was no less moribund east of the Rhine, where laws were yet issued in Latin, and it seems necessary to add further explanations for the vitality of the native tongue. We should perhaps, especially in the North, give some credit to the Irish themselves; it may not be coincidence that the Germanic people most exposed to Irish influence was the one, the Scandinavians apart, to develop its own vernacular furthest.[33] Perhaps, too, the foundations of written English owed something to Theodore, the first effective Archbishop of Canterbury; as a Greek, he may well have been sympathetic to the vernacular, and we know that he was interested in English weights and measures, while his pupil, Tobias of Rochester, was learned, 'Latina, Greca et Saxonica lingua.'[34] However this may be, the status of the pre-Alfredian vernacular should not be exaggerated. Alfred clearly regarded the appearance of those who could read English but not Latin as a recent development; and the king's words suggest that his efforts to establish educational methods for English without concomitant instruction in Latin represented a new departure. Bede had translated the Creed and the Lord's Prayer, and the Council of Clovesho

[31] Trans. D. Whitelock, *English Historical Documents*, i (London, 1955), pp. 818–19.

[32] D. A. Bullough, 'The educational tradition in England from Alfred to Aelfric', *Settimane di Spoleto*, xix (1972), p. 456; F. M. Stenton, *Latin Charters of the Anglo-Saxon Period* (Oxford, 1955), pp. 39–49; and *cf.* Asser, *Vita Alfredi*, xxii, xxiii, ed. W. H. Stevenson (Oxford, repr., 1959), p. 20, for books of Saxon poems at the Wessex court.

[33] *Cf.* C. Donahue, 'Beowulf, Ireland and the Natural Good', *Traditio*, vii (1949–51), pp. 263–77.

[34] Bede, *Historia Ecclesiastica*, v, 8, ed. C. Plummer (Oxford, 1896), pp. 295–96; Bischoff, 'Wendepunkte in der Geschichte der lateinischen Exegese im Frühmittelalter', *Sacris Erudiri*, vi, 1954, pp. 191–94.

(746/7) allowed translations not only of these texts, but also of the offices of Mass and Baptism; but neither say anything to indicate that their work could be read, rather than memorized and recited, by those who were ignorant of Latin.[35] An independent vernacular had begun to emerge, but it had not yet progressed as far as in Ireland.

Above all, the rise of written English proves nothing about lay literacy. The early English law-codes could have been written by clergy (as in the eleventh century) and read out to judges; unlike the early Irish laws, they were substantially christianized.[36] Nor, as we have also seen, do inscriptions, whether runic or Roman, take us much further, interesting and important as are Dr Page's recent suggestions; Anglo-Saxon inscriptions do not, in any case, compare either in scale or content with those of sub-Roman Gaul and Spain.[37] The question must be decided on more concrete evidence, negative and positive.

The first point is that, despite the interesting references in the *Endowments of Men* to the, 'poet endowed with songs', the, 'one who can in the assembly of wise men determine the custom of the people', and the one who, 'knows laws when men deliberate', we can scarcely postulate a class of secular English professionals to compare with the *filid*.[38] Obviously, there were poets and men familiar with legal custom, but we cannot dignify these men with the title of profession, still less that of class. Except in Scandinavia, the traces of the learned order which may once have been common to the Indo-European peoples are extraordinarily difficult to detect among the early medieval Germans. As the Hindu and Irish examples clearly show, it is not in the nature of such classes to leave little or no mark upon the evidence, and one can only conclude that, among the Anglo-Saxons and their continental neighbours, there was no such potential for non-clerical literacy as in Ireland. *Beowulf* may not look like the work of a clerical pen, but it is a good deal more marked by Christianity than is the *Tain*; and it is possible to account for it in terms of the known social and cultural instincts of some early English religious

[35] Cuthbert, *De Obitu Bedae*; Bede, *Epist. ad Egbertum*, v; ed. Plummer, pp. clxii, 409; Council of Clovesho, x, ed. W. Stubbs, *Councils and Ecclesiastical Documents*, iii (Oxford, 1871), p. 366.

[36] Laws of Aethelbert, 1; of Wihtred, Pr.-24; of Ine, Pr.-5:1; 6:1; 13; 15:1; 23:2; 45; 55; 61; 76–76:3; ed. F. Liebermann, *Gesetze der Angelsachsen* (Halle, 1903–16), pp. 3, 12–14, 88–91, 94–99, 108–09, 114–17, 122–23.

[37] R. I. Page, *An Introduction to English Runes* (London, 1973), pp. 96–105; E. Okasha, *A. Handlist of Anglo-Saxon non-Runic Inscriptions* (Cambridge, 1971); E. Le Blant, *Inscriptions Chrétiennes de la Gaule* (Paris, 1856, 1865, 1892); J. Vives, *Inscripciones cristianas de la Espana romana y visigoda* (Barcelona, 1942).

[38] Trans. Whitelock, *Eng. Hist. Docs.*, p. 805.

communities.[39] Ecclesiastical discipline was not so well established in the early Middle Ages that it is usually safe to conclude that a given text, however hair-raising, could not have been written in a monastery.

We do, of course, know of literate laymen before Alfred. Apart from the famous cases of the seventh-century kings, Sigebert of East Anglia and Aldfrith of Northumbria, educated respectively in Gaul and Ireland, we hear, as in Ireland, of noblemen's sons entrusted temporarily to monasteries at Ripon and York.[40] But that these were exceptional cases is strongly argued by Alfred's own experiences. It is not, as often, easy to be sure what Asser means, but it looks as though, for all his enthusiasm, Alfred did not learn to read at all until he was nearly forty, and that he then learnt simultaneously to read English and Latin. When he had already assembled his Mercian scholars, and Waerferth had translated Gregory's *Dialogues*, the king was still read to: '*non enim adhuc aliquid legere inceperat*'. The judges whom Alfred sought to make literate were unable to read even Saxon books (though some had slaves who could), and Asser's account hardly suggests that they shared their ruler's love of letters until their jobs were at stake.[41] Asser thus not only underlines the lack of an independent tradition of vernacular education, but also highlights scarcely less dramatically than Procopius the social and cultural obstructions to barbarian literacy, even in a relatively cultivated court.[42] But to this apparent indifference, there was, if we may believe the most famous of Asser's stories, one conspicuous exception: Alfred's mother. Sceptics have failed to notice how well her efforts to foster her sons' education fit the European background of comparatively more extensive enthusiasm for letters among women.[43] Even though Alfred did not then learn to read, it is not perhaps wholly fanciful to associate his almost obsessive pursuit of literacy subsequently with the psychological impact of his mother, the memory of whose influence he communicated to Asser.

The balance of the evidence thus suggests that Alfred's policy to educate the sons of free men in their own language was something

[39] Whitelock, *The Audience of Beowulf* (Oxford, 1951), pp. 4–21; I discuss this familiar problem further in a forthcoming paper on, 'Bede, *Beowulf* and the Conversion of the Anglo-Saxon aristocracy'.

[40] Bede, *H.E.*, iii, 18; iv, 26; v, 13 (pp. 162–63, 268, 311–13); Eddius, *Vita Wilfridi*, xxi, ed. W. Levison, M.G.H., S.R.M., vi, p. 216; *Vita Alcuini*, iv, ed. W. Arndt, M.G.H., SS., xv, p. 186.

[41] Asser, xxii–xxv, lxxvi, lxxvii, lxxxi, lxxxvii–lxxxix, cvi (pp. 20–21, 59, 62–63, 67, 73–75, 93–95); the interpretation of these passages here adopted was also that of Stevenson, p. 221.

[42] *Cf.* the letters of Servatus Lupus, trans. Whitelock, *Eng. Hist. Docs*, pp. 809–10.

[43] Asser, xxiii (p. 20).

new. When considering this policy itself, the king's use of the vernacular should once again be separated from his educational objectives proper. As Professor Bullough has argued, there is no obvious continental precedent for the new scale on which Alfred planned to exploit his mother-tongue.[44] At the same time, it is worth noting that he explicitly acknowledges foreign example in his reference to the translation of the Divine Law and other books by all Christian nations; Walahfrid Strabo had made a similar point in ninth-century Germany, and had mentioned the work of Wulfila.[45] It is now suggested that an illustrated manuscript of the Old Saxon *Genesis* and *Heliand* may have been available in later ninth-century Wessex, and it is not impossible that Alfred was influenced by East Frankish interest in translations, even if he went much further in developing them.[46] If we are looking for inspiration nearer home, it is suggestive that the ninth century also saw major advances of the vernacular among Celtic peoples: not only, as we have seen, in Ireland, but also in Wales, where, whatever one thinks of the authenticity of the oldest Welsh poems, it is common ground that they were probably written down in this period. One of the most important early Welsh manuscripts ended up in St Dunstan's classbook at Glastonbury, and one is tempted to wonder whether Asser might not only have taught the king to read, and helped him with his translations, but also awakened his interest in the further possibilities of the vernacular.[47] Alfred's letter is not, in any case, an unqualified manifesto of vernacular studies. He implies that it was carelessness and decay in the past which now made translations necessary, and he evidently agreed with the view that one's wisdom was the greater the more languages one knew. He was not content that the spiritual leaders of his people should know no Latin, and at the school where his youngest son was taught, Latin and Saxon were read together.[48] If we read the whole preface, it becomes evident that Alfred translated because he thought he had no choice, and, no more than his continental contemporaries would he have considered the vernacular any long-term substitute for the Latin scholarship which alone could bring true wisdom.

[44] *Op. cit.*, pp. 458–60.

[45] Walahfrid, *De exordiis et incrementis rerum ecclesiasticarum*, viii, ed. V. Krause, M.G.H., Leg. Sect. II, ii, p. 481.

[46] B. Raw, 'The probable derivation . . . of Junius 11 . . .', *Anglo-Saxon England*, v (1976), pp. 133–48.

[47] D. Greene, 'Linguistic considerations in the dating of early Welsh verse', *Studia Celtica*, vi (1971), pp. 1–11; and K. Jackson's reply, *ibid.*, ix (1974), pp. 1–33; also, I. Williams, 'The earliest Welsh poetry', *The Beginnings of Welsh Poetry*, ed. R. Bromwich (Cardiff, 1972), p. 42.

[48] Asser, lxxv (p. 58).

Alfred makes his actual educational ambitions quite clear. Even if the verse preface to the *Pastoral Care* implies that his first concern was to improve clerical standards, there is no reason to doubt that he did intend that the sons of all free men should be taught to read, and the king's school for the sons both of nobles and the basely born was presumably a first step.[49] But *why* was Alfred so concerned to make his subjects literate? Asser's language in his final chapter, on Alfred's attempt to educate his judges, is very similar to that of the passages in which he describes the king's own quest for *sapientia*, and this suggests that what Alfred sought to inspire in his judges was what he had fought so painfully to acquire for himself, namely the wisdom of Solomon, the wisdom that came simply from the ability to read, and thus to familiarize oneself with the Word of God.[50] Alfred's conception of *sapientia*, like that of the Carolingian scholars, who had much to say of it, was therefore something moral and religious, and had very little to do with administrative expertise. It was concerned less (as Riché has well put it when discussing Carolingian manuals for laymen) with the government of the state than the government of oneself.[51] The king's actual law-code, if it was issued in anything like the form in which we now possess it, would not have been at all easy to use in court, but it does begin with a translation of the Mosaic Law, and with a history of its subsequent adaptation by Christ, the Apostles and subsequent legislators, ecclesiastical and secular.[52] The prominence in his own legislation of what Alfred called *seo ae*, *The Law*, neatly reflects what Asser implies to have been the main reason for the king's concern with judicial literacy. Literacy mattered to him, as to Alcuin, because it was the source of wisdom, and wisdom was the key to the favour of God, in this world and the next. It was strictly cultured rather than pragmatic, and derived its inspiration not so much from imperial Rome, as from the City of God.

Even by Carolingian standards, Alfred's policy was very ambitious, and we should conclude by considering whether it resulted in a genuine extension of lay education. It is immediately obvious that the vernacular made massive strides in the tenth and eleventh centuries, entering almost all spheres of religious and secular life, from

[49] *Ibid.*

[50] *Ibid.*, xxii, xxv, lxxvi, lxxvii, lxxxviii, cvi (pp. 20, 21, 60–63, 73, 93–95).

[51] Riché, *De l'education antique à l'education chevaleresque* (Paris, 1968), pp. 44–47; *cf.* W. Edelstein, *Eruditio und Sapientia* (Freiberg, 1965), pp. 65–112, 143–218; and Anton, *op. cit.*, pp. 255–57.

[52] The law-book contains several contradictions between Alfred's own laws and those of Ine, and the whole text is numbered in 120 chapters without much regard for content: Liebermann, iii, pp. 35–36, 40; for Alfred's introduction, *cf. ibid.*, i, pp. 26–47.

the sealed writ to the Bible itself.[53] Even so, it failed to emerge completely from the shadow of Latin. Bishop Aethelwold (+984), whose importance as a patron of English has only recently become clear, felt it necessary to apologize for his translation of the Rule of St Benedict. It was:

> 'Necessary for unlearned laymen who . . . abandon this wretched life, and choose . . . the holy service of this Rule. It certainly does not matter by what language a man is . . . drawn to the true Faith, as long as he comes to God. Therefore, let unlearned natives have the knowledge of this holy Rule by the exposition of their own language, that they . . . have no excuse that they were driven by ignorance to err.'[54]

His pupil, Aelfric, whose achievement as a writer of vernacular prose was without any European parallel for several centuries, repeatedly expressed his embarrassment at his use of the mother-tongue. His educational works were designed to teach Latin, not English, though, as he recognised, his Grammar was bound to be important for English also.[55] If it is true that (as in Ireland) the precocity of native literature was one reason for the relative poverty of later Anglo-Latin scholarship, it is important to notice that this was through no choice of the major English scholars, for whom Latin remained the language of true learning.

Moreover, it does not follow from the ascendancy of the vernacular that lay literacy was now widely established. Of the possible symptoms of a *civilization de l'écrit*, we hear little, after Alfred, of organized schools for laymen as well as clerics. Aelfric was poorly taught by a semi-literate priest; this may be evidence for parish-schools, but we do not know enough about Aelfric's upbringing to be sure.[56] There is no specific demand for the establishment of schools in the laws of the later Anglo-Saxon kings, unlike those of Charlemagne. Wulfstan's *Canons of Edgar* were influenced by the diocesan statutes of Theodulf into making similar provisions for priestly teaching, and Theodulf's

[53] F. Harmer, *Anglo-Saxon Writs* (Manchester, 1952); G. Shepherd, 'English versions of the Scriptures before Wycliffe', *Cambridge History of the Bible*, ii, ed. G. W. H. Lampe (Cambridge, 1969), pp. 366–77.

[54] Trans. Whitelock, *Eng. Hist. Docs*, p. 848; *cf.* H. Gneuss, 'The origin of standard Old English and Aethelwold's school at Winchester', *Anglo-Saxon England*, i (1972), pp. 63–83.

[55] Epilogue to *Catholic Homilies, II*, ed. B. Thorpe (London, 1846), pp. 608–09; Latin Preface to *Lives of the Saints*, ed. W. W. Skeat (Oxford, Early English Texts Society, lxxvi, repr., 1966), pp. 2–3; Preface to Genesis, *The Old English version of the Heptateuch*, ed. S. J. Crawford (Oxford, E.E.T.S., clx, 1922), p. 80. On Aelfric in general: P. Clemoes, 'Aelfric', *Continuations and Beginnings*, ed. E. G. Stanley (London, 1966), pp. 176–209.

[56] Preface to Genesis, pp. 76–77.

decrees were in any case available in English, but we can say nothing about the results.[57] The truth is that Aelfric and his contemporaries were overwhelmingly concerned with the education of the clergy. In a passage from the English preface to his Grammar, Aelfric seems almost to echo Alfred's preface, but he makes it much clearer that it is the supply of clergy with Latin skills that preoccupies him.[58] If, then, lay education existed, and it was certainly not discouraged by Aelfric and Wulfstan, we must accept that it was incidental to the education of the clergy.

What of the evidence for lay readership or ownership of books? We may start with the court itself. The most famous royal book collector of the Anglo-Saxon period was Aethelstan, who was probably himself literate.[59] Yet, in the first place, most of the identifiable constituents of his library were Bibles and Psalters, where Charlemagne's *Hofbibliothek* contained an impressive range of classical authors. Second, there is no reason to suppose that any of these was actually written at court, though we can say as much for Charlemagne; several, indeed, were of foreign origin. Finally, Aethelstan seems to have got rid of his books almost as fast as they came in; his attitude to books, like his attitude to relics, had more in common with the world of gift-exchange than that of the antiquarian. Unlike that of Charlemagne, the will of Eadred, Aethelstan's brother and successor but one, said nothing about a royal library.[60] In this respect, therefore, the English evidence scarcely compares with the Frankish.

Beyond the court, the most attractive evidence for lay bibliophiles is supplied by the patrons of Aelfric. Like Carolingian scholars, Aelfric wrote books for laymen at their request, and his long letter for Sigeweard, a local thegn, is a masterly essay on the lessons of the Bible for the warrior. But he says nothing about Sigeweard actually *reading* his work, and it is good works rather than learning whose importance he mainly stresses; his letter could have been read aloud.[61] One of Aelfric's patrons, however, was almost certainly

[57] *Wulfstan's Canons of Edgar*, li, ed. R. Fowler (Oxford, E.E.T.S., cclxvi, 1972), pp. 12–13; O.E. translation of *Theodulf*, xx, ed. B. Thorpe, *Ancient Laws and Institutes of England* (London, 1840), p. 475.

[58] Ed. J. Zupitza (Darmstadt, repr., 1966), pp. 2–3.

[59] William of Malmesbury, *Gesta Regum*, cxxxii–cxxxiii, ed. W. Stubbs (London, Rolls Series, 1887), pp. 144–45.

[60] J. Armitage Robinson, *The Times of St Dunstan* (Oxford, 1923), pp. 51–71; will of Eadred, trans. Whitelock, *Eng. Hist. Docs*, pp. 511–12; *cf.* Bischoff, 'Die Hofbibliothek Karls des Grossen', *Karl der Grosse*, ii, pp. 42–62; 'Die Hofbibliothek unter Ludwig dem Frommen', *Medieval Learning and Literature*, ed. J. J. G. Alexander and M. T. Gibson (Oxford, 1976), pp. 3–22.

[61] *Old English Heptateuch*, ed. Crawford, pp. 15–75; *cf.* J. Hurt, *Aelfric* (New York, 1972), pp. 91–100.

literate. Ealdorman Aethelweard was apparently the author of a Latin version of the Anglo-Saxon Chronicle; its Latinity has raised more than one scholarly eyebrow, but it is the work of a man with a lively interest in the resources of the Latin language. His son was also a patron of Aelfric, and his grandson-in-law presented books to Crediton.[62] But before we make too much of this dramatic illustration of the possibilities of aristocratic literacy, we should note that this family was of royal descent, and royalty was always rather a special case in the early Middle Ages.[63]

Further than this case, moreover, we cannot easily go. If the illustrated late Saxon manuscripts of the translated or versified Old Testament were indeed aimed at laymen, this is very double-edged evidence for lay literacy.[64] Examination of the vernacular books listed in Ker's *Catalogue* reveals several that may have belonged to laymen, but the only probable non-royal case is, significantly, that of a woman, Aelfgyth; the later medieval picture is much more promising.[65] A Worcester book-list mentions 'Odda's book', and this is likely to have been the mid eleventh-century earl Odda, but he became a monk before his death, and put up the chapel at Deerhurst which bears his name.[66] The will of Bishop Aelfwold of Crediton, before 1012, bequeaths a copy of Hraban and a martyrology to Ordwulf, a layman, but also the uncle of Aethelred II, and the founder of Tavistock. Otherwise the only two secular wills which mention books are those of women.[67] Caution is perhaps advisable here; books might not have been important enough to mention, and the will of Wynflaed does indeed hurry through the bequest of, 'books and such small things', before going on to the horses, suggesting that the priorities of high-born English ladies have not changed much in a thousand years. Yet we are still left with a contrast between clerical and female wills, sometimes mentioning books, and the wills of secular men, which do not. None of the sixty odd Anglo-Saxon wills compares remotely in bibliographical interest with the Carolingian wills mentioned earlier. It is not mere special

[62] *The Chronicle of Aethelweard*, ed. A. Campbell (London, 1962); M. Winterbottom, 'The style of Aethelweard', *Medium Aevum*, xxxvi (1967), pp. 109–18; *The Exeter Book of Old English poetry*, ed. R. W. Chambers, M. Förster and R. Flower (London, 1933), pp. 85–90.

[63] Auerbach, *op. cit.*, p. 263.

[64] Raw, *op. cit.*, p. 135; C. R. Dodwell and P. Clemoes, *The Old English Illustrated Hexateuch* (Copenhagen, Early English MSS. in Facsimile, xviii, 1974), p. 58.

[65] N. R. Ker, *Catalogue of Manuscripts containing Anglo-Saxon* (Oxford, 1957), no. 115, pp. 152–53; *cf.* 137, p. 172; 403, p. 469.

[66] *Anglo-Saxon Charters*, Appendix ii, 5, ed. A. J. Robertson (Cambridge, 1939), pp. 250–51, 456–58, 499.

[67] Whitelock, *Eng. Hist. Docs.*, pp. 536–37; *Anglo-Saxon Wills* (Cambridge, 1930), 3, pp. 14–15; *The Will of Aethelgifu* (Oxford, 1968), p. 6.

pleading, therefore, to suggest that the general impression is not one of extensive lay literacy, and the exceptions tend to explain themselves away: as royalty, as ladies, or as men whose bookishness was shortly to lead them to a wholesale renunciation of secular life. One's conclusion is bound to be affected by where one thinks that the *onus probandi* lies, but my own view is that we need better evidence than this before we can accept that cultured literacy was widely established even in later Anglo-Saxon society.

Finally, we may turn to the difficult problem of the level of pragmatic literacy in pre-Conquest England. It is perhaps anachronistic to suppose that a highly organized government must necessarily have made copious use of written records.[68] Nevertheless, the later Anglo-Saxons do seem to have had some appreciation, like the Carolingians, of the value of documentation. There may, after all, have been an Anglo-Saxon chancery from the mid tenth century.[69] Anglo-Saxon noblemen had documents and seals.[70] Yet the written legislation of Alfred's successors raises many of the same problems as that of the Carolingians, and here too it may have been the *verbum regis* rather than the written text which gave it the force of law. It has been shown that Archbishop Wulfstan wrote most of the later Anglo-Saxon codes.[71] At the end of the Latin paraphrase of Aethelred's sixth code, Wulfstan wrote:

> 'These legal statutes . . . were urgently issued at our synodical council by King Aethelred, and all the magnates . . . swore that they would observe them faithfully; and therefore . . . I have committed them to writing for the memory of posterity, and the benefit of men now and in the future.'[72]

[68] L. Mair, *Primitive Government* (London, repr., 1970), pp. 138–65; but *cf.* M. Bloch, 'Astrology and Writing in Madagascar', Goody, *op. cit.*, pp. 286–88.

[69] Important and as yet unpublished research by Mr Simon Keynes may make it necessary to qualify the strong case of Dr P. Chaplais, 'The Origin and Authenticity of the royal Anglo-Saxon diploma', and, 'The Anglo-Saxon Chancery: from the diploma to the writ', *Journal of the Society of Archivists*, iii (1965–69), pp. 48–61, 160–76. But it will also be necessary to take account of the downgrading of the whole idea of an early medieval Chancery, reflected, *e.g.*, in J. Fleckenstein, *Die Hofkapelle der deutschen Könige*, i (Stuttgart, 1959), pp. 74–95.

[70] For portions of Chirographs in the hands of laymen, *cf.*, *e.g.*, *Anglo-Saxon Charters*, lxxxi, ci (pp. 156–57, 190–91), and Robertson's note to lxxv (p. 394); and *Anglo-Saxon Wills*, xxiv, xxx (pp. 68–69, 78–79); for seals, *cf.* Okasha, *op. cit.*, pp. 107–08, 118–20; for administrative documentation in general, *cf.* J. Campbell, 'Observations on English government from the tenth to the twelfth centuries', *ante*, xxv (1975), pp. 41–42, 48–51.

[71] D. Bethurum, 'Wulfstan', *Continuations and Beginnings*, pp. 210–46, with bibliography of her own, and Professor Whitelock's, discoveries.

[72] Liebermann, i, p. 257.

Nothing is here said about royal promulgation in writing; it was Wulfstan, the king's legal adviser, who was responsible for the text. That this was no exceptional situation is suggested by various features of the other codes. Their manuscript tradition is, by continental standards, very thin, and exclusively dependent on a few great ecclesiastical centres; there is no trace, as there is in Francia, of court manuscripts.[73] The constant formula of tenth-century decrees was, 'we say', and in Aethelstan's sixth code, we find the phrase, 'the king's word'.[74] The corpus of Aethelstan's legislation is as heterogeneous as much of Charlemagne's. In the Grately and Exeter codes, preserved at Winchester and (?) Canterbury, the king makes laws in the first person. But the Faversham code is professedly a record of the Kentish shire-court, addressed to the king in the second person; the Thundersfield code looks like the minutes of a council held on the king's instructions in his absence, and he is referred to throughout in the third person; while the London code represents the decision taken by the local peace-guild under their bishop, and except in one clause, the first person refers to the guild, not the king. It seems likely that each of these codes owes its survival in its extant form to the archives not of the king, but of Archbishop Wulfhelm at Canterbury, who was closely involved in their promulgation, and may even have been responsible for their written composition.[75] Thus, even in later Anglo-Saxon England, formal royal law-making may have remained oral, and our texts may be more in the nature of ecclesiastical records of decisions taken than legislative acts in themselves.

It is true that, like the capitularies of Charlemagne's immediate successors, the English codes after Alfred show some of the marks of a literary legal tradition. We find demands that the codes be used by judges, arrangements for their publication, and cases where they are cited by subsequent decrees.[76] As in Francia, these are important indications of a striving after literate standards of law-making and law-enforcement. Yet, exactly as in Francia the tradition died out after six generations; there is no trace of a further code in the fifty years between the legislation of Cnut and the Conquest, easily the biggest lacuna since Alfred's time. Perhaps the decisive evidence that written law-making was not yet 'natural' is that in not one

[73] Whitelock, *Eng. Hist. Docs.*, p. 329; *cf.* Bischoff, 'Hofbibliothek unter Ludwig', p. 14.

[74] *E.g.* I Edward 1:2, 3, 5; 2; 3; II Aethelstan 5–8, etc.; VI Aethelstan 10; II Edmund 4; 6 (Liebermann, i, pp. 138–41; 152–55; 181; 188–89).

[75] II Aethelstan Epilogue; III Aethelstan Pr.; VI Aethelstan 10; 12:1 (pp. 166–67, 170, 181–83).

[76] *E.g.* I Edward Pr.; II Edward 5; 5:2; IV Edgar 15–15:1 (pp. 138–39, 142–45, 214–15).

Anglo-Saxon law-case known to me was a legal clause cited, either verbally or by reference. The contrast with the *Pays du Droit écrit* in Italy and southern France, or even with some ninth-century North Frankish cases, is very clear.[77] Some Anglo-Saxon kings and bishops may therefore have felt, like Charlemagne and his successors, that the new consecrated and imperial status of English kingship demanded written laws, but neither in its form nor in its effect was Old English legislation ever quite like law-making as Justinian, or even the Lombards and Visigoths, would have understood it. This must affect our estimate of the uses of pragmatic literacy in England before the Conquest.

It is never easy to prove a negative, and early medieval literacy is not a simple issue. But I conclude that the traditional view of restricted literacy is substantially valid for the whole early English period. Given the absence of early Anglo-Saxon *filid*, it was always likely that literacy would remain something of a clerical monopoly, and that Latin would retain its cultural grip on the imaginations of learned Englishmen, however their vernacular flourished. The indifference to education in letters which Alfred experienced as a boy guaranteed the former; the fact that the main source of the literate tradition was Rome and the Latin Church made the latter no less likely, whatever other cultural influences were at work. Indeed, we do no justice to the situation either in England or Europe unless we appreciate that the literacy of the *clergy* could never be taken for granted, and this was much the more urgent priority for the writers and authorities of the early Middle Ages. But if Alfred's youth highlights the obstacles to the development of lay literacy, his reign and achievements show just what an impact Romano-Christian inspiration could have. Alfred learnt from the Franks and from the Bible of the advantages of a written history of his dynasty, and of written law; he also learnt that literacy was essential if he and his subjects were to acquire the wisdom that God demanded, and he attempted more even than Charlemagne to realize this objective. The same lesson was open to others, and we should not be surprised to find shadows of the greatest of English kings among the Anglo-Saxon ruling-classes of the tenth and eleventh centuries. Yet we do not find conclusive evidence of a 'take-off' of literacy in post-Alfredian England, and in several significant respects, we find less evidence than in

[77] *Cf., e.g., Codice Diplomatico Longobardo*, i, 81; ii, 163, 168; iii, 36, ed. L. Schiaparelli and C. R. Brühl (Milan, Fonti della Storia Italica, 1929, 1933, 1974), pp. 237–38, 111–12, 123–24, 223; *Textes relatifs aux institutions privées et publiques aux époques merovingienne et carolingienne*, 88, 114, 128, ed. M. Thévenin (Paris, 1887), pp. 118–19, 167–68, 188–90; *Diplomata Karolinorum*, 216, ed. E. Mühlbacher, M.G.H., Diplomata, i, pp. 288–89.

Carolingian Francia.[78] The potential was there, but we cannot prove that it was fulfilled. We may blame foreign conquest for this failure of promise. Alternatively, we may lay the blame on a resurgence of the old Germanic Adam, to whom the attractions of the *schola humani servitii* remained, for the time being, too strong.

[78] The idea of a 'take-off' of literacy is discussed and illustrated for England after the Conquest by M. T. Clanchy in his forthcoming book, *From Memory to Written Record.*

THE SOCIAL RELATIONS OF TUDOR OXFORD

By Professor J. K. McConica, C.S.B., M.A., D.Phil., F.R.Hist.S.

READ AT THE SOCIETY'S CONFERENCE 17 SEPTEMBER 1976

IF study of the university can have any place in the general history of society, it must be understood as a part of a much larger historical phenomenon, of whose vastness and complexity the university's records themselves make us aware. In the sixteenth century we are conscious of powerful currents of social change and energy upon which the universities floated with little or no power of control: a rapidly growing population, geographically and economically on the move; a burgeoning school system; urban wealth growing and changing location, but always under the massive dominance of London; an active land-market; rise in prices; and the work of governments, both national and local, concerned with education and its consequences. This is the setting of Tudor society, and only special optical devices will enable us to pick out the university and set it in the foreground. In the process some distortion is inevitable. An indication of the problems that occur in university history may be found in the view of a recent student of Tudor Cambridge who, while acknowledging that one contribution of the universities to the complex change within English society was 'the creation of a more refined and integrated cultural and intellectual milieu' centred upon London and the court, finds the truly significant contribution in a more informed, vigorous and tenacious local solidarity in the 'country'.[1] Another historian of Elizabethan England tells us that in the universities, 'the interesting thing, as so often in English life, is the extent and intimacy of the social mixture'.[2] I am inclined to think that all three of these views can be defended at once and consistently, but we are warned that to present a total view will not be done easily.

I chose to describe the present essay as one about the 'social relations' of Tudor Oxford since I hope only to indicate that university's place in the general society of the day. The social *role* of the university,

[1] Victor Morgan, 'Cambridge University and "The Country" 1560–1640' in Lawrence Stone (ed.), *The University in Society*, i (Princeton, 1974), p. 184.

[2] A. L. Rowse, *The England of Elizabeth* (New York, 1951), p. 521.

in the sense defined by Professor Lawrence,[3] remains the subject of speculation still at this date. Its avowed social *purpose*, measured by statutory declarations and other legislation, is remarkably unchanged from the Middle Ages. To be sure, there is an unavowed social purpose of a new kind. It is found more in what was done than what was said, and this new purpose immensely broadened the service of the universities to the nation, in the developments that have come to be known as the 'educational revolution'.[4] In the present attempt to present a general portrait I have confined myself chiefly to two considerations: the interests and careers of Oxford graduates, and the origins of those same men, of the university's scholars and masters. I have not attempted to deal more than incidentally with important matters to which these issues are inextricably connected: studies and curriculum, state policy, and patronage. Even so, we will see how directly the developments of the sixteenth century grew out of the medieval past, and how they rehearse, with new inflexions, the conflicting priorities of education in a society still torn between the useful and the heroic.

'Relatively to Cambridge, Oxford lost by the Reformation: it made the fortune of the younger university.'[5] We may agree with Dr Rowse without fear of contradiction. We should therefore begin with the old professional faculties which have been ignored so far by the students of the 'educational revolution'. That they should have been set aside is quite understandable; as Mark Curtis long ago pointed out, social growth and change was intimately connected with the teaching of Arts, especially in the colleges and off the curriculum. Nevertheless, the older faculties survived and retained 'medieval' functions in the Tudor polity, and Tudor governments were at times much exercised about their welfare. They cannot be ignored in a rounded portrait of the University. What happened to them?

The cataclysm was greatest in Law. It was not simply the ban on Canon Law teaching; the uncertain future of the ecclesiastical courts threatened, 'that reasonable assurance of a living for the merely competent and industrious which is necessary to make a professional faculty prosper', as John Barton has recently written.[6] While it is true that Masterships in Chancery came to be given to civilians, and

[3] In a paper given at the Conference.

[4] I have reviewed bibliography on this question in 'The Prosopography of the Tudor University', *Journal of Interdisciplinary History*, iii:3 (Winter, 1973), pp. 543–54.

[5] Rowse, *op. cit.*, p. 512.

[6] In his as yet unpublished contribution to volume three of the official history of the University of Oxford.

that the reorganized Court of Admiralty must have provided more employment for them than formerly, these were small compensation for that general shock to the profession epitomized in their loss to the lay, common lawyers, of the great offices of Lord Chancellor and Master of the Rolls. When in the early 1540s, Sir Thomas Smith commended the study of Civil Law to the University of Cambridge, he stressed the many opportunities for royal service available to its adepts.[7] Perhaps Smith was not the best advocate; at any rate the lesson seems to have been lost. Smith's successor as public reader, his most distinguished pupil Walter Haddon, was the only man to proceed to the Cambridge doctorate in Civil Law from 1544 to 1551.[8]

At Oxford the situation seems to have been little different and the collapse of the law faculties at both universities was a matter of serious concern to the government of the day. The royal visitors of 1549 intended that Oxford should provide a new college dedicated exclusively to the study of civil law. It was to be created by transferring the legists of New College to All Souls College, and the artists at the latter place to New College. At Cambridge, the same end was to have been served by merging the foundations of Clare Hall and Trinity Hall.[9] The resistance respectively of Nicholas Ridley, as Visitor, and of Stephen Gardiner, as Master of Trinity Hall, helped to defeat the scheme at Cambridge, and provoked from Somerset sonorous lectures on the need for learned civilians. 'And we are sure ye are not ignorant,' he wrote to Ridley on 10 June 1549, 'how necessary a Study that Study of Civil Law is to all Treaties with Foreign Princes and Strangers, and how few there be at this present to do the King's Majesty's Service therein.'[10] And to Gardiner, in March 1548, he wrote, 'For, if many be incorporate to that studie,

[7] J. B. Mullinger, *The University of Cambridge from the Royal Injunctions of 1535 to the Accession of Charles the First*, (Cambridge, 1884), p. 131.

[8] There were only eight B.C.L.'s in the same period; *cf.* Mullinger, *op. cit.*, p. 132. On the doubtful side of Smith's service to the study in Cambridge see Mary Dewar, *Sir Thomas Smith* (London, 1964), p. 21. Haddon's *Oratio quam habuit cum Cantabrigiae legum interpretationem ordiretur* deplores the decline in the study since Smith's depature: '. . . sic excellentissimum hoc studium iuris civilis, quod sincerissimum esse debuit, & quondam sane fuit, nunc contaminatum & oblitum est peregrinitate verborum & rerum, ut Iustinianus ipse si revivisceret, novum incendium inter hos iuris perturbatores excitaturus sit.' See *G. Haddoni . . . lucubrationes passim collectae, & editae* (London, 1567), pp. 78–79 [incorrectly numbered in reverse order in pagination in Huntington Library copy].

[9] Mullinger, *op. cit.*, pp. 133–34.

[10] Printed by Gilbert Burnet, *The History of the Reformation of the Church of England*, The Second Part (London, 1681) [appendix] A collection of Records and Original Papers . . . referred to in the Second Part [separate title, London, 1680], Part II, Book I, No. 60, p. 235.

as you terme yt, amonges the moo peradventure some shall rise well lerned and fyt for the comen wealth; where as now, as they be but few, yt is hard to fynd one, and rather, as we are informed, in dede there is none, whom for excellencie we can have commended unto us.' In the same letter he went on to announce the King's intention to establish a house of civilians in London, recruited from the 'best lerned' of Cambridge and Oxford, to provide counsel and practise in the Admiralty Court, 'or others, as they may.'[11]

The situation at Oxford can be surmised from the Registers. In the five years from 1530 to 1534 inclusive, some ninety persons were presented for degrees in the faculty of Canon Law, and about seventy in Civil Law. The drop in numbers in the years immediately following is dramatic, even if we allow for a torn leaf in Registrum H.[12] In the five years from 1535 to 1539 inclusive, only eight are known to have petitioned in Canon Law, and thirty-nine in Civil Law. Of the latter, thirty-two were bachelors, five more took both the B.C.L. and the doctorate, one was a doctor, and one a doctor incorporated from Cambridge.

The awarding of degrees in Canon Law virtually disappears, of course,[13] and a slight recovery in Civil Law is suggested by the record of fifty-one bachelors' degrees and eight doctorates in the years 1540 to 1544 inclusive. By the later decades of the century, however, the stream had dwindled further. In the five years from 1581 to 1585, inclusive, of the 767 entries that show supplication for or award of a degree in Arts, thirteen reveal that the man later took a degree in law (B.C.L. 9, B.C.L. and D.C.L. 4), a mere 1·7% of the whole. This does not give the whole picture, however, since an additional twenty degrees in law are recorded in the five year period, awarded to men who did not take the pathway through the Arts faculty. Ten of these were bachelors, two doctors, and eight took both degrees (seven being fellows of All Souls College). If we add these twenty degrees to the total, we find that of all the degrees awarded showing study in the two faculties, thirty-three (4.2% of 787) were in law. Comparison with the period from 1591 to 1595 shows only 0.56% of the Arts graduates later taking a degree in law (4 out of 701), and a total of 23, or 2·6% of the degrees awarded in the two faculties, Arts and Law.

The men who took these degrees went on for the most part to

[11] B.L. Add. MS. 28,571 4v–5v; printed by James A Muller in *The Letters of Stephen Gardiner* (Cambridge, 1933) Appendix 3, p. 493.

[12] Rev C. W. Boase (ed.), *Register of the University of Oxford*, i (Oxford, 1885), p. 182.

[13] But not entirely: at least five were granted in the reign of Mary Tudor; *cf.* Boase, *op. cit.*, pp. 227–28, 230, 233.

Doctors' Commons and to judicial appointments in the ecclesiastical courts.[14] Those who did not make careers in law may have taken the degree out of independent interest, or simply because they held one of the many legist fellowships available in the colleges. If we may indicate by one example the possible variety in use made of the faculty we might choose to refer to a non-graduate, William Fulbeck, son of a mayor of Lincoln, who was admitted to Corpus Christi College, Oxford, as a scholar in February 1580, having matriculated from St Alban's Hall in December 1577 as 'plebei filius', aged 17 years. He read the statutory curriculum in Arts, receiving his B.A. in October 1581 and his M.A. in 1584. There is no record of his receiving formal instruction as a civilian, and in fact he went from Oxford to Gray's Inn where he was said to have 'addressed himself to the study of the municipal laws. . . .'[15] His publications testify to the true direction of his interest, since among them are legal works, *A Direction or Preparative to the Study of the Lawe*,[16] *The Pandectes of the Law of Nations*,[17] and, in two parts, *A Parellele or Conference of the Civill Law, the Canon Law and the Common Law of this Realme of England*.[18] Wherever Fulbeck learned his civil law, this last work is curiously reminiscent of one of the provisions of the Edwardian Statutes for civilian doctorates at Oxford, requiring that at every *comitia*, a disputant should determine the question by comparing the provisions of the civil, ecclesiastical and of English law.[19]

The Faculty of Law at Oxford thus served a continuing but sharply reduced function in late Tudor England. In Theology, while the shock to the curriculum was greater, the preoccupations of the day served in the long run to enhance the school. The evidence of undergraduate reading alone testifies to the obsessive interest of university men in theological questions; the surge of vocations to the ministry in the later years of the century provides another indication. This enthusiasm was the atmosphere in which the Faculty itself operated, since its interests were distinct from those of the Faculty of Arts, where the ordinary cleric took his training before ordination.

Like the Faculty of Law, the Faculty of Theology had an endowed base in fellowships long provided for those studying within it. And it was college fellows, almost exclusively, who made up the roster of

[14] John Barton, to whom I owe this information, presents an analysis of careers; *cf.* n. 6 above.

[15] J. Foster, *The Register of Admissions to Gray's Inn, 1521–1889* . . . (London, 1889); William Fulbeck's name appears under 25 November 1584 as of Staple Inn, p. 66 (fo 65).

[16] S.T.C. 11410.

[17] S.T.C. 11414.

[18] S.T.C. 11415, 11415a.

[19] Strickland Gibson (ed.), *Statuta Antiqua Universitatis Oxoniensis* (Oxford, 1931), Statuta Edwardi Sexti, pp. 345–46.

candidates for degrees.[20] This considerable endowment of places was enriched further by the provision of many college statutes ordering their theologians to proceed to the bachelor's or doctor's degree as a condition of retaining their fellowships.

The degree lists indicate the relative prosperity of the Faculty. In the five years from 1581 to 1585 inclusive, we find that among those awarded degrees in Arts, forty-nine (or 6·4%) took the B.D., and forty more (5·2%) took both the B.D. and D.D.; eighty-nine degree-takers all told, or 11·6% of the men presenting themselves for degrees in the Faculty of Arts. In the second representative period, from 1591 to 1595, forty-four of the Arts graduates (6·2%) took the B.D., and an additional thirty-two (4·5% of the whole) took both the B.D. and D.D., all told, 10·8% of the Arts graduates. These statistics include a very few divinity degrees awarded in the same periods to men who had previously, no doubt, graduated in Arts, but the number is too small to affect the percentages significantly. The men in the second period examined were taking their theology degrees in the years of the early seventeenth century when the oversupply of clergy might conceivably have affected their decisions, but the yield of membership for the Faculty is only marginally lower than was that a decade earlier.

We must remember that we are dealing with the best-endowed of the professional faculties, and its fellowships provided avenues to other callings than those of preaching and the ministry. To be sure, among the doctors of divinity in the above samples was that celebrated son of a Reading clothier, William Laud. Among the doctors, too, was Thomas Saunderson, later a translator of the Bible, and among the bachelors, Arthur Lake, son of an esquire of Southampton, who as Warden of New College would establish lecturerships in Hebrew and mathematics at his own expense, and who ended as a notable occupant of the see of Bath and Wells. On the other hand, the B.D.'s also included such as Richard Ball of Magdalen College, who in 1604 became Gresham Professor of Rhetoric in London, and John Morwen of Corpus, who became Greek Reader in that college but shifted to medicine in the reign of Edward VI. His ecclesiastical career, with a strongly Catholic flavour, was however, briefly resumed in the reign of Mary Tudor.

The last of the professional faculties is the least-known, Medicine. While a fresh study of its history in the sixteenth century suggests that its activity and achievement have been underestimated,[21] a dip

[20] I owe this information to Rev Dr Stanley Greenslade, preparing a study of the Faculty for the history of the University; *cf.* n. 6.

[21] Dr R. G. Lewis, St Anne's College, Oxford, is preparing an account of the Faculty for the history of Oxford, volume 3; *cf.* n. 6.

into our representative years shows that it was smaller than Law. Of those passing through the Registers for Arts degrees in the years from 1581 to 1585, three took the B.M. and M.D. and were licensed to practise, six more were licensed to practise only (one of these is doubtful), and two others were admitted to medical degrees: the degree-takers amount to only 0·4% of the total. In the years from 1591 to 1595 there were ten who took degrees, two bachelors (one licensed to practise) and eight who took both degrees (five licensed to practise), and there were three more licensed to practise without degrees. One of these however, George Stevens of Balliol College, is described as a student of medicine of twenty-two years' standing. The degree-takers alone thus number 1·4% of the total number taking or presenting themselves for Arts degrees in this second period. If we add the three who were licensed, the percentage of men showing interest in medicine rises to 1·8%, a significant increase over the earlier period. Among those taking all qualifications in the first group was John Woolton, the eldest son of the bishop of Exeter, who became a fellow of All Souls College and later practised in Exeter. In the latter group was Edward Lapworth of Warwickshire, son of the physician to Henry Berkeley. He had a distinguished career at the university, and after a period of private practice, probably in Faversham, Kent he was designated first Sedleian reader in natural philosophy in 1618, and in August 1619 appointed Linacre physic reader. He spent part of each year in Oxford, with summer in practice, according to his biographer,[22] usually in Bath. And as further evidence of the variety in background, we may notice the William Herleis who was admitted bachelor in Canon Law in 1530, and two years later supplicated for the B.M.[23]

These statistics may be summarized in tabular form as follows. In the earlier period, one hundred and five men who presented themselves in the Arts faculty later took a higher degree (13·6% of the total), and in the period 1591–95, ninety men did so (12·8% of the total), an indication that the higher faculties of the university,

[22] C. L. Kingsford in the *D.N.B.*

[23] Boase, *op. cit.*, p. 171 'Herteis'; *cf.* A. B. Emden, *A Biographical Register of the University of Oxford A.D. 1501 to 1540* (Oxford, 1974), p. 282. Another perspective on the relative importance of the higher faculties may be gained from the Register of an Arts college with a medical tradition. At Merton College in mid-century, of the 141 fellows found in the Register from 1521 to 1567, four later took degrees in civil law, one of them a doctorate; sixteen took the B.M. and a licence to practice, of whom nine later took the doctorate in medicine; and twenty-eight took the B.D., of whom ten later took the D.D. Forty-eight, or 34% of the total number in this select group took degrees in the higher faculties. See J. M. Fletcher (ed.), *Registrum annalium collegii Mertonensis 1521–1567*, Oxford Historical Society, new ser., 23 (Oxford, 1973).

even after the disruptions of the Reformation, continued to draw on a substantial and fairly steady proportion of the university's graduates in Arts, and in the disciplines of law and medicine, trained or licensed others as well.

	1581–85	%	1591–95	%
Total granted (or supplicating for) Arts degrees	767	100	701	100
Arts graduates taking law degrees	13	1·7	4	0·56
Others admitted to law degrees, same period	20		19	
Arts graduates taking bachelor of divinity only	49	6·4	44	6·2
Arts graduates also taking doctor of divinity	40	5·2	32	4·5
Arts graduates taking degrees in medicine	3	0·4	10	1·4
Arts graduates licensed to practise medicine	6	0·8	3	0·4
Others admitted to medical degrees	2		0	
Total arts graduates going on to higher degrees	105	13·6	90	12·8

[All information from A. Clark, *Register of the University of Oxford*, Vol. ii, Part iii (Oxford, 1888).]

With the Faculty of Arts we come to the real growth-point of the Tudor university. Since a degree in Arts was the usual propaedeutic to a professional degree, we can best confront the issue of the origins of men at Tudor Oxford by examining the social composition of the candidates in Arts. We recall, of course, that we must distinguish between those reading the statutory curriculum, who for the most part were future clerics, and men taught less formally in the colleges by special arrangements, who for the most part were acquiring a gentleman's education.[24] We shall see however that even this by now well-established generalization needs some cautious qualification. The two groups virtually coincide with the foundationers—scholars and fellows in clerical orders—and commoners, who paid for the privilege of living in a college and for the personal tuition they there received.

Lawrence Stone's recent survey of Oxford recuitment[25] may perhaps be taken as a convenient and authoritative entry into the literature that has grown up about the 'educational revolution' since Mark Curtis published his invaluable *Oxford and Cambridge in Transition.* In his necessarily brief account of the Tudor period, Professor Stone contrasts the two undergraduate groups, sons of plebeians and sons of gentlemen, as a convenient simplification of the more complex social stratifications. The gentlemen, as all have agreed, wanted no vocational training but came to the universities in response to the diffusion of humanist ideals propagated in the early decades of the

[24] The first developed statement of this view is in Mark H. Curtis, *Oxford and Cambridge in Transition, 1558–1642* (Oxford, 1959).

[25] 'The Size and Composition of the Oxford Student Body, 1580–1910', in *The University in Society*, i: *Oxford and Cambridge from the 14th to the Early 19th Century* (Princeton, 1974), pp. 3–110.

century, to find an appropriate intellectual and social formation as future governors of the state and countryside. This development occurred against the background of 'strong voices and opinions'[26] that felt the universities should be kept for the clergy, and that new and quite different institutions should be established for the sons of the gentry and aristocracy. The complex developments that involved the universities in this profound social and educational change were first explained by Mark Curtis, but numerous as were the gentry, they were a smaller proportion of the men at the university than Curtis thought, a smaller proportion of the whole than those who described themselves as sons of plebeians. These latter are described by Professor Stone as the sons of the 'relatively poor' who found in the university a training-school for professional advancement, chiefly in the church or grammar-school teaching.[27] This conception of the commonest vocations of the Arts graduates, incidentally, may be traced back at least to the St John's College, Cambridge, play, *The Pilgrimage to Parnassus*, in which two undergraduates, Philomusus and Studioso, seeking the Parnassus of the Cambridge B.A., and drawing near to it in the land of Philosophy, encounter Ingenioso, who is disgusted with his own poverty after years of study, and who describes, descending from Parnassus, 'a companie of ragged vicars and forlorne schoole-maisters, who as they walked scrached there unthriftie elbowes, and often putt there handes into there unpeopled pocketes, that had not beene possessed with faces this manie a day.'[28] In his recent account, Professor Stone observes that, 'very few of those who filled these positions in the Elizabethan period were either sons of clergy or sons of gentry.' As we shall see, of sons of the gentry there certainly were some. He goes on, 'These "plebeians" were sons of men in truly modest occupations and with restricted incomes.'[29] This notion of the 'plebeian' is the most problematical topic in the continuing discussion of the late Tudor university's social composition, and I would like to begin my own account of the Arts undergraduate with this issue.

As all are to some degree aware, the difficulty is that among the plebeians we find the sons of townsmen and merchants.[30] However, it is by no means possible to rank these men automatically

[26] See Curtis, *op. cit.*, pp. 65–82.

[27] *Ibid.*, pp. 18–19.

[28] J. B. Leishman (ed.), *The Three Parnassus Plays (1598–1601)* (London, 1949), p. 125, lines 581–85.

[29] *Op. cit.*, pp. 18–19.

[30] Using data from the third and fourth decades of the next century, Stone estimated that slightly under a quarter of the plebeians at Oxford then came from towns; 'The Educational Revolution in England, 1560–1640', *Past and Present*, xxviii (July 1964), p. 62.

among those 'in truly modest occupations and with restricted incomes.' Neither can they be classed simply with those who characteristically seek a professional qualification. The range of wealth and opportunity among the urban born can be illustrated vividly in the career of William Becher,[31] who matriculated at Corpus Christi College, Oxford, in 1594, 'armigeri filius'. His 'esquire' father was Henry Becher, haberdasher, ordinarily in this period designated a 'plebeian', but entitled to the rank his son claimed by virtue of his position as an alderman of London. His own father, a Devonian by birth, had also been a haberdasher and was Sheriff of London later in his life. He was a man of considerable wealth, who left large bequests not only within his family but to charitable, educational and religious institutions. The career of his son, the father of our matriculant, came to an end in 1608, at which point he left William all his lands. In due course, William Becher, who took the B.A. in June 1597 and entered the Inner Temple in 1598, also received most of the estate of his mother Judith Rich, daughter of an apothecary to the Queen. William acquired an estate at Howbery in Bedfordshire and a knighthood in 1619. He married Elizabeth St John, daughter of Oliver Lord St John, for whom he named his eldest son and heir. His eleventh son Howard (of eighteen children) had for godmother the Countess of Peterborough, from whom he was to receive a living if he entered the Church. If the upward movement of this family is especially striking, it is by no means unique, and the history of the Becher generations illustrates vividly how difficult it can be to distinguish effectively between the educational expectations of the gentry and those of the urban well-to-do.

It may be objected justly that I have been less than fair to Professor Stone's generalization by selecting as an example a merchant's son who could properly describe himself, not as the son of a plebeian, but as esquire. In the same recent volume with that essay I furnished information that indicates, in part, how much Sir Thomas White's Oxford foundation, St John's College, was given over to the education of sons of merchants, to the extent that half the total membership, including the commoners, came from towns.[32] Many of these were men of very substantial wealth and with excellent prospects. Almost all of them were described as sons of plebeians. Fortunately, the best single account of early education to survive from this period was left by one of the Merchant Taylors' scholars, a plebeian at St John's College; it is the *Liber famelicus* of Sir James Whitelocke (1570–

[31] For general information see F. A. Page-Turner, 'The Becher Family of Howbury', *Publications of the Bedfordshire Historical Record Society* v (1920), pp. 133–61.

[32] 'Scholars and Commoners in Renaissance Oxford', in *The University in Society*, i, pp. 151–81, especially graph 1, p. 166.

1632).[33] His retrospective family chronicle is highly informative about the aims and ideals of a townsman who was admitted as a scholar on 12 July 1588, 'plebei filius' aged 18 years. He was not conspicuously wealthy, but certainly had substance, and it would seem that his upbringing firmly knitted him to the aspirations and interests of the gentry. He was descended from a substantial Berkshire family. His father, the youngest of four sons, was 'put to London to be broughte up in the trade of marchandise.'[34] He prospered as a merchant adventurer and died of 'a plurisye' on a trading voyage to Bordeaux in 1570, aged 37 years. He left four sons. His widow, already once before the widow of a London merchant who left her 'of competent estate', married for the third time to yet another merchant named Thomas Price. She was the daughter of John Colte of Hertfordshire, like his ancestors a tenant there of the Bouchier family. She was clearly a woman of more than ordinary determination and competence, and more than a match for her third husband Price, who, according to his stepson, was 'a notable unthrift, and a verye unkinde and insolent husband.'[35] The widow kept aside £600 for her sons' provision, secretly bought out Price's interest in certain leases, and by 'suche care and admirable wisdom', says Sir James, 'did bring up all her children in as good sort as any gentleman in England wulde do, as in singing, dancing, playing on the lute and other instruments, the Latin, Greek, Hebrew and Frenche tongues, and to write fair.'[36]

Whitelocke's account of his education at the Merchant Taylors' School under Richard Mulcaster reveals clearly the same understanding of the social implications of his training there.[37] That education, and his later study at St John's College, Oxford, may show more intellectual seriousness than was typical, but we have no way of knowing. In its general contour it conformed perfectly to the pattern of gentry education. Whitelocke's attitude to the social advantages of university training emerges incidentally when he recalls that he was elected probationer of St John's College along with a vintner's son, George Wrighte of Eastcheap, London, who later (in Whitelocke's words) 'having good enheritance descended to him, is now clerk of the king's stable and a knighte, a verye discreet and honest gentleman.'[38]

Whitelocke read Greek and Hebrew at Oxford along with the Latin classics, worked at Logic and 'the artes', especially at history,

[33] *Liber famelicus of James Whitelocke*, ed. J. Bruce (Camden Society, lxx, 1858).
[34] *Ibid.*, p. 4. [35] *Ibid.*, p. 6. [36] *Ibid.*, p. 6.
[37] *Ibid.*, p. 12; notice his account of Mulcaster's presentation of plays at court to teach the boys 'good behaviour and audacitye'.
[38] *Ibid.*, p. 12.

and qualified both in civil law and common law. For two years he kept terms holding a fellowship in civil law, while he did his exercises at the New Inn in London.[39] He was admitted to the Middle Temple in March 1592, and he qualified at Oxford for the B.C.L. in Lent 1594. He spent most of his time after that in London, but kept his Oxford fellowship since he was useful to St John's 'to dispatche them of thear businesses and chargeable journeys to London.'[40] After he was called to the bar in August 1600, the College made him steward of their estates. His later career need not concern us, but it is relevant to recall that he married into substantial county stock with the Bulstrodes of Buckinghamshire, his wife being a woman whose ancestors, Whitelocke boasted, had been 'of verye ancient continuance in Buckinghamshire, and born the best and most worshipfull offices in the countrye.'[41]

The representative interest of this account, which I have much abbreviated, scarcely requires comment. We have the generational background in a younger son from country stock who made an advantageous marriage in London, in order to further his career in business. This is exactly paralleled by the ambition of the next generation, in the person of our memorialist, to resume the county connection. There is also in Whitelocke solid and genuine intellectual interest, piety, and a carefully planned programme of advancement through the law. The use of Oxford to provide both intellectual fare and a needed reassurance about gentle status is clear. All of this seems to cast light on the entries in the Registers of the College recording the benefactions of grateful Merchant Taylors, especially in books and scholarships. To select among them one that seems to show the same intellectual seriousness that marked the career of Whitelocke, we might instance that of Thomas Paradyne, citizen and haberdasher of London, who in addition to an annuityto maintain three poor scholars, gave to the college, 'whear I was broughte uppe, my hieromes workes in 3 volumes, my hebrew concorduance, Alphonsus de Castro, Tertullian, Cyprian and Augustines worckes beinge fyve volumes.'[42] These seem to have been his own books. Even if he had not opened them since he left Oxford, for him to have bought so much at any time was a mark in favour of the College and a sign of his own aspiration.

The College's awareness of the value of these urban connections produced policies like those generated only slightly later for gentleman commoners of landed wealth. In 1590, for example, the President

[39] *Liber famelicus*, p. 14; *cf.* W. R. Prest, *The Inns of Court under Elizabeth I and the Early Stuarte 1590–1640* (London, 1972), p. 134.

[40] *Ibid.*, pp. 14–15.

[41] *Ibid.*, p. 15.

[42] St John's College Oxford, *Munim.* X, fo 33.

and senior fellows at St John's decided that two commoners, William Byrde, son of the mayor of Bristol, and Humfrey May, son of a former master of the Merchant Taylors' Company and 'armigeri filius' at matriculation, should be admitted to the bachelors' table and dispensed from their obligation to attend scholastic exercises within the College, provided that they attend divine service, preserve the peace of the house, give due reverence to their superiors and attend lectures and other exercises of learning—all of this in consideration of former benefits bestowed upon the College, 'as also for and in regard of some good hope conceyved of future good from their parents . . .' It is noted with satisfaction at the foot of this entry that, 'Mr. Byrde gave unto the College a standing cup price £7; and Mr. May gave unto the College £20 and Mrs. May an ale pot price £6.'[43] That was not all. May, who took a B.A. in March 1592 and was later knighted, had a sister who married the first Viscount Camden. From her, Laud, who matriculated at St John's a year later than May and was thus in College with him (and himself, 'plebei filius' of Reading) later procured the living of Great Stoughton for the College.

On close examination, the plebeians at the Tudor university emerge as at least a variegated group, numbering in their ranks men of conspicuous wealth whose taste and ambition it is difficult to distinguish from that of the gentry. Even if we agree with Victor Morgan that 'members of the urban merchant societies were temporal transients'[44] we should be aware of the degree to which urban recruitment and urban wealth helped to shape the fortunes of Tudor Oxford and Cambridge. At Corpus Christi College, Oxford, there was a monument in the chapel to one Francis Colthurst, heir to an extremely wealthy London grocer, who was listed in the college as a 'gentleman commoner' in 1594 and who neither matriculated nor took a degree. He succeeded his father in his business and died unexpectedly in 1602 or 1603. Perhaps because he left two pounds each to twenty-five poor men of Oxford, more likely because he left the College twenty pounds to buy plate, he was buried beneath an inscription describing him as, 'generous, civis et mercator' and 'huius collegii quandam commonarius', a concise and enduring memorial not only to the late Francis, but to the changing social designations of a time when that college, like so many others, exerted the force of a catalyst.[45]

[43] See W. H. Stevenson and H. E. Salter, *The Early History of St John's College Oxford* (Oxford, 1939), p. 273.

[44] *Op. cit.*, p. 211.

[45] *'Survey of the Antiquities of the City of Oxford', Composed in 1661–6, by Anthony Wood*, ed. Andrew Clark, i (Oxford, 1889), p. 551.

If we are to refine our understanding of the social phenomena in these colleges we require more data than the existing records will give. A new perspective on the issue of college recruitment is beginning to emerge from a lengthy study of the members of Corpus Christi College from the time of its foundation to 1604.[46] This study embraces about 600 men—fellows, *discipuli* and commoners—and its first contribution is to try to fill in the social background and careers of the men belonging to a foundation that may be thought to be representative of post-medieval Oxford. This is done from the very early years of the century to the end of the reign, thus promising to alleviate the uncertainty that has hitherto surrounded our speculations about the university before the advent of the Matriculation Registers, effectively in the 1580s. Up to this point approximately 150 dossiers—one quarter of the whole—are reasonably complete, and they fall fortunately with regularity through all the decades of the century. The *discipuli* or undergraduate members on the foundation were recruited, we can see, with remarkable uniformity from the counties and dioceses designated by the Founder. These regions were dictated by the incidents of Fox's career in the Church and by the College's endowments, but they happened to imitate the geographical constituency of the university as a whole. The fact that they are adhered to closely in these early decades suggests that if, as we know from the correspondence of Brian Twyne,[47] the Fellows of Corpus in the 1590s were not above venal persuasion in electing to college places, they or their predecessors at least adhered fairly well to the local communities prescribed by Fox. More importantly, when the commoners at Corpus become visible in significant numbers, they too seem to come from the College's designated zones of recruitment. This is striking testimony to the capacity of lands, livings and schoolmasters to build up local connection even where a college has no notable regional identity.[48]

A disciple at Corpus might be elected at any age from 12 to 19 years, and as his allowance consisted only of meagre commons and two marks a year, he clearly needed additional support from home or some other sponsor. The candidate, who had to be an undergraduate at election, shared the room of a fellow who acted as his tutor. There was no guarantee of promotion to a fellowship for

[46] The general aim of this study is described in the article cited in n. 4 above. I would like here to acknowledge the indispensable work of my collaborator Mr Kenneth Powell in assembling details of biographical information about the members of Tudor Corpus Christi College, Oxford, and the generous financial support of the Canada Council.

[47] See Twyne's letter to his father, 3 August 1601, in *The Bodleian Quarterly Record*, v, no. 56 (4th Quarter, 1927), pp. 218.

[48] *Cf.* Morgan, *op. cit.*, pp. 205–06.

these 'disciples', and my findings differ from the conclusions of the College historian, Dr Henry Fowler, who stated that 'though "externs" were not absolutely excluded' in elections to fellowships, 'in the long experience of the College, it seldom happened.'[49] This was perhaps true in Fowler's day, but I find on the contrary, that of the 300 admitted as *discipuli* between 1517 and the end of Elizabeth's reign, only 95 later became fellows of Corpus, while another 43 were elected from outside. The vast majority of scholars at Corpus went on to careers elsewhere, and this fact may have its bearing on the real educational role of the college from the beginning.

Up to this point (availability of records at Oxford and Cambridge being what it is) we have tended to assume that the resort of the gentry to the universities in significant numbers is almost entirely a phenomenon of the last three decades of the sixteenth century.[50] That such resort in large numbers did not begin until the 1580s seems clear and uncontrovertible. However, it now seems clear that at Corpus at least, the college drew in men of gentle status and substantial means from the very first, and on the foundation too, as *discipuli*. Most of these seem to have been younger sons who went on to careers in the university or the Church. In the early years, up to about 1530, they were probably a small minority, recruited from wealthy yeomen or gentry stock, with the occasional younger son of a knight or esquire.[51] These latter elements become more conspicuous as the century wears on. Even in the early period there is the occasional heir, like Thomas Ogle, who was born about 1525 at Pinchbeck, Lincolnshire, and succeeded to the properties of his esquire father apparently without a degree, although he was admitted as a *discipulus* at Corpus on 29 March 1541 and stayed there for a total of six terms. His father was descended from a cadet branch of the lords Ogle and—already a considerable landowner in Lincolnshire—benefited from the Dissolution to die a very wealthy man. He was wealthy enough, indeed, to provide for a younger son Nicholas, 'yf he wilbe a contynuall student', a lease of the manor of Croyland, apparel, a house with 15 acres and many legal books of his own holding. It suggests a more indulgent attitude toward learning than some famous contemporary accounts of the landed

[49] *The History of Corpus Christi College* (Oxford, 1893), p. 47.

[50] J. H. Hexter noted the exception for those planning careers in the Church, and adds, 'By the third quarter of the sixteenth century the squirarchy has elbowed its way into Oxford in force.' 'The Education of the Aristocracy in the Renaissance', *Journal of Modern History*, xxii (1950), pp. 7–8.

[51] Among men at Corpus who were born before 1525 one might mention as examples, Leonard Arden, William Boughton, Kenelm Deane, Thomas Ogle, Richard Pates, Clement Perrot, Christopher Roper, John Standish and William Wye.

gentry would lead us to expect. In the same will Ogle senior left a horse to Sir William Cecil. His wife, we find, was the sister of Sir Anthony Cooke, Burghley's father-in-law, and perhaps this family tie with the Cecils and Bacons helps to explain the educational interests of this unmistakably gentry family.[52]

A second example of the gentleman foundationer from this early period would be Clement Perrot. His father Robert, a distinguished musician and organist of Magdalen College, Oxford, was a bachelor of music of the University. He was also grandson of Sir Owen Perrot of Haroldston, Pembrokeshire, from an old and knightly family there, and Robert himself, described in his will and epitaph as a gentleman, became a considerable landowner in Oxfordshire as a result of the Dissolution.[53] His son Clement was admitted *discipulus* at Corpus in September 1530, graduated B.A. in 1532 and M.A. in 1535, and became in the same year a fellow of Lincoln College and prebendary of Lincoln Cathedral. In a more usual pattern for one of gentry origins, Christopher Roper, although admitted *discipulus* in July 1524 as the third son of an esquire of Kent, took no degree but was admitted to Gray's Inn in 1528. He entered the service of Reginald Pole and Thomas Cromwell, established himself in Kent where he was M.P. for Rochester in 1553, and raised forces against Sir Thomas Wyatt before his death in 1559.

These examples are illustrative. On a related point, the continuity of gentry admission to the degree registers in Arts can be verified by a cursory examination of those lists. In the year 1591, for example, in addition to William Petre, second Lord Petre and eldest son of Sir John, the petitioners for degrees in Arts included at least four other sons of knights and six eldest sons of esquires, as the registers themselves show. Examination of the background to many entries would undoubtedly reveal more such individuals.

With the biographical register for Corpus Christi College still incomplete, there may be little point in suggesting a figure, but on the basis of what is already known, and assuming that all those for whom no positive identification has yet been made are plebeians, I think it is not misleading to suppose that some 15 to 20% of the men on the foundation at Corpus, in the period before the Matriculation Register begins to function fairly uniformly (about 1575), were the sons at least of wealthy yeomen, and more often of gentlemen, esquires and knights. This figure is conservative, since analysis of the years from 1577 to 1604 reveals that 34% of those on the

[52] The will is dated 8 September 1555, proved 2 December 1556, P.C.C. 25 Ketchyn.

[53] J. R. Bloxam, *A Register of the Presidents, Fellows . . . and other Members of Saint Mary Magdalen College in the University of Oxford*, ii (Oxford, 1857), pp. 182–84.

foundation belonged to the gentry and above.[54] Perhaps a similar proportion of the plebeians were the sons of well-to-do merchants, or notaries, or servants to great families, and we may be reminded here of Alan Everitt's comments on the new professional classes in the towns, men who formed no more than a small fraction of the population, but whose 'wealth, power and prestige increased well beyond their mere rise in numbers'.[55]

If these proportions withstand further investigation, they are large enough to cause us to reassess our views about the social constituency of the Tudor university from years long before the Reformation. It will remind us too that in 1547, Roger Ascham at Cambridge bemoaned the lack of experienced teachers and the predominance of sons of wealthy parents, and Latimer two years later echoed the same complaints.[56] If Bishop Fox's foundation was drawing so steadily on the sons of the propertied classes, can we assume that there were no further links of an informal kind with the eldest sons of such families? Unfortunately, the commoners at Corpus become identifiable only with the advent of the Matriculation Registers. The founder did however provide that the college would take up to six lodgers, sons of nobles or gentlemen. In a list known as the Visus we have the surnames only of those in residence each week for the years 1537 to 1542, and there are other names in the Visus than those of men on the foundation, never more than six. In the five years there are nineteen in all. These men are very elusive, but they seem unmistakably to be the forerunners of the commoners who came in such numbers in later years. In the 1580s the foundation continues to attract the younger sons of the gentry, merchants' sons, the occasional son of a prebendary or other substantial cleric, and even, no doubt, the genuinely poor. It is difficult however to document many cases like that of Sir John Mason, Fellow of All Souls, Chancellor of Oxford and sometime ambassador to Charles V, who was born in 1503 in Abingdon, son of the town cowherd.[57]

This is not the place to develop the theme of the intellectual training experienced by these Arts students, but one notable fact has already emerged. Contrary to our suppositions, well-to-do plebeians like William Becher, James Whitelocke and Humfrey May were sometimes willing to take the statutory requirements and qualify for an Arts degree. Even in this they were not necessarily departing

[54] McConica, *op. cit.*, p. 159.

[55] 'Change in the Provinces: the Seventeenth Century', *Occasional Papers*, 2nd ser, no. 1 (Leicester, 1969), p. 45.

[56] Mullinger, *op. cit.*, pp. 89–90.

[57] Emden, *op. cit. sub nomine*; another example would be Sir Thomas Smith; *cf.* Dewar, *op. cit.*, ch. 1.

from the habits of the gentry, many of whom, we have seen, did the same thing. To our earlier examples we could add that of Richard Stephens, eldest son of a Gloucestershire landowner, who took the B.A. in 1568 and became a fellow of Corpus before leaving the college for a career in law, to end as an M.P.[58] In the later period we have Henry Hawker, a commoner at Corpus whose father was a Kentish gentleman. He matriculated in 1598 and took the M.A. in March 1602 before going on to a career in law.[59] It is probably true that nothing much can be gained by multiplying the stories of individuals unless we can establish at least the outlines of a firm statistical framework. While we hope that such a framework will become available through further work on the membership of Corpus Christi College, we are usefully reminded in the meantime of the size and individuality of the community with which we have to deal.

At this point we may attempt a sketch of the picture that begins to emerge. The old professional faculties continued to function in the sixteenth-century university. Among them the Faculty of Law was hardest hit by the events of the Reformation, but even Law continued to attract able men, assisted in part by the endowment of legal fellowships inherited from the medieval period. The revisions of the Statutes in all of these faculties characteristically reduced the term of years slightly to bring the requirements more in line with the habits of dispensation, and introduced a conservative revision of their curricula. In most essential features, however, the faculties of Theology, Law and Medicine at Tudor Oxford taught many of the same texts, used the old exercises for the most part, and continued to serve the national community. This is true also of the Faculty of Arts which, amidst important changes, continued to serve as a major seminary of the kingdom, and even attracted lay students and, quite regularly, the sons of the well-to-do. If their patronage of the Arts Faculty is a reliable index, indeed, we must believe that humanist theory did not entirely dominate the ideals of the gentry.

In the last decade of the century, some 15 to 20% of the graduates in Arts went on to the professional faculties. This was by no means an insignificant number, and we are wrong to think, as we may tend to do, that the universities were completely out of step with the times except to the degree that they provided extra-statutory teaching to

[58] Information may be found in J. E. Neale, *Elizabeth I and Her Parliaments 1584–1601* (London, 1957), pp. 257–60; *A History of the County of Gloucester*, ed. C. R. Elrington and N. M. Herbert, x (The Victoria History of the Counties of England, Oxford, 1972), p. 128; *The Visitation of the County of Gloucester by Thomas May etc. with additions*, ed. T. F. Fenwick and W. C. Metcalfe (Exeter, 1884), p. 174.

[59] A. Clark, *Register; The Register of Admissions to Gray's Inn*, p. 102 (fo 527), 28 November 1601.

undergraduate commoners. Nevertheless, it was that teaching, and that recruitment, that accounted chiefly for the vast increase in enrolment in the later sixteenth century. As we know already, these were commoners and the sons of well-to-do men, many from landed stock. However, a very substantial and significant proportion even among the commoners is from the towns and 'plebeian' by designation. By the end of the century these men are assimilating themselves to gentry status, and even adopting the designation of 'gentleman'. Their educational aspirations at all times are very difficult to distinguish from the ideals that also impelled the landed families to send their sons to the universities as secular seminaries for civil careers and family service.

Finally, recent work on the membership of Corpus Christi College indicates clearly that resort to the colleges by the well-to-do, both urban and rural, as training schools of humane studies and manners, antedates humanist teaching and the flood-tide of matriculations in the 1570s and 1580s and may, indeed, go back to the very first years of the century. If that is so we are invited to reconsider the social role of the later medieval university as well, and to remember, for example, the advice to Margaret Paston to educate her son both in the Faculty of Arts and at the Inns of Court.[60] At the very least, it is clear that the choices open to the able and ambitious were freer and more numerous than we perhaps tend to think in retrospect, when we look only at the long-term, and forget also the schemes and suggestions that did not, in the event, carry the day.

There is a rather illustrative link between the two worlds of the later middle ages and Elizabethan England in the career of Robert Pursglove. Since it also illustrates the difficulty we have in fixing the notions of 'wealth' and 'station' it will serve as an appropriate conclusion to a discussion intended to suggest the richness of our canvas rather than to provide, at this stage, a wholly new understanding. Pursglove was born about 1500 and was admitted to Corpus Christi College probably at the original foundation, about 1518. He came from no urban centre but from Tideswell, Derbyshire, where he would probably have lived and died but for his maternal uncle William, a shearman and churchwarden of St Michael Cornhill, London. Pursglove received some elementary education from the vicar of Tideswell and then, through his uncle's sponsorship, went next to St Paul's school in London, where he is said to have spent about nine years. From St Paul's school he was admitted to Corpus. After leaving the College he entered Guisborough Priory in North Yorkshire as an Austin Canon Regular, and after the enactment of

[60] James Gairdner (ed.), *The Paston Letters*, (London, 1904), vi, pp. 11–14.

the Royal Supremacy, he became suffragan bishop of Hull. His long, controversial and full ecclesiastical career was ended when he refused to subscribe four times in 1559. He was deprived of all livings and placed under house arrest. Six years later, however, he was given the freedom of York diocese and Derbyshire, and he retired to his native soil at Tideswell. Before he died in 1579 he founded there Tideswell Grammar School and a hospital, and at Guisborough another school,[61] leaving the local boys with just such an opportunity for education as he himself would have missed, but for the accident of his talents and the invisible 'wealth' of his uncle, the shearman, in London. Perhaps his career encourages us to think that we will always fail to impose a tidy conceptual world upon a vibrant past.

[61] On Pursglove's later career see J. C. H. Aveling, *Catholic Recusancy in the City of York 1558–1791* (Catholic Record Society, St Albans, 1970), pp. 298–99.

THE MAGIC OF MEASUREMENT: MENTAL TESTING AND ENGLISH EDUCATION 1900–40*

By Gillian Sutherland, M.A., Ph.D.

READ AT THE SOCIETY'S CONFERENCE 17 SEPTEMBER 1976

I

IT has been a characteristic of studies of social policy-making in England to lay considerable stress on the importance of quantification, of precise measurement, in the evolution of any given policy. It has been suggested that the power of the evidence, once properly assembled and measured, could on occasion be sufficient to dissolve previous certainties and act as a catalyst of new thought.[1] It is perhaps not entirely fanciful to see links between this aspect of the historiography of social policy and the preoccupation of English social thought with empiricism, a preoccupation which led sometimes to the presentation of empiricism as an alternative to social theory.[2] All of this enhances the importance of attempts to assess the role of measurement in any given field of policy and to confront directly the questions of its autonomy and the power of its advocates.

Education provides a key field in which to test hypotheses about social policy-making.[3] It is by definition a social activity; and it can involve some of the most elaborate, extended and expensive social

* The work upon which this paper is based is being financed by the Social Science Research Council and I wish to acknowledge their generous support. I would like also to emphasize that the paper is an *interim* report from work in progress. Completion of the research may well lead to modifications in some of the hypotheses advanced.

[1] *E.g.* O. R. McGregor, 'Social Research and Social Policy in the Nineteenth Century', *British Journal of Sociology*, viii (1957), pp. 146–57; O. O. G. M. MacDonagh, 'The Nineteenth Century Revolution in Government: a Reappraisal', *Historical Journal*, i (1958), pp. 52–67.

[2] *Cf.* Philip Abrams, *The Origins of British Sociology: 1834–1914* (Chicago, 1968); Eileen Yeo, 'Social Science and Social Change: A Social History of Some Aspects of Social Science and Social Investigation in Britain 1830–1890', unpublished Sussex D.Phil. thesis, 1973; M. J. Cullen, *The Statistical Movement in Early Victorian Britain: the Foundations of Empirical Social Research* (Hassocks, Sussex, 1975).

[3] *Cf.* Gillian Sutherland, 'The Study of the History of Education', *History*, liv (1969), pp. 49–59.

engineering. An investigation of the initial impact on English education of mental testing, that is, the techniques associated with the psychology of individual differences for measuring the capacities and aptitudes of individuals, thus has obvious attractions. The interest and importance of the study are enhanced, moreover, by the close involvement of mental testing with some of the major innovations in statistical method of the early twentieth century, with the application of the normal curve of distribution to social phenomena, the development of correlation and of factor analysis.

II

It may be helpful to begin with a brief chronology of the development of mental tests. The first person to preoccupy himself systematically with differences in the abilities of individuals and ways of measuring them was Francis Galton, a cousin of Charles Darwin. Galton was principally interested in heredity and experimented only with tests of sensory perception. But he proceeded from what was known about physical characteristics to formulate two hypotheses for the study of mental attributes of the first importance. Studies of height and chest measurements in various populations had shown that their distribution followed the Gaussian or normal curve. Galton argued that the distribution of mental abilities in a population was likely to follow the same pattern. He also occupied himself with characterizing and expressing precisely the relationship between any two attributes possessed by one individual, making the earliest attempt to calculate correlation coefficients.[4]

The use of correlation in mental testing specifically was taken further by Carl Spearman. In his article, '"General Intelligence" Objectively Determined and Measured', in the *American Journal of Psychology* in 1904, he reported on the results of measuring promiscuously any large number of different abilities and pooling the results together. This gave, he argued, evidence that human abilities are the compound of two factors, one of which is specific to the ability, the other general to all.[5] This paper marked the formal opening of a debate extending to the Second World War about the factors of the mind and their nature and ordering. The development of factor

[4] D. W. Forrest, *Francis Galton: The Life and Work of a Victorian Genius* (London, 1974), p. 197. Forrest's book is the most recent general study of Galton. But a more vivid picture of one of the last of those Victorians who were both amateurs and polymaths is conveyed by Galton's own *Memories of My Life* (London, 1908), while the classical biography remains Karl Pearson, *The Life, Letters and Labours of Francis Galton* (Cambridge, 1914–30), 4 vols.

[5] Vol. xv, pp. 201–92.

analysis which accompanied it, entailed the computation and manipulation of matrices of correlation coefficients.[6]

Spearman's initial battery of tests had been in fact rather limited, consisting of attainment and sensory perception tests. At virtually the same time Alfred Binet and Victor Simon were pursuing the hypothesis that the higher and more complex mental processes could only be measured by tests which engaged them directly. Attempting to devise tests of vocabulary, spatial perception, memory, inductive and deductive reasoning, and even 'judgement' and 'moral sense', they tried them out on hundreds of Paris school children, relating the results to what the teachers told them about normal and abnormal performances, revising, re-designing and adjusting. In 1905 they published a first series of tests, with an age-related scale for scoring the results. A further revision followed in 1908 and a third in 1911.[7]

The impact of this was immediate and world-wide. The German psychologist Wilhelm Stern made it easier to assimilate Binet's stress on the complex to Spearman's notion of general intelligence by the device of the IQ or intelligence quotient. He divided mental age by chronological age, multiplied by 100 to eliminate the fractions and came up with a single number which could be used to describe the potential of one individual and contrast him with any other. In California Lewis Terman and in Liverpool Cyril Burt began work on the standardization of Binet and Simon's tests on American and English school children respectively. They began also to experiment with the possibility of a group test, that is, one that could be administered in written form, not orally, to a number of people simultaneously and the results scored by an unskilled individual, or even a machine. A dramatic demonstration of the possibilities of such tests was given in 1917 and 1918, when the Alpha and Beta Tests devised by the consultant psychologists to the American Army enabled the overwhelmed authorities to begin to distinguish between the recruits who were not to be trusted with a rifle and those who were potential officer material.[8]

Thus by the end of the First World War the idea that intelligence could be tested and measured and two types of test, the group and

[6] For a fuller discussion of factor analysis, see A. W. Heim, *The Appraisal of Intelligence* (2nd edn, Slough, 1970), ch. V.

[7] Theta H. Wolf, 'The Emergence of Binet's Conceptions and Measurement of Intelligence: A Case History of the Creative Process', *Journal of the History of the Behavioral Sciences*, v (1969), pp. 113–34, 207–37.

[8] *A History of Psychology in Autobiography* (Worcester, Mass., 1930–36, 1952), 4 vols., vols. 1–3, ed. C. A. Murchison, vol. 4, ed. E. G. Boring, H. S. Langfeld, H. Werner, R. M. Yerkes; P. H. DuBois, *A History of Psychological Testing* (Boston, Mass., 1970).

the individual, were all in existence; and the term 'intelligence test' was beginning to be used.

III

This, then, in the crudest outline is mental testing. To what uses was it put in the English educational system? What was its relationship to policy change and innovation? The two most obvious uses are the identification of the sub-normal child, as a prelude to special treatment and the classification of normal children, again as a prelude to differential treatment. I propose to examine these two uses separately not simply, or even primarily, for convenience. They form two distinct case-studies with their own phasing and the juxtaposition and comparison helps underline the peculiarities of each.

The earliest use of mental testing was in the precise identification of the subnormal child. Binet and Simon's early work and lobbying was of great importance in leading to the creation of the French Ministerial Commission on the Abnormal, for whom, formally, the 1905 scale was produced.[9] In England, however, a preoccupation with the identification and separate treatment of such children considerably ante-dated the development of sophisticated diagnostic tools. The Royal Commission on the Elementary Education Acts, the Cross Commission, which sat from 1886 to 1888, had recognized the problem represented by these children and invited the Royal Commission on the Blind, Deaf and Dumb, with which it coincided, to consider their treatment in more detail. This Commission, reporting in 1889, firmly recommended special classes and where appropriate, special schools for those whom they called 'educable imbeciles' and 'the feeble-minded.'[10]

Emboldened by this, the London School Board began in 1891 to group subnormal children in special schools. Following the legislation authorizing special provision and grants for blind and deaf children in 1893, they embarked on a campaign for special powers and increased grant to treat mentally defective children. By the time a departmental Committee of the Education Department met to consider the position in 1898, special classes and/or special schools had been started in Leicester, Birmingham, Bristol, Bradford, Brighton, Nottingham and Plymouth, as well as in London.[11]

[9] Wolf, *loc. cit.*

[10] Parliamentary Papers (P.P.), 1889, xix, *Report of the Royal Commission on the Blind, Deaf and Dumb*, paras. 709–24.

[11] P.P. 1898, xxvi, *Report and Minutes of Evidence of the Departmental Committee on Defective and Epileptic Children*, paras 4, 6 and 7 and qq. 3569–72; Public Record Office (P.R.O.), Education Department Papers (class Ed), Ed 14/43.

Coincident with this were a series of investigations of defective children sponsored first by the British Medical Association, then by the Charity Organization Society and finally by an International Congress on Hygiene and Demography held in London in 1892. Dr Francis Warner figured prominently in all of these. But as he readily admitted to the 1898 Committee, the children investigated were selected—and thus effectively defined as defective—by their teachers. His subsequent examination and analysis was almost exclusively anthropometric, concerned with physical defects and peculiarities as indices of abnormality.[12]

The departmental Committee duly recommended legislation. The main difficulty in drafting and carrying a bill proved to be the lack of a precise and rigorous definition of mental deficiency. As the Permanent Secretary had to admit, none of the Committee's witnesses was able 'to offer any verbal definition of that degree of want of intelligence which constitutes a defective child'. Notwithstanding, in 1899 a permissive bill was carried, giving local education authorities power, if they chose, to create special classes and schools for children 'who, not being imbecile and not being merely backward or dull children are, by reason of mental defect, incapable of receiving proper benefit from the instruction in ordinary schools'. The teacher was formally associated with the medical officer of health in the identification of such children.[13]

A number of local education authorities chose to exercise their powers under this Act. By 1903 London and fifty other authorities were making provision of some kind,[14] and some teachers and medical officers of health were beginning in an unsystematic way to ask questions like some of those in Binet's 'hotchpotch'.[15]

Here, then, was another potential audience for Binet and Simon, besides that of the academic psychologists, and the response was rapid and complete. In his Report for 1910 Dr George Newman, Medical Officer of Health to the Board of Education, drew attention in general terms to Binet and Simon's work. In his Report for 1911 he presented his usual summary of the items to be included in the

[12] P.P. 1898, xxvi, qq. 717, 720–26; Francis Warner, *The Nervous System of the Child* (New York, 1900).

[13] P.R.O. Ed 31/16, quotation from Permanent Secretary's Memorandum II, 25 January 1899; 62 and 63 Vict. c. 32.

[14] P.P. 1903, xx, Cd 1763, *Annual Report of the Board of Education for 1902–3* (A.R.), f. 392.

[15] P.P. 1908, *Report and Minutes of Evidence of the Royal Commission on the Care and Control of the Feeble-Minded*, xxxv, Cd 4215, pp. 485–87, 690 papers accompanying qq. 8364, 3614, xxxvi, Cd 4216, q. 12984, xxxviii, Cd 4219, pp. 211–25, Appendix V; P.P. 1910, xxiii, Cd 5426, Appendix to Medical Officer of Health's Report (M.O.H.R.) for 1908.

properly conducted physical examination of a child thought to be mentally defective, then continued: 'in assessing the intelligence, however, which is, broadly speaking, the chief criterion for differentiation of the normal child from the feeble-minded, the mental tests designed by Binet and Simon are recommended'. He went on to set out the scheme of tests in the 1911 version, to give a lucid and succinct account of the method of calculating the mental age of the child from the results and concluded by stressing that the tests should supplement and not replace the teacher's report and the phsyical examination.[16] The discovery of a sophisticated diagnostic tool thus *followed* the first legislation for the separate education of mentally defective children by over a decade. The development of mental testing had a reinforcing rather than an innovative effect.

The scope for the use of this tool, however, and for possible new developments, was dramatically enlarged almost straight away. The growing concern with the identification and care of the sub-normal at the end of the nineteenth century had not, of course, been confined to children. Dark predictions by various kinds of social darwinists about the deterioration of the race were fed by studies of heredity of the type conducted by Galton and his friend and disciple, Karl Pearson. The early disasters of the Boer War gave considerable impetus to more general discussions of national efficiency and these formed part of the context for the Royal Commission on the Care and Control of the Feeble-Minded, 1904–1908.[17] Their report recommended major legislation and was enthusiastically championed within the Cabinet by Winston Churchill, who, for the duration of his spell at the Home Office at least, was an ardent propagandist for eugenics.[18] The result was two pieces of legislation, one in 1913 and one in 1914, the bulk of which dealt with adult mental defectives but which also laid upon local education authorities the duty of ascertaining the mental competence of all children between seven and sixteen. Those deemed ineducable became the charge of new mental deficiency authorities; but for the educable defective children all local education authorities were now *required* to provide appropriate training.[19]

[16] P.P. 1911, xvii, Cd 5925, M.O.H.R. ch. X; P.P. 1912–13, xxi, Cd 6530, M.O.H.R., Appendix E.

[17] On the general context, see Bernard Semmel, *Imperialism and Social Reform: English Social-Imperialist Thought 1895–1914* (London, 1960), G. R. Searle, *The Quest for National Efficiency: A Study in British Politics and British Political Thought 1899–1914* (Oxford, 1971) and Kathleen Jones, *A History of the Mental Health Services* (London, 1972), pp. 185–98.

[18] See *e.g.* P.R.O. Ed 24/167.

[19] P.R.O. Ed 24/620, 24/622, 24/640, 31/190, 31/196; 3 and 4 Geo. V c. 28, 4 and 5 Geo. V c. 45; Kathleen Jones *op. cit.*, pp. 198–212.

The outbreak of war prevented much being done immediately. But in 1919 George Newman began to exhort local authorities to honour their obligations under the Act and his reports regularly carried a chapter on the problems of sub-normal children and advances in their diagnosis and treatment.[20] Nor was he alone in his interest. From the first, he had encouraged individual medical officers of health to undertake research projects linked to their work and his reports from 1921 onwards regularly devoted a section to these. In 1932 Newman estimated that 1322 research projects had been undertaken during his twenty-three years of service, mental defect being the second most frequently chosen area of investigation, outstripped only by rheumatism and heart disease.[21]

Despite this interest and the sophistication of the tools available, estimates of the incidence of mental deficiency varied almost as wildly from area to area in the twenties as they had done before the War.[22] This was yet another of the indefatigable Newman's preoccupations. In 1923 he exploited his unique position of authority as Chief Medical Officer simultaneously to the Board of Education and the Ministry of Health, to set up a specialist committee to investigate the subject. The Committee, known after its Chairman as the Wood Committee, spent four years at work and sponsored probably the most comprehensive investigation ever of the incidence of mental deficiency, both child and adult, over the country as a whole. Six sample areas were chosen, each with a population of approximately 100,000. The investigators looked not only at children in institutional care, special schools and classes, but also at those in ordinary schools as well. The class teachers in the elementary schools in each area were asked to select the fifteen per cent of their class who were the most backward. These children were then examined by a group test and those with the lowest scores were given further individual tests and in extreme cases a physical examination also. On the basis of this it was concluded that besides the 33,000 defective children already identified by medical officers and teachers, only half of whom were actually in special schools, there were another 18,000 unascertained.[23]

Following this, the Wood Committee engaged in a discussion of

[20] See especially P.P. 1920, xv, Cmd 995, M.O.H.R. 1919, ch. VI, P.P. 1921, xi, Cmd 1522, M.O.H.R. 1919–20, s. VIII. From 1921 onwards the report of the Medical Officer was published as a semi-official paper under the title *The Health of the School Child* (H.S.C.). H.S.C. 1925 (London, 1926), s. VII.

[21] H.S.C. 1932 (London, 1933), Appendix A.

[22] P.P. 1914–16, xviii, Cd 7730, M.O.H.R. 1913, para. 242; H.S.C. 1923 (London, 1924), n. 23, cont. s. VI; *Report of the Mental Deficiency Committee* (London, 1929), 3 vols. (Wood Cttee), I, ch. I, para. 2.

[23] *Ibid.*, III.

mental defect far more elaborate than any in the pre-war period, their language showing the impress of developments in both medicine and psychology in the interval. They distinguished between congenital defects, the consequences of brain damage, and the possible temporary effects of mental illness, all of which could impair what they called 'independent social adaptation'. This, in turn, they defined as dependent upon certain inborn capacities, amongst the most important of which was 'general intelligence'.[24] When they got down to practical recommendations concerning the treatment of children, they wanted to make a number of changes. Conventionally, local education authorities had come to regard children with I Qs of below 70 as certifiable either for segregation in special schools or for referral to the local mental deficiency authority as 'ineducable'. The Committee wanted only children with an I Q of 50 or under to be certified as defective and referred to the care of the local mental deficiency authority. Children with I Qs between 50 and 70 should be grouped together with those with I Qs between 70 and 80, hitherto conventionally identified as the 'dull and backward'; and this new category, labelled 'retarded' should be given special care within the framework of the ordinary school, not segregated into a special school. They wanted also to extend the compulsory school life for these children.[25]

There was no serious challenge either to the Committee's methods or findings. But their impact on policy was nil. Attempts were made within the Board of Education to prepare plans of action and memoranda of advice to local authorities. But as they found, practically all the Wood Committee's recommendations required legislation; and proposals to raise the school leaving age for retarded children could not be separated from the highly contentious question of the raising of the school leaving age in general. They took it for granted that no government, whatever its political complexion, would be willing to legislate; and at this point they gave up.[26]

Underlying this fatalism was the problem of finance. For the kind of reorganization envisaged by the Wood Committee would not only have required legislation but would also have cost a great deal of money. The postponement of the raising of the school leaving age for all children—first projected in 1918, implemented only after the Second World War—is the classic illustration of the impact of financial crisis and economic depression on educational policy in the inter-war years. This impact was immediate and affected all aspects of the Board's work. It explains why the Board brought no pressure

[24] *Ibid.*, I, ch. I, para. 16.
[25] *Ibid.*, I, ch. IX, s. II.
[26] P.R.O. Ed 24/1365.

—other than Newman's exhortations—to bear upon local education authorities at the end of the War to meet their legal obligations under the Act of 1913. Wood did his best to argue that the research of his Committee might reveal a way out of this impasse, writing to the Permanent Secretary: 'you will see we are not wild men about finances. In fact we have shown over and over again that we are trying to reduce impossible statutory obligations within the bounds of possibility'.[27] Treasury scepticism was reflected in the annual struggle for sums never exceeding £1,000 to enable the Committee to continue its work.[28] And since the Committee's way of 'reducing impossible statutory obligations' turned out to be to create new ones, its recommendations fell on deaf ears.

Mental testing thus initially powerfully reinforced and extended an already developing policy for the identification and separate treatment of defectives. But its widespread acceptance and increasingly elaborate and sophisticated use was not sufficient to prevent the onset of stagnation.

IV

In the case of the uses of mental testing in the classification of normal children, the beginnings are similar but the development rather different. Constraints of time and space make it possible to look only at such classification in its extreme form, that is, in selection for secondary education: mental testing and 'streaming' deserve a separate discussion.

Initially the effect of mental tests was again to reinforce and extend a trend towards such classification already apparent. The creation of scholarships, awarded on examination, to enable children from public elementary schools to proceed to secondary schools can be traced back to the work of the Endowed Schools Commission and the 1870 Education Act. By 1900 approximately 5,500 such children were receiving help from public funds in this way.[29] The Education Act of 1902 and the creation of local authority secondary schools provided further impetus, as did the celebrated Free Place Regulations of 1907. These increased grants to secondary schools but made it a condition of the receipt of the full grant that a minimum of 25% of the school's places should be free and open only to children from elementary schools. The effect of this was that by 1912 49,120 children, or 32% of the total population of maintained secondary

[27] P.R.O. Ed 24/1199, ms. note accompanying typewritten Note, Wood to Permanent Secretary 23.10.25.

[28] P.R.O. Ed 23/319.

[29] P.P. 1913, Cd 6707, A.R. 1911–12, ch. I, para. 13.

schools, were former public elementary school pupils receiving free tuition. Between 1912 and 1920 the proportion of free-placers did not increase but their absolute numbers nearly doubled, to 72,386 in a total maintained secondary school population of 246,000.[30]

In 1907, in order, as they put it, 'to secure that this provision shall not have the effect of lowering the standard of the education provided by the school' the Board of Education had laid down that 'applicants for free places . . . may be required to pass an entrance test of attainments and proficiency'.[31] Such tests became known as free place examinations. In 1912 the Board stressed that the intention of the free place regulations was not 'to create a scholarship system for the intellectual elite of the Elementary Schools', but to bring 'higher education' within the reach of some children of 'the poorer classes'.[32] But this view of a free place examination as simply a qualifying test was never more than a pious hope. As the figures already quoted suggest, the demand for free places expanded steadily and rapidly, along with the general demand for secondary education, turning the free place examination into an intensely competitive scholarship examination right from the start.

In 1919 the Bradford County Borough Education Committee, which had inherited the progressive mantle of the old school board, added to the scholastic tests in their free place examination several group tests originally devised for research purposes by Burt in Liverpool between 1911 and 1913.[33] In 1920 the Northumberland Education Committee invited Godfrey Thomson, Professor of Education at Newcastle to advise them 'how', as he put it, 'with most justice to select eleven year old children in the primary schools for the privilege of free secondary school education.' Specifically, they were worried about missing children of ability from remote and unsophisticated rural households and schools. Thomson devised a group test, by which a few dozen high scorers were selected. To these he and his research students then administered individual Binet Tests; and finally a cautious education authority was persuaded to offer a dozen of the highest scorers free places.[34]

Thomson published an account of the Northumberland experiment in the *British Journal of Psychology* for 1921.[35] In the same year

[30] P.P. 1920, xv, Cmd 968, *Report of the Departmental Committee on Scholarships, Free Places and Maintenance Allowances* (Hilton Young Cttee), para. 13.

[31] P.P. 1908, xxvi, Cd 3862, A.R. 1906–07, p. 67.

[32] P.P. 1913, xx, Cd 6707, A.R. 1911–12, ch. I, para. 34.

[33] Cyril Burt, 'The Use of Psychological Tests in England' in *Essays on Examinations* (London, International Institute Examinations Enquiry, 1936), p. 103.

[34] Thomson, *A History of Psychology in Autobiography*, iv, pp. 284–85.

[35] 'The Northumberland Mental Tests', *B.J.P.*, xii (1921–22), pp. 201–22.

Cyril Burt brought out the first edition of his handbook, *Mental and Scholastic Tests*. These two publications may be said to inaugurate group testing as an industry, both in the research sense and the more conventional money-making sense. A growing number of students clustered round Burt and Spearman at the University of London.[36] Thomson put the fees paid him as an examiner by Northumberland and other authorities which followed suit, into a trust fund to finance the development and publication of further tests; and after his move to Edinburgh in 1925, the tests supported by this fund became familiar as the Moray House Tests.[37]

Group tests did not have their Newman; but the response of the Board of Education was rapid and sympathetic. As early as 1919 E. K. Chambers had suggested 'the use of psychological tests of educable capacity in the public school system' as an ideal subject for investigation by the Board of Education's advisory Committee of independent experts, the Consultative Committee.[38] A sub-committee of the Consultative Committee duly considered the matter between 1920 and 1924. Thomson was one of the witnesses, stating in his proof of evidence that, 'Intelligence tests would be perhaps of greatest value in selecting types of children for different forms of education'.[39] Burt was actually a coopted member of the sub-committee and ended up writing a large part of the Report.[40]

The Report declared that tests of intelligence, which the Committee was careful to distinguish from scholastic tests and tests of particular vocational aptitudes, 'are to be regarded as an attempt to apply a knowledge of psychology and statistical methods to examinations intended primarily to discover ability rather than attainments'. They recommended that intelligence tests be included in selection examinations on an experimental basis and their results correlated with those of attainment tests.[41] This recommendation was reiterated and strengthened by the Board of Education in the Memorandum of guidance for local authorities on the conduct of free place examinations, published in 1928. This advocated the use of intelligence tests to discover children who had not done themselves justice

[36] See the prominence of these students among those applying for permission to carry out experimental work in L.C.C. schools—Greater London Council Record Office, Education Office Papers (class EO), EO/PS/1/21–25.

[37] Thomson in *A History of Psychology in Autobiography*, iv, p. 286.

[38] P.R.O. Ed 24/1228, list of 'Suggested References to the Consultative Committee' 6.8.19.

[39] P.R.O. Ed 24/1226, notes of evidence to be given 20 January 1921.

[40] P.R.O. Ed 24/1224 and 24/1226.

[41] *Report of the Consultative Committee on Psychological Tests of Educable Capacity and their possible use in the public system of education* (London, 1924) pp. 136–37, 141.

in the attainments tests and to discriminate between borderline candidates.[42] The revised version of the Memorandum for local authorities on what were now called 'special place examinations', issued in 1936 was more positive still and recommended that an intelligence test be included in *every* examination for the award of special places.[43]

Yet by 1936 only 34 out of 146 County and County Borough Councils in England and Wales were using an intelligence test in their special place exams;[44] and there seems to have been no rush to follow the Board of Education's advice in the last years before the War. It is not quite stagnation but it is very slow growth indeed; and the explanation is more complex and less obvious than in the case of testing and the care of sub-normal children.

There are no obvious geographical patterns, either of region, density of population, or type of economic activity. Economic depression is but one of a number of factors. It is part of the explanation for the muted role of government. Undoubtedly the most effective way to get local education authorities to use intelligence tests would have been to attach a financial carrot. But, as the case of subnormal children has already shown, the Board of Education spent much of the inter-war period frozen into postures of quiescence, lest any act of theirs should generate more expenditure. In theory they could have done it the other way round, adjusting the scale of secondary school grants to penalise authorities whose selection procedures they considered inadequate. But this would have caused political uproar. It would also have run clean counter to a stance they had been developing well before the economic crisis hit them. In many ways the nineteenth-century Education Department was an aggressive body. This was not so much the product of conscious choice as a role developed and forced upon them by the system of grants known as payment by results and the dual system of board and voluntary schools. By 1890 they were dealing directly and regularly with well over 3,000 local authorities and quasi-local-authorities of one kind or another. It was excessively time-consuming, wildly uneconomic and frequently acrimonious.[45] Not the least of the pressures leading to the legislation of 1902 was the wish for

[42] *Free Place Examinations*, Board of Education Pamphlet No. 63 (London, 1928), p. 55.

[43] *Special Place Examinations*, p. 7.

[44] My calculations from the data in s. IA, Sir Philip Hartog and Gladys Roberts, *A Conspectus of Examinations in Great Britain and Northern Ireland* (London, International Institute Examinations Enquiry, 1937).

[45] See Gillian Sutherland, *Policy-Making in Elementary Education 1870–95* (London, 1973), esp. chs. 7, 8 and 9.

administrative rationalization.[46] Among other things that Act reduced the number of local authorities with which the Board of Education had to deal to just over 200 and gave them considerable financial autonomy. Subsequently both politicians and officials took a great deal of trouble to re-establish the Board in the role of adviser and guide, rather than that of watchdog and antagonist. Such roles are always easier to sustain when there is some money to distribute —the free place regulations are a classic example. If there is no money and exhortation and encouragement meet with no response, a frustrated passivity is the only course of action left.

Finance is very little help at all in making sense of the widely diverging responses of local authorities. The use of intelligence tests would not have added significantly to the cost of the actual examination. Trial free place examinations conducted by the government inspectorate 1931–34 showed that the scholastic tests organized by some authorities could be reduced in number and in length and an intelligence test added with neither loss of efficiency nor increase in cost.[47] Nor did the inclusion of an intelligence test imply any drastic and expensive reorganization of secondary schools. Moreover, as the onset of depression slowed the expansion in secondary school places, so the competition intensified.[48] The Board of Education had long since ceased to argue that the examination was not an elitist exercise and in 1936 declared baldly: 'the purpose of the examination is the selection at the age of 11+, of children fit to profit by secondary education. The importance of accurate selection is vital and the main business is to get the right children.'[49] In such a situation one might have expected local education authorities to adopt intelligence tests if only to be able to deploy in their own defence the claims of the psychometrician to objectivity and scientific validity.

However, some local authorities remained resolutely deaf to arguments about the necessity of selecting the best and/or equal opportunity. In 1928, for example, the Board's inspectorate conducted a detailed investigation of the free place examinations at Stockport and were appalled at what they found. It was left to parents to decide whether they wanted their children to enter and the examination was very poorly publicised. Only 12% of those eligible actually

[46] See J. R. Fairhurst, 'Some Aspects of the Relationship between Education, Politics and Religion 1895–1906' (unpublished Oxford D.Phil. thesis, 1974).

[47] P.R.O. Ed 10/152, V5 (53).

[48] Between 1908 and 1918 provision nearly doubled; between 1928 and 1938 it increased by just over a quarter—B. R. Mitchell and H. G. Jones, *Second Abstract of British Historical Statistics* (Cambridge, 1971), p. 215. See also the discussion of demand in P.R.O. Ed 24/1625, 24/1637, 24/1644, 24/1647–51.

[49] *Special Place Examinations*, p. 4.

did enter. The written papers in English and Arithmetic were badly set and worse marked by examiners from the Northern Universities' Joint Matriculation Board, and were followed by some extremely idiosyncratic interviewing. 'As it stands', the inspectors concluded, 'the Examination has almost every possible fault.' They got nowhere in their efforts to persuade the authority to remedy it. The senior inspector left an extremely frank and bitter minute of two days of meetings with the Chairman and Secretary of the local education authority. The Chairman displayed a total and uncaring ignorance. The Secretary opposed every suggestion and denounced the idea that the authority might like to try the experiment of examining all children of 11+ as 'socialistic' and guaranteed to lead to 'a nation on the dole'.[50]

In other places the authority seems to have been willing but the constituents were uninterested. In 1924, for example, the inspectorate reported on the free-place examination in the Isle of Ely, where the head teachers of the elementary schools nominated the candidates. Only 11% of the eligible age group sat the examination; but the district H.M.I. stressed that this did not mean that heads were holding back able children. There was, he lamented, no zeal for education in the Fens. Many of the leaders of local public opinion boasted of being self-made men; while the extremes of agricultural depression made it difficult for some families to contemplate a secondary school education for their children even with free places.[51]

Neither of these conditions, a reactionary authority—and I quote the divisional H.M.I. on Stockport—or an uninterested constituency obtained in Wales. Welsh local authorities were in the van among those pressing for an extension of the free and special place system. By 1938 78% of the children in Welsh secondary schools had partial or total exemption from fees, as contrasted with 56% of the children in English secondary schools; while eleven Welsh local authorities filled their schools entirely with holders of special places.[52] Yet the only Welsh authority to use intelligence tests was Monmouthshire,[53] beginning in 1925. The more generous provision of special places may have taken some of the edge off the competition. But there was probably more to it than that. Historically the Welsh counties had been committed to a system of secondary education far less elitist than England. Welsh County Councils acquired powers to set up

[50] P.R.O. Ed 77/26; *cf.* entry for Stockport in s. IA of Hartog and Roberts, *Conspectus of Examinations*.

[51] P.R.O. Ed 77/21.

[52] P.P. 1938–39, x, Cmd 6013, A.R. 1938, ch. II, para. 9, ch. X para 16.

[53] Reply by the Director of Education for Gwent to questionnaire (G.S.Q.) sent in 1975.

secondary schools under the Welsh Intermediate Education Act of 1889, thirteen years before English counties acquired comparable powers; and their jealous protection of 'their' schools was acknowledged and reflected in separate treatment by the Board of Education from 1907 onwards.[54]

Although Monmouthshire County Council acknowledged the force of the English example, their intelligence tests were very much a domestic affair, being designed until 1947 by the Rev. A. Donald Amos, Master of Educational Method at University College, Cardiff.[55] This particular example provides a clue to another jealously protective vested interest, which operated as powerfully in England as in Wales, the teachers. Here the contrast with the doctors is instructive. There is no evidence that medical officers of health opposed or resisted the use of Binet tests in the diagnosis of subnormal children. But it must be remembered, first, that by 1900 doctors were securely established as a profession; and second, that the tests could be easily integrated into their existing pattern of medical examination, giving them, indeed, some kind of cross-check on the teacher's report on the child's school performance. Neither of these two statements can be made about teachers and the administration of group tests. The teachers were professionally insecure. By 1900 they had only just succeeded in emancipating themselves from a situation in which for forty years the work of public elementary schools had been dominated by annual examinations, conducted by the government inspectors, which determined the size of the school's annual grant. The fight against this had enabled the National Union of Teachers to become an effective national organization.[56]

The involvement of the teachers in the free-place examinations was thus a political necessity accepted by all local authorities. The extreme example of this is Newcastle, before the First World War, where a proportion of the free places were allotted simply on the basis of the elementary head teachers' recommendations. The system that operated in the Isle of Ely, whereby the elementary school heads nominated the candidates for the exam, was widely paralleled. Elsewhere, as in Reading, where entry for the examination was

[54] Leslie Wynne Evans, 'The Evolution of Welsh Educational Structure and Administration 1881–1921' in *Studies in the Government and Control of Education since 1860* (London, History of Education Society, 1970). *Cf.* also Sir Wynn Wheldon and Sir Ben Bowen Thomas, 'The Welsh Department, Ministry of Education 1907–1957', *Transactions of the Honourable Society of Cymmrodorion* session 1957, pp. 18–36.

[55] Gwent reply to G.S.Q. 1975; Gwent County Record Office, A. Donald Amos, *A Preparatory Guide to the Gwent Intelligence Tests* (Newport, 1937).

[56] See the early chapters of A. Tropp, *The School Teachers* (London, 1957).

compulsory, the elementary school heads marked the written papers of the first stage of the exam. In addition, until 1935 the N.U.T. was prepared to undertake the entire organization of their free-place examination for any local authority who requested it.[57]

The teachers' first priority was, naturally enough, to maintain and extend their involvement. They devoted a great deal of time and energy, both locally and nationally, to efforts to give the child's school record an assigned and substantial place in the selection process. It is no exaggeration to say that ways of doing this were canvassed every time the mechanics of the free-place examination were discussed, despite the scepticism of the government inspectorate about the objectivity and reliability of head teachers' reports in the mass.[58]

This preoccupation with the school record in turn provides some clues about teachers' attitudes to group tests. The head teacher formed his view of the child after prolonged observation and tested it by familiar attainment tests: this was his expertise. What was he to make of a group test, devised perhaps by someone who had never seen his school or the child? It was easy to administer a group test; but in marking the answers the key allowed him no discretion. To turn raw scores into IQs he had to use a set of mysterious tables. Finally, there were the difficulties of reconciling this IQ with the results of observation and attainments tests. Not only were there practical problems, but the immutability attaching to the notion of intelligence could be seen as reducing, if not challenging outright, the teacher's role and power as the cultivator and moulder of the child's abilities. The introduction of group intelligence tests into free-place examinations was thus likely to present teachers with problems in maintaining a hard-won but still precarious authority.

Time, experience and the inclusion of mental testing in the curricula of Colleges and University Departments of Education no doubt brought adaptation; but the signs are that the process was only barely under way by 1940. Monmouthshire, as we have seen, faced the difficulty by inviting a local man, training local teachers, to devise their tests. Wiltshire in 1933 invited an expert from the University of Birmingham to work with a committee of local teachers and officials, on the most appropriate method of introducing intelligence tests into their selection procedures.[59] The London Junior County

[57] P.P. 1913, Cd 6707, A.R. 1911–12, ch. 1; P.R.O. Ed 77/18, 22/127, No. 426, 22/128, No. 455; Hartog and Roberts, *Conspectus of Examinations*, p. 3.

[58] *E.g. Free Place Examinations* (1928), pp. 60–63; *Special Place Examinations* (1936), pp. 8–9; P.R.O. Ed 22/108, No. 332, Ed 22/138, No. 578, Ed 10/151, esp. U5 (21) and U5 (35), and Ed 10/152, V5 (53).

[59] Reply by Director of Education for Wiltshire to G.S.Q. 1975.

Scholarship Examination, on the other hand, included no intelligence test in the period before the Second World War. The L.C.C., whose medical services were one of the strongholds of individual testing, ran a series of experiments with group tests between 1917 and 1931, involving head teachers at every step. But they did not succeed in resolving adequately the question of the relative weights to be attached to intelligence tests, attainments tests, school record and head teacher's report.[60] The urge to experiment also eventually manifested itself in the Isle of Ely. In 1938 the Director of Education there added to the written tests in English and Arithmetic an Intelligence Test he had composed himself, by selecting questions from most of the well-known published tests. As the government inspectors reported, 'it did not give the help that had been expected in selecting the candidates'. In discussing the examination afterwards with Ely officials and teachers, they found that none of them appreciated fully what standardization meant, or that tests were designed and balanced as wholes; and several of the teachers more or less admitted that if the results of the intelligence tests did not match the results of the attainments tests, they were not interested in them.[61]

This last example shows problems of vested interest and understanding intertwined. It also makes it plain that problems of understanding were by no means confined to the teachers. Even in cases where local authorities were prepared to fetch in the outside expert, they were by no means always prepared to take all of his advice. Godfrey Thomson made it a regular policy to advise local authorities using Moray House tests, to administer them to an entire age group, to ensure adequate standardization. But they were not always prepared to do this; and on occasion—for example, in the Oxfordshire test in 1934—he had to try to form the standard for translating raw scores into IQs by using the results of tests carried out on larger groups elsewhere—in this particular case, Edinburgh and Halifax.[62]

The advantages of testing the whole age group usually dawned on the authority after a year or two.[63] But the advantages of the experts' advice were not always so plain; and, indeed, the experts might disagree. In the great debate about factor analysis Thomson was much closer to the Americans than to Burt and other English psychologists. Expertise is not a monolith. Explaining the rejection of it as primarily or simply the product of ignorance and/or vested interest may come

[60] Greater London Council Record Office EO/PS/3/36–38.

[61] P.R.O. Ed 77/22.

[62] Godfrey Thomson Unit for Academic Assessment, Edinburgh, Moray House Papers (M.H.P.) IV, ff. 18 and 24; but see also *passim*.

[63] *E.g.* M.H.P. III–VI, Birmingham entries.

close to arrogant hindsight. Throughout the period, group testing continued to present some very real technical problems, not all of which the experts themselves succeeded in resolving. This is perfectly exemplified in an exchange of letters between the Education Officer for Darlington and Godfrey Thomson in 1931. Whalley, the Education Officer, took an informed interest in the whole subject of testing and wrote to Thomson on 1 April 1931:

> 'I enclose statement showing the percentage of children in Darlington in the 11–12 age group who obtained an IQ 115 and over during the last three years. I have been examining these figures with reference to the question of provision for secondary education and am struck by the difference between these percentages and those given by Burt in the report of the Medical Research Council on Vocational Guidance, which, if I remember rightly, is 12%. I understand that the figure given by him a few years ago before the British Association was 15%.
>
> Can you throw any light on the matter?'

Thomson replied five days later:

> 'Your letter . . . raises a problem which, in a wider form than you give it, has been troubling me for some years. I fear I must write at some length about it.
>
> No doubt the figures which you quote from memory from Burt are what he gave—12% or 15% at and over IQ 115. In the group of very nearly 1000 Californian children upon whom Terman carefully standardized the Stanford Revision of the Binet Test, the standard deviation of IQ was almost exactly 13 points, which corresponds, with normal distribution, to about 13% of the candidates attaining or exceeding IQ 115, which falls between Burt's two figures.
>
> The reasons for the departure from this at Darlington are to be found in one or more of the following. The phenomenon is not peculiar to Darlington, but I find it more marked there than almost anywhere:
>
> (1) Darlington children, as I frequently told you, do very well in the group tests, often beating the expectation based on trials at other places.
>
> (2) The Intelligence Quotients meant by Burt, and also those obtained by Terman, are Binet IQs, obtained by individual testing. Group test IQs seem to show a wider scatter.
>
> (3) There is a connection between the scatter of IQs and the age-allowance which the IQ procedure carries with it, and the endeavour to give the correct age-allowance implies permitting

the scatter of the IQs to rise if there is to be consistency in the conversion of raw score into IQ.

(4) The conditions of testing are different, at an examination upon which very much depends, and for which the schools have been preparing, from the conditions of testing envisaged by Burt; and the results therefore artificial and distorted from his point of view, though perhaps correct from that of the educational administrator.

(5) It is possible that the scatter of intelligence is actually, and not merely apparently, wider than Burt and Terman think.'[64]

He spent another four pages expanding these points and the letter, in fact, represents the first draft of what was to be one of his most celebrated articles in the *British Journal of Educational Psychology* in 1932, on the problems of comparing IQs obtained by group and individual tests.[65]

The work done so far, therefore, has tended to diminish the autonomy and authority I was initially inclined to attribute to mental testing. The psychometrician now appears not as the sorcerer but as the sorcerer's apprentice, and an apprentice, seemingly, more welcome to the doctor than to the teacher. An examination of the uses of mental testing in the education system proves to be yet another way of confronting the extent of the impact of the inter-war depression, its contribution to an educational process characterized by intensive selection and the forces which put control of this lock, stock and barrel, into the hands of individual local authorities.

[64] M.H.P. I, f. 44.

[65] 'The Standardization of Group Tests and the Scatter of Intelligence Quotients: A Contribution to the Theory of Examining', *British Journal of Educational Psychology*, ii (1932), pp. 92–112, 125–37.

MASS EDUCATION AND MODERNIZATION—THE CASE OF GERMANY 1780–1850

The Prothero Lecture

By Professor Thomas Nipperdey, Dr.Phil.

READ AT THE SOCIETY'S CONFERENCE 17 SEPTEMBER 1976

'You alone are to blame for all the misery that has befallen Prussia in the past year. You and your pseudo education, your impious platitudes which you disseminate as true wisdom, have eradicated the faith and loyalty in the minds of my subjects and have turned their hearts from me. This pompous, sham-education has always been abhorrent to me, and as sovereign I have done my utmost to suppress it. It is not the rabble I fear, but rather the profane doctrines of the modern, frivolous worldly-wisdom which have poisoned and undermined the loyalty of a group of officials [the teachers] of whom I previously believed I could be proud.' So Frederick William IV, king of Prussia, told a delegation of directors of teacher training colleges in January 1849.[1]

IN the 1850s, school policy enjoyed very high priority in the fight against the revolution. The elementary school was to be brought back to simple subject matter, firmly grounded truths and to an education stressing authority; above all the teachers were to be given as simple a training as possible.

In 1866, a journalist came up with the slogan[2] that it was the Prussian elementary school teacher who won the Battle of Königgrätz. This opinion was often repeated internationally and played a major role in the discussions within governments and parliaments in Germany. What was meant was not an education producing obedience, for this was no weaker in Austria, but rather a systematic education and an education producing technical-rational precision.

Both opinions describe two sides of the phenomenon that we today call modernization. The first opinion holds that mass education through the elementary school has in part caused and in part accompanied the social and political change which has led from the subject to the citizen, from authoritarian government to democratic participation, from the dynastic particular state to the liberal national state, from the dominance of religion to the secular relation

[1] *Reden und Trinksprüche Friedrich Wilhelms IV* (1855), pp. 344–45.

[2] Oskar Peschel, *Ausland*, 29, 17 July 1866; F. Stiehl, *Meine Stellung zu den drei preussischen Regulatiren* (1872), pp. 49–50.

of man to his world. At the same time, according to the other opinion, mass education has led to the modernization of the armies and in general to the prevalence of individual behaviour-patterns which correspond to the technical-industrial mastering of the world. If Keynes could truthfully say that Bismarck founded the German Reich, not with blood and iron, but with iron and coal,[3] it is equally valid to connect this to the industrial training of the masses which decisively loosened the traditional patterns of behaviour.

Proof that the correlation between the elementary school system and modernization in German was not a subsequent construction of the historians, a bogey of the conservatives of 1848, or an object of pride to the victors of 1866 is demonstrated by the fact that, in the decades before 1848, Germany was one of the countries most sought out by international experts in education from government, administration or academia. The later French Minister of Education Victor Cousin,[4] who reformed the French elementary schools, and Horace Mann,[5] the founder of the public school system in the U.S.A. (in Massachusetts), were the two most important, but by no means the only such experts, who studied developments in Prussian-Germany in order to modernize education in their own countries.

I intend here to present a case study related to the problem of modernization though I do not want to enter into the shallows and depths of the subject. I believe it is still too early to develop further theories before we have exact empirical knowledge about the specific histories of particular societies and countries. In particular the question of whether there is a normative model of modernization that applies outside Europe and the U.S.A., *i.e.* in the developing countries, can be left open. It is certain, however, that since the so-called industrial revolution and in the age of the democratic revolution we find a disintegration or transformation of tradition-dominated societies, which we can tentatively call modernization—and this somewhat vague concept will perhaps become more concrete, as I present my story. I also do not want to involve myself in a systematic discussion about the relationship between mass education and modernization. The close connection between the technological modernization of society and elementary education is a truism in the West, in the East (in the Soviet Union as well as in China) and in the third world. So far we have only hypotheses on the possible correlation between mass education and revolution. These hypo-

[3] John M. Keynes, *The Economic Consequences of the Peace* (London, 1920), pp. 74–75.

[4] Victor Cousin, *Bericht des Herrn Victor Cousins über den Zustand des öffentlichen Unterrichts in einigen Ländern Deutschlands, besonders in Preussen* (Altona, 1832).

[5] Horace Mann, *Report of an Educational Tour* (London, 1846).

theses state that all modern revolutions rest on a specific relation between increasing literacy and still prevalent illiteracy. There is certainly today a distinction between technical modernization and democratic-participatory modernization, as we know from experience with dictatorships, communist systems and developing countries. Whether and how the two work necessarily together is still an open question. I shall, however, refrain from giving this problem general consideration. In the nineteenth century, at least, the theory of the relationship between social and political progress and elementary education belonged to the liberal democratic creed as well as to the nightmares of the conservatives. In this respect the Prussian-German example comes as a surprise, indeed a paradox: here is a case where an authoritarian, non-democratic state itself introduced the modern, potentially revolutionary, elementary school system. It was a state that attempted to keep such schools under firm control, sought to permeate them with authority and obedience as primary values, and wished to carry out sectional modernization without endangering its conservative structure: mass emancipation in a conservative, status-quo orientated system, in fact through such a system—that is a seeming paradox. The intentions of the actors and the effects of their actions were opposed to each other, as we shall see. A sectional modernization which could reduce and eliminate the element of participation was impossible in the first half of the nineteenth century, as I shall demonstrate.

I

Education in the old, traditional world, the 'world we have lost', did not take place in the school It occurred in the world of home and social standing; the individual grew to maturity not by systematic learning, but through action and imitation. The patterns of behaviour and discipline and the mastering of present and future were established by tradition, not by reflection; not by abstract notions, but by tangible, visible example including the gallows and public executions even in the smaller towns. The total realm of life was where teaching and learning took place. In the village, therefore, all the older people could alternatively take on the function of the teacher. Instruction was a sideline; the school and the teacher were of secondary importance, auxiliaries of the extended household. Whatever was needed to give meaning to life was found in the Bible. Reading and learning Bible passages were enough to orient the individual in his world. The world of common man was a static one.

It was already under these conditions during the eighteenth century that the state began to assume responsibility for the school. The school became an affair of the state and subject to its administration. The state founded schools and prescribed compulsory education as the subjects' duty. Existing schools were put under government control. Ecclesiastical inspection of the schools was now carried out under the state's commission. At the same time a certain secularization of Christian educational objectives made itself apparent. A man's capability and usefulness in his social rank now became secular goals of education, even in the elementary school. But in the eighteenth century one can see only the beginnings of this development. The administration was much too weak to overcome the feudal and local, corporative and communal powers. Compulsory education could not be carried out because of opposition from nearly all parents. Many places had no schools at all, and where they existed they were schools controlled by the local magistrates, or which only functioned in winter, with an old craftsman acting as teacher; or schools which were an auxiliary institution of the home. Bureaucratic centralization was still not able to prevail over the quasi-natural variety of particular relations.

II

It was not until 1790 to 1815—a period between enlightened absolutism and bureaucratic reform—that a general, relatively uniform elementary school system on a modern basis developed, a system that turned into a specific subsystem of culture and society, apart from the institution of the extended family. This was the era of fundamental school reform. The lead in this reform was taken by the state.

There are a variety of reasons for this development. I shall group them into three categories.

(a) Linked to the demographic revolution, agrarian structural changes and the beginning of a factory system social problems arose which could not be solved in the world of tradition. A class emerged below the peasantry that was no longer integrated into the social framework of the village. Rural occupations became overcrowded and more dependent on technology and economic fluctuation. Poverty seemed to become a collective and no longer an individual fate. There was the problem of child labour in the factories. So-called industry-schools that combined factory work with schooling grew out of this situation. The famous Swiss educator Pestalozzi developed his educational concept of individual autonomy from his experience of the decline of the extended household in the traditional village society and the loosening of family bonds. The Prussian Chancellor Hardenberg in 1817 initiated an inquiry into child-labour.[6] His idea was that a one-sided occupational training made the children incapable of adjusting to the changing situations of modern life and predestined them to become part of a proletariat. The only remedy would be a broad and general, formal education. Intertwined with these social problems was the demand for an increase in economic productivity, first of all in the agrarian sector. The means to this was greater rationality, and a prerequisite seemed to be a general and formal education with rationality as its goal. In brief, there were social and economic challenges to the traditional system of bringing up children; these challenges did not, of course, 'cause' the new educational system but the improvement of the schools was one possible response.

(b) The importance of this response is related to intellectual developments. In the late Enlightenment—Enlightenment is, by the way, a pedagogical concept—public discussion was dominated by pedagogical topics and by the theme of public education in particular. Education became a separate sector of society and at the same time a planned and institutionalized system. The philosophical movements of Neo-Humanism and Idealism which took over in Germany from the Enlightenment retained this priority. A new pedagogical theory emerged—Pestalozzi who took Kant as his starting point was its champion for the elementary school—and this theory corresponded to the changes actually occurring in society. Man was no longer seen as bound by home and social status, by the world and the tradition into which he was born. He took on what contemporaries called 'personal standing', his behaviour was to be autonomously controlled; the inner-directed man became the ideal. Man was viewed as the product of his own efforts. The world was no longer treated as given, but rather as a thing to be planned and formed. One no longer oriented oneself on the past or on birth, but rather on the future. We might call this a new concept of the person or of humanity. The consequences for education were not to pass on patterns, but rather to call forth abstraction, reflection and spontaneity; not to convey useful rules for given situations, but rather to enable people to see through new situations and to choose autonomously a suitable course of action.

Skills now took priority over knowledge; general formal education over occupational training. Such a theory placed enormous demands on the school. The school received an historical function; it became the preliminary stage for a new kind of human existence. Today this might be considered exaggerated or a specifically Ger-

[6] J. Kuczynski, *Hardenbergs Umfrage über die Lage der Kinder in den Fabriken* (Berlin, 1960), p. 23.

man metaphysic, but it is only from these ideas that we can explain the intensity of the Prussian reforms. Characteristic for Germany was the fact that this intellectual movement, this pedagogical commitment permeated the state very quickly because the state was based on academically educated civil servants. These civil servants were the ones who transformed the lofty educational theories of pedagogical writers into administrative principles and formed the necessary institutions. And not only the Prussian reforms with their philosophical superstructure followed these ideas, but also the more prosaic reforms in Napoleonic Germany.

(c) Of course the states were not such monstrous entities in which philosophers were kings. They had considerable political interest in the new school system. Even Absolutism wanted to improve its subjects in order to increase their economic efficiency and the amount of taxes they could pay and in order to reduce crime. Now the state wanted to wake and increase the entire potential power of society. And that meant that the emancipation, the release of individual and above all economic strength must be designed to benefit the state. The freeing of the peasants, general conscription and mass education stood in a very close relation to each other. In 1817 Süvern, the Prussian civil servant responsible for the elementary schools, called the school reform 'the most important of all ventures which, though not necessarily at the moment, will inevitably yield abundant interest'.[7]

It was the minister of war, Boyen, who, when commenting on the danger of revolution in 1819, demanded that all available means should be concentrated on the improvement of the elementary schools.[8] Modernization, which made the individual freer and more capable, and in practice, therefore, the school, was intended to strengthen the state. Another interest the state had in the new school system was that it would help to integrate the old and new provinces as well as the churches into the state, to assert the latter's sovereignty against all feudal and corporate powers, and to establish an immediate relationship between the state and its subjects. The schools, with the state controlling them and enforcing compulsory attendance upon everybody, served the construction of the modern, bureaucratic state. Compulsory education is similar to conscription and tax liability as an expression of the demands which the modern state makes on all its citizens.

Certainly there were differences and tensions within these reform tendencies, within the alliance between intellectual reformers and

[7] W. Süvern, *J. W. Süvern* (1929), p. 218.

[8] E. Müsebeck, *Das preussische Kultusministerium vor hundert jahren* (1918), p. 203.

the established ruling groups. The intellectuals expected the state to serve as the agent for modernizing the existing feudal and corporate society in which reformed education formed a vital element. For the liberal intelligentsia this modernizing always implied an element of participation. For large parts of the ruling *élite*, however, the necessary modernizing should be limited to what could be done without disrupting the existing political structure. Education should increase economic and social capabilities but at the same time instil a new and more internalized respect for authority. These contradictory purposes were implicit in the synthesis of the reforms.

It is not necessary to describe the implementation of school reforms, the foundation and improvement of the schools, the actual enforcement of compulsory education and school attendance against public resistance, from parents as well as children, the introduction of special city schools, the construction of a system of school administration and school inspection, the financing of the schools. This was a long process that took decades. The state required much time and caution to put through the new system against the communities who had to bear the financial burden. The bureaucracy understood itself as the advocate of the masses, the future citizens and the children, even as the advocate of the 'real' interests of contemporary society, and they put through the new school system against opposition from society. They constituted, we may say, a kind of educational dictatorship. In the final analysis, or so it seemed, the reform was successful down to 1848. The rate of illiteracy declined decisively, Army statistics showing a rate of less than 10–15% as compared with figures for France and Britain of 40–45%.[9] The number of children who actually and regularly attended school from the age of six to twelve or fourteen rose to 82% by 1846 with a concurrent increase in population of 50%, which meant a particular growth at the young end of the scale.[10] The first reduction of child labour in favour of school attendance in 1838, however, was achieved by the school administration only when the military insisted that its recruits receive a reasonable school education. The most important aspect of this reform was that the state created a new social class, the teachers. In place of marginally and haphazardly selected, untrained and grossly uneducated persons there emerged a new class of systematically trained experts: the essence of the reform was expressed by the founding of forty teachers' colleges in Prussia. And although liberal contemporaries and later historians stress the flaws

[9] Literacy in Prussia meaning the ability to read and write; in France only to read.

[10] Peter Flora, *Indikatoren der Modernisierung* (1975), p. 67; *Mitteilungen des statistichen Büros in Berlin* (1849), p. 3.

of the system (one-room village schools, etc.) the historically remarkable aspect is above all the positive result.

III

After 1817–19 the peak of the era of the reforms was over; the so-called 'Restauration' began: a conservative backlash against decades of liberalism. Our question is: what happens to progressive reform in such a period of conservative reorientation? The conservatives had their doubts about the modern school and school reform. They even fought against it, because it seemed revolutionary in its results. According to the conservatives the reforms were intended to bring about the autonomy of the individual, they fostered criticism and independence and thereby destroyed the bonds of tradition, received truths and authorities. They produced an obsession with criticism and ratiocination, and endangered moral character by their sole stress on the intellectual element. The conservatives thought that it was a fundamental error to believe that more freedom meant more happiness; instead, emancipation from tradition and bonds would not make a man happy. The outcome of modern school education, it was charged, was a concern with too many subjects and at the same time a decline of real knowledge as against the so-called skills; what results is only a pseudo-education. And this pseudo-education itself was part of the revolutionary ferment, because it traced man's permanent discontent to his particular situation. Furthermore the modern school pre-supposed a principled equality of education; however the equality of the school is artificial, breeding only competition and demands, and standing in opposition to the inequalities in every society. The modern school, it was alleged, did not help man to conform to the existing conditions, it did not stabilize society and persons, but rather created mobility and insecurity.

Although much of the criticism of the contemporary school was justified, it was essentially a fear of education for the masses. The conservatives suggested remedies: on the one hand, Authority, received truths, firm knowledge, modesty, contentment, stability, and on the other, reduce the amount of education, eliminate all excesses, cut out the natural sciences, literature and history, as well as formal practice in mathematics or languages, believed to be practice in reflection. The knowledge of the masses should not exceed an elementary and basic level. Not education as such but rather the limits of education formed the focal point of the conservative arguments. Seen positively, the school should generate conservative character. The means to this was religious instruction freed from all forms of rationalism. There were too many schools already, it was argued, but as long as they were there they should be conservative; they should not promote modernity, but rather immunize against modernity. Teachers' training stood in the centre of the struggle. Science and theoretical thought, philosophy and literature should not dominate; the aim should be to produce simple and competent craftsmen. Only in this way could the teachers avoid alienating themselves from the way of life of those they were meant to educate. We may note that once the school becomes a general institution the typical struggle for the school begins; since the school is a formative force in society, the political powers in society compete for control of this institution.

The conservative 'Restauration' achieved partial success in Prussia. The expansion slowed down. The position of the church was strengthened, numerous moderating decrees stressed the limitation of education. Appointment and promotion policy tried at least to influence teacher training in this sense. Nevertheless, this policy had no lasting effects until the 1840s. The elementary school system remained pluralist, did not become conservative, and maintained the liberal–rational character which made it an ally of the 1848 Revolution. This was caused by a number of factors which are related to special German conditions. I can only touch on them very briefly.

(a) The conservatives were opposed to centralizing and bureaucratizing and rejected general laws. In 1819, Beckedorff, one of the highest officials, wrote that the state should not intend to force its projected form of education on the entire nation. That would be an expression 'of bureaucratic suspicion of our ancestors, our descendants as well as our contemporaries'. The state could only 'warn out of love, never command or co-erce, even if it meant helping a man to achieve his salvation'. Who was 'to guarantee that the end result would not be an inquisition or burning at the stake?' Mistakes could not be abolished by decree but rather should be so handled that they correct themselves.[11] The Ministry of Education refused to set up a central publishing house for school books, because they did not want to restrict free development, or to set up a monopoly which would be incompatible with the other institutions of the state. Neither for the primary schools nor for the teachers' colleges were there binding curricula, timetables or textbooks; the administration operated with individual decrees, recommendations, admonitions or warnings, only in extreme cases resorting to regulations or orders. In brief, one avoided using effective means to put through one's own objectives. Instead, Beckedorff founded a journal and in this way made

[11] E. Quittschau, *Geschichte des Evangelischen Religions—unterrichts in den preussischen Lehrerseminaren*, Phil.Diss. (Griefswald, 1931), pp. 246, 303, 305.

his appeal to the public.[12] For his opponents the same principle of appealing to the public applied so that the opposition was able to express views contrary to those of the Ministry in journals for liberal civil servants.

(b) The ruling establishment was by no means uniform. The man who remained Kultusminister was Altenstein, a man of reform who although modifying his reform concept of education in a conservative direction, nevertheless carried on in office and prevented a conservative reaction. This applied all the more to the predominantly middle-class civil servants in the provinces, and above all in the school administrations. The bureaucracy stood as an independant factor outside the government and more progressive in educational matters. They saw no danger to the political order in the advancing school education. Therefore they failed really to carry out the wishes of the central government, or when they did, acted only very slowly.

(c) Much the same was true of the church. The conservatives supported the orthodox or the revivalists, but at the same time there were rationalists and liberals who maintained a strong position in the church administration up to the middle of the century. This applied especially to school affairs. The enlightened catholic as well as protestant theologians who had adopted the cause of the elementary schools now occupied crucial positions. The educated civil servants were on their side. They were opposed to orthodoxy and clericalism, and that assisted the rationalists and liberals.

(d) Furthermore, the school system became an area with autonomous tendencies. The experts, above all the teachers at the teachers' colleges, became a political group with its own influence; as civil servants in Germany they could virtually not be removed from office. This pedagogical establishment stood under the impact of the Enlightenment, Pestalozzi and the reform movement. Being young in 1810 these people were still in office in 1840 and determined school practice. Most of the text books, even books on religion, came from these circles. Even the experts on whom the conservative government tried to rely were one-time reformers who had turned conservative. They still held to certain ideals of the reform movement.

(e) Finally there was the self-government of the cities which had set up their own and to some extent independent school system and even in the 1830s and 1840s were able to prevent the reaction from encroaching too far.

In brief, the state was no monolithic block. Even the established powers, the bureaucracy and the church, were not uniformly conservative, but rather pluralistic. Within this relative pluralism, the

[12] *Jahrbücher für das preussische Volksschulwesen*, 1825–1828.

reforms could continue to exist. A characteristic example is found in the career of Diesterweg, the leader of the liberal teachers. In 1822 he was nominated director of the teachers' college. The Ministry of Education was against him because he was not a theologian, and because he was a rationalist. However, the provincial administration and the ecclesiastical authorities after much argument secured his appointment. For ten years he successfully held his liberal line against constant criticism from the Ministry of Education. In 1827 he founded the leading liberal school-journal. In 1832 he was appointed by the Minister of Education on the recommendation of a leading churchman to one of the most important new positions; he became director of a special college for city school teachers in Berlin. It was not until 1844–45—a new extremely conservative minister having taken over—that attempts were made to throw him out, but for the time being the principle still prevailed that no one could be removed from office for holding the opinions he had held when he was appointed. It was not until 1847 that he was finally removed from office. More remarkable than his dismissal, which aroused public protest at the time, was the fact that the man had been able to work in leading positions for three decades. Of course, the conservatives gained more and more influence in the school system, and above all the course became stricter after 1840. Books, certain subjects and teachers' organizations were banned, strict, conservative partisans were appointed, the moving of the teachers' colleges to small towns and a new emphasis on gardening as a means against revolution were in preparation. These conservative measures, however, in a non-totalitarian system met with the heated opposition of the teachers and increased their activism.

In principle, the situation in the other German states was similar to that in Prussia, even in the catholic states. Two cases may be mentioned. There were states that had no school system, like Hanover, and states that did not accept the new concept of the elementary school, like Austria. Where no modern schools existed, no struggles arose. Then, in the south-west and in central Germany, the liberal school practice remained in effect as a result of the leading position of rationalism in the church. The ultramontane catholic demands on the school, above all in the 1840s, led to tensions between the two conservative powers, between state and church. As a result liberal school policy enjoyed an important degree of independence.

IV

Up to now I have tried to show that the founding and reforming of the elementary school system was a grand, large-scale reform with the goal of mobilizing and modernizing society economically and socially and in a wider sense modernizing it politically, that is, of winning the voluntary and active loyalty of the citizen for the state. The conservatives clearly recognized the tradition-destroying, modernizing, revolutionary character of this reform and opened the battle over the schools. They wanted to reduce the school and organize it on conservative principles. Even though the German states were ruled conservatively and even though the highest school officials followed this course, nevertheless strong opposition, the plurality of the establishment and the plurality of objectives, prevented such a policy from being more than partially successful. In principle the reform continued, even if slowly and hindered by financial problems.

To turn briefly to another question: what was the response of the liberal bourgeois to the accusation, that the school promoted revolution? A lively discussion over the elementary school developed in the 1830s as a result of the contemporary interest in questions regarding the impoverished masses, the new social questions and the fear of revolution. A good public education as the antidote to the revolution, was the quintessence of this discussion. It was argued that the school had no immediate effects on society; on the contrary it depended on society. The school did, however, effect society indirectly by encouraging man to rely on his personal abilities. The change the school set in motion was an evolutionary kind of change. 'Where the school prospers, there progress is assured; a slow, gradual, but inevitable progress.' Or, the school was said to be the foundation of a permanent reform because—according to the optimism of the time—governments would eventually have to submit to an educated public.[13] The school, according to the leading liberal industrialist Harkort,[14] assisted the individual in making use of his possibilities in a varied and flexible manner, helped him achieve economic independence, increased productivity and ability to consume and managed to eliminate pauperism and the proletariat. And secondly, not too much education, but too little education would lead to revolution—the half-educated is the revolutionary; only the ignorant person stood at odds with society and was susceptible to the demagogy of socialism and communism. True obedience to the law and a commitment to society and the nation were grounded on an understanding of society and politics. Only an educated Every-

[13] A. Diesterweg, *Sämtliche Werke*, ed. H. Deiters, H. Ahrbeck *et al.*, i (1956), pp. 4, 179, 183.

[14] F. Harkort, *Bemerkungen über die preussische Volksschule und ihre Lehrer* (1842); *Bemerkungen über die Hindernisse der Civilisation und Emancipation der unteren Klassen* (1844).

man was likely to know that his well-being and that of all citizens depended on submission to the law. Whoever wished to avoid or fight revolution, political as well as social, had to improve the school; it was necessary to combat its deficiencies, not its excesses. Therefore, more money was needed for the school, the curriculum had to be more realistic, the ecclesiastical influence had to be reduced, the teachers had to be given better training. In brief, the school was regarded as the foundation of a reform policy that objected to both Revolution and Reaction. Hoffman, the leading statistician in Prussia, reduced the problem to a formula: the wealthy classes must bear the costs of education much more than formerly, because the security of life and property was guaranteed primarily by the school. Of course, there were liberal communities and groups of rising liberal industrialists who held different opinions.[15] Two leading Rhineland entrepreneurs spoke out against improving the educational level of the lower classes and making them aware of their rights, as opposed to their duties. No liberal of the time would have argued against this emphasis on duties, but the majority of liberals did not follow the line of such arguments in favour of restriction.

V

Up to now we have discussed whether the system of mass education had a modernizing effect from the standpoint of the reformers, the conservatives and the liberals. I must now attempt to take the analysis of the problem beyond the views and intentions of the actors. There are two main questions:

(a) What role was played by the teachers? The attitude of the teacher depended greatly on his social status. This status was characterized by an enormous discrepancy between self-conception, self-assessment, and role expectancy on the one hand, and socio-economic position on the other. As a result of their education, the teachers had a high awareness of their task, their civilizing function. They were to transform the tradition-guided society by combating prejudice and superstition. They were to bring about more rational and effective behaviour patterns, to spread culture and humanity, to elevate ethics and character. And they viewed themselves as educated people in touch with the general culture, as mediators of objective *Geist*. This self-confidence was the heritage of the reforming pathos which remained in effect even in the rhetoric. Colleges and administrations which first had to build up a new class of teachers, constantly apostrophized the special significance and responsibility

[15] J. Köster, *Der rheinische Frühliberalismus und die soziale Frage* (Berlin, 1938), pp. 31, 73, 86.

of the teacher in this sense. They should influence 'the reform of the whole life of the people, as well as the rebirth of the age.'[16] They felt themselves to be, as one contemporary critically remarked,[17] 'world-saviours'. This self-confidence was also strengthened by the fact that teachers acquired a new social status. They stemmed from the rural proletariat, from small peasants or craftsman families; they were advanced by the state quickly and at an early age, and set to higher functions; they were called the 'new' teachers as opposed to the teachers of the old school. This was reason enough for the teachers to be critical of tradition. They themselves had no tradition and no established roles, they were *homines novi*. Their identity and self-confidence were the result of reflection on their 'task'. It was the separation from their rural and plebeian origin that led them to view their profession more ideologically. And, in addition, their self-confidence was upheld by the fact that they had command of a special kind of knowledge by virtue of their Pestalozzian methods; they developed the pride of achievement characteristic of the expert. Finally, their self-confidence may have been increased by an attempt to compensate for the uncertainty resulting from the discrepancy between the demands and expectations implicit in their education on the one hand and their achievement and actual education on the other.

This role-awareness stood in sharp opposition to their miserable social and economic conditions. The legal status of teachers was insecure, their pay was miserable—less than the income of a sergeant, a rural constable or a bailiff, in most cases less than the pay of a skilled worker, and in the countryside it was often just barely level with the wages of farm labourers, day labourers, or apprentices. Their salaries contrasted sharply with the most modest claims to a social prestige corresponding to their function. Furthermore, the teachers were given tasks that seemed degrading to their new self-esteem, such as serving the church as vergers. Their relationship to the pastor was, therefore, already strained. In addition, the pastors had the job of supervising the work of the teachers, but did not exercise this supervision properly because, according to the teachers, they understood nothing of modern pedagogy. In many places the teachers had to struggle with their superiors for decades in order to be addressed by the formal 'Sie' and the title 'Herr'. Their position was also weak against the majority in the communities, which often viewed them as a financial burden. For this reason their chances of marrying were not favourable. They were generally isolated in

[16] F. Thiersch, *Über den gegenwärtigen Zustand des öffentlichen Unterrichts* i, (1838), p. 34.

[17] W. Curtmann, *Die Schule und das Leben* (Friedberg, 1842), p. 83.

social intercourse as discipline required them to be particularly serious in demeanour. This can be put more abstractly: The teachers emerged from a layer beneath the actual traditional estates, but they were not yet integrated into the civil society of occupation and class. They constituted a new class. For this reason the difficulties we have mentioned emerged in the same form in almost all societal systems of the day, *e.g.* in the democratic cantons of Switzerland.

Many teachers conformed to these conditions or withdrew to the idyll of bee-keeping or cultivated eccentricity, a theme often handled in the literature of the period. But many accentuated their role as modernizers, developing revolutionary feelings against the existing conditions. W. H. Riehl, a particularly clear-sighted contemporary (one could call him a nostalgic sociologist) spoke of a seminarian and third-rate education that had exterminated the peasant character of the teacher and filled him with modern sentiment so that he felt uneasy and constantly tried to break through the barriers of his class and vocation and even saw 'himself as the personified call for the reconstruction of society'. Elsewhere Riehl spoke of the 'minor official, who wants to reform society because he is not able to reform his own meagre salary'.[18] Such an interpretation is one-sided. For the teachers' personal existence was not isolated, but rather was inseparably linked with the existence of the school. And it was also the interest of the school that let the teachers press for an emancipation, even for a transformation of the state, for the participation of the people and the intelligentsia, for the priority of the cultural budget over the military budget, for the separation of their institution from a church that had become too conservative. But Riehl's description of the feeling among the teachers is basically correct. There was a revolutionary disposition. And because the society was not yet segmented in a variety of different social groups as it later was, but rather had relatively clear dividing lines, the majority of the teachers entered into an alliance with the liberal-democratic forces in society.

From the modernizing role of the teacher developed a revolutionary politicizing of the entire profession. This can be clearly seen in the history of the teachers' organizations. Originally, such organizations developed from government initiative. It is an odd phenomenon, that the state should have founded free associations for its minor civil servants. These associations were at first devoted to further education, they were to stabilize the brief training of the new teachers, and bring new methods and the 'rolling reform' into the schools. This lay in the interest of the state as well as that of the teachers. The associations also served the social contacts of the isolated teachers.

[18] W. H. Riehl, *Die bürgerliche Gesellschaft* (1854), pp. 80, 339.

Typically, choral societies were formed in the 1820s and 1830s and teachers' festivals held. In the late 1830s the associations freed themselves from government influence. They began to represent the interests of their class and they made salary claims. Eventually, demands relating to school policy in general were presented: a more strongly realistic orientation, less obedient passivity and more independence from the children. The 'inner emancipation' of the teacher, it was claimed, should be brought about by more comprehensive and scientific training at the teachers' colleges, emancipation from ecclesiastical inspection should be granted and the autonomy of the school guaranteed. The development of a school press, the founding of specialized journals for teachers and their generally more critical tone point in the same direction. Teachers' festivals, such as the anniversary in 1845 of Diesterweg's appointment or the Pestalozzi celebration of the same year, became acts of political representation. The government's attempt to suppress this movement increased the opposition of the teachers all the more. Thus, before the revolution of 1848 the very teachers who had been trained by the state, and who were supervised by and dependent on it, were, on the whole, part of the opposition movement against this magisterial state. This applied even to states like Baden and Saxony that had relatively liberal school policies or an essentially rationalistic school administration. Precisely here, the revolutionary movement of the teachers was particularly strong. This fact shows that on the whole the structural conditions for the modern school and its teachers were more important than the respective measures of the administration. The state had created a new class in order to modernize. This class had no secure status in society. As the state began to cut down or block modernization, the teachers, with their modernizing potential, developed into a group prone to revolution. For a time the teachers played a prominent part in the revolution, although society and above all the common man were not particularly friendly towards the school. In the countryside, it was the teachers who, apart from the ecclesiastical establishment were the relatively educated persons. Any revolutionary propaganda had, at first, to win over this group. Thanks to their origins they were particularly close to the lower classes and to their social problems and as they were not yet affected by conservative ideology they were particularly inclined to the radical democratic wing.

(b) My final question asks whether the effect of the teachers' work in school was itself modernizing and revolutionary? In other words let us look at the pupils instead of the teachers. Riehl maintained that the teacher attempted to communicate 'the state of pseudo-education, which he had acquired, even to the ignorant peasants and tried to liberate them completely from their customs and traditions'. The teacher carried a feeling of 'muddle-headedness and bitterness into the village'. In the role of the worthless 'man of letters' he had the power to tear away the otherwise staid peasant from the grasp of custom and tradition. He acted as an 'evil demon' to the degenerate and run-down peasantry. His appearance often led to a division in the village. While the older people and the 'aristocracy' of the village rejected the teachers, groups of young people gathered around them.[19] In such an interpretation, observation and conservative opinion are mixed. However, we can verify some of his observations from other witnesses. With the modern teacher there appeared a new authority for the child and young people in the pre-industrial world; an authority that claimed an independent importance next to the authority of father, family and home on the one hand, and the all-encompassing authority of pastor and church on the other. At first a kind of counter-authority to the traditional world emerged. The institutional school was something new, and it developed in opposition to the traditional world. Even the poor school that only taught the three Rs and religion stood in opposition to the traditional behaviour patterns. The school offered the children another interpretation of the world and another model for behaviour. Even the most rudimentary amount of critical reflection connected with the new method had this result. The competition between two interpretations of the world, offered to the individual at an early stage, enabled the individual to assume a critical, artificial attitude towards society. If modernization is the loosening of traditional ties and if these ties are removed by reflection or by new information, then the schools had a modernizing effect; this effect was strongest in the initial phase, in a predominantly agricultural world, because here tradition and modernity stood in sharp opposition to each other. Later, tradition was no longer so traditional, and modernity no longer so modern. Subsequently, other institutions affecting the socialization process and the integration into society such as occupation, class, trade unions, parties and ideologies were to prove stronger than the school.

The school conveyed content, ideas, perhaps even concepts, that connected everyday reality with the realities of culture and the *Zeitgeist*, without requiring the mediation of the church. Even the elimination of illiteracy brought about this effect. Thereby, current and even political affairs penetrated the traditional world, and in this way thoughts and ideas were mobilized. The setting-up of a new counter-authority with its tendency for politicizing had revolu-

[19] W. H. Riehl, *Die bürgerliche Gesellschaft* (1854), pp. 80, 106.

tionary effect in a period of transition. This was independant of the more or less conservative orientation of school policies and teacher training. The school and the teachers were not yet fully integrated into society and state, were not yet subject to an ideology which politically neutralized the modernity of the school and limited its modernizing effect to the economic-technical sphere, or, like the later German nationalism, blocked for a time the democratic implications of modernity. Hence, the school could at first have no stabilizing effect, but rather was dynamic in its results. Mass education was a vehicle for unrest, and because it produced unrest, it was also an object of unrest. It was a particularly superb instrument for modernization, at least for a certain time.

It remains astonishing that it was the conservative states that set this process in motion. Society in Germany at the beginning of the nineteenth century was still much too traditional, and after the middle of the century perhaps too middle-class to initiate modernization through mass education by its own efforts. In this it was different essentially from the Anglo-Saxon world. The state contained an element of the modern educational dictatorship, even when directed against existing society. It had to do so because it had to modernize in order to be able to exist. It created the modern school system in and out of its own interests; but it was not able to retain the potential thereby released under control, despite the great efforts it undertook in this direction. Its own structure, the structure of its ally the church, the independent tendencies of the school and the socially underprivileged teachers, the effect the new institution had on the traditional society, all this prevented the limiting of the school to the goal of releasing economic, technical, and military powers and maintaining the existing political structure. The spirit of the school turned against its initiator and promoter, the preconstitutional and only partially liberalized state. The state bred the very people that revolutionized it. It created the powers that changed it. This was not an accident, it was inevitable.

WAR AND SOCIETY IN THE TENTH CENTURY: THE MALDON CAMPAIGN*

By Eric John, M.A., F.R.Hist.S.

READ 15 OCTOBER 1976

A general study of the effects of the Viking Wars on Anglo-Saxon society is much to be desired. These wars lasted from the last years of the Mercian hegemony to the last months of the life of William the Conqueror. It has been abundantly shown that the English did not catch institutions from the Vikings like a sort of social measles, but common-sense alone suggests that a three hundred years war with little more than one generation's respite must have had consequences. Such a study is far too large for a single paper. What I have sought to do, therefore, is take a single campaign, that culminating in the famous battle of Maldon, which occurred at a moment of intense crisis and to try to set this campaign in a context of the relevant political and military problems of the day, and most of what I have to say relates to the much-dismissed, little studied, but well-evidenced, reign of Æthelred II.

After a generation of peace the Viking raids were renewed within a matter of months of the accession of Æthelred. It is noticeable that amongst the first places they attacked were Southampton[1] and Cheshire,[2] both places protected by early tenth-century burghs. The burghal system had up till now been a resounding success but in the next year the sacking of London cast still more doubt on the credibility of such defences; and this may perhaps have been intended. In 994 Olaf Tryggvason and Swein of Denmark again attacked London and, apparently to their surprise, were unable to take it.[3] This check did not stop them ravaging in Essex, Kent, Sussex and Hampshire.[4] By now Southampton was at their command and it is there that they collected £16,000 tribute. In 988 Watchet had been ravaged,[5] a burgh of the first generation.[6] It is almost as though the

* I have to thank Mr J. Campbell and Dr C. R. Hart for reading and commenting on this paper.

1 *Chronicle*, C, s.a. 980.

2 *Ibid.*

3 *Op. cit.*, s.a. 994.

4 *Ibid.*

5 *Op. cit.*, s.a. 988.

6 *Anglo-Saxon Charters*, ed. A. J. Robertson (Cambridge, 1939), p. 246.

dismantling of the burghal system were a first object of the Vikings. In any case it is clear that the new campaigns were differently directed from the old campaigns the burghal system had been designed to contain. The Vikings, for the first time, did not avoid pitched battles and usually won them. Their attacks were, in the beginning at any rate, directed on the coastal areas and fell overwhelmingly on Wessex and its closest dependencies: the South-West, the old kingdom of Kent, and the East Anglian or East Mercian 'half-kingdom' that had been under the control of the family of Æthelstan 'Half-King', of West Saxon origin, for most of the century.[7] Mercia proper, that is, I take it, the dioceses of Worcester, Hereford and Lichfield, was hardly touched.[8]

According to the C text of the *Chronicle*, after the defeat of Ealdorman Byrhtnoth at Maldon in 991, geld amounting to £10,000 was paid to the Danes to gain peace for the first time. Plummer was right to point out[9] that this is not strictly correct: even the great Ælfred had purchased peace on occasion. But let us not be pedantic. The last mention of money amassed, if not spent, for this purpose is in King Eadred's will[10] nearly half a century earlier. Besides the *scandlice nydgylde* as Archbishop Wulfstan called it[11] was collected on a scale and with a frequency quite unprecedented: £10,000 in 991; £16,000 in 994; £24,000 in 1002; £36,000 in 1007; £48,000 in 1012 rising to the climax of the £80,000-odd pounds paid to Cnut's army. These are only the spectacular occasions: there seems also to have been smaller, perhaps local, tributes. These Vikings were after loot, not homes, and when their ambitions rose with their success it was not a new Danelaw they sought but control of the royal government itself. It was the goose that laid the golden eggs they wanted and a study of Mr Campbell's recent paper to this Society[12] will show why.

I have spoken of 'Vikings' as is customary, as though they were a more or less homogeneous group subsisting through the ages. In fact there is reason to think that the Vikings who attacked the England of Æthelred II were men with more sophisticated training and methods than their predecessors. Up to 991 and the defeat at Maldon the English, it seems to me, expected to win and supposed the defences they possessed were adequate. It is after this defeat that the temper and mood of the English slides into defeatism and division.

[7] *Anglo-Saxon England*, ii (1975), pp. 115–45.

[8] H. M. Chadwick, *Anglo-Saxon Institutions* (Cambridge, 1905), p. 196.

[9] *Two Saxon Chronicles*, ed. C. Plummer, ii (Oxford, 1892), p. 174.

[10] *Select English Historical Documents*, ed. F. E. Harmer (Cambridge, 1914), no. xxi.

[11] *Sermo Lupi ad Anglos*, ed. D. Whitelock (London, 1952), l. 109.

[12] *Transactions of the Royal Historical Society*, 5th series, xxv (1975), pp. 39–54.

The Viking commander at Maldon was Olaf Tryggvason:[13] in 994 Olaf was joined by Swein of Denmark who holds the centre of the stage for the remainder of his life. This unity of command and steadfastness of purpose, this capacity to fight long campaigns that, at first, only paid off handsomely after months or even years, is quite new. We could, therefore, reasonably guess that the governance of the Vikings as well as the English had undergone something of a transformation but we do have a little hard evidence.

Scandinavian tradition, notably the *Jomsvikinga Saga*, makes it clear that about this time important changes in Viking organization and objectives took place. As Mr Hunter Blair put it: '. . . something new and more formidable appeared. This was the highly trained army of professional soldiers whose purpose was not to colonize but to spend their lives in fighting.'[14] The *Saga* tells of the foundation of a remarkable fortress called Jomsborg that has never been found but is believed to stand near the mouth of the Oder. The founder was a Danish Viking called Palna-toki, who cannot certainly be identified outside the *Saga*, though it is possible to connect him and some of his exploits directly or indirectly with real men and real deeds. It is on the other hand quite impossible to extract a viable chronology out of all this and some at least of Palna-toki's career as described in the *Saga* must be fiction. It is the fiction of political myth, however, not the fiction of the adventure story. The *Saga* gives a detailed account of the fantastic fortress Palna-toki constructed at Jomsborg and the ferocious discipline exacted from its garrison. Archaeologists have found four fortresses in Denmark proper that go a long way to

[13] There has been some confusion over the presence or absence of Olaf at this battle. Plummer, *op. cit.*, p. 173, thought that the *Parker Chronicle* confused the events of 991 and 994. The late Professor Campbell, *The Anglo-Saxon Chronicle*, ed. D. Whitelock, D. C. Douglas, and S. I. Tucker (London, 1961), p. 82, showed that the annal, with its reference to Olaf, was meant to stand under the year 991. The treaty, usually cited as II *Æthelred*, names Olaf amongst the Viking leaders and Archbishop Sigeric amongst the English. Liebermann showed conclusively that the treaty must be referred to the year 991, *Die Gesetze der Angelsachsen*, ed. F. Liebermann, iii (Berlin, 1903–16), pp. 149–50. The 994 fighting was still raging at its height in September and Sigeric died late in October. But the treaty says that Sigeric negotiated the terms of the tribute: this chimes in with the *Abingdon Chronicle*, s.a. 991. In 994 the same source says that the bishop of Winchester was the ecclesiastical negotiator. In 994 Olaf became a Christian and Æthelred became his godfather; there is no reference to this in the treaty. In 994 Swein was the most powerful of the Viking leaders: he is not mentioned in the treaty. There is, then, no doubt that Olaf Tryggvason was at Maldon.

[14] P. Hunter Blair, *Introduction to Anglo-Saxon England* (Cambridge, 1956), p. 93. A. S. Napier and W. H. Stevenson, *The Crawford Charters* (Oxford, 1895), pp. 139 *et seq.*, present an English summary of most of the historical evidence that can be extracted from the *Jomsviking Saga*.

confirm the authenticity of the *Saga* here.[15] I entirely agree with Mr Hunter Blair when he suggests that: '... the plan and construction of the fortresses suggests they were built and occupied by military communities of the kind described in the saga of the Jomsvikings'.[16] The aspiring Jomsviking had to be a proved warrior: on admission he had to take an oath that he would avenge his fellow-members as his own brothers: the operations of the feud were suspended: as was the normal pattern of family life—no women were allowed in the fortress and no member of the garrison could have more than three nights away without special leave. What we have here is the ancient *comitatus* made into a new institution by the intensity and permanence of the military life prescribed and what we might call the hardware that enshrined this life. These fortresses are unparalleled anywhere in the early middle ages and compare with those of Rome in her hey-day. It is not surprising that thegns who never spent less than three-quarters of the year at home on their estates were no match for these professionals whose survival depended on the loot they could win.

Articulate Anglo-Saxon opinion offered a different explanation of the English record of consistent failure. According to Archbishop Wulfstan's well-known *Sermon*: '... we have entirely despoiled God's houses inside and out. And the servants of God are everywhere deprived of respect and protection ...'[17] By servants of God Wulfstan meant: 'bishops and abbots, monks and nuns, priests and women under religious vows'[18] and he was referring to the anti-monastic reaction that followed King Edgar's premature death. We cannot dismiss Wulfstan's rhetoric as what Marc Bloch called 'the natural pessimism of sacred oratory'. What appeared to Wulfstan as the golden age of Edgar was far from golden to some: to some indeed it was worse than the Vikings since *they* could be bought off with money which was not true of Archbishop Wulfstan's friends. Before I explain what I mean let me point out that I am not offering an explanation of the Benedictine Reform in political or institutional terms merely, or even any general explanation at all of that complex and ill-understood movement. What I want to point out is the undoubted consequences of King Edgar's ecclesiastical policies that any such explanation will have to take into account. There is really no doubt that these policies affected some members of the landholding classes

[15] *English and Norse Documents relating to the reign of Æthelred the Unready*, ed. M. Ashdown (Cambridge, 1930), p. 186, ll. 35–36. It is a pity that the whole *Saga* is not more accessible to English scholars.

[16] *Loc. cit.*

[17] Ed. D. Whitelock, l. 31.

[18] *English Historical Documents*, ed. D. Whitelock (London, 1955), p. 855, n. 3.

at every level. Indeed if some of Wulfstan's sentiments and concerns were ever translated into action even the thralls were affected, and whatever they gained their masters lost.[19] There can, in any case, be no doubt that some ordinary thegns found their social and economic status reduced.

The 'immense estate at Taunton, which from early times had belonged to the church of Winchester'[20] had in part passed to the Crown before the Benedictine Reform. According to Queen Ælfthryth[21] this meant that some or all of it had been granted out to the King's thegns, who had presumably held by landbook since the Queen speaks of the one in whom she had an interest as relinquishing his *boc*. The thegns were now subject to the bishop. It seems fair to assume that obligations were created or increased and certain that, in place of bookright that granted security of tenure and hereditary succession, the thegns became tenants at will. One of them, Leofric, a man of the highest connections, pleaded grace and favour, and got a new charter that guaranteed him, but not his heirs, against dispossession by Bishop Æthelwold's successors. The implication is that the less favoured tenants were not so guaranteed.

[19] '. . . and poor men are sorely deceived and cruelly defrauded and sold far and wide out of this country into the power of foreigners . . . and the rights of slaves are restricted . . .' ed. D. Whitelock, ll. 43 *et seq.*, to which the version in CCC.201, which if it is not actually by Wulfstan is a contemporary gloss, *Homilies of Wulfstan*, ed. D. Bethuram (Oxford, 1957), p. 23, and reflects the provisions of laws known to be his, Whitelock, *Sermo*, note to l. 48: '... slaves are not allowed to keep what they have gained by toil in their own free time, or what good men have granted them in God's favour', adds point. If the rights of slaves were protected the rights of masters suffered. Wulfstan's *Institutes of Policy*, ed. B. Thorpe, *Ancient Laws*, ii (London, 1840), p. 320, says it is reeves who are the instigators of the injustices castigated in the *Sermo* and by reeves he means principally ealdormen. In VII *Æthelred*, 2.3, Wulfstan says that slaves may be exempt from labour services on the three days special fast the code prescribes *et operetur sibimet quod vult*. VI *Æthelred* 22.1 forbids *worldlicra weorca* on Sundays: these two laws taken together suggest Wulfstan thought that slaves should have holidays from labour services on fasts and festivals but could work on their own account. The reformers seem to have increased the number of festivals to be observed: 'all St. Mary's high festivals shall be worthily observed', VI *Æthelred* 22.2 and the *Handbook of Dates* lists nine of them. Edward the martyr's day was added to the calendar and the fasts of Ember days were revived. It is worth noting that the anti-reforming publicist, Bishop Adalbero of Lâon, accused the reforming monks—he appears to be referring to Abbo of Fleury's writings in particular and Abbo had influence and importance in English reforming circles—of undue sympathy with the labouring classes and tampering with the proper order of society. Unfortunately we have no means of knowing what difference, if any, these concerns and the laws they gave rise to, made.

[20] *Anglo-Saxon Writs*, ed. F. E. Harmer (Manchester, 1952), p. 380, and E. John, *Bulletin of John Rylands Library*, xlvii (1965), pp. 404 *et seq.*

[21] *Writs*, no. 108.

Further insight into the tenurial consequences of King Edgar's support for the monks comes from Worcester. I shall leave aside all mention of the disputed *Altitonantis* charter, CS 1135, in this connection;[22] instead, I shall rely on St Oswald's *Indiculum*, or memorandum, of the liberty of Oswaldslow as Hemming calls it.[23] Professor Galbraith, for once agreeing with Round, unlike most commentators, thinks the *Indiculum*, CS 1136, a forgery.[24] Dr Galbraith's arguments seem to me unconvincing and to some extent to derive their force in advance from their conclusion. He says it is incongruously placed by Hemming with the Domesday documents. This incongruity arises from the fact that: 'the letter was fabricated ten years or more after the Domesday Inquest'. If we ask how he knows the memorandum was fabricated I fear we should be told that it is incongruously placed in Hemming. It seems to me that the *cartula*, of which an abbreviated version was included in Domesday Book itself and which Hemming gave the same title as he did to the memorandum, *Indiculum Libertatis de Oswales Lawes Hundred*, is itself derived from CS 1136, which is thus the source of the Domesday account of Oswaldslow and there is no incongruity, far from it, in its placing in Hemming. The two texts are related in subject-matter and vocabulary[25] but significantly the *cartula* is modern where CS 1136 is antique. *Beneficium* is replaced by *feudum*, terms like *redditiones*, *socarum*, *vicecomes*, and phrases like *ad dominicum victum* occur which are quite inappropriate for the tenth century but essential for the late eleventh. If Dr Galbraith were right then the fabricator of CS 1136 did a unique job in eliminating every modern technical term from his forgery and substituting periphrases of impeccably tenth-century origin. There is not a single word or phrase in CS 1136 that could not, rather does not, belong to the time of Oswald and Edgar. In any case when the record had been made *in autentica regis cartula*, witnessed by the Domesday commissioners, included with the *totius Anglie descriptionibus* in the royal treasury and Domesday Book, which Dr Galbraith has taught us was certainly compiled many fewer than ten years after the Domesday Inquest, what conceivable point was there in fabricating a letter from St Oswald to King Edgar that could have no legal force in Anglo-Norman England, if it ever had any in Anglo-Saxon England? But such a letter from a famous saint might well have helped persuade the King and his agents into giving the state of affairs in Oswaldslow as the church of Worcester said it

[22] The authenticity of the charter is discussed in the Appendix to the present article, p. 192–93 below.

[23] *Hemingi Chartularium Wignorniensis*, ed. T. Hearne (1723), pp. 292–96.

[24] V. H. Galbraith, *E.H.R.*, lxii (1967), pp. 100–01.

[25] E. John, *Land Tenure in Early England* (Leicester, 1960), pp. 142–43.

should be—and the witness of the shire did not disagree—the compelling legal authority it enjoyed after 1086.[26] It seems to me that Oswald's letter is genuine.[27]

The Oswaldslow letter makes it clear there has been a quarrel and that the Bishop has won. The Oswaldslow thegns, like those of Taunton, hold precariously although they have the right to nominate two heirs. Various obligations of tenure are listed in terms that suggest they are either more onerous or simply new. This letter is supplemented by what is probably a nearly complete set of loan charters granted by Oswald. Some of them are strange hybrid documents recording loans for three lives, as the letter does, but otherwise cast in the language of the landbook.[28] Landbooks, it is worth recalling since so many writers on this period do not seem to grasp the point, are granted by kings, and by kings only, 'for ever'. These loans masquerade as landbooks but are in fact episcopal grants for three lives only. In almost every case the services listed are fewer than those in the *Indiculum*. A surprising number of them claim to be granted to relatives or connections of Oswald himself. Consequently it is hard to suppose that they were tenants of the church of Worcester before Oswald became bishop, and it follows that some of them replaced tenants expelled to make way: precisely what the Taunton document promised Leofric will not happen to him. At the other end of the country the *Liber Eliensis* 'gives a clear, though not attractive picture of Bishop Æthelwold'[29] and the lawsuits there recorded, though from a part of the country where the establishment was very much on the side of the monks, suggest good reasons for discontent amongst the smaller landholders.

Most important of all were the great magnates, the ealdormen and king's thegns, who were the prime losers of ecclesiastical patronage on the terms of reformers' notions of abbatial elections and the lords of the disaffected thegns. They must also have borne the brunt of providing for the well-born and 'lascivious' clerks together with their off-spring whom the reformers expelled by the dozen. These

[26] Dr Galbraith, *loc. cit.*, points out that the *Indiculum* was drawn up in tripartite form and copies deposited in Winchester and Canterbury. He remarks rightly that procedure was sometimes followed for wills and then makes what seem to me unnecessary difficulties by pointing to the absence of the essentials of a will in the *Indiculum*. But the letter does not purport to be a will and this tripartite form was used for other documents than wills—the object was to attain greater security and the motivation was not in the ordinary sense legal. *Orbis Brittaniae*, p. 260, n. 3.

[27] I do not understand why Mr Sawyer ignores CS 1136 in his paper on the Worcester Archive, *op. cit.*

[28] Land Tenure, p. 129 *et seq.*

[29] *Liber Eliensis*, ed. E. O. Blake, Royal Historical Society Camden Series, xcii (London, 1962), p. xii.

men had been provided for by the exercise of family patronage and were at one stroke cast back upon the family for support and maintenance. If these men accepted conversion then presumably their families still had to be provided for and the evidence suggests the reforming monk-bishops felt little responsibility for them. Scholars have jibbed at facing the consequences of Edgar's reforms and treated them as though they were a storm in the tea-cup of Barsetshire proportions. But compared with the confrontation of Edgar's new men and the old brigade, the tensions between Archdeacon Grantly and Bishop Proudie were very small beer.

Obviously we cannot quantify the effects of the reform because we have not enough evidence. But this is a period in which evidence of anything is rare and all of it comes from sources favourable to, or emanating from, the reforming churchmen, and is concerned to play down the discontent and totally reject its justice. In such conditions there is really too much evidence surviving from too many and too significant parts of the country to justify minimizing it. Even the sources we have, favourable to the monks as they are, cannot conceal what hard men Æthelwold and Oswald were. There were, too, far more new liberties than there were records. I have cited evidence from three reformed communities, Winchester, Ely and Worcester but there were more than forty altogether. There must have been many shires south of the Trent with disaffected thegns, unhappy exclerks, and wrathful families. What is more, at the top of society at least, the cost of the new order was neither fairly distributed nor equally borne.

We must at this point look at the shipsokes, the culmination on one level of the defensive plans against the Vikings and on another a buttress for the monks against their enemies. Perhaps, also, on a rather different level one of those brilliant pieces of political sleight of hand supposed to kill two birds with one stone that do incalculable damage to the cause it was meant to promote. The so-called Laws of Henry I remark incidentally that England was divided into shipsokes.[30] The division of the country into triple hundreds required to provide ships and crews are first recorded in a source of unimpeachable integrity in Æthelred II's fifth code, generally believed to date from 1008. But the letter of Bishop Æthelric of Sherborne shows that these shipsokes were earlier than this and the late Dr Harmer gathered impressive supporting evidence.[31] Bishop Æthelric reveals that all, or at least most, bishops were given such a liberty together with attendant responsibilities· It may be questioned whether only bishops got these liberties since the original endowment of Per-

[30] *Leges Henrici Primi*, ed. L. J. Downer (Oxford, 1972), p. 96.
[31] Writs, pp. 266–68.

shore was a triple hundred in Worcestershire that is not known before the reformers got to work on founding or reforming it.[32] It may be that abbots, as well as bishops, had such liberties.

These shipsokes served first a military function. It is reasonable to connect Edgar's command of the fleet they provided him with and the peaceful character of his reign, and more interestingly with the peculiar form of homage done to him by Scottish princelings after his coronation. They also made the holder of the liberty, the head of the soke, the possessor of *haute justice* and the lord of the military tenants. The ealdorman and his subordinates, called in the sources exactors, lost the right of entry into the liberty and the power to recoup their losses in the guise of fines for evasion of service. It was long ago pointed out[33] that in Edgar's reign the ealdorman of Mercia and the ealdorman of East Anglia, and the ealdorman, or earl, of Northumbria, were vice-regents of their respective areas of authority under the king. They certainly had other ealdormen subject to them. The first *Life* of St Oswald implies that this vice-regal position goes back to the time of Æthelstan,[34] and it looks very much as though the system was a result of the comparatively sudden enlarging of the kingdom. The most important region was what had once been the heart of Offa's Mercia, the land between the Humber and the Thames. This was divided by Edgar's day into two: the western portion, that is the sees of Worcester, Hereford and Lichfield, which is usually called Mercia in the sources and the eastern portion called, misleadingly, East Anglia in our text books but by contemporaries, more revealingly, eastern Mercia.[35] Both these sensitive half-kingdoms seem to have been ruled by families with strong West Saxon connections.[36] However, for reasons I do not understand, King Edgar greatly preferred the eastern to the west Mercian dynasty.

It seems to have been in Edgar's reign that the diocese of Lindsey and that of Dorchester were combined into the unwieldy amalgam ruled until the Conqueror's day from a small town on its southern extremity. When the abbey of Ramsey, which was so closely attached to the East Mercian establishment,[37] was a going concern, its first

[32] *English Place Name Society*, iv, A. Mawer and F. M. Stenton, *The Place-Names of Worcestershire* (Cambridge, 1927), p. 183.

[33] H. M. Chadwick, *Anglo-Saxon Institutions* (Cambridge, 1905), p. 178, n. i: E. John, *Orbis Brittaniae*, p. 221–22: Hart, *op. cit.*, p. 121.

[34] *Historians of the Church of York*, Rolls Series (London, 1879), ed. J. Raine, i, p. 428.

[35] *Ibid.*, p. 444.

[36] Hart, *op. cit.*, p. 116 and *The Early Charters of Northern England and the North Midlands* (Leicester, 1975), p. 260 and p. 299.

[37] C. R. Hart, 'Eadnoth, First Abbot of Ramsey', *Proceedings of the Cambridge Antiquarian Society*, lvi–lvii (1964), pp. 61–67.

abbot, Eadnoth became bishop of the new monster diocese, and the see remained a Ramsey perk until 1049. Thus eastern influence was pushed right to the boundaries of the west Mercian sees of Lichfield and Worcester. But Worcester was itself held by the east Mercian, Oswald. If he were not related to Ealdorman Æthelwine of East Mercia, and no evidence survives that he was, he was certainly related to one of Æthelwine's right-hand men, Æthelstan Manessune,[38] members of whose family dominated Ramsey and Dorchester for generations. Bishop Oswald also got a liberty, unless we are to suppose he was exceptionally underprivileged compared with his colleagues, whose geographical location deserves study. Oswaldslow completely surrounded Ealdorman Ælfhere's *burh* at Worcester. If we may count the first abbot of Pershore, Foldbriht, as part of Oswald's political connection, then half of Worcestershire was quite out of the ealdorman of Western Mercia's control. St Oswald's position in the ancient kingdom of the Hwicce was very solidly based and the loans of land he gave to his relatives cannot have reduced his advantage in the balance of power. If we turn to the east and to Oswald's 'foundation' at Ramsey it is a very different political story. No doubt the monks lived a very different life from the old ways, unless the first *Life* of Oswald represents the view of its author and a tiny minority of the monks only. None the less promotions were kept strictly within the family. So long as he lived Ealdorman Æthelwine enjoyed the direct power of an *advocatus* in total contravention of the commands of the *Regularis Concordia*. The great, if lesser, abbey of Ely[39] was also refounded or revived on Æthelwine's patch by St Æthelwold himself. It got a great liberty of five and half hundreds at Wicklow[40] but unlike Oswaldslow, no sooner was it granted than it was farmed out to Ealdorman Æthelwine for a modest pension. Ealdorman Ælfhere would, no doubt, have found the erection of Oswaldslow tolerable on such terms. There is more that could be said but this is sufficient for my purpose.

When Edgar died and was succeeded by his eldest son Edward, the candidate of the monastic party, the reformers must bear some of the blame for the unpopularity of a young man whom they had treated as illegitimate until necessity compelled a change of front.[41] A great deal of bitterness must have been left behind from top to bottom of the landholding classes. Some monasteries in western

[38] C. R. Hart, 'Eadnoth, First Abbott of Ramsey', *Proceedings of the Cambridge Antiquarian Society*, lvi–lvii (1964), p. 61.

[39] *Ibid.*, p. 66.

[40] *Orbis Brittaniae*, pp. 210–33, and J. Pope, *England Before the Conquest*, ed. P. Clemoes and K. Hughes (Cambridge, 1971), pp. 85–113.

[41] *Orbis Brittaniae*, pp. 271–76.

Mercia were destroyed and some fell at least partly into the hands of local kindred groups.[42] Then came the renewal of the Viking attacks and these were directed precisely at Wessex—where we may reasonably conjecture there were some, perhaps a great many, disaffected thegns—and East Anglia where there were not only disaffected thegns but thegns alienated from their immediate lords. It is difficult to believe that western Mercia's ambiguous role in the wars of Æthelred's reign was solely due to its ealdorman's knavish tricks or that Æthelred's lack of success against the Vikings was solely due to ill counsel.

The sources are agreed that the raids were renewed in Æthelred II's reign and not earlier.[43] It is very easy to suppose that from the renewal of the raids to the succession of Cnut the tale is one of unimpeded Viking success and unrelieved English defeat. In fact thirty-four years passed before the flight of Æthelred and the acceptance of Swein as king of the English. Fourteen of those years passed before Swein appeared in England in 994[44] and it is significant that we immediately hear tales of treachery by English landholders in his interest.[45] For the next twenty years the tale is the same, Viking invasions and English treachery, until Swein ultimately wins all only to die straightaway. In other words we have a series of Viking invasions augmented by what amounted to an endemic civil war. Nor were all the divisions on one side. In 994 Swein arrived accompanied by Olaf Tryggvason, usually reckoned to be a Jomsviking leader.[46] But a year later Olaf became a Christian, accepted King Æthelred as his godfather, and never fought against him again. But he could and did fight against Swein. Just before Swein's moment of triumph, forty-five shiploads of Vikings led by another Jomsviking, Thorkell the Tall, left him to fight for Æthelred.[47] Until Cnut was firmly established on the English throne Thorkel continued to play an independent and equivocal role in English affairs. It is quite clear that the Viking progress in Æthelred's reign was much slower and more tortuous than is commonly supposed. The contrary impression is largely derived from an over-reliance on the C text of the *Chronicle*, or the *Abingdon Chronicle* to give its traditional and useful name.

The *Abingdon Chronicle* gives a picture of the reign as one of unrelieved gloom conveyed very skilfully in a narrative a good deal

42 *Life of Oswald*, pp. 443 *et seq.*, J. Stevenson, *Chronicon Monasterii de Abingdon*, Rolls Series (London, 1858), i, p. 357.

43 *Life* of Oswald, p. 455, and *cf. Chronicle*, C, s.a. 980 and D, s.a. 981.

44 *Chronicle*, C, s.a. 994.

45 *Anglo-Saxon Wills*, ed. D. Whitelock (Cambridge, 1930), no. xvi, 2.

46 *Epitome of the Sagas of the Kings of Norway*, Ashdown, *Documents*, p. 146.

47 *Crawford Charters*, p. 139, *Writs*, p. 574.

more artful than appears at first reading. It is evident that the annals for the earlier part of the reign were written when defeat had become a habit. The annal for 991, which records amongst other things the English defeat at Maldon, also says that this was the year it was *first* decided to pay tribute to the Danes, so its author plainly knows the shape of things to come. In fact only one further payment of tribute is recorded, 994, before 1002. Not surprisingly the Chronicler presents Maldon as simply an English defeat. 'In this year Ipswich was ravaged and very soon afterwards Ealdorman Byrhtnoth was killed at Maldon'.[48] Miss Ashdown was right to say: 'The *Chronicle* does not suggest that the battle was considered of the first importance'.[49] But the *Abingdon Chronicle* does not tell the whole story.

The *Winchester Chronicle*, that is the *Parker Chronicle* or A text, reveals that Olaf Tryggvason came to Ipswich with ninety-three ships having first ravaged Folkestone, Sandwich, and their environs *en route*. The text of the treaty made with the Vikings after the Maldon defeat has also survived.[50] The *Abingdon Chronicle* says that the tribute was paid on the advice of Archbishop Sigeric of Canterbury and the Winchester text shows why he should be involved. The treaty itself shows that two West Saxon ealdormen, Ælfric and Æthelweard, were the main English agents involved, and none of the sources I have so far examined suggest anything to explain why a Hampshire and a Devon magnate should take the lead here. Under the year 988, however, the *Abingdon Chronicle* tells us that Watchet was ravaged and Goda, a Devonshire thegn, was killed. The first *Life* of St Oswald, usually thought to have been written by Byrhtferth of Ramsey and a source at least as near to the events it records as any text of the *Chronicle*, is more illuminating. It gives no dates but it records the taking of Watchet and the death of one Stremwold, a *miles fortissimus*.[51] Florence of Worcester, conflating information from a text of the *Chronicle* with the *Life*, adds the name of Goda, here described as a satrap, to that of Stremwold, showing that he took the *Life* to be referring to the taking of Watchet in 988.[52] The *Life* goes on to say that after a few months had passed there was another great battle in the east of this famous region—he means what he calls East Anglia or Eastern Mercia elsewhere

[48] S.a. 991.

[49] *Documents*, p. 3.

[50] II Æthelred in A. J. Robertson, *The Laws of the Kings of England from Edmund to Henry I* (Cambridge, 1925), pp. 57–63. Not all this text is an authentic part of the treaty.

[51] *Op. cit.*, pp. 455 *et seq.*

[52] *Florentii Wignorniensis Chronicon ex Chronicis*, ed. B. Thorpe (London, 1848), i, p. 148.

—*in quo primatum pugnae tenuit gloriosus dux Byrihtnodus cum commilitionibus suis*. Then Byrhtferth goes on to describe Byrhtnoth's appearance and to explain how he was 'supported by the manifold faithfulness of the Lord since he was worthy'. The tenor of the passage suggests that this battle took place only a few months after the Devonshire affair, not like Maldon three years later. Further, where the *Abingdon Chronicle* without actually saying the English were defeated in 988 suggests this was so, the *Life* is quite explicit that the English won and the Vikings withdrew. It conveys there was some sort of connection between Byrhtnoth's battle and the Viking defeat in Devonshire and that Byrhtnoth was supported by God as he deserved. Thus we should expect Byrhtferth to be telling us of a victory won by Byrhtnoth but he suddenly concludes his passage by telling us that many English and Danes were killed, including Byrhtnoth, whose companions then fled. Thus the passage concludes with what can only be a reference to the battle of Maldon, 991 having begun with a battle at or near Watchet in 988. For good measure we are then given an obituary of St Dunstan, who died in fact 19 May 988:[53] Byrhtferth relates his death to this martial activity and seems to mean that he died after the battle of Maldon. We can make some sense out of this extraordinary passage.

Byrhtferth is an author whose reach occasionally outdistances his grasp. In particular he essays a trendy pre-Gregorian ideology, tricked out in words and themes familiar neither to many of his contemporaries nor to his modern readers. Here the key passage is the sentence I quoted in Latin. What did Byrhtferth mean by *primatus pugnae*? This is usually taken to mean he commanded the army but the passage cannot be translated coherently if this were so. Byrhtnoth shares the *primatus* with his fellow-soldiers so it cannot refer to his rank as general. The only sense I can make from it is that Byrhtferth means us to know that Byrhtnoth and his companions won the battle that took place shortly after the Watchet victory. This isn't conventional Latin of any period but Byrhtferth is thinking of the English as having the supremacy of the battlefield (this is the battle after which Dunstan died, I believe), and the battle in which Byrhtnoth had, as he deserved (he was a leader of the pro-monastic party) the favour of God, a passage that makes nonsense if referred to the description of the Maldon defeat that follows. If both the battles Byrhtnoth took part in took place at Maldon most of the confusion is explicable enough. The *Life* is not alone in supposing that Maldon, 991, was the climax of a campaign or that there were two battles at Maldon. Much the fullest account

[53] *Ibid.*, p. 148.

of the Maldon business is to be found in the *Liber Eliensis*[54] and to this we must now turn.

The extant version cannot be much younger than two centuries after the battle of Maldon[55] which makes it no more, if no less, than a tradition. It needs to be remembered that the *Liber* drew on a mass of much earlier written materials so that it would be dangerous to assume that all of them have been identified. We must look at what it tells us and I believe we must take that information very seriously because quite a lot of it can be corroborated from other sources and there is little evidence of myth or myth-making. It also needs pointing out that the story makes sense. We are told that the Danish invasions erupted again in several localities and that the magnates of other provinces chose Byrhtnoth to lead them—much as the *Life* of Oswald has it. Byrhtnoth heard the Vikings had landed at Maldon, he met them there, beat them, and sent the remnants scuttling back to where they came from: he, himself, went to Northumbria. If my reading of the *Life* is correct, again the two sources are in virtual agreement and entire independence. In the fourth year after this the Vikings came again (it is important here that no sources speak of any Viking activity in 989 or 990) and the leaders are named, and named accurately. The same names are given by Florence of Worcester, who took them from the text of the treaty.[56] Florence could be the source of the *Liber Eliensis* here but I do not believe that he is. Byrhtnoth hears of their arrival—they are seeking revenge—in the North and hurries down to meet them, being unwilling to yield an inch of territory: as well he might not be since he and probably the majority of his companions were major landholders in eastern England. On the way he arrived at the abbey of Ramsey and sought hospitality for himself and his men. The Abbot would only cater for Byrhtnoth himself and seven of his men so Byrhtnoth rejected his offer and went to Ely, where the abbot was more forthcoming. In return Byrhtnoth left them a substantial legacy of landed property. To anyone familiar with sources of this kind it will come as no surprise that Ely's windfall is the point of the story to which the rest is merely the legacy's *Sitz in Leben*. The estates are listed and correctly described. Now the Ramsey tradition, entirely independently of any Ely source, tells much the same story, ruefully regretting what was lost and claiming that

[54] *Liber Eliensis*, pp. 133–36.

[55] *Ibid.*, p. xlviii. The author of the account says specifically he is using *historiae* in the English tongue: I do not believe it can be shown that the well-known poem, *Maldon*, is one of them.

[56] II Æthelred and *Florence*, i, p. 149, and Plummer, *Two Chronicles*, ii, p. 173.

Byrhtnoth gave them a single gift of land.[57] It is inconceivable that two late traditions should chime together as the Ely and Ramsey sources do if the traditions were legends. Fairy tales from different and later sources do not corroborate each other.

After what is plainly the point of his story the Ely writer sends Byrhtnoth into battle at Maldon. The tactics are briefly and plausibly described. The description tallies in places with that of the well-known vernacular poem on the battle and some scholars have supposed that the poem was composed, or at any rate known, at Ely. But in the last substantial study and edition of the poem, that of the late Professor E. V. Gordon, it is pointed out that the Ely account differs quite markedly from the poem, and in my opinion at least as good a case can be made out for supposing the poem to have come from Ramsey as from Ely. The abbot of Ely hears the outcome of the battle and he and some monks go to the battlefield and remove Byrhtnoth's headless body, the Vikings having taken the head with them. We have the best of testimonies to Byrhtnoth's burial at Ely, his widow's will,[58] which, moreover, does not survive in an Ely text. The body, still headless, was still there in the eighteenth century[59] where it still bore traces of *post mortem* decapitation. Thus the Ely tradition, too, thought the battle in 991 the climax of something that started three years or so earlier and that the English campaign was initially successful. There is only one major detail entirely without corroboration and that is the *Liber*'s claim that Byrhtnoth was ealdorman of Northumbria, not Essex.

All the books say that Byrhtnoth was ealdorman of Essex, usually without citing sources. The fact, if fact it is, depends on a single source, written at least a century after Byrhtnoth's death, Florence of Worcester. Now Florence, for this part of his chronicle, had a version of the Anglo-Saxon Chronicle, the *Life* of Oswald, the text of the treaty that followed the English defeat in 991, and if Dr Gordon's account of the language of the MS is acceptable—it certainly is to me—probably the vernacular poem on Maldon too.[60] If Florence got his claim that Byrhtnoth was ealdorman of Essex from his annals then he is probably correct but it seems to me that he probably based his assertion on the poem.

[57] *Chronicon Abbatiae Rameseiensis*, Rolls Series (London, 1886), ed. W. D. Macray, pp. 116–17.

[58] *Wills*, no. xv taken from B.L., Harley Charter 43, C.4 a Bury charter. The only point on which the *Liber Eliensis* can be shown to be wrong is the name of the reigning abbot, for which Dr Blake offers an explanation, *ibid.*, p. 422.

[59] *The Battle of Maldon*, ed. E. V. Gordon (London, 1937), p. 21 and *Liber Eliensis*, p. 136, n. 1.

[60] Gordon, *Maldon*, p. 33.

Everyone agrees that the poem is nearly contemporary[61] and in line 69 the English army is described as 'the flower of the East Saxons'. Florence may well have made the reasonable assumption that this implied that the leader of the East Saxon *fyrd* was the ealdorman of Essex. Byrhtnoth came from this part of the world, most of his property lay in the area and his leading vassals would in all probability be of eastern provenance themselves. But first of all what was meant by Essex in 991? Certainly a much wider area than either the modern or medieval shire of Essex[62] and at least one of the flower of the East Saxon *fyrd* was the descendant of a Mercian ealdorman.[63] Byrhtnoth had for most of his career been a right-hand man, and subordinate of the local half king, Æthelwine. Now the poem also proves he had a connection with Northumbria since he had a Northumbrian hostage who fought with him.[64] The curious episode of Byrhtnoth's arrival at Ramsey certainly suggests he was coming down from the North. It would not be difficult to see how and why Byrhtnoth became earl of Northumbria. The Edgarian earl had a Danish name and disappears about the time of the crisis over Edward the Martyr's succession. Byrhtnoth may well have been promoted to one of the three super shires: broad acres and vassals in eastern England would no more come amiss to a man who aspired to rule Northumbria in the southern interest than the lands and vassals of the church of Worcester did to the northern archbishops.[65] In the end I prefer to believe what an Ely monk said about one of his abbey's greatest benefactors whose memory was still green centuries later, to a maker of annals whose motives we do not yet understand.

Thus if we base our account of Maldon on the *Life* of Oswald and the *Liber Eliensis* taken together then it is apparent that the English defeat at Maldon has to be taken in connection with the English success of 988, for which the Viking raid of 991 was a comeback. Moreover it may have been a desperate come-back if the papal letter

[61] The total absence of the defeatist tone of the later sources for Æthelred's reign; the fact that the poet did not know the name of the Viking leaders, even the famous Olaf Tryggvason (it is true that the poem is incomplete but the central section of the poem would work much more easily if he had been able to use names for the Vikings as he could for the English); as well as the fact that within a few years no one was likely greatly to care who fell or who fled from Maldon, suggest that the impression is pretty solidly based.

[62] *Orbis Brittaniae*, p. 222 *et seq.*

[63] *Maldon*, ll. 211 *et seq.* Hart, *Charters of Northern England*, p. 328, for Ælfwine's kindred. He was a nephew of Ealdorman Ælfhere of Mercia, the enemy of the monks.

[64] *Maldon*, ll. 265 *et seq.*

[65] Earlship and ealdormanship in relation to Byrhtnoth and Thored is discussed in the Appendix to the present article, p. 193–95 below.

of John XV, JL/3840, is authentic.[66] This letter says the Pope has heard of discord between the duke of Normandy and King Æthelred. It is not clear whether they had actually fought but Duke Richard's tolerance of the use of his ports as Viking bases was certainly at the bottom of the discord. The Pope sent a legate, who arrived in Normandy, Christmas 990 and a treaty of peace was made 1 March 991 between Norman and English plenipotentiaries. The terms are general but would preclude—if they were observed—thc use of Normandy as a Viking base. England had already been free of raids for two years, and this I have suggested was due to Byrhtnoth's successes in the field. Presumably something, either an English expedition that has gone entirely unrecorded which seems to me improbable, or simply the credibility of English arms established by Byrhtnoth, had persuaded Duke Richard to come to terms. No doubt the Pope reminded him that if he wanted to be accepted as part of Christendom—and as a powerful vassal very much more involved in the West Frankish kingdom than our text-books tell us that was important to him—he could not be the ally of pagans against Christians. But whatever Richard's motives he made an alliance only a few months before the Vikings re-appeared in Kent. It looks very much as though for Olaf and his Vikings it was now or never and equally probable that had Byrhtnoth won the story of the reign of Æthelred would have been very different.

Thus Maldon was more than a local encounter but a battle whose participants had purposes and connections covering a large part of England, and on whose outcome much depended. It is on this view intelligible that its result should have led to a Kentish archbishop and two South-Western magnates undertaking peace negotiations and advocating the payment of a general tribute. On a wider front we must be on our guard against the deceptive picture painted by the *Abingdon Chronicle* in the light of the aftermath of Maldon and its author's general pessimism.

Abingdon was after all St Æthelwold's first foundation and the cradle of the reform movement[67] and its chronicler is not going to admit that the epidemic of treachery and mutual mistrust he so vividly conveys owed anything to the excesses of the reformers, let alone that St Æthelwold himself must bear some of the responsibility for the miseries of the times. Nor did he care to spoil or complicate

[66] *Memorials of St Dunstan*, Rolls Series (London, 1874), pp. 397–98. Stubbs noted the exceptional form of this bull, JL/3840, and contented himself with citing Jaffé to the effect that it was authentic. It is very exceptional in form and a pedantic form-critic would reject it out of hand, but common-sense would ask what conceivable motive would anyone have had for forging it?

[67] F. M. Stenton, *Early History of Abingdon* (Oxford, 1913), p. 7.

his story by insisting that the Danish success was something less than the triumphant progress he describes. English victories and Danish dissensions were of little importance in the hindsight of Swein's triumph. There is, moreoever, a lot more to the Maldon business than he tells us.

The Maldon campaign was a turning-point in the history of the times. Up to then the English, I think, expected to win. There is no Abingdon defeatism in either the *Life* of Oswald or the poem. Sometimes they did win. It looks as though resistance to the Danes was led by the leaders of the monastic party, of whom Byrhtnoth, now pretty senior, was perhaps the most able-bodied. He was an able man without hesitation, successful, rich, pro-monastic, religious, and very much *persona grata* to a source like the *Life* of Oswald. But with his death and defeat the scene changed. Immediately two West Saxon magnates inaugurate the new policy of paying tribute and an era of feeble defiance alternating with the craven payment of protection money in escalating sums. With Byrhtnoth, too, went the pro-monastic aristocracy. It is possible to find the kinsfolk of Byrhtnoth and Æthelwine in the eleventh-century sources, but they are no longer major figures in the Establishment, if they are members of the Establishment at all.[68] When the wars were over, as they effectively were with the accession of Cnut, England is a world of new men with new interests. The Establishment that was overthrown in 1066 was not one with very deep roots in English society, though we need much more prosopographical research to determine how deep-rooted, how old, that Establishment was. But to some extent it goes back to the initial success and terminal failure of the Maldon campaign.

King Æthelred himself may well have been ineffective but he was hardly ill-advised in spite of his nickname. Such policy options as he had he pursued, and if he failed in the end, he had his successes. If the papal bull of John XV is genuine as it is generally held to be Æthelred took some action against the French Danelaw, Normandy, which the Vikings were using as their base, before Christmas 990. Thus he tried to deny this important piece of coastline to the Vikings

[68] Dr Hart, *Anglo-Saxon England*, 2, p. 116, writes: 'Æthelstan "Half King" at the height of his power governed in virtual autonomy a province the size of Normandy, and owned in addition extensive estates outside his earldom . . . nevertheless his family was completely bereft of influence before the end of the century.' And p. 135 notes, too, the importance of the death of Byrthnoth and Æthelwine as turning points in the history of the reign. When the prosopographical studies, so necessary for the increase of knowledge of this crucial period, get under way, they will need to be based on the prodigious labours of Dr Hart on the source materials of Eastern England, to be found in the books and articles cited in this paper.

and after his marriage to the Norman princess, Emma, in 1002, he certainly secured his objective. The fateful connection between England and Normandy had begun and Æthelred had secured for the house of Cerdic its last and most reliable allies. He tried with some success to divide his enemies. He certainly back-pedalled on Edgar's way with monastic patronage and contrived in doing so not to lose the support of the monks. The traditions of some of the greatest houses, supplemented by Æthelred's charters, show that the local great families re-gained some of their influence. The abbots, who regularly witness Edgar's charters with precedence over the ealdormen, are demoted, sometimes excluded, for a time. Although they crept back soon enough they never re-gained their old status. The King used all the traditional military means, the *burh* and the *shipfyrd*, and even the *Abingdon Chronicle* doesn't blame him for the subsequent debacles.

The foundations of West Saxon power, laid by a series of rulers from Ælfred to Edgar, were no longer adequate. The Vikings barred from the Continent by the Saxon rulers of East Francia and excluded from England by the deployment of *burh* and shipsoke, could only make a come-back by turning themselves into an utterly professional, basically mercenary, army. In their turn the English kings found the mecessary counter-measures, the greater and greater reliance on armies of mercenaries paid for by the first national land tax since the palmy days of the Carolingians: and it was Æthelred who set the process in motion. In the process the English acquired a new Establishment, including no fewer than three royal kindred groups, with a new outlook. At the same time the old provincial divisions of Wessex and Mercia and so on were greatly weakened. Excessively insular policies were not possible: no English government could afford to ignore what was happening in Scandinavia, Flanders and Normandy. I suspect instability was built into the new system though more work on the landholding classes is needed to make sure. If that instability was cured for ever by the events of 1066 it begins at Maldon. The Norman Conquest and the settlement that follows it will never be understood until the events and social structure of the intervening period have been adequately investigated.

APPENDIX

I. *The authenticity of the Altitonantis Charter*

I devoted an elaborate and lengthy study to the *Altitonantis* Charter, *C*[*artularium*] *S*[*axonicum*], ed. W. de G. Birch (London, 1885–93), iii, no. 1135, suggesting that an authentic charter underlay this obvious fabrication, and seeking to identify some of it, *BJRL*, xli (1958), pp. 53 *et seq.* Professor P. H. Sawyer, *Tenth-Century Studies*, ed. D. Parsons (London, 1975), 'The Worcester Archive', pp. 85–87, repeating the same point made by Professor V. H. Galbraith, *English Historical Review*, lxxii (1967), pp. 100 *et seq.*, and Professor M. Deansley, *The Pre-Conquest Church in England* (London, 1961), p. 318, n. i, preferred to suppose CS 1135 a total fabrication because it was not included in Hemming's Cartulary. Only Dr Galbraith, however, took into account Dr N. R. Ker's demonstration, *Essays Presented to F. M. Powicke* (Oxford, 1948), pp. 49 *et seq.*, that Hemming's Cartulary is really two separate cartularies, the first being compiled very shortly after 1000. He suggested that the effect of Dr Ker's discovery 'is to enhance the reliability of those charters found in Tib. i (that is the pre-Conquest cartulary to which the late Professor Finberg gave the more elegant name of *Liber Wignorniensis*) and to deepen our suspicions regarding the pre-Conquest charters not found in Tib. i', *op. cit.*, p. 100. Archive provenance is, in my opinion, only one factor to be taken into account and can never be a substitute for an examination of the text formula by formula. I do not believe medieval filing methods were any more error-proof than modern ones and it will not do to suppose that the absence of a document from a cartulary where one would expect it to be filed proves either deliberate and significant omission or the non-existence of the unfiled document at the date of the cartulary's compilation. In the case of the two Oswaldslow documents, however, special problems arise. It is true that charters not apparently forged that 'ought' to have been in the *Liber Wignorniensis* are omitted, Ker, *op. cit.*, p. 69, n. i, but CS 1135 and CS 1136 are such important documents casual omission does not seem probable. CS 1136 is, of course, included in the Domesday material in Tib. ii and I have argued above that Galbraith and Round were wrong in rejecting the otherwise near-unanimous opinion that CS 1136 is authentic. But CS 1136 is not included in the *Liber*—nor does this most-discussed of all the documents connected with St Oswald get a mention in Mr Sawyer's essay on the Worcester Archive. The *Liber* is not primarily concerned with the claims and counter-claims of the church of Worcester and the Crown but with the claims of the church of Worcester upon its tenants. It is noticeable that Oswaldslow is not mentioned in the *Liber* though the shipsokes, of which Oswaldslow was only one, must antedate the *Liber*. The latest possible date for dividing of England into shipsokes is 1008. I do not know of any major attempt to call out the sea-fyrd after 1008 and after the inauguration of the *heregeld* as a regular tax in 1012 immunity from the collectors of the geld must have been one of the most important privileges conferred by the liberty, yet CS 1135, whilst it prohibits the intrusion of secular 'exactors' into the liberty never mentions the geld. I suggested, *art. cit.*, that an important clue to the reasons for the fabrication of the *Altitonantis* charter was its implied claim that (a) Oswald ejected the clerks from Worcester in 964, and (b) that Wynsige was made prior in the same year. Wynsige had been priest of one of the principal Worcester churches, St Helen's. The status of this church, and all the other 'churches, lands, tithes, burial-dues, as well as other ecclesiastical customs or perquisites' that were then transferred to the right of the monks had long been in dispute by the year

1092, when the aged St Wulfstan came to a definitive settlement with the community, *Hemming*, pp. 527 *et seq*. The settlement was the work of a committee of arbitration, appointed by St Wulfstan and headed by the monks' leader, the Prior, and the Bishop's representative, the Archdeacon. They agreed that Oswald had established monks at Worcester in 969 but that no prior was appointed for three years. This the community had evidently disputed since Florence of Worcester s.a. 969 says that in this year Oswald established monks in the cathedral and also appointed the first prior Wynsige. Florence claims he had Oswald's own testimony for all this. The implications are made clear by Wulfstan's acceptance of the fact that Oswald conceded to Wynsige 'and to all his successors the priors of this church, namely that no archdeacon should insert himself into matters concerning the clerks or churches of the monks: the prior, just as high dean of the bishop, was to pay (direct) to the bishop (what was due) on behalf of these churches.' In other words the dispute was an early example of a type of litigation that was a common feature of twelfth-century ecclesiastical life, the attempt of monastic communities to claim privilege and exemption from the ordinary jurisdiction of bishop and archdeacon. The settlement does not say when the dispute began, only that it was of long-standing. The claim that the cathedral was purged of clerks in 969 and that Wynsige's appointment as prior coincided precisely with the introduction of monks was based on two doctored Oswald loan charters, CS 1243, which adds to a commonplace Oswald charter of 969 the sentence that it was witnessed by Wynsige and all the monks at Worcester, and CS 1298, a loan charter of 974 that calls Wynsige *decanus*. The title of dean clearly echoes the claim of 1092 that the prior should be high dean and that the archdeacon and any other dean should have no rights over the community's churches. But CS 1243—which is certainly doctored—and CS 1298—which could be genuine (just) but is also doctored, I believe—are both found in the *Liber Wignorniensis*, so that in some form the dispute had started before the composition of the *Liber* and had already produced fabricated documents. Thus from before the composition of the *Liber* to 1092 when the date got definitive acceptance the monks had contended that 969 was the date of the monachization of the cathedral and that Wynsige was appointed prior in the same year. CS 1135 agrees that Wynsige was prior in the same year that the monks came to Worcester but puts all this five years earlier in 964. I cannot believe that the fabricated portions of CS 1135 could have been added once the date 969 had become a basic proposition of the monks' case for independence or exemption, and 969 was the monks' date from before the compilation of the *Liber* to the definitive settlement in 1092. I can only explain the date 964 by supposing that it is the genuine date for the conversion of Worcester, and the witness-lists of the loan charters offer some support here. It is easy to explain why the monks altered the date of the conversion. Knowledge of the Ramsey material, notably the first Life of Oswald, meant that Wynsige's inconvenient period of training at Ramsey could not be ignored, and Ramsey was not founded until 969. (Eadmer, in his *Vita Oswaldi*, deliberately informs us that Wynsige's stay at Ramsey was a short one.) It is hardly surprising that no version of the *Altitonantis* charter was included in the *Liber*. When I wrote about CS 1135 originally, Edgar's reference in the preamble to an Irish expedition he had successfully made seemed highly implausible. In view of recent work on the Norse kingdoms of Dublin and York one can no longer dismiss this passage with the same confidence.

II. *Earlship and ealdormanship: Byrhtnoth and Thored*

The poem normally calls Byrhtnoth *earl* but in l. 218 Ealhelm is called *ealdorman* (of Mercia). This may be significant. Before the reign of Cnut the title *earl* is reserved for men of Viking name and men of authority in the Danelaw (Chadwick,

Anglo-Saxon Institutions, pp. 162 *et seq.*). IV Edgar 15 neatly illustrates the point here. Ælfhere of Mercia and Æthelwine of East Anglia are called ealdormen but Oslac of Northumbria is called earl. Dr Whitelock, 'The Dealings of the Kings of England with Northumbria', *The Anglo-Saxons*, ed. P. Clemoes (London, 1959), pp. 78 *et seq.*, points to a passage that implies Oslac's son, Thorth or Thored, was a resident—and presumably a landholder—in Cambridgeshire (*Liber Eliensis*, ii, c. 32). She suggests: 'As in their choice of archbishops, the kings may have considered Anglo-Danes from this region particularly suited for office in the Northern Danelaw.' She also points to a passage from Gaimar's *Lestorie des Angles* that claims Edgar sent Ealdorman Æthelwold of East Anglia to York to rule Northumbria. Plainly the *Liber Eliensis*' location of Byrthnoth's *scir* is not ill-informed speculation, if it is speculation at all. An Earl Thored signs charters occasionally, as *dux*, 979–88 and was one of the leaders of the disastrous expedition of 992, after which he is not heard of again. It is usually said that Thored was earl of Northumbria in this period and was identical with the Thored, son of Gunnar, who, as earl of Northumbria, ravaged Westmorland in 966 and was replaced immediately afterwards. Plummer was rightly sceptical on both these counts, see *Chronicle*, D.E., s.a. 966, and Plummer's comments. Thored, son of Gunnar, is supposed to have been deposed for ravaging Westmorland, and to have been restored on Oslac's banishment in 975 (Whitelock, *loc. cit.*). This Thored was plainly an older and senior man to Oslac and must therefore have been a very aged man to be entrusted with the command against the Vikings in 992. The *Chronicle* gives no hint that King Edgar expressed any animus against Thored for ravaging Westmorland nor makes the slightest suggestion that he was deposed. It would be most naturally taken to mean that Thored was replaced because he either lost his life in the raid or died soon afterwards. Gaimar, again, claims he was killed in the raid. In this case Oslac would most probably be related to him and 'Thored' a family name. Oslac's banishment must be connected with the crisis of 975 and must mean he took the opposite side to the prevailing party of Æthelwine, Byrhtnoth, and Oswald. Thored signs as *dux* from 979. I suggest he was Oslac's son of the same name who gained at least partial restoration with the accession of Æthelred and partial eclipse of the reformers' party. Where was Thored's *scir*? He held land both in East Anglia and the North, since he gave estates to St Cuthbert (*Charters*, lx). That his *scir* was in Northumbria rests on a single piece of evidence, Mr Neil Ker's reconstruction of the damaged text, printed as *Charters*, liv, *Catalogue of MSS Containing Anglo-Saxon* (Oxford, 1957), p. 302. If Mr Ker is right then St Oswald complains the see of York was robbed of a number of estates in southern Northumbria when Thored came to power. Dr Whitelock, *English Historical Documents* (London, 1955), p. 522, read the MS as claiming the robbery took place when Æthelred succeeded: this would destroy the sole reason for placing Thored amongst the northern earls, and the conventional habit of referring to Thored as earl of Northumbria without any qualification is to be deplored. He seems to have been succeeded, however, by a Mercian thegn, who was earl of the southern part of Northumbria, and Dr Hart, who accepts Mr Ker's reconstruction, places Thored as earl of Deira (*Early Charters of Northern England*, p. 258), which seems reasonable and careful. Thored cannot have succeeded to the superior position of Oslac. He attests fewer charters than the other *duces* and always with low precedence: usually he signs last. I suggest that Byrhtnoth, a great East Anglian magnate, and one of the chief members of the party of Edward the martyr and the monastic reformers succeeded to Oslac as earl of Northumbria with the same status as Ælfhere and Æthelwine (these three virtually always take precedence over the other ealdormen in the early charters of Æthelred's reign) and in 979, with the set-back to the triumph of that party, was forced to accept as colleague and subordinate Thored, the son of the former earl of Northumbria, a man of a different party who could serve as counter-balance and who certainly harried St Oswald if Mr Ker is correct. In 992 Thored made his final appearance in history as the leader of an expedition against the Vikings mustered at London. He looks much more like an East Anglian than a Northumbrian magnate. The other participants were all southern or south-eastern—Ælfric of Hampshire, the bishop of Dorchester and another south-eastern bishop. The *Chronicle* speaks as though all the ships present were either East Anglian or from London: there is no trace of either Northumbrian or Mercian participation.

PRESIDENTIAL ADDRESS
By Professor G. R. Elton, M.A., Ph.D., Litt. D., F.B.A.

THE HISTORIAN'S SOCIAL FUNCTION

READ 19 NOVEMBER 1976

THERE is said to be a crisis in historical studies whose collapse some predict. I think myself that the word crisis gets over-used, and I am convinced that history as a subject of study and instruction will survive. We may find fewer students of it in schools and universities, but we shall stop well short of the retreat (itself, it seems to me, now halted) that has befallen the classical languages. People will continue to read history, even serious history, and people will continue to write history, even good history. Still, there are enemies, some lurking in thickets, some boldly skirmishing across the plain, and while their peashooters cannot kill they can and do hurt. Those sufficiently out of date still to think that what gets the customers is relevance continue to proclaim that history is irrelevant to a forward-looking—indeed, a progressive—society; and since their numbers include a good many who decide what happens in colleges of education, in schools, and (worst of all) in the Department of Education and Science, their obscurantism is not to be ignored. I do not here, in this company, need to defend or justify the study of history, but I feel urged to warn historians that they would be well advised to consider and state their case: at the very least we cannot any longer take it for granted that society will as a matter of course accept us at our own valuation and therefore support us. Today, therefore, on this last occasion that I address this body as President, I should like to consider the grounds on which I would argue that no healthy society can afford to abandon the professional study of the past at its highest, most intensive, and to all appearances least practical level. I cannot now also attend to the history that is told to the generality: one thing at a time.

There are a number of traditionally used justifications which I have come to regard as either insufficient or untrue. Historians have been said to serve society in a variety of ways. They record the actions of men and preserve their memory for posterity. Some people like to be preserved for posterity (to the point of failing to destroy incriminating tapes) and some do not; but unfortunately this preservation of the past is just what the philistines regard as the dangerous effect of a concern with history. Thus there can be little point in emphasizing this function, however well we may think of it. Historians, as Charles Beard put it, are themselves the memory of mankind, and he was right in thinking that without memory man is mindless and inhuman: unable to remember, he cannot look forward, he lacks a third dimension, he is paper-thin. True indeed, but our critics not only are paper-thin but content to be so. These are therefore insufficient justifications because they rest on claims, true enough in themselves and attractive to those so inclined, which only underscore the objections used by others to attack the continued use and usefulness of historical studies.

As for the commonest defence employed in our behalf, it is unfortunately my belief that it will not stand up to inspection. This is the illusion that, to quote Bacon, history makes men wise. Is it not very widely held that a knowledge of past events and developments forms the best foundation for assessing the present and perhaps even the future: that historians are the teachers of mankind? A nice thought, if only it were true. The chief purpose of historical studies lies, it is believed, precisely there: we should study history in order to understand the present. In a desperate attempt to gain social approval, historians themselves have done much to give currency to such beliefs, to the point where some will offer themselves as persons able to look into the roots of present discontents and discern the shape of things to come. Present-directed history is on the increase; even ancient historians and medievalists have been known to proclaim to the world that the twentieth century cannot understand itself unless it attends to the effects of the Peloponnesian War or the coronation of Charlemagne upon (I suppose) the policy of the Kremlin or the balance-of-payments crisis. Perhaps I exaggerate, but not by much. Those less assured than they should be of the justice of their cause are always liable to pin the hostile slogan over their hearts with a slightly sickly smile.

Still, though I deplore them I can understand these aspirations which place the study of the past under the guiding star of the present, but I must point out that they rest on assumptions which experience all the time denies to be true. What proof is there that an understanding of the past improves a man's understanding of his present? The many excellent historians of nineteenth-century Germany who put their learning at the service of nation and politics made ghastly mistakes, displayed appalling misconceptions, caused disastrously false convictions to settle in the public mind, but anyone who for that reason would deny their quality as historians would be guilty of an equal misjudgment. I vividly remember that good man and excellent historian, Alfred Cobban, rubbing his hands in glee when Labour won the 1964 election, ecstatically convinced that a new dawn had risen for the universities of this country, a day of glorious, government-supported expansion and virtue. Twelve years later, facing the consequences of an egalitarian contempt for 'elitism' and 'excellence', we know him for a poor prophet, but we do not need to think him a worse historian for all that. Sometimes I think that only historians of a naturally pessimistic turn of mind ever manage to forecast things correctly, but even a consistent expectation that things will get worse can be sadly disappointed. Even what might appear to be obvious links between a man's experience in the study and the needs of his active calling seem far from sure to offer beneficial instruction: I remain to be persuaded that a minister of foreign affairs is better able to discharge his office because he once investigated the career of Metternich.

Of course, I agree that history, by enlarging a man's acquaintance, enlarges his experience and thus can improve his judgment and his vision, but I find no grounds for thinking that this happens necessarily and good grounds for fearing that a conscious preoccupation with wishing it to happen works the other way. Knowing history does not make you a better prophet, but trying to serve as adviser and prophet can spoil your work as an historian. It matters little what political allegiance may have stirred the scholar into wanting to use his learning about the past in order to assist and explain the present: both Seeley and Tawney would have been better historians if they had not so firmly fixed their purpose on being immediately serviceable to their own society. By allowing their history to serve their politics they reduced the worth of their contribution to both. In fact, I believe that there are fundamental reasons why historians cannot make better prophets than might be the practitioners of other forms of learning—reasons closely connected with the manner in which history must be investigated. I shall come back to this.

I have thrown down the claims which most of us make when challenged to justify our labours: have I left us naked to our enemies? I propose now to construct a covering garment of much superior quality, to be worn not so much with pride as with arrogance. And I propose to do so by going to the roots of our existence as historians. If there is a claim to be entered on behalf of history, it must start by demonstrating that history exists as an intellectual enterprise and discipline distinguishable from other pursuits and not to be replaced by them, for that is just what the adversary denies; and I would maintain that that demonstration depends on showing that history operates by a method peculiar to itself. History has often been denied disciplinary status because there is said to be no such thing as historical method: historians, it is alleged, employ no more than a form of common sense, sharpened and directed by the borrowing of methods from real disciplines. I disagree. Certainly we borrow techniques of all kinds first developed by other scholars—by linguists, bibliographers, philosophers, mathematicians, anthropologists, psychologists and so forth. Dealing with the whole experience of mankind, the historian cannot but use whatever technical devices mankind has developed for understanding itself. But being concerned with his proper task, the study of the past, the historian would not be discharging it faithfully unless he subjected all these techniques, chosen for their usefulness in solving this problem or that, to the general rules of his own method, developed to solve the universal problems of investigating that which has gone beyond recall.

The historian's task is to discover, reconstruct and explain what has happened in the past from such survivals of the past as are found in the present. The pervasive problems facing him are two: the extant evidence is always incomplete and usually highly ambiguous, and in trying to understand and explain that evidence he inescapably introduces the (possibly distorting) subjectivity of his own mind. These barriers stand squarely in the way of every effort to produce an account of the past which comes as close as possible to a truthful reconstruction, independent of the observer, of past situations and events. They are universals and arise no matter what particular type of event is being investigated, what historical age or region is studied, or what line of approach (political, economic, intellectual and so forth) is employed. All historians face these special difficulties, the condition of their calling. And since the difficulties are universal, so is their solution: historical method is the method deliberately devised for use by all historians so that they can minimize the effects of incompleteness, ambiguity and subjectivity in the treatment of extant evidence. It is therefore on the treatment of evidence that the method concentrates, and it does so in three respects: discovery, comprehension and interpretation.

The first task of the historian is to find such evidence as may be available to answer his questions, and in doing so he at once confronts the worst hazard of the whole enterprise. Since it must be he who decides what is relevant to his enquiry, how can he avoid the danger of allowing the terms of the enquiry to dictate the discovery, with the result that he will come to do no more than document an answer at which he had already arrived on the basis of little evidence or none? We all know how frequently this happens in practice, especially when the historian finds himself proving a case in which he is emotionally involved. But there is an answer, and it lies in three categorical imperatives of the method. One: the first approach to the evidence must be void of specific questions directing the search which should rather at this stage be an open investigation looking to the evidence to suggest questions. Two: all the available and potentially relevant evidence must be seen. Three: no evidence must be constructed additional to that which is found extant in its own right. These are hard demands. But let it be noted at once that they clearly distinguish the historical method from that of the experimental sciences (which construct experiments—artificial occurrences—in order to test conjectured consequences), of the social sciences with their preliminary instruments (models and questionnaires) and their manipulation by quantification, or of the philosophical sciences which employ logic in order to draw out the implications of propositions set up as the start of the enquiry. The historian starts by not knowing where he is going; all that he knows is that there is an area of history to be investigated, and that there are historical materials to be worked through from which he will learn the particular questions he should pursue.

Of course, I know that this analysis contradicts the advice usually given to beginners, namely that they must formulate questions before reading. Both experience and reflection have taught me that, on the contrary, one must in the first instance read solely to open the mind to questions arising from the evidence—a mind kept clear of all but the most general questions (such as: I wonder what is in these documents which I have chosen to read because I want to know what the people living in that place and time were doing about governing themselves, or earning a living, or dealing with crime). 'Real'—that is, pointed—questions will soon rise up like an exhalation, at which point the mind, hitherto relatively passive, becomes dominant in the purposeful pursuit of the problems thus established as interesting and valid. Only if the historian works in this way can he be sure that his answers were not put there from the first by himself; only thus can he avoid the dangers of what J. H. Hexter has called 'source-mining', the search for convenient evidence to support a conclusion already arrived at. It follows, secondly, as I have said, that in order to eliminate accident and bias so far as he may he must investigate all the possibly relevant evidence, a prescription which in English history, for instance, becomes very difficult in the twelfth century and soon thereafter impossible. It nevertheless remains the only sound rule, and where it cannot be followed (except at the cost of eternal silence) the historian is obliged to devise ways for reducing the mass without prejudging the results of the enquiry. Briefly, I hold that this again is best done by interpolating a stage at which the choice of what is studied is not governed by the ultimate questions to be answered but perhaps by an archival criterion: one may choose to work through a given sector of the mass—as it might be the files of an institution or the correspondence of a certain person—with no limit to the issues thought relevant, before selectively investigating the remainder under the direction of the questions which the first reading has brought forward. Much, naturally, will depend on the soundness of the choice made in identifying a dominant archive. These again are hard rules, but I know from experience that they can be observed at least with that approximation to precision that is the best that we as historians, operating in the imprecisions of men's fortunes, can ever hope to achieve.

Perhaps I need not say much on the third point, that which prohibits the creation of evidence. It may seem obvious and trite. However, a good deal especially of the more ambitious history one reads derives from such constructed evidence, put in where natural evidence deserts us, and those who advocate the use of theory—for instance psychological or economic theory—are particularly prone to that practice. Erikson's notorious book on Luther presents a picture of the man which owes almost everything to the author's (rather particular and limited) psychoanalytical doctrine and almost nothing to the evidence which the sixteenth century has left behind. An emphasis on technical statistics, insofar as it involves extrapolation rather than calculation, or on anthropological analogies, can have similar effects. I am not, of course, decrying the usefulness of such techniques; I am only asserting that they need to be applied under the continuous and careful control of the strict historical method if they are to help the enterprise rather than pervert it. Any historian will use speculation and conjecture in order to fill gaps in the knowledge based on evidence, and the more sophisticated his mind and his understanding of the technique become the more intelligent and possibly persuasive his gap-filling will be. But it remains conjecture, and in erecting arguments upon figures, analogies and theories the historian must himself remain aware of a difference which also he should not allow the reader to forget.

Discovery is followed by comprehension, by which I mean understanding what the details of evidence brought to light really mean. I do not need here to repeat familiar points about the criticism of sources, but I should like to remind you that it depends upon the rigorous observation of one principle: the material must be evaluated in its own terms and in relation to what surrounds it, that is with reference to the meaning it had at the time it was deposited in the record and not with reference to the historian's own present. Lawyers, for instance, whose training efficiently creates an a-historical cast of mind, notoriously read old law under the guidance of present significance, a habit proper to themselves but so wrong for the historian that large parts of our constitutional history still need rescuing from the consequences of historians' humble prostration before the shrine of legal mystery. Or take the literature of protest, a recurring phenomenon in history and therefore too readily divorced from its historical context. Whether they are inclined to protest themselves or to the repression of protest, historians have too often managed to read such writings as though they bore only some eternal, politico-philosophical, meaning. The social thought of the sixteenth century, for instance, has been ill-treated by instinctive defenders of an existing order who concentrate upon its hierarchic concepts without realizing that the prevalence of these really reflects their absence in the politics of the day; it has been worse treated by radicals who describe its moral outrage against oppression while forgetting that the men giving voice to that outrage denounce just those practices of resistance and rebellion which the radical historians regard as the proper reply to oppression. Either way we do not get what the sixteenth century thought and wrote. However, when I assert that we have a duty to understand the past for its own sake and in its own terms, I had better, to prevent misunderstanding, add that I do not wish us to ignore the past's relationship with the present, perhaps with eternity. We must fulfil that duty so that the past which we relate to the present shall be, as far as possible, the real past.

Lastly, in this brief sweep over historical method, I turn to the problem of interpretation—of making sense of what we have found out. In practice, most historical interpretation comes down to discovering and describing various forms of causal relationships—the ways in which various phenomena acted upon one another so as to produce the discovered result. (I know we are not supposed to talk of causes, but despite the philosophers no other concept in fact so comprehensively describes historians' main analytical preoccupation.) Here again the historical method is peculiar in two ways. The historian never argues from cause to effect, always from effect to cause; and he operates by multiplying causes. He argues from effect to cause because he is always trying to explain an event (or complex of events) known to him, by reference to its antecedents which he needs to disentangle if he is to understand what he already knows. Although we may write that the arms race before 1914 helped to bring about the outbreak of war, we really arrived at that statement the other way round: we argue that the war (which we happen to know took place) derived in part from the arms race. This manner of reasoning is necessarily true of all historical enquiry because until one knows what happened one has no occasion to seek causes and influences. It is this peculiarity of the historical method—its inability to argue forward, to predict—that deprives the historian of any professional claims to play the prophet. Nothing in his method, and (if he is honest) nothing in his experience, entitles him to say that from a given set of circumstances he can forecast what will happen. On the contrary, all his experience has taught him how powerful the contributions are of the unexpected, the unforeseen, the contingent, the accidental and the unknowable, in shaping the fates of men and the course of events. Trained, and rightly trained, to hindsight—to working from effect from cause—the historian, confronted with the question, 'what will come of this?', can only humbly answer, 'your guess is as good as mine'—an answer which more usually he hides behind his favourite phrase, 'well, it all depends'.

Secondly, in seeking to discover his causes the historian works by multiplication and cumulation. Two sound philosophic precepts are anathema to him: the injunction to look for the essence of a problem, and the injunction to avoid multiplying entities beyond necessity. His necessity knows no end: he throws away Ockham's razor and grows his epistemological beard, sprouting in all directions. Reduction to essence is wrong because it has been found that historical phenomena cannot be different from what they are, namely a particular manifestation which is the product of all antecedents, discovered or as yet undiscovered. You may really not take away any element in the complex, however trivial it may appear, without altering the phenomenon itself from the shape which the process of investigation has shown it to possess. This, of course, is one reason why history throws up so many controversies which often circle around rival emphases in the vast mish-mash of relevant contributory and explanatory detail; but it is also why historical knowledge progresses through such controversies which operate by adding rather than reducing. It is very rare in history for what one man has said about an event to be altogether discarded in the progress of better knowledge; rather it gets subsumed into an ever growing agglomerate of interpretation in which it continues to occupy a place.

It will have become clear in this analysis of method that I am confining the term history to one of the two disciplines that lay claim to it. These two I may call empirical or thesis-free, and determinist or thesis-dominated. By thesis I here mean a general scheme of interpretation, regarded as universally applicable, as derived from laws discoverable in the historical process, and as possessed of powers of prediction. The most important current example, of course, is Marxist-Leninist history (in its various forms), but other such universal schemes—as the Toynbean, the Islamic or the Christian—have or have had large vogues. I am not for one moment suggesting that the empirical discipline is free of all forms of thesis: it involves the production of generalizations which can set up an interpretative thesis. This, however, is limited to the single problem for which it is constructed and has no power to predict. Insofar as it employs alleged general laws, these are loose and large views of human behaviour derived from experience and devoid of that normative power which a law must possess to deserve the name. In empirical history, universals form the beginning of understanding; in determinist history, the end of it. My reason for treating history as though it were necessarily of the former kind is simple enough: thesis-free history is fully concerned with the proper subject matter of history, namely the past, whereas thesis-dominated history is not. Men adopt thesis-dominated historical schemes not because they want to understand the past—the ease with which they accommodate or eliminate awkward facts in order to preserve the thesis proves this—but because they want to gain information about the future. It is the predictive power of the thesis, supposedly proved from earlier predicting successes, which attracts: prophecy, not history, is the proper concern of thesis-dominated history, from Joachim da Fiore to the Russian sextet who so informed their audience at the San Francisco Congress of 1975. It is therefore not really history at all.

Let me sum up my definition of the method peculiar to history proper, a definition which, as I am well aware, has had to be a crudely compressed account of possibly controversial views. The historical method consists of an approach to the material to be studied which involves broadfronted attacks without preconceptions, and not linear forays determined by specific enquiry; it involves an understanding of things in terms of the time when the material was created; and it involves interpretation proceeding from effect to cause and by means of the multiplication of causes rather than by distinguishing between essentials and accidentals. If it is objected that this method is also used by people who are not historians, I reply that in that case they miscall themselves. Much present-day sociology uses historical method (of a sort), but that is because it is really social history; empirically inclined economists sometimes operate like historians, but that is because they are in fact practising economic history. Not surprisingly the results sometimes suggest that these fish have slipped from water into an element not altogether familiar to them. In particular they are likely not to realize—even more than genuine historians are found not to realize—the consequences which for the historian flow from the nature of his materials and method: consequences which to some may seem like limitations that call the whole enterprise in question, but which to me constitute the foundations of the historian's claims upon his society.

In the first place, historians have to accept that not everything they would wish to know can be known. There are perfectly good historical questions which we cannot answer. Thanks to the expansion of the profession, the growing number of sharp intelligences in it, the accumulation of knowledge, the fructifying effects of new questions, and also occasionally the usefulness of newly adopted techniques, the tally of unanswered questions once thought unanswerable shrinks all the time; but a residue of truly unanswerable questions will remain. This should worry only those who seek in history a universal bible, and they would be well advised to turn to its thesis-dominated version. Secondly, we must resign ourselves to the fact that even where we know we shall never know completely; our best understanding of any remotely complex historical situation will always be imperfect. But this again need trouble no historian who stops short of wishing to have his views and reconstructions treated as holy writ, the more so because it leads to the third important consequence which is that in history there are in effect no closed issues. Any answer we may give to historical questions is always liable to be at least altered by new knowledge and new thought, quite often in adjacent territory rather than in work on the question itself; the progress of historical learning is as endless and as ever in flux as is history itself; there is never an end and always more to learn. The historian's intellectual life terminates only with his physical existence. When we remember that this is very far from true for colleagues in other disciplines, especially in the natural sciences where problems can get finally solved, we ought to thank our Muse for saving us from such disaster by the characteristically ironic device of a built in and inescapable uncertainty in everything we do.

However: I think that the true significance of that uncertainty remains insufficiently recognized, a fact for which we historians are in measure to blame. History being an unending double dialogue—a dialogue between the scholar and his sources, and a dialogue between scholars—and historians being men of passion, it follows that to the innocent eye of the by-stander historical debate looks like the battles of theologians: as though the disputants were defending rival certainties when in reality they are advancing various hypothetical interpretations from whose collisions better knowledge and clearer understanding may (and usually do) emerge. These idiosyncrasies of the profession, which, I regret to say, sometimes deceive even its members, have disguised the basic truth about historical study which derives directly from the nature of its materials, the methods used to work on them, and the ultimate open-ended uncertainty that is our fate. Because there are no certainties there can be no authorities: history is free. There is, indeed, only one authority whose word is law, and that is the historical evidence: but it is typically an ambiguous authority whose word sounds differently in different ears and whose law disconcertingly changes shape as various obedient subjects endeavour to abide by it. I do not wish to be misunderstood: I do not subscribe to the frivolous, even nihilist, notion of relativism which thinks that historical understanding is only what happens in the observer's mind and varies casually from historian to historian. I think that there is a historical reality which we seek to grasp and can come closer and closer to grasping; and I think that the willingness of historians to agree on so much, as well as the special unwillingness of the relativists to have their own interpretations doubted, support my belief. But that is another large question which here I must put aside.

In history there are no authorities: history is a free study in which no man can claim rule, or credence for his mere *ipse dixit*, and in which the only true sin is to deny a hearing to views with which one happens to disagree. This truth, too, eliminates those forms of history which suppose that to cite Scripture or Zarathustra or Engels on a disputed point of historical truth is to settle the issue. I have always regretted that common parlance calls works of history 'the authorities', for that is exactly what they are not. I may believe what Professor X has written and doubt what Dr Y has replied, but my faith owes nothing to any submission to authority or even to any choice between rival authorities. If Professor X is to be believed it is only because his management of the evidence is more convincing; and when a still more convincing interpretation comes along all his apparent authority will avail him nothing. When, far too many years ago, I was examined on my dissertation, one of my examiners, apropos of some statement of mine, said very courteously, 'But that is not what Pollard says'. Rather taken aback I replied, somewhat rudely, 'But that is only what Pollard says'. In retrospect, I confess, I am less shocked by my rudeness than by the examiner's attitude which supposed that the issue was not what the evidence meant but how one could possibly dissent from authority. None of us hold authority; none of us have any right to pronounce upon problems *ex cathedra*; all of us have the right to argue freely and to be judged solely by the quality of our argument; all of us live under the single obligation faithfully to heed the one authority there is, the historical record.

History, then, is by its inmost nature a free study in which nothing is solved by citing edicts or rules. Does this exhilarating truth tell us anything of the function the historian must discharge in his social capacity? It does indeed, but in order to make my meaning plain I must briefly digress to consider the nature of other intellectual disciplines. And here I am guided by Thomas Kuhn whose views,

I am sure, are by now familiar enough. Kuhn, you will remember, argues that a science becomes 'mature' (that is, worthy of the name) when it achieves what he calls a paradigmatic structure. By this he means a generally agreed framework of theoretic interpretation—a structured view of that world which the science in question studies—within which the process of research (called by him accurately, though a little irreverently, puzzle-solving) is carried out. The paradigm not only determines the lines of research but distinguishes between successful and unsuccessful research; it becomes an authoritative structure which separates orthodoxy from heresy by calling things true and false; and it can be removed only by a revolution when it will be replaced by another paradigm. This, of course, is a crude summary of subtle enough ideas but it is accurate; and I think Kuhn is right partly because observation confirms his analysis, and partly because scientists have told me that indeed this is how they operate.

The paradigmatic principle and method are general throughout both the natural and the social sciences, varied only by the occasional coexistence of more than one paradigm in temporary rivalry one with another (during a pre-revolutionary stage); 'maturing' tends to reduce the several to one. Indeed, it is the stated aspiration of both kinds of science to build such structures: their express ambition is to find a framework which will explain every phenomenon found within it. Sociologists are quite as eager to elevate their science to that kind of maturity as are physicists. Revealingly enough, the main intellectual assault upon history from social scientists concentrates on denying us the status of a science because we do not operate with such compelling frameworks. I have read social scientists so caught up in the paradigmatic predicament that they cannot at all understand how any non-paradigmatic science can claim to exist; they simply have no means of grasping that there are valid forms of knowledge which achieve their ends in other ways. Again, I do not wish to be misunderstood: all disciplines are fully entitled to employ whatever to them seem the right methods for their kind of enquiry, provided they grant the same right to others. Developed interpretative frameworks are a dominant feature in practically every intellectual enterprise; but they are, or they should be, totally absent from history. As I have already hinted, the interpretative structures we build explain nothing except the particular set of circumstances from which they are inferred; each piece of history as treated by every historian has a scheme applicable only to itself and not transferable to any other set of historical questions. The only use of such transfers consists in applying apparent analogies in order to open questions: they are the beginning of study, not the end of it, and no historical problem is solved by being subsumed under a general paradigm. Thus, for instance, an understanding of the prehistory of the Russian revolution may suggest to the student of seventeenth-century England questions and lines of research that may be worth exploring; but only disaster results if he instead assumes that a 'theory of revolutions' worked out from what happened in 1917, or 1848, or 1789, will provide usable answers for his own investigations. We may be stimulated into a particular enquiry by somebody else's mini-paradigm, but we are not obliged to come up with answers that fit it nor should we be wise to treat the paradigm as guide or crutch. If our results fit it, this is by accident—because for once empirical study supported rather than refuted the initial theory. (Of course, it is better to have no initial theory: but let that pass.) The only large paradigmatic structure to which historians adhere consists of a world-view which says that human beings are rational, irrational, divers, like-minded, wise, foolish, brave, timid, moderate, violent, ambitous, submissive, kindly and vicious—a structure so fluid and unauthoritative that it eliminates no answers and can create no heresies. Even the historian who confounds the probabilities of nature and of men's minds by claiming that all civilization derives from the teaching of visitors from Venus is no heretic, though we may think him ill-advised and ask in vain for his proof.

Thus the historian's freedom from authority is not confined to his relations with other historians; it is the very inward essence of his craft and distinguishes him singularly from practitioners in adjacent intellectual enterprises. To this freedom he has surrendered the very human desire to discover great schemes, large answers, words that may save or damn mankind: he will be limited, particular—and free. And it is this freedom that he contributes to society and with which he repays society's willingness to support him. Paradigmatic sciences are fascinating, valuable, inescapable—and dangerous. As a method of research the use of world-views, frameworks and models may be entirely unexceptionable. But these things do not stay within the region to which they belong; they escape into the political and social lives of men. The social scientists who seek to discover the true structure of society rapidly transform an instrument of research into a norm for the society studied; what is thought to be the reality of social relationships discovered by enquiry becomes reality by being imposed (with the authority of science) upon those relationships—a happy instance of self-legitimation—or alternatively is set up as a supposedly real bogeyman for political attack. It is here that the historian's proper function and true service enter: possessed of intellectual freedom he must resist the imposition of intellectual dictatorship and its social consequences. As all the disciplines rush after paradigms, there are not many such free men left around; and among those left free only the historian—still possessed of influence, capable of just the sort of questions to which paradigm-mongers are vulnerable, and available in sufficient numbers—can successfully stand up to the claims and pressures of developed science. Our peculiar method of working, which renders us incapable of seeking 'maturity' in the production of a universal law or system, enables us, and our social duty obliges us, to subject the paradigmatic structures of others to criticism and if necessary to demolition by applying our own unhindered, unauthoritative, pragmatic and sometimes simplistic doubts to their claims to authority—especially when that authority moves from intellectual concerns (where after all it constrains only other practitioners of the same discipline) to political, where it constrains us all. History is sceptical—sceptical of anything that cannot be demonstrated by rational proof; universal structures in human existence, which assuredly cannot be demonstrated, can as certainly be asserted and imposed; historians are—or rather, should be—continually sceptical of them. And since universal structures are by their nature enemies to freedom—the freedom of the mind and ultimately of the body—the survival of liberty in thought, in speech, in speculation, in every aspect of life, comes to depend on the continued existence of historians, questioning all authoritative statements and alleged laws of existence by asking their simple question: what actually happened?

But if historians are to discharge this function they need to take care. They can do so only if they follow their own trade honestly and faithfully, without regard to favour, without fear of consequences, above all without respect to the supposed needs and calls of the passing day. Only if they obey the legitimate demands of their own science can they successfully undertake to criticize the sciences of others. Those who would with to make history acceptable and socially serviceable by directing its thoughts to the present day and the alleged demands of contemporary society unfortunately, with the best of intentions, lead it straight to destruction and damnation. The more we turn from studying the past for the sake of understanding that past to the use of the past for the purposes of the present, the more we abandon our proper role and the less useful and justified do our labours, do our lives, become. It is not our task to produce panaceas: the world is full of people—from scientists through pundits to gurus—willing to do that. What society has a right to expect from us is that we should act as mankind's intellectual conscience, helping in our sceptical way to sort the true from the untrue, the useful from the pernicious, the valid from the pretentious, and teaching others (especially our students) those proper standards of sceptical questioning which alone can protect freedom. It is our task to undermine self-appointed certainties and to break the shackles of structures, whether they dominate the mind or all of life. If the world of the mind contained nothing but historians it would be a wild anarchy; but it does not contain only historians, and without them it would become a collection of despotisms. The balance between order and freedom, especially in an age which finds the first easier to preserve than the second, depends, I suggest to you, on the continued practice of conventional, empirical historical study. The nations are today much beset by the claims of absolutist system-builders, whether they be political dictators or social equalizers or fanatics for any cause from the sole usefulness of wheat-germ to that enslavement which has stolen the name of liberation. To those still willing to listen the historian, trained to freedom, offers the gift of sceptical criticism, which is liberty. How can any society afford to lose its historians?

THE ROYAL HISTORICAL SOCIETY

REPORT OF COUNCIL, SESSION 1975–76

THE Council of the Royal Historical Society has the honour to present the following report to the Anniversary Meeting.

A conference on 'Colonies' was held at Dale Hall, University of Liverpool, from 18 to 20 September 1975. The papers read were:

'English Contributions to Renaissance Colonisation', by Professor D. B. Quinn.

'Scandinavian Settlement in Western Britain—An Archaeological point of view', by Professor D. M. Wilson.

'Colonialism as a context for the understanding of alien societies: the image of Africa and the image of Europe', by Professor T. Ranger.

'The French Colonialist Movement during the Third Republic', by Dr C. M. Andrew.

'Colonies: an Attempt at a Typology', by Professor M. I. Finley.

Forty members of the Society and twelve guests attended. The University held a reception for them on 19 September. It was decided to hold the seventh annual conference at Clare College, Cambridge, from 16 to 18 September 1976, on the topic 'Education and its Social Purposes'.

An evening party was held for Fellows and guests at University College London on 2 July 1975 for which 125 acceptances were received.

During the year, Sir Francis Hill resigned as Honorary Solicitor of the Society, a position he had held for twenty years. Council wishes to record its appreciation of the long and valuable service he has given to the Society. Mr J. S. Roper has accepted Council's invitation to fill the vacancy.

The representation of the Society upon various bodies was as follows: Professor G. E. Aylmer and Mr A. T. Milne on the Joint Anglo-American Committee exercising a general supervision over the production of the *Bibliographies of British History*; the President, Professor C. N. L. Brooke, Professor Sir Goronwy Edwards and Professor J. C. Holt on the Advisory Committee of the new edition of Gross, *Sources and Literature of English History*; Professor G. W. S. Barrow, Dr P. Chaplais and Professor P. H. Sawyer on the Joint Committee of the Society and the British Academy established to prepare an edition of Anglo-Saxon charters; Professor E. B. Fryde on a committee to regulate British co-operation in the preparation of a new repertory of medieval sources to replace Potthast's *Bibliotheca Historica Medii Aevi*; Professor P. Grierson on a committee to promote the publication of photographic records of the more significant collections of British coins; Professor A. G. Dickens on the Advisory Council on the Export of Works of Art; the President and Mr K. V. Thomas on the British National Committee of the International Historical Congress; Professor G. H. Martin on the Council of the British Records Association; Professor A. M. Everitt on the Standing Conference for Local History; Mr M. R. D. Foot on the Committee to advise the publishers of *The Annual Register*; Dr P. D. A. Harvey on the Ordnance Survey Archaeological Advisory Committee, and Miss K. Major on the Lincoln Archaeological Trust. Council received reports from these representatives.

Professor W. N. Medlicott represents the Society on the Court of the University of Exeter and Professor J. A. S. Grenville on the Court of the University of Birmingham.

The Vice-Presidents retiring under By-law XVI were Dr P. Chaplais and Professor D. Hay. Sir John Habakkuk and Mrs D. M. Owen were elected to replace them. The members of Council retiring under By-law XIX were Mr T. H. Aston, Professor J. McManners, Professor P. H. Sawyer and Professor F. M. L. Thompson. Professor Margaret Gowing, Mrs Jenifer Hart, Professor H. G. Koenigsberger and Professor R. L. Storey were elected to fill the vacancies. Messrs Beeby, Harmar & Co. were appointed auditors for the year 1975–76 under By-law XXXVIII.

Early in the session, Messrs Dawson had given notice that they wished to relinquish the distribution and sale of part of our publications. Negotiations have been conducted with D. S. Brewer Ltd and a new contract for the sale and distribution of all of the Society's publications has been agreed with them.

During the past year Council has urged upon the Trustees of the Wiener Library that they should renew efforts to maintain that unique collection in London. The Society has co-operated in an investigation being made by the Royal Society and the British Academy into the position of learned societies in the present difficult economic situation.

Publications, and Papers Read

This year Council has signed a contract with Harvester Press for the reprinting of Pargellis and Medley: *Bibliography of British history: 1714–89*, and Conyers Read: *Bibliography of British history: Tudor Period, 1485–1603*. It is expected that the first volume of the *Annual Bibliography of British and Irish History* mentioned in the last Report will be published in the summer of 1976.

Council has made plans during the year to create a means for the publication of works of history at a time when traditional publishers are increasingly loath to do so. Circulation of the Fellowship at the time of the last Anniversary Meeting elicited a good deal of support for the scheme. Entitled STUDIES IN HISTORY, it has an Editorial Board under the chairmanship of Professor G. R. Elton and a part-time Editorial Assistant, Mrs Janet Godden. Members of the Board and Fellows acting as readers of manuscripts are giving their time and labour without remuneration. The Board hopes that the first books will appear early in 1977. The printers of the series, who will also distribute it, are Swift Printers Ltd. This promising venture would not have got so far without considerable financial support from the British Academy, The Twenty-Seven Foundation, the American Embassy, The Pilgrim Trust, the Wolfson Foundation, as well as a number of individual anonymous donors, who have together raised nearly £10,000 to provide launching capital for the scheme.

Financial support for a bibliography of British History from 1914 mentioned in the last Report has not so far been found.

The following works were published during the session: *Transactions*, Fifth Series, volume 26; *The Account Book of Beaulieu Abbey* (Camden Fourth Series, volume 16) and *A Calendar of Western Circuit Assize Orders, 1629–48* (Camden, Fourth Series, volume 17).

At the ordinary meetings of the Society the following papers were read:

'The Eighteenth-Century Debate on Parliamentary Supremacy', by Dr. H. T. Dickinson. (17 October 1975.)

'Urban Decline in Late Medieval England', by Dr R. B. Dobson. (6 February 1976.)

'The Mid-Victorian Newspaper', by Dr Lucy Brown. (5 March 1976.)

'Gregory King and the Social Structure of pre-industrial England', by Professor G. S. Holmes. (14 May 1976.)

At the Anniversary Meeting on 21 November 1975 the President, Professor G. R. Elton, delivered an address on 'Tudor Government: The points of Contact: 3. The Court'.

The Alexander Prize was awarded to Dr Brendan Bradshaw, S.M., for his essay 'Cromwellian reform and the origins of the Kildare rebellion, 1533–34' which was read on 11 June 1976; Mr Keith Haines's essay 'Attitudes and Impediments to Pacifism in Mediaeval Europe' was judged *proxime accessit.*

Membership

Council records with regret the death of 28 Fellows and 3 Associates since 30 June 1975. Among these Council would mention especially Professor the Rev. F. Dvornik and Professor O. Halecki, Corresponding Fellows; Professor Sir Goronwy Edwards and Professor Sir John Neale, Honorary Vice-Presidents; Dr G. S. R. Kitson Clark, a former Vice-President. The resignation of 7 Fellows, 1 Associate and 10 Subscribing Libraries was received.

54 Fellows and 9 Associates were elected, 9 Libraries were admitted and 1 Library re-admitted. The membership of the Society on 30 June 1976 comprised 1,290 Fellows (including 104 Life Fellows and 39 Retired Fellows), 29 Corresponding Fellows, 166 Associates and 768 Subscribing Libraries (1,271, 31, 161 and 768 respectively on 30 June 1975). The Society exchanged publications with 15 Societies, British and foreign.

Finance

Over the year, the Society's income increased by only £1,533 or 6%, whereas expenditure increased by £8,274 or 45%. Consequently, although the financial year ended with a small surplus of £592, this was achieved only by using the whole of the income from the Browning Fund to meet current expenditure. All areas of expenditure contributed to the increase, but especially publications, where the increase in net expenditure was £6,413 or 83%, due largely to the escalation of printing and publishing costs but also to the appearance for the first time of a full year's preparation expenses for the *Annual Bibliography of British and Irish History* and to a decrease in the proceeds of sales of publications from last year's exceptionally high figure. By contrast secretarial and administrative expenses increased by only £1,487 or 15%.

To minimize the effect of future increases in printing and publishing costs Council has agreed to the use of new printing techniques and some minor changes in format, which will produce economies without affecting significantly the quality of the Society's publications. Also in due course the *Annual Bibliography* is expected to become self-supporting (the STUDIES IN HISTORY scheme is separately funded and will be self-supporting from the outset) and increased revenue from sales of the Society's other publications is expected following the new distribution agreement with D. S. Brewer Ltd.

However, while Council continues to seek possible economies, these can have but a marginal effect upon anticipated future increases in overall expenditure. Council has, therefore, decided after a careful review of the situation that in order to maintain a full publications programme it is necessary to increase the subscription of subscribing libraries from £7 to £12 with effect from 1 July 1976 and to recommend to the Anniversary Meeting increases in the subscriptions of Fellows from £7 to £10 and of Associates from £3 to £4 with effect from 1 July 1977.

The Society's Balance Sheet takes into account for the first time the bequest by the late Professor A. S. Whitfield of £8,000 to be devoted to an annual prize for an historical essay on a subject connected with England or Wales. Council is considering the form which this prize should take.

ROYAL HISTORICAL SOCIETY

Balance Sheet as at 30 June 1976

30.6.75 £						£
			ACCUMULATED FUNDS			
			General Fund			
47,323			As at 1 July 1975			55,478
822			Royalties from reprints of the Society's publications received and treated as Capital in 1975, now treated as income			—
7,333			Add Excess of Income over Expenditure and Provisions for the year			592
55,478						56,070
			Sir George W. Prothero Bequest		£	
	13,852		As at 1 July 1975		14,710	
	857		Surplus on sale of Investment		157	
14,709						14,867
			Reddaway Fund			
5,000			As at 1 July 1975			5,000
			Andrew Browning Fund			
	73,776		As at 1 July 1975		74,429	
	156		Add Sale of Stamp Collection (Balance)		75	
	497		Profit on sale of Investment		—	
74,429						74,504
149,616						150,441
			A. S. Whitfield Prize Fund			
			Bequest received from the Executors		8,000	
			Interest Received		466	
						8,466
£149,616						£158,907
			REPRESENTED BY:			
			Investments			
	125,696		Quoted Securities—at cost		139,475	
			Market Values £173,709 (1975: £133,571)			
	13,500		Money on 7-day Deposit		12,500	
	128		Due from Stockbrokers		186	
139,324						152,161
			Current Assets			
			Balances at Bank:			
	2,975		Current Accounts		5,789	
	14,127		Deposit Accounts		10,312	
	68		Cash in Hand		39	
	1,419		Income Tax Repayment due		1,569	
	195		Payments in advance		133	
	2,311		Stock of paper in hand		1,155	
	21,095				18,997	
			Less Current Liabilities			
		1,430	Subscriptions received in advance . .	2,273		
		103	Conference Fees in advance . .	502		
		975	Sundry Creditors	76		
		8,295	Provision for publications in hand .	9,400		
	10,803				12,251	
10,292						6,746
£149,616						£158,907

Note: The cost of the Society's Library, Furniture and Office Equipment and the stock of its publications has been written off to the Income & Expenditure Account as and when required.

ROYAL HISTORICAL SOCIETY

INCOME & EXPENDITURE ACCOUNT FOR THE YEAR ENDED 30 JUNE 1976

30.6.75 £	£			£	£
		INCOME			
	410	Subscriptions for 1975/76: Associates		417	
	4,801	Libraries		4,887	
	7,362	Fellows		7,702	
12,573					13,006
		(The Society also had 104 Life Fellows at 30 June 1976)			
909		Tax recovered on Covenanted Subscriptions (includes 3 years' Transitional Relief)			1,699
1,650		Arrears of Subscriptions recovered in year			1,156
10,033		Interest and Dividends received and Income Tax recovered			10,535
161		Royalties and Reproduction Fees			287
355		Donations and Sundry Receipts			531
£25,681					£27,214
		EXPENDITURE			
		SECRETARIAL & ADMINISTRATIVE EXPENSES			
	7,666	Salaries, Pension contributions and National Insurance		8,514	
	844	General Printing and Stationery		1,214	
	484	Postage, Telephone and Sundries		684	
	405	Accountancy and Audit		521	
	70	Office Equipment		—	
	118	Insurance		130	
	311	Meeting and Conference Expenses		322	
9,898					11,385
		PUBLICATIONS			
	225	Directors' Expenses		275	
		Publishing Costs in year:			
		Transactions, Fifth Series, Vol. 25 (total cost)	4,420		
		Camden, Fourth Series, Vol. 15 (total cost)	3,518		
		Camden, Fourth series, Vol. 16 (total cost)	6,301		
			14,239		
		Less Provision made 30 June 1975	8,295		
	2,656			5,944	
		Provision for Publications in Progress:			
		Transactions, Fifth Series, Vol. 26	4,250		
		Camden, Fourth Series, Vol. 17	5,150		
	8,295			9,400	
	71	Preparation expenses *Annual Bibliography*		937	
	11,247			16,556	
	3,528	*Less* Sales of Publications		2,424	
7,719					14,132
£17,617		*Carried forward*			£25,517

EXPENDITURE (contd.)

30.6.75				£
17,617		*Brought forward*		25,517
		LIBRARY AND ARCHIVES		
	327	Purchase of Books and Publications	700	
	344	Library Assistance and Equipment	329	
	671		1,029	
	—	*Less* Sale of Books	15	
671				1,014
		OTHER CHARGES		
	17	Alexander Prize and Expenses	39	
	18	Subscriptions to other bodies	27	
	25	Prothero Lecture Fee	25	
60				91
18,348		TOTAL EXPENDITURE		26,622
25,681		INCOME AS ABOVE		27,214
£7,333		EXCESS OF INCOME OVER EXPENDITURE AND PROVISIONS FOR THE YEAR		£592

R. ELTON, *President*.
. ROPER, *Treasurer*.

We have examined the foregoing Balance Sheet and Income and Expenditure Account with e books and vouchers of the Society. We have verified the Investments and Bank Balances ppearing in the Balance Sheet. In our opinion the foregoing Balance Sheet and Income and xpenditure Account are properly drawn up so as to exhibit a true and fair view of the state of fairs of the Society according to the best of our information and the explanations given to us d as shown by the books of the Society.

BEEBY, HARMAR & CO.,
Chartered Accountants

, LEONARD STREET,
NDON, EC2A 4QS
h August 1976

THE DAVID BERRY TRUST

Receipts and Payments Account for the Year Ended 30 June 197

30.6.75 £	£	*Receipts*	£	£
		Balances in Hand 1 July, 1975:		
		Cash at Bank:		
	14	Current Account	3	
	66	Deposit Account	103	
	530	483.63 Shares Charities Official Investment Fund .	530	
610	—		—	63
78		Dividend on Investment per Charity Commissioners .		9
8		Interest Received on Deposit Account		
£696				£73

£	£	*Payments*	£	£
10		Meetings and Sundry Expenses		–
	37	Advertising—*The Times*		–
	13	*The Scotsman*		–
50	—			
		Balance in Hand 30 June 1976:		
		Cash at Bank:		
	3	Current Account	3	
	103	Deposit Account	202	
	530	483.63 Shares Charities Official Investment Fund (Market Value 30.6.76 £545)	530	
636	—		—	73
£696				£73

We have examined the above account with the books and vouchers of the Trust and find it
be in accordance therewith.

BEEBY, HARMAR & CO.,
Chartered Accountants

79, Leonard Street,
London, EC2A 4QS
6th August 1976

The late David Berry, by his will dated 23rd day of April, 1926, left £1,000 to provide in eve three years a gold medal and prize money for the best essay on the Earl of Bothwell or, at t discretion of the Trustees, on Scottish History of the James Stuarts I to VI in memory of h father, the late Rev. David Berry.

The Trust is regulated by a scheme sanctioned by the Chancery Division of the High Court Justice dated 23rd day of January, 1930, and made in an action 1927 A. 1233 David Anders Berry deceased, Hunter and another *v.* Robertson and another.

The Royal Historical Society is now the Trustee. The Investment held on Capital Accou consists of 634 Charities Official Investment Fund Shares (Market Value £715).

The Trustee will in every second year of the three year period advertise in the *Times Litera Supplement* inviting essays.

ALEXANDER PRIZE

The Alexander Prize was established in 1897 by L. C. Alexander, F.R.Hist.S. It consists of a silver medal awarded annually for an essay upon some historical subject. Candidates may select their own subject provided such subject has been previously submitted to and approved by the Literary Director. The essay must be a genuine work of original research, not hitherto published, and one which has not been awarded any other prize. It must not exceed 6,000 words in length and must be sent in on or before 1 November 1977. The detailed regulations should be obtained in advance from the Secretary.

LIST OF ALEXANDER PRIZE ESSAYISTS (1898–1976)[1]

1898. F. Hermia Durham ('The relations of the Crown to trade under James I').
1899. W. F. Lord, B.A. ('The development of political parties in the reign of Queen Anne').
1901. Laura M. Roberts ('The Peace of Lunéville').
1902. V. B. Redstone ('The social condition of England during the Wars of the Roses').
1903. Rose Graham ('The intellectual influence of English monasticism between the tenth and twelfth centuries').
1904. Enid W. G. Routh ('The balance of power in the seventeenth century').
1905. W. A. P. Mason, M.A. ('The beginnings of the Cistercian Order').
1906. Rachel R. Reid, M.A. ('The Rebellion of the Earls, 1569').
1908. Kate Hotblack ('The Peace of Paris, 1763').
1909. Nellie Nield, M.A. ('The social and economic condition of the unfree classes in England in the twelfth and thirteenth centuries').
1912. H. G. Richardson ('The parish clergy of the thirteenth and fourteenth centuries').
1917. Isobel D. Thornley, B.A. ('The treason legislation of 1531–1534').
1918. T. F. T. Plucknett, B.A. ('The place of the Council in the fifteenth century').
1919. Edna F. White, M.A. ('The jurisdiction of the Privy Council under the Tudors').
1920. J. E. Neale, M.A. ('The Commons Journals of the Tudor Period')
1922. Eveline C. Martin ('The English establishments on the Gold Coast in the second half of the eighteenth century').
1923. E. W. Hensman, M.A. ('The Civil War of 1648 in the east midlands').
1924. Grace Stretton, B.A. ('Some aspects of mediæval travel').
1925. F. A. Mace, M.A. ('Devonshire ports in the fourteenth and fifteenth centuries').
1926. Marian J. Tooley, M.A. ('The authorship of the *Defensor Pacis*').

[1] No award was made in 1900, 1907, 1910, 1911, 1913, 1914, 1921, 1946, 1948, 1956, 1969 and 1975. The prize Essays for 1909 and 1919 were not published in the *Transactions*. No Essays were submitted in 1915, 1916 and 1943.

1927. W. A. Pantin, B.A. ('Chapters of the English Black Monks, 1215–1540').
1928. Gladys A. Thornton, B.A., Ph.D. ('A study in the history of Clare, Suffolk, with special reference to its development as a borough').
1929. F. S. Rodkey, A.M., Ph.D. ('Lord Palmerston's policy for the rejuvenation of Turkey, 1839–47').
1930. A. A. Ettinger, D.Phil. ('The proposed Anglo-Franco-American Treaty of 1852 to guarantee Cuba to Spain').
1931. Kathleen A. Walpole, M.A. ('The humanitarian movement of the early nineteenth century to remedy abuses on emigrant vessels to America').
1932. Dorothy M. Brodie, B.A. ('Edmund Dudley, minister of Henry VII').
1933. R. W. Southern, B.A. ('Ranulf Flambard and early Anglo-Norman administration').
1934. S. B. Chrimes, M.A., Ph.D. ('Sir John Fortescue and his theory of dominion').
1935. S. T. Bindoff, M.A. ('The unreformed diplomatic service, 1812–60').
1936. Rosamund J. Mitchell, M.A., B.Litt. ('English students at Padua, 1460–1475').
1937. C. H. Philips, B.A. ('The East India Company "Interest", and the English Government, 1783–4').
1938. H. E. I. Phillips, B.A. ('The last years of the Court of Star Chamber, 1630–41').
1939. Hilda P. Grieve, B.A. ('The deprived married clergy in Essex, 1553–61').
1940. R. Somerville, M.A. ('The Duchy of Lancaster Council and Court of Duchy Chamber').
1941. R. A. L. Smith, M.A., Ph.D. ('The *Regimen Scaccarii* in English monasteries').
1942. F. L. Carsten, D.Phil. ('Medieval democracy in the Brandenburg towns and its defeat in the fifteenth century').
1944. Rev. E. W. Kemp, B.D. ('Pope Alexander III and the canonization of saints').
1945. Helen Suggett, B.Litt. ('The use of French in England in the later middle ages').
1947. June Milne, B.A. ('The diplomacy of Dr John Robinson at the court of Charles XII of Sweden, 1697–1709').
1949. Ethel Drus, M.A. ('The attitude of the Colonial Office to the annexation of Fiji').
1950. Doreen J. Milne, M.A., Ph.D. ('The results of the Rye House Plot, and their influence upon the Revolution of 1688').
1951. K. G. Davies, B.A. ('The origins of the commission system in the West India trade').
1952. G. W. S. Barrow, B.Litt. ('Scottish rulers and the religious orders, 1070–1153').
1953. W. E. Minchinton, B.Sc.(Econ.) ('Bristol—metropolis of the west in the eighteenth century').
1954. Rev. L. Boyle, O.P. ('The *Oculus Sacerdotis* and some other works of William of Pagula').
1955. G. F. E. Rudé, M.A., Ph.D. ('The Gordon riots: a study of the rioters and their victims').
1957. R. F. Hunnisett, M.A., D.Phil. ('The origins of the office of Coroner').
1958. Thomas G. Barnes, A.B., D.Phil. ('County politics and a puritan *cause célèbre*: Somerset churchales, 1633').

1959. Alan Harding, B.Litt. ('The origins and early history of the Keeper of the Peace').
1960. Gwyn A. Williams, M.A., Ph.D. ('London and Edward I').
1961. M. H. Keen, B.A. ('Treason trials under the law of arms').
1962. G. W. Monger, M.A., Ph.D. ('The end of isolation: Britain, Germany and Japan, 1900–1902').
1963. J. S. Moore, B.A. ('The Domesday teamland: a reconsideration').
1964. M. Kelly, Ph.D. ('The submission of the clergy').
1965. J. J. N. Palmer, B.Litt. ('Anglo-French negotiations, 1390–1396').
1966. M. T. Clanchy, M.A., Ph.D. ('The Franchise of Return of Writs').
1967. R. Lovatt, M.A., D.Phil., Ph.D. ('The *Imitation of Christ* in late medieval England').
1968. M. G. A. Vale, M.A., D.Phil. ('The last years of English Gascony, 1451–1453').
1970. Mrs Margaret Bowker, M.A., B.Litt. ('The Commons Supplication against the Ordinaries in the light of some Archidiaconal Acta').
1971. C. Thompson, M.A. ('The origins of the politics of the Parliamentary middle group 1625–1629').
1972. I. d'Alton, B.A., ('Southern Irish Unionism: A study of Cork City and County Unionists, 1884–1914').
1973. C. J. Kitching, B.A., Ph.D. ('The quest for concealed lands in the reign of Elizabeth I').
1974. H. Tomlinson, B.A. ('Place and Profit: an Examination of the Ordnance Office, 1660–1714').
1976. B. Bradshaw, M.A., B.D. ('Cromwellian reform and the origins of the Kildare rebellion, 1533–34').

DAVID BERRY PRIZE

The David Berry Prize was established in 1929 by David Anderson-Berry in memory of his father, the Reverend David Berry. It consists of a gold medal and money prize awarded every three years for Scottish history. Candidates may select any subject dealing with Scottish history within the reigns of James I to James VI inclusive, provided such subject has been previously submitted to and approved by the Council of the Royal Historical Society. The essay must be a genuine work of original research not hitherto published, and one which has not been awarded any other prize. The essay should be between 6,000 and 10,000 words, excluding footnotes and appendices. It must be sent in on or before 31 October 1979.

LIST OF DAVID BERRY PRIZE ESSAYISTS (1937–76)[1]

1937. G. Donaldson, M.A. ('The polity of the Scottish Reformed Church *c.* 1560–1580, and the rise of the Presbyterian movement').
1943. Rev. Prof. A. F. Scott Pearson, D.Th., D.Litt. ('Anglo-Scottish religious relations, 1400–1600').
1949. T. Bedford Franklin, M.A., F.R.S.E. ('Monastic agriculture in Scotland, 1440–1600').
1955. W. A. McNeill, M.A. (' "Estaytt" of the king's rents and pensions, 1621').
1958. Prof. Maurice Lee, Ph.D. ('Maitland of Thirlestane and the foundation of the Stewart despotism in Scotland').
1964. M. H. Merriman ('Scottish collaborators with England during the Anglo-Scottish war, 1543–1550').
1967. Miss M. H. B. Sanderson ('Catholic recusancy in Scotland in the sixteenth century').
1970. Dr Athol Murray, M.A., LL.B., Ph.D. ('The Comptroller, 1425–1610').
1973. Dr J. Kirk ('Who were the Melvillians: A study in the Personnel and Background of the Presbyterian Movement in late Sixteenth-century Scotland').
1976. Dr A. Grant ('The Development of the Scottish Peerage').

[1] No Essays were submitted in 1940. No award was made in 1946, 1952 and 1961.

THE ROYAL HISTORICAL SOCIETY

(INCORPORATED BY ROYAL CHARTER)

OFFICERS AND COUNCIL—1976

Patron

HER MAJESTY THE QUEEN

President

PROFESSOR G. R. ELTON, MA, PhD, LittD, FBA.

Honorary Vice-Presidents

PROFESSOR SIR HERBERT BUTTERFIELD, MA, LLD, DLitt, DLit, LittD, FBA.
PROFESSOR C. R. CHENEY, MA, DLitt, FBA.
SIR CHARLES CLAY, CB, MA, LittD, FBA, FSA.
PROFESSOR R. A. HUMPHREYS, OBE, MA, PhD, DLitt, LittD, DLitt, DUniv
THE HON SIR STEVEN RUNCIMAN, MA, DPhil, LLD, LittD, DLitt, LitD, DD, DHL, FBA, FSA.
SIR RICHARD SOUTHERN, MA, DLitt, LittD, DLitt, FBA.
DAME LUCY SUTHERLAND, DBE, MA, DLitt, LittD, DCL, FBA.

Vice-Presidents

PROFESSOR J. M. WALLACE-HADRILL, MA, DLitt, FBA
PROFESSOR G. E. AYLMER, MA, DPhil, FBA.
PROFESSOR R. H. C. DAVIS, MA, FBA, FSA.
PROFESSOR F. J. FISHER, MA.
PROFESSOR J. C. HOLT, MA, DPhil, FSA.
PROFESSOR J. HURSTFIELD, DLit.
SIR JOHN HABAKKUK, MA, FBA.
MRS D. M. OWEN, MA, FSA.

Council

J. P. W. Ehrman, MA, FBA, FSA.
B. H. Harrison, MA, DPhil.
A. F. Thompson, MA.
D. E. R. Watt, MA, DPhil.
Professor T. C. Barker, MA, PhD.
R. F. Hunnisett, MA, DPhil.
Professor D. W. J. Johnson, BA, BLitt.
Professor D. C. Watt, MA.
J. M. Roberts, MA, DPhil.
K. V. Thomas, MA.
Professor W. L. Warren, MA, DPhil, FRSL.
Professor Joyce A. Youings, PhD.
Professor Margaret Gowing, MA, DLitt, BSc(Econ), FBA.
Mrs J. M. Hart, MA.
Professor H. G. Koenigsberger, PhD.
Professor R. L. Storey, MA, PhD.

Honorary Secretary

C. J. Holdsworth, MA, PhD, FSA.

Literary Director

Professor Valerie Pearl, MA, DPhil, FSA.

Assistant Literary Director

C. T. Allmand, MA, DPhil.

Honorary Treasurer

M. Roper, MA.

Honorary Librarian

E. L. C. Mullins, OBE, MA.

Honorary Solicitor

John S. Roper, MA.

Executive Secretary

Mrs J. Chapman

Library and Offices

University College London, Gower Street, London WC1E 6BT

Bankers

Barclay's Bank Limited.

STANDING COMMITTEES—1976

Finance Committee

PROFESSOR T. C. BARKER.
C. E. BLUNT, OBE, FBA, FSA.
SIR JOHN HABAKKUK
R. F. HUNNISETT.
N. J. WILLIAMS, MA, DPhil, FSA.
And the Officers.

Publications Committee

PROFESSOR G. E. AYLMER.
PROFESSOR F. J. FISHER.
SIR JOHN HABAKKUK
B. H. HARRISON.
PROFESSOR D. W. J. JOHNSON.
MRS D. M. OWEN.
PROFESSOR R. L. STOREY.
K. V. THOMAS.
PROFESSOR D. C. WATT.
And the Officers.

Library Committee

PROFESSOR G. E. AYLMER.
PROFESSOR F. J. FISHER.
SIR JOHN HABAKKUK.
J. M. ROBERTS.
And the Officers.

LIST OF FELLOWS OF THE ROYAL HISTORICAL SOCIETY

(CORRECTED TO 31 DECEMBER 1976)

Names of Officers and Honorary Vice-Presidents are printed in capitals. Those marked have compounded for their annual subscriptions.*

Abbott, A. W., CMG, CBE, Frithys Orchard, West Clandon, Surrey.
Adair, J. E., MA, PhD, 1 Crockford Park Road, Addlestone, Surrey.
Adam, R. J., MA, Cromalt, Lade Braes, St Andrews, Fife.
Addison, P., MA, DPhil, Dept of History, The University, William Robertson Building, George Square, Edinburgh EH8 9JY.
*Addleshaw, G. W. O., The Very Rev. the Dean of Chester, MA, BD, FSA, The Deanery, Chester CH1 2JF.
Ainsworth, Sir John, Bt, MA, c/o National Library, Kildare Street, Dublin 2, Ireland.
Akrigg, Professor G. P. V., BA, PhD, FRSC, Dept of English, University of British Columbia, Vancouver 8, B.C., Canada.
Alcock, Professor L., MA, FSA, 29 Hamilton Drive, Glasgow G12 8DN.
Alder, Professor G. J., BA, PhD, Dept of History, The University, Whiteknights, Reading RG6 2AA.
Alderman, G., MA, DPhil, 172 Colindeep Lane, London NW9 6EA.
Allan, D. G. C., MSc(Econ), FSA, 45 Hambalt Road, London SW4 9EQ.
Allen, D. H., BA, PhD, 105 Tuddenham Avenue, Ipswich, Suffolk IP4 2HG.
Allen, Professor H. C., MC, MA, School of English and American Studies, University of East Anglia, University Plain, Norwich NOR 88C.
ALLMAND, C. T., MA, DPhil, (*Assistant Literary Director*), 111 Menlove Avenue, Liverpool L18 3HP.
Altholz, Professor J., PhD, Dept of History, University of Minnesota, 614 Social Sciences Building, Minneapolis, Minn. 55455, USA.
Altschul, Professor M., PhD, Case Western Reserve University, Cleveland, Ohio 44106, USA.
Anderson, Professor M. S., MA, PhD, London School of Economics, Houghton Street, London WC2 2AE.
Anderson, Mrs O. R., MA, BLitt, Westfield College, London NW3.
Andrew, C. M., MA, PhD, Director of Studies, Corpus Christi College, Cambridge.
Andrews, K. R., BA, PhD, Dept of History, University of Hull, Cottingham Road, Hull HU6 7RX.
Anglesey, The Most Hon., The Marquess of, FSA, FRSL, Plas-Newydd, Llanfairpwll, Anglesey LL61 6DZ.
Anglo, S., BA, PhD, FSA, Dept of History of Ideas, University College, Swansea.
Annan, Lord, OBE, MA, DLitt, DUniv, University College, Gower Street, London WC1 6BT.
Annis, P. G. W., BA, 70 Northcote Road, Sidcup, Kent DA14 6PW.

Appleby, J. S., Little Pitchbury, Brick Kiln Lane, Great Horkseley, Colchester, Essex CO6 4EU.

Armstrong, Miss A. M., BA, 7 Vale Court, Mallord Street, London SW3.

Armstrong, C. A. J., MA, FSA, Hertford College, Oxford.

Armstrong, Professor F. H., PhD, University of Western Ontario, London 72, Ontario.

Armstrong, W. A., BA, PhD, Eliot College, The University, Canterbury, Kent.

Arnstein, Professor W. L., PhD, Dept of History, University of Illinois at Urbana-Champaign, 309 Gregory Hall, Urbana, Ill. 61801, U.S.A.

Ashton, Professor R., PhD, The Manor House, Brundall, near Norwich NOR 86Z.

Ashworth, Professor W., BSc(Econ), PhD, Dept of Econ. and Soc. History, The University, Bristol.

Aston, Mrs M. E., MA, DPhil, Castle House, Chipping Ongar, Essex.

Aston, T. H., MA, FSA, Corpus Christi College, Oxford OX1 4JF.

Auchmuty, Professor J. J., CBE, MA, PhD, DLitt, LLD, MRIA, FAHA, 9 Glynn Street, Hughes, ACT 2605, Australia.

Austin, M. R., BD, MA, PhD, The Glead, 2a Louvain Road, Derby DE3 6BZ.

Avery, D. J., MA, BLitt, 6 St James's Square, London SW1.

Axelson, Professor E. V., DLitt, University of Cape Town, Rondebosch, S. Africa.

*Aydelotte, Professor W. O., PhD, State University of Iowa, Iowa City, Iowa, U.S.A.

Aylmer, Professor G. E., MA, DPhil, FBA, University of York, Heslington, York YO1 5DD.

Bahlman, Dudley W. R., PhD, Dept of History, Williams College, Williamstown, Mass., U.S.A.

Baillie, H. M. G., MBE, MA, FSA, 12B Stanford Road, London W8 3QJ.

Bailyn, Professor B., MA, PhD, LittD, LHD, Widener J. Harvard University, Cambridge, Mass. 02138, U.S.A.

Baker, L. G. D., MA, BLitt, Dept of Medieval Hist., The University, Edinburgh.

Baker, T. F. T., BA, Camden Lodge, 50 Hastings Road, Pembury, Kent.

Ballhatchet, Professor K. A., MA, PhD, 11 The Mead, Ealing, London W13.

Banks, Professor J. A., MA, Dept of Sociology, The University, Leicester LE1 7RH.

Barber, M. C., BA, PhD, Dept of History, The University, Reading, Berks. RG6 2AA.

Barker, E. E., MA, PhD, FSA, 60 Marina Road, Little Altcar, Formby, via Liverpool, Lancs. L37 6BP.

Barker, Professor T. C., MA, PhD, Minsen Dane, Brogdale Road, Faversham, Kent.

Barkley, Professor the Rev. J. M. MA, DD, 2 College Park, Belfast, N. Ireland.

*Barlow, Professor F. MA, DPhil, FBA, Middle Court Hall, Kenton, Exeter.

Barnes, Miss P. M., PhD, Public Record Office, Chancery Lane, London WC2.

Barnes, Professor T. G., AB, DPhil, University of California, Berkeley, Calif., 94720, U.S.A.

*Barnes, Professor Viola F., MA, PhD, LLD, 16 North Sycamore Street, South Hadley, Mass. 01075, U.S.A.

Barratt, Miss D. M., DPhil, The Corner House, Hampton Poyle, Kidlington, Oxford.

Barron, Mrs C. M., MA, PhD, 35 Rochester Road, London NW1.

Barrow, Professor G. W. S., MA, DLitt, FBA, The Old Manse, 19 Westfield Road, Cupar, Fife KY15 5AP.

Bartlett, C. J., PhD, 5 Strathspey Place, West Ferry, Dundee DD5 1QB.

Batho, G. R., MA, Dept of Education, The University, 48 Old Elvet, Durham DH1 3JH.

Baugh, Professor Daniel A., PhD, Dept of History, McGraw Hall, Cornell University, Ithaca, N.Y. 14850, U.S.A.

Baxter, Professor S. B., PhD, 608 Morgan Creek Road, Chapel Hill, N.C. 27514 U.S.A.

Baylen, Professor J. O., MA, PhD, Georgia State University, 33 Gilmer Street S.E., Atlanta, Georgia 30303. U.S.A.

Beales, D. E. D. MA, PhD, Sidney Sussex College, Cambridge CB2 3HU.

Beales, H. L., DLitt, 16 Denman Drive, London NW11.

Bealey, Professor F., BSc(Econ), Dept of Politics, Taylor Building, Old Aberdeen AB9 2UB.

Bean, Professor J. M. W., MA, DPhil, 622 Fayerweather Hall, Columbia University, New York, N.Y. 10027, U.S.A.

Beardwood, Miss Alice, BA, BLitt, DPhil, 415 Miller's Lane, Wynnewood, Pa. U.S.A.

Beasley, Professor W. G. PhD, FBA, 172 Hampton Road, Twickenham, Middlesex TW2 5NJ.

Beattie, Professor J. M., PhD Dept of History, University of Toronto, Toronto M5S 1A1, Canada.

Beaumont, H., MA, Silverdale, Severn Bank, Shrewsbury.

Beckett, Professor J. C., MA, 19 Wellington Park Terrace, Belfast 9, N. Ireland.

Beckingsale, B. W., MA, 8 Highbury, Newcastle upon Tyne NE2 3DX.

Bédarida, F., Professeur à l'Institut d'Etudes Politiques, 13 rue Jacob, 75006 Paris, France.

Beddard, R. A., MA, DPhil, Oriel College, Oxford.

Beeler, Professor J. H., PhD, 1302 New Garden Road, Greensboro, N.C. 27410, U.S.A.

*Beer, E. S. de, CBE, MA, DLitt, FBA, FSA, 31 Brompton Square, London SW3 2AE.

Beer, Professor Samuel H., PhD, Faculty of Arts & Sciences, Harvard University, Littauer Center G-15, Cambridge, Mass. 02138, U.S.A.

Begley, W. W., 17 St Mary's Gardens, London SE11.

Behrens, Miss C. B. A., MA, Dales Barn, Barton, Cambridge.

Bell, P. M. H., BA, BLitt, The School of History, The University, P.O. Box 147, Liverpool L69 3BX.

Beller, E. A., DPhil, Dept of History, Princeton University, N.J., 08540, U.S.A.

Beloff, Professor M., DLitt, FBA, The Univ. College at Buckingham, Hunter Street, Buckingham MK18 1EG.

Bennett, Capt. G. M., RN(ret.), DSC, Stage Coach Cottage, 57 Broad Street, Ludlow, Salop. SY8 1NH.
Bennett, Rev. Canon G. V., MA, DPhil, FSA, New College, Oxford.
Bennett, R. F., MA, Magdalene College, Cambridge.
Bethell, D. L. T., MA, Dept of Medieval History, University College, Belfield, Dublin 4, Ireland.
Bethell, L. M., PhD, University College, Gower Street, London WC1E 6BT.
Biddiss, M. D., MA, PhD, The University, Leicester LE1 7RH.
Biddle, M, MA, FSA, Winchester Research Unit, 13 Parchment Street, Winchester.
Bidwell, Brig. R. G. S., OBE, Royal United Services Institute, Whitehall, London SW1A 2ET.
Bindoff, Professor S. T., MA, 2 Sylvan Gardens, Woodlands Road, Surbiton, Surrey.
Binney, J. E. D., DPhil, 6 Pageant Drive, Sherborne, Dorset.
Birch, A., MA, PhD, University of Hong Kong, Hong Kong.
Bishop, A. S., BA, PhD, 254 Leigham Court Road, Streatham, London SW16 2RP.
Bishop, T. A. M., MA, The Annexe, Manor House, Hemingford Grey, Hunts.
Black, Professor Eugene C., PhD, Dept of History, Brandeis University, Waltham, Mass. 02154 U.S.A.
Blair, P. Hunter, MA, LittD, Emmanuel College, Cambridge CB2 3AP.
Blake, E. O., MA, PhD, Roselands, Moorhill Road, Westend, Southampton SO3 3AW.
Blake, Professor J. W., CBE, MA, DLitt, Willow Cottage, Mynoe, Limavady, Co. Londonderry, N. Ireland.
Blake, Lord, MA, FBA, The Provost's Lodgings, The Queen's College, Oxford OX1 4AW.
Blakemore, H., PhD, 43 Fitzjohn Avenue, Barnet, Herts.
*Blakey, Professor R. G., PhD, c/o Mr Raymond Shove, Order Dept, Library, University of Minnesota, Minneapolis, Minn., U.S.A.
Blakiston, H. N., BA, 6 Markham Square, London SW3.
Blaxland, Major W. G., Lower Heppington, Street End, Canterbury, Kent CT4 7AN.
Blewett, Professor N., BA, DipEd, MA, DPhil, School of Social Sciences, Flinders University of S. Australia, Bedford Park, 5042, S. Australia.
Blomfield, Mrs K., 8 Elmdene Court, Constitution Hill, Woking, Surrey GU22 7SA.
Blunt, C. E., OBE, FBA, FSA, Ramsbury Hill, Ramsbury, Marlborough, Wilts.
*Bolsover, G. H., OBE, MA, PhD, 7 Devonshire Road, Hatch End, Middlesex.
Bolton, Miss Brenda, BA, Dept of History, Westfield College, London NW3 7ST.
Bolton, Professor G. C., MA, DPhil, 6 Melvista Avenue, Claremont, Western Australia.
Bolton, Professor W. F., AM, PhD, FSA, Douglass College, Rutgers University, New Brunswick, N.J. 08903, U.S.A.
Bond, M. F., OBE, MA, FSA, 19 Bolton Crescent, Windsor, Berks.
Borrie, M. A. F., BA, 14 Lancaster Gate, London W2.
Bossy, J. A., MA, PhD, Dept of Modern History, The Queen's University, Belfast BT7 1NN, N. Ireland.

Bottigheimer, Professor Karl S., Dept of History, State University of New York at Stony Brook, Long Island, N.Y., U.S.A.

Boulton, Professor J. T., BLitt, PhD, Dept of English, The University, P.O. Box 363, Birmingham B15 2TT.

Bowker, Mrs M., MA, BLitt, The Cottage, Bailrigg Lane, Lancaster.

Bowyer, M. J. F., 32 Netherhall Way, Cambridge.

*Boxer, Professor C. R., DLitt, FBA, Ringshall End, Little Gaddesden, Berkhamsted, Herts.

Boyce, D. G., BA, PhD, Dept of Political Theory and Government, University College, Swansea SA2 8PP.

Boyle, Professor the Rev. L. E., DPhil, STL, Pontifical Institute of Mediaeval Studies, 59 Queen's Park, Toronto 181, Canada.

Boynton, L. O. J., MA, DPhil, FSA, Westfield College, London NW3.

Brading, D. A., MA, PhD, 28 Storey Way, Cambridge.

Bradshaw, B., MA, BD, PhD, Mary Immaculate College of Education, Limerick, Ireland.

Bramsted, E. K., PhD, DPhil, Woodpeckers, Brooklands Lane, Weybridge, Surrey KT13 8UX.

Brandon, P. F., BA, PhD, Greensleeves, 8 St Julian's Lane, Shoreham-by-Sea, Sussex BN4 6YS.

Breck, Professor A. D., MA, PhD, LHD, DLitt, University of Denver, Denver, Colorado 80210, U.S.A.

Brentano, Professor R., DPhil, University of California, Berkeley, Calif., U.S.A.

Brett, M., MA, DPhil, 7 Bardwell Road, Oxford OX2 6SU.

Brett-James, E. A., MA, Royal Military Academy, Sandhurst, Camberley, Surrey.

Bridge, F. R., PhD, The Poplars, Rodley Lane, Rodley, Leeds.

Briggs, Lord, BSc(Econ), MA, DLitt, Provost, Worcester College, Oxford.

Briggs, J. H. Y., University of Keele, Staffs ST5 5BG.

Briggs, R., MA, All Souls College, Oxford OX1 4AL.

Brock, M. G., MA, 31 Linton Road, Oxford OX2 6UL.

Brock, Professor W. R., MA, PhD, Department of History, University of Glasgow, Glasgow 2.

Brodie, Miss D. M., PhD, 137 Roberts Road, Pietermaritzburg, Natal, South Africa.

Brogan, D. H. V., MA, University of Essex, Colchester CO4 3SQ.

*Bromley, Professor J. S., MA, Merrow, Dene Close, Upper Bassett, Southampton.

*Brooke, Professor C. N. L., MA, LittD, FBA, FSA, Westfield College, London NW3 7ST.

Brooke, J., BA, 63 Hurst Avenue, Chingford, London E4 8DL.

Brooke, Mrs R. B., MA, PhD, c/o Westfield College, London NW3 7ST.

Brooks, F. W., MA, FSA, The University, Hull.

Brooks, N. P., MA, DPhil, The University, St Andrews, Fife.

Brown, Professor A. L., MA, DPhil, The University, Dept of History, Glasgow G12 8QQ.

Brown, G. S., PhD, 1720 Hanover Road, Ann Arbor, Mich., 48103, U.S.A.

Brown, Jennifer M., MA, PhD, Dept of Scottish History, University of Glasgow, Glasgow G12.

Brown, Judith M., MA, PhD, Dept of History, The University, Manchester M13 9PL.

Brown, K. D., BA, MA, PhD, Dept of Econ. and Soc. History, The Queen's University, Belfast BT7 1NN, N. Ireland.

Brown, Miss L. M., MA, PhD, 93 Church Road, Hanwell, London W7.

Brown, Professor M. J., MA, PhD, 333 South Candler Street, Decatur, Georgia 30030, U.S.A.

Brown, P. R. Lamont, MA, FBA, Hillslope, Pullen's Lane, Oxford.

Brown, R. A., MA, DPhil, FSA, King's College, Strand, London WC2.

Bruce, J. M., MA, 6 Albany Close, Bushey Heath, Herts, WD2 3SG.

Bryant, Sir Arthur (W. M.), CH, CBE, LLD, 18 Rutland Gate, London SW7.

Bryson, Professor W. Hamilton, School of Law, University of Richmond, Richmond, Va. 23173, U.S.A.

Buckland, P. J., MA, PhD, 6 Rosefield Road, Liverpool L25 8TF.

Bueno de Mesquita, D. M., MA, PhD, Christ Church, Oxford.

Bullock, Sir Alan (L.C.), MA, DLitt, FBA, St Catherine's College, Oxford.

Bullough, Professor D. A., MA, FSA, Dept of Mediaeval History, 71 South Street, St Andrews, Fife.

Burke, U. P., MA, 15 Lower Market Street, Hove, Sussex, BN3 1AT.

Burleigh, The Rev. Professor J. H. S., BD, 21 Kingsmuir Drive, Peebles, EH45 9AA.

Burns, Professor J. H., MA, PhD, 39 Amherst Road, London W13.

Burroughs, P., PhD, Dalhousie University, Halifax, Nova Scotia, Canada.

Burrow, J. W., MA, PhD, Sussex University, Falmer, Brighton.

Bury, J. P. T., MA, LittD, Corpus Christi College, Cambridge.

Butler, Professor L. H., MA, DPhil, Principal, Royal Holloway College, Englefield Green, Surrey.

Butler, R. D'O, CMG, MA, All Souls College, Oxford.

BUTTERFIELD, Professor Sir Herbert, MA, LLD, DLitt, DLit, LittD, FBA, 28 High Street, Sawston, Cambridge CB2 4BG.

Bythell, D., MA, DPhil, 23–26 Old Elvet, The University, Durham DH1 3HY.

Cabaniss, Professor J. A., PhD, University of Mississippi, Box No. 253, University, Mississippi, U.S.A.

Calvert, Brig. J. M. (ret.) MA, 6A Gregory Place, Kensington, London W8 4NG.

Calvert, P. A. R., MA, PhD, AM, Dept of Politics, University of Southampton, Highfield, Southampton SO9 5NH.

Cameron, Professor K., PhD, The University, Nottingham.

Campbell, Professor A. E., MA, PhD, School of History, University of Birmingham, P.O. Box 363, Birmingham B15 2TT.

Campbell, J., MA, Worcester College, Oxford.

Campbell, Professor Mildred L., PhD, Vassar College, Poughkeepsie, N.Y., U.S.A.

Campbell, Professor R. H., MA, PhD, University of Stirling, Scotland.

Cant, R. G., MA, 2 Kinburn Place, St Andrews, Fife.

Cantor, Professor Norman F., PhD, Office of the Academic Vice President, State University of New York at Binghamton, New York 13901, U.S.A.

Capp, B. S., MA, DPhil, Dept of History, University of Warwick, Coventry, Warwickshire CV4 7AL.

Cargill-Thompson, Professor W. D. J., MA, PhD, Dept of Ecclesiastical History, King's College, Strand, London WC2.

*Carlson, Leland H., PhD, 255 S. Avenue 50, Los Angeles, Cal. 90042, U.S.A.
Carlton, Professor Charles, Dept of History, North Carolina State University, Raleigh, N.C. 27607, U.S.A.
Carman, W. Y., FSA, 94 Mulgrave Road, Sutton, Surrey.
Carr, A. D., MA, PhD, University College of North Wales, Dept of Welsh History, Bangor, Gwynedd.
Carr, A. R. M., MA, St Antony's College, Oxford.
Carr, W., PhD, 16 Old Hay Close, Dore, Sheffield S17 3GQ.
Carrington, Miss Dorothy, 3 Rue Emmanuel Arene, 20 Ajaccio, Corsica.
Carter, Mrs A. C., MA, 12 Garbrand Walk, Ewell, Epsom, Surrey.
Cartlidge, Rev. J. E. G., Sunnyside House, Snowhill, St George's, Oakengates, Salop.
*Carus-Wilson, Professor E. M., MA, FBA, FSA, 14 Lansdowne Road, London W11.
Catto, R. J. A. I., MA, Oriel College, Oxford.
Chadwick, Professor W. O., DD, DLitt, FBA, Selwyn Lodge, Cambridge.
Challis, C. E., MA, PhD, 14 Ashwood Villas, Headingley, Leeds 6.
Chambers, D. S., MA, DPhil, Warburg Institute, Woburn Square, London WC1.
Chandaman, Professor C. D., BA, PhD, St David's University College, Lampeter, Cardiganshire.
Chandler, D. G., MA, Hindford, Monteagle Lane, Yately, Camberley, Surrey.
Chaplais, P., PhD, FBA, FSA, Wintles Farm House, 36 Mill Street, Eynsham, Oxford OX8 1JS.
Charles-Edwards, T. M., DPhil, Corpus Christi College, Oxford.
*CHENEY, Professor C. R., MA, DLitt, FBA, 236 Hills Road, Cambridge CB2 2QE.
Chibnall, Mrs Marjorie, MA, DPhil, 6 Millington Road, Cambridge CB3 9HP.
Child, C. J., OBE, MA, PhM, 94 Westhall Road, Warlingham, Surrey CR3 9HB.
Chrimes, Professor S. B., MA, PhD, LittD, 24 Cwrt-y-Vil Road, Penarth, Glam. CF6 2HP.
Christie, Professor I. R., MA, 10 Green Lane, Croxley Green, Herts. WD3 3HR.
Church, Professor R. A., BA, PhD, School of Social Studies, University of East Anglia, Norwich NOR 88C.
Cirket, A. F., 71 Curlew Crescent, Bedford.
Clanchy, M. T., PhD, FSA, The University, Medieval History Dept, Glasgow G12 8QQ.
Clark, A. E., MA, 32 Durham Avenue, Thornton Cleveleys, Blackpool FY5 2DP.
Clark, Professor Dora Mae, PhD, 134 Pennsylvania Ave., Chambersburg, Pa. 17201, U.S.A.
Clarke, P. F., MA, PhD, Dept of History, University College, Gower Street, London WC1E 6BT.
*CLAY, Sir Charles (T.), CB, MA, LittD, FBA, FSA, 30 Queen's Gate Gardens, London SW7.
Clementi, Miss D., MA, DPhil, Flat 7, 43 Rutland Gate, London SW7 PB1.
Clemoes, Professor P. A. M., BA, PhD, Emmanuel College, Cambridge CB2 3AP.

Cliffe, J. T., BA, PhD, 263 Staines Road, Twickenham, Middx. TW2 5AY.
Clive, Professor J. L., PhD, 38 Fernald Drive, Cambridge, Mass. 02138, U.S.A.
Clough, C. H., MA, DPhil, School of History, The University, 8 Abercromby Square, Liverpool 7.
Cobb, H. S., MA, FSA, 1 Child's Way, Hampstead Garden Suburb, London NW11.
Cobban, A. B., MA, PhD, School of History, The University, 8 Abercromby Square, Liverpool 7.
Cockburn, J. S., LLB, LLM, PhD, c/o Public Record Office, Chancery Lane, London WC2A 1LR.
Cocks, E. J., MA, Middle Lodge, Ardingly, Haywards Heath, Sussex.
*Code, Rt Rev. Monsignor Joseph B., MA, STB, ScHistD, DLitt, 3441 Esplanade Avenue, New Orleans, Louisiana 70119, U.S.A.
Cohn, H. J., MA, DPhil, University of Warwick, Coventry CV4 7AL.
Cohn, Professor N., MA, DLitt, 61 New End, London NW3.
Cole, Dame Margaret, 4 Ashdown, Clivedon Court, Clevelands, London W13 8DR.
Coleman, B. I., MA, PhD, Dept of History, The University, Exeter.
Coleman, Professor D. C., BSc(Econ), PhD, FBA, Over Hall, Cavendish, Sudbury, Suffolk.
Collier, W. O., MA, FSA, 34 Berwyn Road, Richmond, Surrey.
Collins, Mrs I., MA, BLitt, School of History, 8 Abercromby Square, Liverpool 7.
Collinson, Professor P., MA, PhD, Keynes College, The University, Canterbury, Kent CT2 7NP.
Colvin, H. M., CBE, MA, FBA, St John's College, Oxford.
Conacher, Professor J. B., MA, PhD, 151 Welland Avenue, Toronto 290, Ontario, Canada.
Congreve, A. L., MA, FSA, Orchard Cottage, Cranbrook, Kent TN17 3NW.
Connell-Smith, Professor G. E., PhD, 7 Braids Walk, Kirkella, Hull, Yorks. HU10 7PA.
Constable, G., PhD, 25 Mount Pleasant Street, Cambridge, 40, Mass, U.S.A.
Conway, Professor A. A., MA, University of Canterbury, Christchurch 1, New Zealand.
Cook, A. E., MA, PhD, 20 Nicholas Road, Hunter's Ride, Henley-on-Thames, Oxon.
Cook, C. P., MA, DPhil, 182 Stoneleigh Park Road, Ewell, Epsom, Surrey.
Cooke, Professor J. J., PhD, Dept of History, College of Liberal Arts, University of Mississippi, University, Miss. 38677, U.S.A.
Coolidge, Professor R. T., MA, BLitt, History Dept, Loyola Campus, Concordia University, 7141 Sherbrooke Street West, Montreal, Quebec H4B 1R6, Canada.
Cooper, J. P., MA, Trinity College, Oxford.
Cope, Professor Esther S., PhD, Dept of History, Univ. of Nebraska, Lincoln, Neb. 68508, U.S.A.
Copeland, Professor T. W., PhD, Dept of English, Univ. of Massachusetts, Amherst, Mass. 01002, U.S.A.
Cornford, Professor J. P., Dept of Politics, University of Edinburgh, William Robertson Bldg., George Sq., Edinburgh EH8 9JY.

Cornwall, J. C. K., MA, 1 Orchard Close, Copford Green, Colchester, Essex.
Corson, J. C., MA, PhD, Mossrig, Lilliesleaf, Melrose, Roxburghshire.
Costeloe, M. P., BA, PhD, Hispanic and Latin American Studies, The University, 83 Woodland Road, Bristol.
Cowan, I. B., MA, PhD, University of Glasgow, Glasgow, G12 8QH.
Cowdrey, Rev. H. E. J., MA, St Edmund Hall, Oxford OX1 4AR.
Cowie, Rev. L. W., MA, PhD, 38 Stratton Road, Merton Park, London SW19 3JG.
Cowley, F. G., PhD, 17 Brookvale Road, West Cross, Swansea.
Craig, R. S., BSc(Econ), 27 Ridgmount Gardens, Bloomsbury, London WC1E 7AS.
Cramp, Professor Rosemary, MA, BLitt, FSA, Department of Archaeology, The Old Fulling Mill, The Banks, Durham.
Craton, Professor M. J., BA, MA, PhD, Dept of History, University of Waterloo, Waterloo, Ontario, Canada.
*Crawley, C. W., MA, 1 Madingley Road, Cambridge.
Cremona, His Hon. Chief Justice Professor J. J., DLitt, PhD, LLD, DrJur, 5 Victoria Gardens, Sliema, Malta.
Crittall, Miss E., MA, FSA, 16 Downside Crescent, London NW3.
Crombie, A. C., BSc, MA, PhD, Trinity College, Oxford OX1 3BH.
Cromwell, Miss V., MA, University of Sussex, Falmer, Brighton, Sussex.
Cross, Miss M. C., MA, PhD, University of York, York YO1 5DD.
Crowder, C. M. D., MA, DPhil, Queen's University, Kingston, Ontario, Canada.
Crowe, Miss S. E., MA, PhD, St Hilda's College, Oxford.
Cruickshank, C. G., MA, DPhil, 15 McKay Road, Wimbledon Common, London SW20.
Cruickshanks, Eveline G., PhD, Full Point, Off Clarendon Road, Sevenoaks, Kent.
Cumming, Professor I., MEd, PhD, The University, Auckland, New Zealand.
Cummins, Professor J. S., PhD, University College, Gower Street, London WC1E 6BT.
Cumpston, Miss I. M., MA, DPhil, Birkbeck College, Malet Street, London WC1.
Cunliffe, Professor M. F., MA, BLitt, Dept of American Studies, University of Sussex, Falmer, Brighton BN1 9QN.
Cunningham, Professor A. B., MA, PhD, Simon Fraser University, Burnaby 2, B.C., Canada.
Curtis, Professor L. Perry, PhD, Dept of History, Brown University, Providence, R.I. 02912, U.S.A.
Curtis, M. H., PhD, Scripps College, Claremont, Calif., U.S.A.
Cushner, Rev. N. P., SJ, MA, 168 West Humboldt, Buffalo, New York 14214, U.S.A.
*Cuttino, Professor G. P., DPhil, Department of History, Emory University, Atlanta 22, Ga., U.S.A.

Dakin, Professor D., MA, PhD, 7 Langside Avenue, London SW15.
Darlington, Professor R. R., BA, PhD, FBA, FSA, Warrenhurst, Twyford, Reading.
Davies, Professor Alun, MA, 46 Eaton Crescent, Swansea.
Davies, C. S. L., MA, DPhil, Wadham College, Oxford.
Davies, I. N. R., MA, DPhil, 22 Rowland Close, Wolvercote, Oxford.

Davies, P. N., MA, PhD, Cmar, Croft Drive, Caldy, Wirral, Merseyside.
Davies, Professor R. R., DPhil, University College of Wales, Dept of History, 1 Laura Place, Aberystwyth.
*Davis, G. R. C., MA, DPhil, 214 Somerset Road, London SW19 5JE
Davis, Professor R. H. C., MA, FBA, FSA, 56 Fitzroy Avenue, Harborne, Birmingham B17 8RJ.
Davis, Professor Richard W., Dept of History, Washington University, St Louis, Missouri 63130, U.S.A.
*Dawe, D. A., 46 Green Lane, Purley, Surrey.
*Day, P. W., MA, 2 Rectory Terrace, Gosforth, Newcastle upon Tyne.
Deane, Miss Phyllis M., MA, Newnhan College, Cambridge.
*Deanesly, Professor Margaret, MA, FSA, 196 Clarence Gate Gardens, London NW1.
*Deeley, Miss A. P., MA, 41 Linden Road, Bicester, Oxford.
de la Mare, Miss A. C., MA, PhD, Bodleian Library, Oxford.
Denham, E. W., MA, 27 The Drive, Northwood, Middx, HA6 1HW.
Dennis, Professor P. J., MA, PhD, Dept of History, The Royal Military College of Canada, Kingston, Ont. K7L 2W3. Canada.
Denton, J. H., BA, PhD, The University Manchester M13 9PL.
Dickens, Professor A. G., CMG, MA, DLit, FBA, FSA, Institute of Historical Research, University of London, Senate House, London WC1E 7HU.
Dickinson, H. T., MA, PhD, Dept of Modern History, The University, Edinburgh.
Dickinson, Rev. J. C., MA, FSA, The University, Birmingham 15.
Dickson, P. G. M., MA, DPhil, St Catherine's College, Oxford.
Diké, Professor K. O., MA, PhD, Dept of History, Harvard University, Cambridge, Mass, 02138, U.S.A.
Dilks, Professor D. N., BA, Dept of International History, The University, Leeds.
Dilworth, Rev. G. M., OSB, MA, PhD, The Abbey, Fort Augustus, Inverness-shire PH32 4DB, Scotland.
Dobson, Professor R. B., MA, DPhil, Department of History, The University, Heslington, York YO1 5DD.
*Dodwell, Miss B., MA, The University, Reading.
Dodwell, Professor C. R., MA, PhD, FSA, History of Art Department, The University, Manchester M13 9PL.
Dolley, Professor R. H. M., BA, MRIA, FSA, The Queen's University, Belfast BT7 1NN, N. Ireland.
Don Peter, The Right Revd. Monsignor W. L. A., MA, PhD, Archbishop's House, Colombo 8, Sri Lanka.
Donald, Professor M. B., MSc, Rabbit Shaw, 6 Stagbury Avenue, Chipstead, Surrey CR3 3PA.
*Donaldson, Professor G., MA, PhD, DLitt, FBA, Preston Tower Nursery Cottage, Prestonpans, East Lothian EH32 9EN.
*Donaldson-Hudson, Miss R., BA, (address unknown).
Donoghue, B., MA, DPhil, 7 Brookfield Park, London NW5 1ES.
Dore, R. N., MA, Holmrook, 19 Chapel Lane, Hale Barns, Altrincham, Cheshire WA15 0AB.
Douglas, Professor D. C., MA, DLitt, FBA, 4 Henleaze Gardens, Bristol.
Douie, Miss D. L., BA, PhD, FSA, Flat A, 2 Charlbury Road, Oxford.
Downer, L. J., MA, LLB, Mediaeval Studies, Australian National University, Canberra.

Doyle, A. I., MA, PhD, University College, The Castle, Durham.
Doyle, W., MA, DPhil, Dept of History, University of York, Heslington, York YO1 5DD.
Driver, J. T., MA, BLitt, 25 Abbot's Grange, Off Liverpool Road, Chester CH2 1AJ.
*Drus, Miss E., MA, The University, Southampton.
Du Boulay, Professor F. R. H., MA, Broadmead, Riverhead, Sevenoaks, Kent.
Duckham, B. F., MA, Hillhead Cottage, Balfron, Stirlingshire G63 0PH.
Duggan, C., PhD, King's College, Strand, London WC2.
Dugmore, The Rev. Professor C. W., DD, King's College, Strand, London WC2.
Duke, A. C., MA, Dept of History, The University, Southampton SO9 NH5.
Duly, Professor L. C., PhD, Dept of History, University of Nebraska, Lincoln, Neb. 68508, U.S.A.
Dumville, D. N., MA, PhD, Dept of Welsh, University College of Swansea, Singleton Park, Swansea SA2 8PP.
Dunbabin, J. P. D., MA, St Edmund Hall, Oxford.
Duncan, Professor A. A. M., MA, University of Glasgow, 9 University Gardens, Glasgow G12 8QH.
Dunham, Professor W. H., PhD, 200 Everit Street, New Haven, Conn. 06511, U.S.A.
Dunn, Professor R. S., PhD, Dept of History, The College, University of Pennsylvania, Philadelphia, Pa., 19104, U.S.A.
Dunning, R. W., BA, PhD, FSA, 16 Comeytrowe Rise, Taunton, Somerset.
Durack, Mrs I. A., MA, PhD, University of Western Australia, Crawley, Western Australia.
Dykes, D. W., MA, Cherry Grove, Welsh St Donats, nr Cowbridge, Glam. CF7 7SS.
Dyos, Professor H. J., BSc(Econ), PhD, 16 Kingsway Road, Leicester.

Eastwood, Rev. C. C., PhD, Heathview, Monks Lane, Audlem, Cheshire.
Eckles, Professor R. B., PhD, P.O. Box 3035, West Lafayette, Indiana, 47906, U.S.A.
Ede, J. R., MA, Public Record Office, Chancery Lane, London WC2A 1LR.
Edmonds, Professor E. L., MA, PhD, Dean of Education, Univ. of Prince Edward Island, Charlottetown, Prince Edward Island, Canada.
Edwards, F. O., SJ, BA, FSA, 114 Mount Street, London W1Y 6AH.
Edwards, Professor R. W. D., MA, PhD, DLitt, 21 Brendan Road, Donnybrook, Dublin 4, Ireland.
Ehrman, J. P. W., MA, FBA, FSA, Sloane House, 149 Old Church Street, London SW3 6EB.
Elliott, Professor J. H., MA, PhD, FBA, King's College, Strand, London WC2.
Ellis, R. H., MA, FSA, Cloth Hill, 6 The Mount, London NW3.
Ellul, M., BArch, DipArch, 'Pauline', 55 Old Railway Road, Birkirkara, Malta.
Elrington, C. R., MA, FSA, Institute of Historical Research, Senate House, London WC1E 7HU.
ELTON, Professor G. R., MA, PhD, LittD, FBA (*President*), 30 Millington Road, Cambridge CB3 9HP.

Elvin ,L., 10 Almond Avenue, Swanpool, Lincoln.
*Emmison, F. G., MBE, PhD, DUniv, FSA, 8 Coppins Close, Chelmsford, Essex CM2 6AY.
d'Entrèves, Professor A. P., DPhil, Strada Ai Ronchi 48, Cavoretto, Torino, Italy.
Erickson, Charlotte J., PhD, London School of Economics, Houghton Street, London WC2.
*Erith, E. J., Shurlock House, Shurlock Row, Berkshire.
Erskine, Mrs A. M., MA, BLitt, FSA, 44 Birchy Barton Hill, Exeter EX1 3EX.
Evans, Mrs A. K. B., PhD, FSA, White Lodge, 25 Knighton Grange Road, Leicester LE2 2LF.
Evans, Sir David (L.), OBE, BA, DLitt, 2 Bay Court, Doctors Commons Road, Berkhamsted, Herts.
Evans, Miss Joan, DLitt, DLit, LLD, LittD, FSA, Thousand Acres, Wootton-under-Edge, Glos.
Evans, R. J. W., MA, PhD, Brasenose College, Oxford.
Evans, The Very Rev. S. J. A., CBE, MA, FSA, The Old Manor, Fulbourne, Cambs.
Everitt, Professor A. M., MA, PhD, The University, Leicester.
Eyck, Professor U. F. J., MA, BLitt, Dept of History, University of Calgary, Alberta T2N IN4, Canada.

Fage, Professor J. D., MA, PhD, Centre of West African Studies, The University, Birmingham B15 2TT.
Fagg, J. E., MA, 47 The Avenue, Durham DH1 4ED.
Farmer, D. F. H., BLitt, FSA, The University, Reading.
Farr, M. W., MA, FSA, 12 Emscote Road, Warwick.
Fearn, Rev. H., MA, PhD, Holy Trinity Vicarage, 6 Wildwood, Northwood, Middlesex.
Fenlon, D. B., BA, PhD, Gonville and Caius College, Cambridge.
Fenn, Rev. R. W. D., MA, BD, FSAScot, The Rectory, Staunton-on-Wye, Hereford.
Ferguson, Professor A. B., PhD, Dept of History, 6727 College Station, Duke University, Durham, N.C. 27708, U.S.A.
Feuchtwanger, E., MA, PhD, Highfield House, Dean, Sparsholt, nr Winchester, Hants.
Fieldhouse, D. K., MA, Nuffield College, Oxford.
Finer, Professor S. E., MA, Dept of Government and Public Administration, All Souls College, Oxford OX1 4AL.
Fink, Professor Z. S., PhD, 6880 Hawthorne Circle, Tucson, Arizona 85710, U.S.A.
Finlayson, G. B. A. M., MA, BLitt, 11 Burnhead Road, Glasgow G43 2SU.
Finley, Professor M. I., MA, PhD, DLitt, FBA, 12 Adams Road, Cambridge CB3 9AD.
Fisher, D. J. V., MA, Jesus College, Cambridge CB3 9AD.
Fisher, Professor F. J., MA, London School of Economics, Houghton Street, London WC2.
Fisher, F. N., Duckpool, Ashleyhay, Wirksworth, Derby DE4 4AJ.
Fisher, J. R., BA, MPhil, PhD, 6 Meadway, Upton, Wirral, Merseyside L49 6JG.
Fisher, Professor S. N., PhD, Box 162, Worthington, Ohio 43085, U.S.A.

Fitch, Dr M. F. B., FSA, 37 Avenue de Montoie, 1007 Lausanne, Switzerland.
Fletcher, A. J., MA, 59 Ranmoor Crescent, Sheffield S10 3GW.
*Fletcher, The Rt Hon The Lord, PC, BA, LLD, FSA, The Barn, The Green, Sarratt, Rickmansworth, Herts. WD3 6BP.
Flint, Professor J. E., MA, PhD, Dalhousie University, Halifax, Nova Scotia, B3H 3J5, Canada.
Flint, Valerie I. J., MA, DPhil, Dept of History, The University, Private Bag, Auckland, New Zealand.
Fogel, Professor R. W., PhD, Dept of Economics, Harvard University, 1737 Cambridge Street, Cambridge, Mass. 02138, U.S.A.
Foot, M. R. D., MA, BLitt, 88 Heath View, London N2 0QB.
Forbes, D., MA, 89 Gilbert Road, Cambridge.
Ford, W. K., 48 Harlands Road, Haywards Heath, West Sussex RH16 1LS.
Forster, G. C. F., BA, FSA, The University, Leeds 2.
Foster, Professor Elizabeth R., AM, PhD, 205 Strafford Avenue, Wayne, Pa. 19087, U.S.A.
Fowler, Professor K. A., BA, PhD, 2 Nelson Street, Edinburgh 3.
Fox, L., OBE, DL, LHD, MA, FSA, FRSL, Silver Birches, 27 Welcombe Road, Stratford-upon-Avon.
Fox, R., MA, DPhil, The University, Bailrigg, Lancaster LA1 4YG.
Francis, A. D., CBE, MVO, MA, 21 Cadogan Street, London SW3.
Franklin, R. M., BA, Baldwins End, Eton College, Windsor, Berks.
*Fraser, Miss C. M., PhD, 39 King Edward Road, Tynemouth, Tyne and Wear NE30 2RW.
Fraser, Miss Maxwell, MA, Crowthorne, 21 Dolphin Road, Slough, Berks. SL1 1TF.
Fraser, P., BA, PhD, Dept of History, Dalhousie University, Halifax, 8 Nova Scotia, Canada.
Frend, Professor W. H. C., TD, MA, DPhil, DD, FSA, Marbrae, Balmaha, Stirlingshire.
Fryde, Professor E. B., DPhil, Preswylfa, Trinity Road, Aberystwyth, Dyfed.
*Fryer, Professor C. E., MA, PhD, (address unknown).
Fryer, Professor W. R., BLitt, MA, 68 Grove Avenue, Chilwell, Beeston, Notts.
Frykenberg, Professor R. E., MA, PhD, 1840 Chadbourne Avenue, Madison, Wis. 53705, U.S.A.
*Furber, Professor H., MA, PhD, History Department, University of Pennsylvania, Philadelphia, Pa., U.S.A.
Fussell, G. E., DLitt, 55 York Road, Sudbury, Suffolk, CO10 6NF.
Fyrth, H., BSc(Econ.), Dept of Extra Mural Studies, University of London, 7 Ridgemount Street, London WC1.

Gabriel, Professor A. L., PhD, FMAA, CFIF, CFBA, P.O. Box 130, Charles Street Station 'F', Toronto, Ontario M4Y 2L4, Canada.
*Galbraith, Professor J. S., BS, MA, PhD, University of California, Los Angeles, Calif. 90024, U.S.A.
Gale, Professor H. P. P., OBE, PhD, 6 Nassau Road, London SW13 9QE.
Gale, W. K. V., 19 Ednam Road, Goldthorn Park, Wolverhampton WV4 5BL.
Gallagher, Professor J. A., MA, Trinity College, Cambridge.

Gann, L. H., MA, BLitt, DPhil, Hoover Institution, Stanford University, Stanford, Calif. 94305, U.S.A.
Ganshof, Professor F. L., 12 Rue Jacques Jordaens, Brussels, Belgium.
Gash, Professor N., MA, BLitt, FBA, Gowrie Cottage, 73 Hepburn Gardens, St Andrews.
Gee, E. A., MA, DPhil, FSA, 28 Trentholme Drive, The Mount, York YO2 2DG.
Gerlach, Professor D. R., MA, PhD, University of Akron, Akron, Ohio 44325, U.S.A.
Gibbs, G. C., MA, Birkbeck College, Malet Street, London WC1.
Gibbs, Professor N. H., MA, DPhil, All Souls College, Oxford.
Gibson, Margaret T., MA, DPhil, School of History, The University, Liverpool L69 3BX.
Gifford, Miss D. H., PhD, FSA, Public Record Office, Chancery Lane, London WC2A 1LR.
Gilbert, Professor Bentley B., PhD, Dept of History, University of Ill. at Chicago Circle, Box 4348, Chicago, Ill. 60680, U.S.A.
Gilbert, M., MA, The Map House, Harcourt Hill, Oxford.
Gilley, S., BA, DPhil, Dept of Ecclesiastical History, St Mary's College, University of St Andrew's, St Andrew's, Fife.
Ginter, D. E., AM, PhD, Dept of History, Sir George Williams University, Montreal 107, Canada.
Girtin, T., MA, Butter Field House, Church Street, Old Isleworth, Mddx.
Gleave, Group Capt. T. P., CBE, RAF(Ret.), Willow Bank, River Gardens, Bray-on-Thames, Berks.
*Glover, Professor R. G., MA, PhD, Carleton University, Ottawa 1, Canada.
*Godber, Miss A. J., MA, FSA, Mill Lane Cottage, Willington, Bedford.
Godfrey, Professor J. L., MA, PhD, 231 Hillcrest Circle, Chapel Hill, N.C., U.S.A.
Goldthorp, L. M., MA, Wilcroft House, Pecket Well, Hebden Bridge, West Yorks. HX7 8QY.
Gollancz, Miss M., MA, 41 Crescent Court, Surbiton, Surrey, KT6 4BW.
Gollin, Professor A., DLitt, University of California, Dept of History, Santa Barbara, Calif. 93106, U.S.A.
Gooch, John, BA, PhD, Dept of History, The University, Bailrigg, Lancaster LA1 4YG.
Goodman, A. E., MA, BLitt, Dept of Medieval History, The University, Edinburgh.
Goodspeed, Professor D. J., BA, 164 Victoria Street, Niagara-on-the-Lake, Ontario, Canada.
*Gopal, S., MA, DPhil, 30 Edward Elliot Road, Mylapore, Madras, India.
Gordon, Professor D. J., MA, PhD, Wantage Hall, Upper Redlands Road, Reading.
Gordon-Brown, A., Velden, Alexandra Road, Wynberg, C.P., South Africa.
Goring, J. J., MA, PhD, Little Iwood, Rushlake Green, Heathfield, East Sussex TN21 9QS.
Gorton, L. J., MA, 41 West Hill Avenue, Epsom, Surrey.
Gosden, P. H. J. H., MA, PhD, The University, Dept of Education, Leeds 2.
Gowing, Professor Margaret, MA, DLitt, BSc(Econ), FBA, Linacre College, Oxford.

*Graham, Professor G. S., MA, PhD, DLitt, LLD, Hobbs Cottage, Beckley, Rye, Sussex.

Gransden, Mrs A., MA, PhD, FSA, The University, Nottingham NG7 2RD.

Grassby, R. B., MA, Jesus College, Oxford.

Grattan-Kane, P., 12 St John's Close, Helston, Cornwall.

Graves, Professor Edgar B., PhD, LLD, 318 College Hill Road, Clinton, New York 13323, U.S.A.

Gray, J. W., MA, Dept of Modern History, The Queen's University of Belfast, Belfast BT7 1NN.

Gray, Miss M., MA, BLitt, 10 Clod Lane, Haslingden, Rossendale, Lancs. BB4 6LR.

Greaves, Mrs R. L., PhD, 1920 Hillview Road, Lawrence, Kansas 66044, U.S.A.

Greaves, Professor R. W., MA, DPhil, 1920 Hillview Road, Lawrence, Kansas 66044, U.S.A.

Green, H., BA, 16 Brands Hill Avenue, High Wycombe, Bucks HP13 5QA.

Green, Rev. V. H. H., MA, DD, Lincoln College, Oxford.

Greene, Professor Jack P., Dept of History, Johns Hopkins University, Baltimore, Md. 21218, U.S.A.

Greenhill, B. J., CMG, BA, FSA, National Maritime Museum, Greenwich, London SE10 9FN.

Greenleaf, Professor W. H., BSc(Econ), PhD, University College, Singleton Park, Swansea, Glam. SA2 8PP.

Gregg, E., MA, PhD, Dept of History, University of South Carolina, Columbia, S.C. 29208, U.S.A.

Grenville, Professor J. A. S., PhD, University of Birmingham, P.O. Box 363, Birmingham 15.

Gresham, C. A., BA, DLitt, FSA, Bryn-y-deryn, Criccieth, Caerns. LL52 0HR.

Grierson, Professor P., MA, LittD, FBA, FSA, Gonville and Caius College, Cambridge.

Grieve, Miss H. E. P., BA, 153 New London Road, Chelmsford, Essex.

Griffiths, J., MA, Springwood, Stanley Road, New Ferry, Wirral, Cheshire L62 5AS.

Griffiths, R. A., PhD, University College, Singleton Park, Swansea.

Grimble, I., PhD, 13 Saville Road, Twickenham, Mddx.

Grimm, Professor H. J., PhD, Department of History, 216 North Oval Drive, The Ohio State University, Columbus, 10, Ohio, U.S.A.

Grisbrooke, W. J., MA, 1 Whetstone Close, Farquhar Road, Birmingham B15 2QL.

*Griscom, Rev. Acton, MA, (address unknown).

Gum, Professor E. J., PhD, 2043 N.55th Street, Omaha, Nebraska 68104, U.S.A.

Gundersheimer, Professor W. L., MA, PhD, 507 Roumfort Road, Philadelphia, Pa. 19119, U.S.A.

HABAKKUK, Sir John (H.), MA, FBA (*President elect*), Jesus College, Oxford OX1 3DW.

Haber, Professor F. C., PhD, 3026 2R Street NW, Washington, DC 20007, U.S.A.

Hackett, Rev. M. B., OSA, BA, PhD, Austin Friars School, Carlisle CA3 9PB.

*Hadcock, R. N., DLitt, FSA, Winchcombe Farm, Briff Lane, Bucklebury, Reading.
Haffenden, P. S., PhD, 36 The Parkway, Bassett, Southampton.
Haigh, C. A., BA, PhD, Dept of History, The University, Manchester M13 9PL.
Haight, Mrs M. Jackson, PhD, 8 Chemin des Clochettes, Geneva, Switzerland.
Haines, Professor R. M., MA, MLitt, DPhil, FSA, Dalhousie University, Halifax, N.S., Canada.
Hair, P. E. H, MA, DPhil, The School of History, The University, P.O. Box 147, Liverpool L69 3BX.
Halcrow, Miss E. M., MA, BLitt, Achimota School, Achimota, P.B.11, Ghana, West Africa.
Hale, Professor, J. R., MA, FSA, University College, Gower Street, London WC1E 6BT.
Haley, Professor K. H. D., MA, BLitt, 15 Haugh Lane, Sheffield 11.
Hall, Professor A. R., MA, PhD, 23 Chiswick Staithe, London W4 3TP.
Hall, Professor B., MA, PhD, FSA, St John's College, Cambridge CB2 1TP.
Hall, Professor D. G. E., MA, DLit, 4 Chiltern Road, Hitchin, Herts.
Hallam, Professor H. E., MA, PhD, University of Western Australia, Nedlands 6009, Western Australia.
Haller, Professor W., PhD, Rte 2, Southbridge, Holland, Mass. 01550, U.S.A.
Hamer, Professor D., MA, DPhil, History Dept, Victoria University of Wellington, P.O. Box 196, Wellington, New Zealand.
Hamilton, B., BA, PhD, The University, Nottingham NG7 2RD.
Hammersley, G. F., BA, PhD, University of Edinburgh, William Robertson Building, George Square, Edinburgh EH8 9JY.
Hampson, Professor N., MA, Ddel'U, 305 Hull Road, York YO1 3LB.
Hand, Professor G. J., MA, DPhil, Instituto Universitario Europeo, Badia Fiesolana, 50016 San Domenico di Fiesole, Firenze, Italy.
Hanham, H. J., MA, PhD, The Dean, School of Humanities and Social Science, Massachusetts Institute of Technology, Cambridge, Mass. 02139, USA.
Hanke, Professor L. U., PhD, University of Massachusetts, Amherst, Mass. 01002, U.S.A.
Harding, A., MA, BLitt, 3 Tantallon Place, Edinburgh EH9 1NY.
Harding, F. J. W., MA, BLitt, FSA, Brynrhos, 187 Mayals Road, Swansea SA3 5HQ.
Harding, H. W., BA, LLD, 39 Annunciation Street, Sliema, Malta.
Hargreaves, Professor J. D., MA, 146 Hamilton Place, Aberdeen.
Hargreaves-Mawdsley, Professor W. N., MA, DPhil, FSA, The University, Brandon, Manitoba, Canada.
Harkness, Professor D. W., MA, PhD, Dept of Irish History, The Queen's University, Belfast BT7 1NN.
Harman, Rev. L. W., 20 Brooksby Street, London N1.
Harris, Mrs J. F., BA, PhD, Dept of Social Science and Administration, London School of Economics, London WC2.
Harris, Professor J. R., MA, PhD, The University, P.O. Box 363, Birmingham B15 2TT.
Harrison, B. H., MA, DPhil, Corpus Christi College, Oxford OX1 4JF.
Harrison, C. J., BA, PhD, The University, Keele, Staffs. ST5 5BG.
Harrison, Professor Royden, MA, DPhil, 4 Wilton Place, Sheffield S10 2BT.
Harriss, G. L., MA, DPhil, Magdalen College, Oxford.

Hart, C. J. R., MA, MB, DLitt, Goldthorns, Stilton, Peterborough, Northants PE7 3RH.
Hart, Mrs J. M., MA, St Anne's College, Oxford.
Harte, N. B., BSc(Econ), University College, Gower Street, London WCIE 6BT.
Hartwell, R. M., MA, DPhil, Nuffield College, Oxford OX1 1NF.
Harvey, Miss B. F., MA, BLitt, Somerville College, Oxford OX2 6HD.
Harvey, Margaret M., MA, DPhil, St Aidan's College, Durham DH1 3LJ.
Harvey, P. D. A., MA, DPhil, FSA, 9 Glen Eyre Close, Bassett, Southampton SO2 3GB.
Harvey, Sally P. J., MA, PhD, St Hilda's College, Oxford.
Haskell, Professor F. J., MA, FBA, Trinity College, Oxford.
Haskins, Professor G. L., AB, LLB, JD, MA, University of Pennsylvania, The Law School, 3400 Chestnut Street, Philadelphia, Pa. 19104 U.S.A.
Haslam, E. B., MA, 1 Lakeside, Beckenham, Kent BR3 2LX.
Hassall, W. O., MA, DPhil, FSA, The Manor House, 26 High Street, Wheatley, Oxford OX9 1XX.
Hastings, Professor Margaret, PhD, 9 Silverwood Terrace, South Hadley, Mass. 01075, U.S.A.
Hatcher, M. J., BSc(Econ), PhD, Eliot College, The University, Canterbury, Kent.
Hattersley, Professor A. F., MA, DLitt, 1 Sanders Road, Pietermaritzburg, S. Africa.
Hatton, Professor Ragnhild M., PhD, London School of Economics, Houghton Street, London WC2.
Havighurst, Professor A. F., MA, PhD, 11 Blake Field, Amherst, Mass. 01002, U.S.A.
Havran, Professor M. J., MA, PhD, Corcoran Dept of History, Randall Hall, University of Virginia, Charlottesville, Va. 22903, U.S.A.
Hay, Professor D., MA, DLitt, FBA, Dept of History, The University, Edinburgh EH8 9JY.
Hayes, P. M., MA, PhD, Keble College, Oxford OX1 3PG.
Hazlehurst, G. C. L., BA, DPhil, FRSL, Inst. of Advanced Studies, R.S.S.S., Australian National University, Box 4, P.O. Canberra, ACT, 2600 Australia.
Headlam-Morley, Miss A., BLitt, MA, 29 St Mary's Road, Wimbledon, London SW19.
Hearder, Professor H., PhD, University College, Cathays Park, Cardiff.
Hembry, Mrs. P. M., PhD, Pleasant Cottage, Crockerton, Warminster, Wilts. BA12 8AJ.
Hemleben, S. J., MA, DPhil, (address unknown).
Henderson, A. J., AM, PhD, 247 North Webster, Jacksonville, Ill. 62650, U.S.A.
Hendy, M. F., MA, The Barber Institute of Fine Arts, The University, Birmingham B15 2TS.
Henning, Professor B. D., PhD, Saybrook College, Yale University, New Haven, Conn., U.S.A.
Hennock, Professor E. P., MA, PhD, School of History, University of Liverpool, Lancs.
Hexter, Professor J. H., PhD, Dept of History, 237 Hall of Graduate Studies, Yale University, New Haven, Conn. 06520, U.S.A.
Highfield, J. R. L., MA, DPhil, Merton College, Oxford.

Hill, Sir (J. W.) Francis, CBE, MA, LLD, LittD, FSA, The Priory, Lincoln.
Hill, J. E. C., MA, DLitt, FBA, The Master's Lodgings, Balliol College, Oxford.
Hill, Professor L. M., MA, PhD, 5066 Berean Lane, Irvine, Calif. 92664, U.S.A.
*Hill, Miss M. C., MA, Crab End, Brevel Terrace, Charlton Kings, Cheltenham, Glos.
*Hill, Professor Rosalind M. T., MA, BLitt, FSA, Westfield College, Hampstead, London NW3.
Hilton, Professor R. H., DPhil, University of Birmingham, P.O. Box 363, Birmingham 15.
Himmelfarb, Professor Gertrude, PhD, The City University of New York Graduate Center, 33 West 42 St, New York, N.Y. 10036.
*Hinsley, Professor F. H., MA, St John's College, Cambridge.
Hockey, The Rev. S. F., BA, Quarr Abbey, Ryde, Isle of Wight PO33 4ES.
*Hodgett, G. A. J., MA, FSA, King's College, Strand, London WC2.
*Hogg, Brigadier O. F. G., CBE, FSA, 1 Hardy Road, Blackheath, London SE3.
HOLDSWORTH, C. J., MA, PhD, FSA (*Hon. Secretary*), West End House, 56 Totteridge Common, London N20 8LZ.
Hollaender, A. E. J., PhD, FSA, 119 Narbonne Avenue, South Side, Clapham Common, London SW4 9LQ.
*Hollingsworth, L. W., PhD, Flat 27, Mayfair, 74 Westcliff Road, Bournemouth BH4 8BG.
Hollis, Patricia, MA, DPhil, 30 Park Lane, Norwich NOR 47F.
Hollister, Professor C. Warren, MA, PhD, University of California, Santa Barbara, Calif. 93106, U.S.A.
Holmes, G. A., MA, PhD, 431 Banbury Road, Oxford.
Holmes, Professor G. S., MA, BLitt, Tatham House, Burton-in-Lonsdale, Carnforth, Lancs.
Holt, Miss A. D., Fasga-na-Coille, Nethy Bridge, Inverness-shire.
Holt, Professor J. C., MA, DPhil, FSA, University of Reading, Whiteknights Park, Reading, Berks RG6 2AA.
Holt, Professor P. M., MA, DLitt, FBA, School of Oriental and African Studies, Malet Street, London WC1E 7HP.
Hook, Mrs Judith, MA, PhD, Dept of History, Taylor Building, King's College, Old Aberdeen AB9 2UB.
Hope, R. S. H., 25 Hengistbury Road, Bournemouth, Hants BH6 4DQ.
Hopkins, E., MA, PhD, 77 Stevens Road, Stourbridge, West Midlands DY9 0XW.
Horwitz, Professor H. G., BA, DPhil, Dept of History, University of Iowa, Iowa City, Iowa 52240, U.S.A.
*Howard, C. H. D., MA, 15 Sunnydale Gardens, London NW7.
*Howard, M. E., MC, MA, FBA, The Homestead, Eastbury, Newbury, Berks.
Howarth, Mrs J. H., MA, St Hilda's College, Oxford.
Howat, G. M. D., MA, BLitt, Old School House, North Moreton, Berks.
Howell, Miss M. E., MA, PhD, 10 Highland Road, Charlton Kings, Cheltenham, Glos. GL53 9LT.
Howell, Professor R., MA, DPhil, Bowdoin College, Brunswick, Maine 04011, U.S.A.
Howells, B. E., MA, Whitehill, Cwm Ann, Lampeter, Dyfed.

Hufton, Professor Olwen H., PhD, 40 Shinfield Road, Reading, Berks.

Hughes, Professor, J. Q., BArch. PhD, Loma Linda, Criccieth, Caerns., North Wales.

Hughes, Miss K. W., MA, PhD, LittD, FSA, Newnham College, Cambridge CB3 9DF.

Hull, F., BA, PhD, Roundwell Cottage, Bearsted, Maidstone, Kent ME14 4EU.

Hulton, P. H., BA, FSA, 46 St Paul's Road, London N1.

HUMPHREYS, Professor R. A., OBE, MA, PhD, DLitt, LittD, DUniv, 13 St Paul's Place, Canonbury, London N1 2QE.

Hunnisett, R. F., MA, DPhil, 54 Longdon Wood, Keston, Kent BR2 6EW.

Hurst, M. C., MA, St John's College, Oxford OX1 3JP.

Hurstfield, Professor J., DLit, 7 Glenilla Road, London NW3.

Hurt, J. S., BA, BSc(Econ), PhD, 66 Oxford Road, Moseley, Birmingham B13 9SQ.

*Hussey, Professor Joan M., MA, BLitt, PhD, FSA, Royal Holloway College, Englefield Green, Surrey.

Hyams, P. R., MA, DPhil, Pembroke College, Oxford.

Hyde, Professor F. E., MA, PhD, Heather Cottage, 41 Village Road, West Kirby, Wirral, Cheshire.

*Hyde, H. Montgomery, MA, DLit, Westwell, Tenterden, Kent.

Hyde, J. K., MA, PhD, The University, Manchester.

Ingham, Professor K., OBE, MA, DPhil, The Woodlands, 94 West Town Lane, Bristol BS4 5DZ.

Ives, E. W., PhD, 214 Myton Road, Warwick.

Jack, Professor R. I., MA, PhD, University of Sydney, Sydney, N.S.W., Australia.

Jack, Mrs Sybil M., MA, BLitt, University of Sydney, N.S.W., Australia.

Jackman, Professor S. W., PhD, FSA, 1065 Deal Street, Victoria, British Columbia, Canada.

Jackson, E. D. C., FSA, (address unknown).

James, M. E., MA, University of Durham, 43–45 North Bailey, Durham.

James, Professor Robert R., MA, FRSL, United Nations, N.Y. 10017, U.S.A.

Jasper, The Very Rev. R. C. D., DD, The Deanery, York YO1 2JD.

Jeffs, R. M., MA, DPhil, 25 Lawson Road, Sheffield S10 5BU.

Jenkins, D., MA, LLM, LittD, Dept of Law, Hugh Owen Building, Univ. College of Wales, Aberystwyth, Cards. SY23 2DB.

Jeremy, D. J., BA, MLitt, 16 Britannia Gardens, Westcliff-on-Sea, Essex SS0 8BN.

Jewell, Miss H. M., MA, PhD, 30 Heathfield, Adel, Leeds LS16 6AQ.

John, Professor A. H., BSc(Econ), PhD, London School of Economics, Houghton Street, London WC2.

John, E., MA, The University, Manchester M13 9PL.

Johnson, D. J., BA, 41 Cranes Park Avenue, Surbiton, Surrey.

Johnson, Professor D. W. J., BA, BLitt, University College, Gower Street, London WC1E 6BT.

*Johnson, J. H., MA, Whitehorns, Cedar Avenue, Chelmsford.

Johnson, W. Branch, FSA, Hope Cottage, 22 Mimram Road, Welwyn, Herts.

Johnston, Professor Edith M., MA, PhD, Dept of History, Macquarie Univ. North Ryde, N.S.W. 2113, Australia.
Johnston, Professor S. H. F., MA, Fronhyfryd, Llanbadarn Road, Aberystwyth.
Jones, D. J. V., BA, PhD, Dept of History, University College of Swansea, Singleton Park, Swansea SA2 8PP.
Jones, Dwyryd W., MA, DPhil, The University, Heslington, York YO1 5DD.
Jones, Revd. F., BA, PhD, 4A Castlemain Avenue, Southbourne, Bournemouth.
Jones, G. A., MA, PhD, Dept of History, Faculty of Letters, University of Reading, Whiteknights, Reading, Berks.
Jones, Professor G. Hilton, PhD, Dept of History, Eastern Ill. University, Charleston, Ill. 61920, U.S.A.
Jones, G. J., The Croft, Litchard Bungalows, Bridgend, Glam.
Jones, H. W., MA, PhD, 32 Leylands Terrace, Bradford BD9 5QR.
Jones, Professor I. G., MA, 12 Laura Place, Aberystwyth, Cards.
Jones, Professor J. R., MA, PhD, School of English and American Studies University Plain, Norwich NOR 30A.
Jones, Professor M. A., MA, DPhil, Dept of History, University College, Gower Street, London WC1E 6BT.
Jones, M. C. E., MA, DPhil, The University, Nottingham NG7 2RD.
Jones, The Rev. Canon O. W., MA, The Vicarage, Builth Wells LD2 3BS, Powys.
Jones, P. J., DPhil, Brasenose College, Oxford.
Jones, Professor W. J., PhD, Dept of History, The University of Alberta, Edmonton T6G 2E1, Canada.
Jordan, Professor P. D., PhD, LLD, 26 Cascade Terrace, Burlington, Iowa 52601, U.S.A.
Judson, Professor Margaret A., PhD, 8 Redcliffe Avenue, Highland Park, N.J. 08904, U.S.A.
Jukes, Rev. H. A. Ll., MA, The Vicarage, Tilney All Saints, nr King's Lynn, Norfolk.

Kamen, H. A. F., MA, DPhil, The University, Warwick, Coventry CV4 7AL.
*Kay, H., MA, 16 Bourton Drive, Poynton, Stockport, Cheshire.
Keeler, Mrs Mary F., PhD, The Center for Parliamentary History, Yale University, Box 1603A, Yale Station, Conn. 06520, U.S.A.
Keen, L. J., 14 Fairfield's Close, Roe Green, London NW7.
Keen, M. H., MA, Balliol College, Oxford.
Kellas, J. G., MA, PhD, Dept of Politics, Glasgow University, Adam Smith Building, Glasgow G12 8RT.
Kellaway, C. W., MA, FSA, 2 Grove Terrace, London NW5.
Kellett, J. R., MA, PhD, Dept of Economic History, University of Glasgow, G12 8QQ.
Kelly, Professor T., MA, PhD, FLA, Oak Apple House, Ambleside Road, Keswick, Cumbria CA12 4DL.
Kemp, Miss B., MA, FSA, St Hugh's College, Oxford.
Kemp, B. R., BA, PhD, 12 Redhatch Drive, Earley, Reading, Berks.
Kemp, The Right Rev. E. W., DD, The Lord Bishop of Chichester, The Palace, Chichester, Sussex PO19 1PY.
Kemp, Lt-Commander P. K., RN, Malcolm's, 51 Market Hill, Maldon, Essex.

Kennedy, J., MA, 14 Poolfield Avenue, Newcastle-under-Lyme, Staffs. ST5 2NL.

Kennedy, P. M., BA, DPhil, University of East Anglia, Norwich NOR 88C.

Kent, Rev. J. H. S., MA, PhD, Dept of Theology, University of Bristol, Senate House, Bristol BS8 1TH.

Kenyon, Professor J. P., PhD, Nicholson Hall, Cottingham, Yorks.

Ker, N. R., MA, DLitt, FBA, FSA, Slievemore, Foss, by Pitlochry, Perthshire.

Kerling, Miss N. J. M., PhD, 26 Upper Park Road, London NW3.

Kerridge, E. W. J., PhD, 6 Llys Tudur, Myddleton Park, Denbigh LL16 4AL.

Ketelbey, Miss C. D. M., MA, 18 Queen's Gardens, St Andrews, Fife.

Khanna, Kahan Chand, MA, PhD, 3-B Mathura Road, New Delhi 14, India.

Kiernan, Professor V. G., MA, University of Edinburgh, William Robertson Building, George Square, Edinburgh EH8 9JY.

*Kimball, Miss E. G., BLitt, PhD, Drake's Corner Road, Princeton, N.J., U.S.A.

King, E. J., MA, PhD, Dept of History, The University, Sheffield S10 2TN.

King, P. D., BA, PhD, Lancaster View, Bailrigg, Lancaster.

Kinsley, Professor J., MA, PhD, DLitt, FBA, University of Nottingham, Nottingham NG7 2RD.

Kirby, D. P., MA, PhD, Manoraven, Llanon, Cards.

Kirby, J. L., MA, FSA, 209 Covington Way, Streatham, London SW16 3BY.

Kitchen, Professor Martin, BA, PhD, Dept of History, Simon Fraser University, Burnaby, B.C., V5A 1S6 Canada.

Klibansky, Professor R., MA, PhD, DPhil, FRSC, 608 Leacock Building, McGill University, P.O. Box 6070, Station A, Montreal, H3C 3G1, Canada.

Knafla, Professor L. A., BA, MA, PhD, Dept of History, University of Calgary, Alberta, Canada.

Knecht, R. J., MA, 22 Warwick New Road, Leamington Spa, Warwickshire.

*Knight, L. Stanley, MA, Little Claregate, 1 The Drive, Malthouse Lane, Tettenhall, Wolverhampton.

Knowles, C. H., PhD, University College, Cathays Park, Cardiff CF1 1XL.

Kochan, L. E., MA, PhD, 237 Woodstock Road, Oxford OX2 7AD.

Koenigsberger, Professor H. G., PhD, Dept of History, Kings College, Strand, London WC2.

Koeppler, Professor H., CBE, DPhil, Wilton Park, Wiston House, Steyning, Sussex.

Korr, C. P., MA, PhD, 4466 West Pine Avenue, St Louis, Mo. 63108, U.S.A.

Koss, Professor S. E., Dept of History, Columbia University, New York, N.Y. 10027, U.S.A.

Kossmann, Professor E. H., DLitt, Rijksuniversiteit te Groningen, Groningen, The Netherlands.

Lambert, M. D., MA, 17 Oakwood Road, Henleaze, Bristol BS9 4NP.

Lamont, W. M., PhD, 9 Bramleys, Kingston, Lewes, Sussex.

Lancaster, Miss J. C., MA, FSA, 43 Craigmair Road, Tulse Hill, London SW2.

Lander, J. R., MA, MLitt, Social Science Centre, University of Western Ontario, London, Ont. N6A 5C2, Canada.
Landes, Professor D. S., PhD, Widener U, Harvard University, Cambridge, Mass, 02138, U.S.A.
Landon, Professor M. de L., MA, PhD, The University, Mississippi 38677 U.S.A.
La Page, J., FSA, Craig Lea, 44 Bank Crest, Baildon, Yorkshire.
Larkin, Professor the Rev. J. F., CSV, PhD, Univ. College, De Paul University, 2323 N. Seminary Avenue, Chicago, Ill. 60614, U.S.A.
Larner, J. P., MA, The University, Glasgow W2.
Latham, Professor R. C., MA, Magdalene College, Cambridge.
Lawrence, Professor C. H., MA, DPhil, Bedford College, Regent's Park, London NW1.
*Laws, Lieut-Colonel M. E. S., OBE, MC, Bank Top Cottage, Seal Chart, Sevenoaks, Kent.
Leddy, J. F., MA, BLitt, DPhil, University of Windsor, Windsor, Ontario, Canada.
Lee, J. M., MA, BLitt, Dept of Politics, Birkbeck College, 7–15 Gresse Street, London W1A 2PA.
Lees, R. McLachlan, MA, Kent Cottage, Harbridge, Ringwood, Hants.
Legge, Professor M. Dominica, MA, DLitt, FBA, 191A Woodstock Road, Oxford OX2 7AB.
Lehmann, Professor J. H., PhD, De Paul University, 25E Jackson Blvd., Chicago, Ill. 60604, U.S.A.
Lehmberg, Professor S. E., PhD, Dept of History, University of Minnesota, Minneapolis, Minn. 55455, U.S.A.
Lenanton, Lady, CBE, MA, FSA, Bride Hall, nr Welwyn, Herts.
Le Patourel, Professor J. H., MA, DPhil, Ddel'U, FBA, Westcote, Hebers Ghyll Drive, Ilkley, West Yorkshire LS29 9QH.
Leslie, Professor R. F., BA, PhD, 23 Grove Park Road, London W4.
Levine, Professor Mortimer, PhD, 529 Woodhaven Drive, Morgantown, West Va. 26505, U.S.A.
Levy, Professor F. J., PhD, University of Washington, Seattle, Wash. 98195, U.S.A.
Lewis, Professor A. R., MA, PhD, History Dept, University of Massachusetts, Amherst, Mass, 01003, U.S.A.
Lewis, Professor B., PhD, FBA, Near Eastern Studies Dept, Jones Hall, The University, Princeton, N.J. 08540, U.S.A.
Lewis, C. W., BA, FSA, University College, Cathays Park, Cardiff.
Lewis, P. S., MA, All Souls College, Oxford.
Lewis, R. A., PhD, University College of North Wales, Bangor.
Leyser, K., MA, Magdalen College, Oxford.
Lhoyd-Owen, Commander J. H., RN, 37 Marlings Park Avenue, Chislehurst, Kent.
Liebeschütz, H., MA, DPhil, Dockenhuden, Mariners Road, Liverpool L23 6SX.
*Lindsay, Mrs H., MA, PhD (address unknown).
Linehan, P. A., MA, PhD, St John's College, Cambridge.
Lipman, V. D., DPhil, FSA, Flat 14, 33 Kensington Court, London W8.
Livermore, Professor H. V., MA, Sandycombe Lodge, Sandycombe Road, St Margarets, Twickenham, Middx.
Lloyd, H. A., BA, DPhil, The University, Cottingham Road, Hull HU6 7RX.

Loades, D. M., MA, PhD, Oatlands, Farnley Mount, Durham.
Lobel, Mrs M. D., BA, FSA, 16 Merton Street, Oxford.
Lockie, D. McN., MA, Chemin de la Panouche, Saint-Anne, Grasse, Alpes Maritimes, France.
Logan, Rev. F. D., MA, MSD, Emmanuel College, 400 The Fenway, Boston, Mass, 02115, U.S.A.
London, Miss Vera C. M., MA, Underholt, Westwood Road, Bidston, Birkenhead, Cheshire.
Longford, The Right Honble The Countess of, MA, DLitt, Bernhurst, Hurst Green, Sussex.
Longley, D. A., BA, King's College, The University, Old Aberdeen AB9 2UB.
Loomie, Rev. A. J., SJ, MA, PhD, Fordham University, New York, N.Y. 10458, U.S.A.
Lourie, Elena, MA, DPhil, (address unknown).
Lovatt, R. W., MA, DPhil, Peterhouse, Cambridge.
Lovell, J. C., BA, PhD, Eliot College, University of Kent, Canterbury.
Lovett, A. W., MA, PhD, Dept of History, University College, Belfield, Dublin 4, Ireland.
Lowe, P. C., BA, PhD, The University, Manchester.
Loyn, Professor H. R., MA, FSA, 196 Fidlas Road, Llanishen, Cardiff.
Lucas, C. R., MA, DPhil, Balliol College, Oxford OX1 3BJ.
Lucas, P. J., MA, PhD, University College, Belfield, Dublin 4, Ireland.
Luft, The Rev. H. M., MA, MLitt, Merchant Taylor's School, Crosby, Liverpool 23.
Lumb, Miss S. V., MA, Torr-Collin House, 106 Ridgway, Wimbledon, London SW19.
Luscombe, Professor D. E., MA, PhD, 129 Prospect Road, Totley Rise, Sheffield S17 4HX.
Luttrell, A. T., MA, DPhil, Dept of History, The Royal University of Malta, Msida, Malta.
Lyman, Professor R. W., PhD, Office of the President, Stanford University, Stanford, Calif. 94305, U.S.A.
Lynch, Professor J., MA, PhD, University College, Gower Street, London WC1E 6BT.
Lyon, Professor Bryce D., PhD, Dept of History, Brown University, Providence, Rhode Island 02912, U.S.A.
Lyons, Professor F. S. L., MA, PhD, LittD, The Provost, Trinity College, Dublin, Ireland.
Lyttelton, The Hon, N. A. O., BA, St Antony's College, Oxford.

Mabbs, A. W., Public Record Office, Chancery Lane, London WC2.
McBriar, Professor A. M., BA, DPhil, FASSA, Dept of History, Monash University, Clayton, Victoria 3168, Australia.
MacCaffrey, Professor W. T., PhD, 745 Hollyoke Center, Harvard University, Cambridge, Mass. 02138, U.S.A.
McCaughan, Professor R. E. M., MA, BArch, DSc., Rowan Bank, Kingsley Green, nr Fernhurst, West Sussex.
McConica, Professor J. K., CSB, MA, DPhil, Pontifical Institute of Medieval Studies, 59 Queen's Park, Toronto, Ont. M5S 2C4, Canada.
McCord, N., PhD, 7 Hatherton Avenue, Cullercoats, North Shields, Northumberland.
McCracken, Professor J. L., MA, PhD, New University of Ulster, Coleraine, Co. Londonderry, N. Ireland.

McCulloch, Professor S. C., MA, PhD, 2121 Windward Lane, Newport Beach, Calif. 92660, U.S.A.

MacCurtain, Margaret B., MA, PhD, Dept of History, University College, Belfield, Dublin 4, Ireland.

McCusker, J. J., PhD, c/o Institute of United States Studies, 31 Tavistock Square, London WC1.

MacDonagh, Professor O., MA, PhD, RSSS, Australian National University, Box 4 GPO, Canberra, ACT, Australia.

MacDonald, Professor D. F., MA, DPhil, Queen's College, Dundee DD1 4HN.

McDonald, Professor T. H., MA, PhD, T. H. McDonald Enterprises, 514 Magnolia Street, Truth or Consequences, New Mexico 87901, U.S.A.

McDowell, Professor R. B., PhD, LittD, Trinity College, Dublin.

Macfarlane, A., MA, DPhil, PhD, King's College, Cambridge CB2 1ST.

Macfarlane, L. J., PhD, FSA, King's College, University of Aberdeen, Aberdeen.

McGrath, P. V., MA, University of Bristol, Bristol.

MacGregor, D. R., BA, FSA, 99 Lonsdale Road, London SW13 9DA.

McGurk, J. J. N., BA, MPhil, Conway House, Stanley Avenue, Birkdale, Southport, Lancs.

McGurk, P. M., PhD, Birkbeck College, Malet Street, London WC1E 7HX.

Machin, G. I. T., MA, DPhil, Dept of Modern History, University of Dundee, DD1 4HN.

MacIntyre, A. D., MA, DPhil, Magdalen College, Oxford.

McKendrick, N., MA, Gonville and Caius College, Cambridge.

McKenna, Professor J. W., MA, PhD, 1444 Old Gulph Road, Villanova, Pa. 19085, U.S.A.

Mackesy, P. G., MA, Pembroke College, Oxford.

McKibbin, R. I., MA, DPhil, St John's College, Oxford OX1 3JP.

*Mackie, Professor J. D., CBE, MC, MA, LLD, FSAScot, 67 Dowanside Road, Glasgow W2.

McKinley, R. A., MA, 42 Boyers Walk, Leicester Forest East, Leics.

Mackintosh, Professor J. P., MA, DLitt, MP, House of Commons, London SW1A 0AA.

McKisack, Professor May, MA, BLitt, FSA, 59 Parktown, Oxford.

Maclagan, M., MA, FSA, Trinity College, Oxford.

Maclean, J. N. M., BLitt, PhD, 21 Drummond Place, Edinburgh EH3 6PN.

MacLeod, R. M., AB, PhD, Dept of History and Social Studies of Science, Physics Bldg, University of Sussex, Falmer, Brighton BN1 9QH.

McManners, Professor J., MA, Christ Church, Oxford OX1 1DP.

MacMichael, N. H., FSA. 2B Little Cloister, Westminster Abbey, SW1.

MacNiocaill, G., PhD, Dept of History, University College, Galway, Ireland.

McNulty, Miss P. A., BA, St George's Hall, Elmhurst Road, Reading.

Macpherson, C. B., BA, MSc(Econ), DSc(Econ), DLitt, LLD, FRSC, University of Toronto, Toronto, M5S 1A1, Canada.

McRoberts, Rt Rev. Monsignor David, STL, DLitt, FSA, 16 Drummond Place, Edinburgh EH3 6PL.

Madariaga, Miss Isabel de, PhD, 27 Southwood Lawn Road, London N6.

Madden, A. F. McC., DPhil, Nuffield College, Oxford.
Maddicott, J. R., MA, DPhil, Exeter College, Oxford.
Maehl, Professor W. H., PhD, College of Liberal Studies, Office of the Dean, 1700 Asp Avenue, Suite 226, Norman, Oklahoma 73037, U.S.A.
Maffei, Professor Domenico, MLL, Dr Jur, Via delle Cerchia 19, 53100 Sienna, Italy.
Magnus-Allcroft, Sir Phillip, Bt. CBE, FRSL, Stokesay Court, Craven Arms, Shropshire SY7 9BD.
Mahoney, Professor T. H. D., AM, PhD, MPA, Massachusetts Institute of Technology, Cambridge, Mass. 02138, U.S.A.
Major, Miss K., MA, BLitt, LittD, FSA, 21 Queensway, Lincoln.
Mallett, M. E., MA, DPhil, University of Warwick, Coventry CV4 7AL.
Malone, Professor J. J., PhD, 110-4th Street N.E., Washington, D.C. 20002, U.S.A.
Mann, Miss J. de L., MA, The Cottage, Bowerhill, Melksham, Wilts.
Manning, B. S., MA, DPhil, The University, Oxford Road, Manchester.
Manning, Professor R. B., PhD, 2848 Coleridge Road, Cleveland Heights, Ohio 44118, U.S.A.
Mansergh, Professor P. N. S., OBE, MA, DPhil, DLitt, LittD, FBA, The Master's Lodge, St John's College, Cambridge.
Marchant, The Rev Canon R. A., PhD, BD, Laxfield Vicarage, Woodbridge, Suffolk IP13 8DT.
Marder, Professor A. J., PhD, University of California, Irvine, Calif. 92664, U.S.A.
Marett, W. P., BSc(Econ), BCom, MA, PhD, 20 Barrington Road, Stoneygate, Leicester LE2 2RA.
Margetts, J., DipEd, DrPhil, 5 Glenluce Road, Liverpool L19 9BX.
Markus, Professor R. A., MA, PhD, The University, Nottingham NG7 2RD.
Marriner, Sheila, MA, PhD, Dept of Economic History, Eleanor Rathbone Building, Myrtle Street, P.O. Box 147, Liverpool L69 3BX.
Marsden, A., BA, PhD, 9 Fort Street, Dundee DD2 1BS.
Marshall, J. D., PhD, 16 Westgate, Morecambe, Lancs.
Marshall, P. J., MA, DPhil, King's College, Strand, London WC2.
Martin, E. W., Crossways, 41 West Avenue, Exeter EX4 4SD.
Martin, Professor G. H., MA, DPhil, 21 Central Avenue, Leicester LE2 1TB.
Marwick, Professor A. J. B., MA, BLitt, Dept of History, The Open University, Walton Hall, Walton, Bletchley, Bucks.
Mason, F. K., 147 London Road, St Albans, Hertfordshire.
Mason, J. F. A., MA, DPhil, FSA, Christ Church, Oxford OX1 1DP.
Mason, T. W., MA, DPhil, St Peter's College, Oxford OX1 2DL.
Mather, F. C., MA, 69 Ethelburt Avenue, Swaythling, Southampton.
Mathias, Professor P., MA, All Souls College, Oxford.
*Mathur-Sherry, Tikait Narain, BA, LLB, 3/193–4 Prem-Nagar, Dayalbagh, Agra-282005 (U.P.), India.
Matthew, D. J. A., MA, DPhil, The University, Durham.
Matthew, H. C. G., MA, DPhil, Christ Church, Oxford.
Mattingly, Professor H. B., MA, Dept of Ancient History, The University, Leeds LS2 9JT.
Mayr-Harting, H. M. R. E., MA, DPhil, St Peter's College, Oxford.
Medlicott, Professor W. N., MA, DLit, DLitt, 2 Cartref, Ellesmere Road, Weybridge, Surrey.

Meller, Miss Helen E., BA, PhD, 2 Copenhagen Court, Denmark Grove, Alexandra Park, Nottingham NG3 4LF.
Meekings, C. A. F., OBE, MA, 42 Chipstead Street, London SW6.
Merson, A. L., MA, The University, Southampton.
Mews, Stuart, PhD, Dept of Religious Studies, Cartmel College, Bailrigg, Lancaster.
Micklewright, F. H. A., MA, 228 South Norwood Hill, London SE25.
Midgley, Miss L. M., MA, 84 Wolverhampton Road, Stafford ST17 4AW.
Miller, E., MA, LittD, 36 Almoners Avenue, Cambridge CB1 4PA.
Miller, E. J., BA, FSA, 37 Aldbourne Road, London W12 0LW.
Miller, Miss H., MA, 32 Abbey Gardens, London NW8.
Milne, A. T., MA, 9 Frank Dixon Close, London SE21 7BD.
Milne, Miss D. J., MA, PhD, King's College, Aberdeen.
Milsom, Professor S. F. C., MA, FBA, 23 Bentley Road, Cambridge CB2 2AW.
Milward, Professor A. S., MA, PhD, Inst. of Science and Technology, University of Manchester, PO Box 88, Sackville Street, Manchester M60 1QD.
Minchinton, Professor W. E., BSc(Econ), The University, Exeter EX4 4PU.
Mingay, Professor G. E., PhD, Mill Field House, Selling Court, Selling, nr Faversham, Kent.
Mitchell, C., MA, BLitt, LittD, Woodhouse Farmhouse, Fyfield, Abingdon, Berks.
Mitchell, L. G., MA, DPhil, University College, Oxford.
Mitchison, Mrs R. M., MA, Great Yew, Ormiston, East Lothian EH35 5NJ.
*Moir, Rev. Prebendary A. L., MA, 55 Mill Street, Hereford.
Momigliano, Professor A. D., DLitt, FBA, University College, Gower Street, London WC1E 6BT.
Moody, Professor T. W., MA, PhD, Trinity College, Dublin, Ireland.
Moore, B. J. S., BA, University of Bristol, 67 Woodland Road, Bristol BS8 1UL.
Moore, Professor Cresap, University of California, Los Angeles, California 90024, U.S.A.
Moore, R. I., MA, The University, Sheffield S10 2TN.
*Moorman, Mrs, MA, 22 Springfield Road, Durham DH1 4LR.
Morey, Rev. Dom R. Adrian, OSB, MA, DPhil, LittD, Benet House, Mount Pleasant, Cambridge CB3 0BL.
Morgan, B. G., BArch, PhD, 29 Gerard Road, Wallasey, Wirral, Merseyside L45 6UQ.
Morgan, K. O., MA, DPhil, The Queen's College, Oxford OX1 4BH.
Morgan, Miss P. E., 1A The Cloisters, Hereford, HR1 2NG.
*Morrell, Professor W. P., MA, DPhil, 20 Bedford Street, St Clair, Dunedin SW1, New Zealand.
Morrill, J. S., MA, DPhil, Selwyn College, Cambridge.
Morris, The Rev. Professor C., MA, 53 Cobbett Road, Bitterne Park, Southampton SO2 4HJ.
Morris, G. C., MA, King's College, Cambridge.
Morris, J. R., BA, PhD, Little Garth, Ashwell, nr Baldock, Herts.
Morris, Professor R. B., PhD, Dept of History, Colombia University in the City of New York, 605 Fayerweather Hall, New York, N.Y. 10552 U.S.A.

Morton, Miss C. E., MA, MLS, FSA, Fairview Cottage, Buckland St. Mary, Chard, Somerset TA20 3LE.
Morton, Professor W. L., MA, BLitt, LLD, DLitt, 10A 300 Roslyn Road, Winnipeg, Manitoba R3L 0H4, Canada.
Mosse, Professor G. L., PhD, Dept of History, The University of Wisconsin, 3211 Humanities Bldg., 435 N. Park Street, Madison, Wis. 53706 U.S.A.
Mosse, Professor W. E. E., MA, PhD, Dawn Cottage, Ashwellthorpe, Norwich, Norfolk.
MULLINS, E. L. C., OBE, MA (*Librarian*), Institute of Historical Research, University of London, Senate House, London WC1E 7HU.
Muntz, Miss I. Hope, FSA, Fairview Cottage, Buckland St. Mary, Chard, Somerset TA20 3LE.
Murray, A., BA, BPhil, The University, Newcastle upon Tyne NE1 7RU.
Murray, Athol L., MA, LLB, PhD, 33 Inverleith Gardens, Edinburgh EH3 5PR.
Myers, Professor A. R., MA, PhD, FSA, Rosemount, 3 Cholmondeley Road, West Kirby, Wirral, Cheshire.
Myres, J. N. L., CBE, MA, LLD, DLitt, DLit, FBA, PSA, The Manor House, Kennington, Oxford OX1 5PH.

Naidis, Professor M., PhD, 10847 Canby Avenue, Northridge, California 91324.
Nath, Dwarka, MBE, 30 Crowther Road, South Norwood, London SE25.
Nef, Professor J. U., PhD, 2726 N Street NW, Washington, DC 20007, U.S.A.
New, Professor J. F. H., Dept of History, Waterloo University, Waterloo, Ontario, Canada.
Newman, A. N., MA, DPhil, 33 Stanley Road, Leicester.
Newsome, D. H., MA, Christ's Hospital, Horsham, Sussex.
Newton, K. C., MA, Moonrakers, Recreation Road, Sible Hedingham, Halstead, Essex CO9 3NL.
Nicholas, Professor H. G., MA, FBA, New College, Oxford.
Nicholl, Professor D., MA, Rosthene, Common Lane, Betley, nr Crewe, Cheshire.
Nicol, Professor D. M., MA, PhD, King's College, London WC2R 2LS.
Noakes, J. D., MA, DPhil, Queen's Bldg, The University, Exeter EX4 4OJ.
Norman, E. R., MA, PhD, Peterhouse, Cambridge.

Obolensky, Prince Dimitri, MA, PhD, FSA, Christ Church, Oxford.
O'Connell, Professor D. P., BA, LLM, PhD, LLD, All Souls College, Oxford.
*Offler, Professor H. S., MA, 28 Old Elvet, Durham.
O'Gorman, F., BA, PhD, The University, Manchester M13 9PL.
Olney, R. J., MA, DPhil, Historical Manuscripts Commission, Quality Court, Chancery Lane, London WC2.
Orme, N. I., MA, DPhil, The University, Exeter EX4 4OJ.
*Orr, J. E., MA, ThD, DPhil, 11451 Berwick Street, Los Angeles, Cal. 90049, U.S.A.
Osborn, Professor J. M., DLitt, LHD, FSA, Beinecke Library, 1603A Yale Station, New Haven, Conn. 06520, U.S.A.
Otway-Ruthven, Professor A. J., MA, PhD, 7 Trinity College, Dublin, Ireland.

Outhwaite, R. B., MA, PhD, Gonville and Caius College, Cambridge CB2 1TA.

Ovendale, R., MA, DPhil, Dept of International Politics, University College of Wales, Aberystwyth SY23 3DB.

Owen, A. E. B., MA, 79 Whitwell Way, Coton, Cambridge CB3 7PW.

Owen, Mrs D. M., MA, FSA, 79 Whitwell Way, Coton, Cambridge CB3 7PW.

Owen, G. D., MA, PhD, Casa Alba, Wray Lane, Reigate, Surrey.

Owen, J. B., BSc, MA, DPhil, Academic Vice-President, St Mary's University, Halifax, Nova Scotia, B3H 3C3, Canada.

*Packard, Professor S. R., PhD, DrJur, DHL, 126 Vernon Street, Northampton, Mass., U.S.A.

Pagden, A. R. D., BA, Merton College, Oxford OX1 4JD.

Palliser, D. M., MA, DPhil, 14 Verstone Croft, Birmingham B31 2QE.

Pallister, Miss Anne, BA, PhD, The University, Reading RG6 2AA.

Palmer, J. J. N., BA, BLitt, PhD, 59 Marlborough Avenue, Hull.

Parker, N. G., MA, PhD, Dept of Modern History, St Salvator's College, The University, St Andrew's, Fife.

Parker, R. A. C., MA, DPhil, The Queen's College, Oxford OX1 4BH.

Parker, The Rev. Dr T. M., MA, DD, FSA, 36 Chalfont Road, Oxford OX2 6TH.

*Parkinson, Professor C. N., MA, PhD, Les Caches House, St Martins, Guernsey, C.I.

Parris, H. W., MA, PhD, 15 Murdoch Road, Wokingham, Berks. RG11 2DG.

Parry, E. Jones, MA, PhD, 3 Sussex Mansions, Old Brompton Road, London SW7.

Parry, Professor J. H., MA, PhD, Pinnacle Road, Harvard, Mass. 01451, U.S.A.

Parsloe, C. G., MA, 1 Leopold Avenue, London SW19 7ET.

Patterson, Professor A. T., MA, The Sele, Stoughton, Chichester, Sussex.

Peake, Rev. F. A., DD, DSLitt, Dept of History, Laurentian University, Sudbury, Ontario, P3E 2C6, Canada.

PEARL, Professor Valerie, MA, DPhil, FSA, (*Literary Director*), 11 Church Row, Hamstead, London NW3 6UT.

Pearn, B. R., OBE, MA, The White House, Beechwood Avenue, Aylmerton, Norfolk NOR 25Y.

Peaston, Rev. A. E., MA, BLitt, The Manse, Dromore, Co. Down, N. Ireland.

Peek, Miss H. E., MA, FSA, FSAScot, Taintona, Moretonhampstead, Newton Abbot, Devon TQ13 8LG.

Pelham, R. A., MA, PhD, Orchard End, Church Road, West Lavington, Midhurst, West Sussex GU29 0EH.

Pennington, D. H., MA, Balliol College, Oxford.

Perkin, Professor H. J., MA, Borwicks, Caton, Lancaster.

Peters, Professor E. M., PhD, Dept of History, University of Pennsylvania, Philadelphia 19174, U.S.A.

Petrie, Sir Charles, Bt, CBE, MA, 190 Coleherne Court, London SW5 0DU.

Petti, Professor A. G. R., MA, DLit, Dept of English, University of Calgary, Alberta, T2N 1N4, Canada.

Philip, I. G., MA, FSA, 28 Portland Road, Oxford.

Philips, Professor Sir Cyril (H.), MA, PhD, DLitt, 3 Winterstoke Gardens, London NW7.

Phillips, Sir Henry (E. I.), CMG, MBE, MA, 34 Ross Court, Putney Hill, London SW15.
Phillips, J. R. S., BA, PhD, Dept of Medieval History, University College, Dublin 4, Ireland.
Pierce, Professor G. O., MA, Dept of History, University College, P.O. Box 95, Cardiff CF1 1XA.
Pitt, H. G., MA, Worcester College, Oxford.
Platt, C. P. S., MA, PhD, FSA, 24 Oakmount Avenue, Highfield, Southampton.
Platt, Professor D. C. St M., MA, DPhil, St Antony's College, Oxford.
Plumb, Professor J. H., PhD, LittD, FBA, FSA, Christ's College, Cambridge.
Pocock, Professor J. G. A., PhD, Johns Hopkins University, Baltimore, Md. 21218, U.S.A.
Poirier, Professor Philip P., PhD, Dept of History, The Ohio State University, 216 North Oval Drive, Columbus, Ohio 43210, U.S.A.
Pole, J. R., MA, PhD, 6 Cavendish Avenue, Cambridge CB1 4US.
Pollard, Professor S., BSc(Econ), PhD, Dept of Economic History, The University, Sheffield S10 2TN.
Polonsky, A. B., BA, DPhil, Dept of International History, London School of Economics, Houghton Street, London WC2A 2AE.
Porter, B. E., BSc(Econ), PhD, Dept of International Politics, University College of Wales, Aberystwyth SY23 3DB.
Porter, H. C., MA, PhD, Selwyn College, Cambridge.
Postan, Professor M. M., MA, FBA, Peterhouse, Cambridge CB2 1RD.
*Potter, Professor G. R., MA, PhD, FSA, Herongate, Derwent Lane, Hathersage, Sheffield S30 1AS.
Powell, W. R., BLitt, MA, FSA, 2 Glanmead, Shenfield Road, Brentwood, Essex.
Powicke, Professor M. R., MA, University of Toronto, Toronto 5, Ont., Canada.
Prest, W. R., MA, DPhil, Dept of History, University of Adelaide, North Terrace, Adelaide, 5001 S. Australia.
Preston, Professor A. W., PhD, Dept of History, Royal Military College of Canada, Kingston, Ontario K7L 2WE, Canada.
*Preston, Professor R. A., MA, PhD, Duke University, Durham, N.C., U.S.A.
Prestwich, J. O., MA, The Queen's College, Oxford.
Prestwich, Mrs M., MA, St Hilda's College, Oxford.
Prestwich, M. C., MA, DPhil, Dept of Medieval History, The University, St Andrews, Fife.
Price, A. W., 19 Bayley Close, Uppingham, Rutland LE15 9TG.
Price, F. D., MA, BLitt, FSA, Keble College, Oxford.
Price, Professor Jacob M., AM, PhD, University of Michigan, Ann Arbor, Michigan 48104, U.S.A.
Pritchard, Professor D. G., PhD, 11 Coedmor, Sketty, Swansea, Glam. SA2 8BQ.
Procter, Miss Evelyn E. S., MA, Little Newland, Eynsham, Oxford.
Pronay, N., BA, School of History, The University, Leeds.
Prothero, I. J., BA, PhD, The University, Manchester M13 9PL.
Pugh, Professor R. B., MA, DLit, FSA, 67 Southwood Park, London N6.
Pugh, T. B., MA, BLitt, 28 Bassett Wood Drive, Southampton SO2 3PS.
Pullan, Professor B. S., MA, PhD, The University, Manchester M13 9PL.

Pulman, M. B., MA, PhD, University of Denver, Colorado 80210, U.S.A.
Pulzer, P. G. J., MA, PhD, Christ Church, Oxford OX1 1DP.

Quinn, Professor D. B., MA, PhD, DLit, DLitt, St Mary's College of Maryland, St Mary's City, Maryland 20686, U.S.A.

Rabb, Professor T. K., MA, PhD, Princeton University, Princeton, N.J. 08540, U.S.A.
Radford, C. A. Ralegh, MA, DLitt, FBA, FSA, Culmcott, Uffculme, Cullompton, Devon EX15 3AT.
*Ramm, Miss A., MA, Somerville College, Oxford OX2 6HD.
*Ramsay, G. D., MA, DPhil, 15 Charlbury Road, Oxford OX2 6UT.
Ramsey, Professor P. H., MA, DPhil, Taylor Building, King's College, Old Aberdeen.
Ranft, Professor B. McL., MA, DPhil, 16 Eliot Vale, London SE3.
Ranger, Professor T., MA, DPhil, The University, Manchester M13 9PL.
Ransome, D. R., MA, PhD, Rill Cottage, Great Bealings, Woodbridge, Suffolk.
Ransome, Miss M. E., MA, 16 Downside Crescent, London NW3.
Rathbone, Eleanor, PhD, Flat 5, 24 Morden Road, London SE3.
Rawley, Professor J. A., PhD, University of Nebraska, Lincoln, Nebraska 68508, U.S.A.
Ray, Professor R. D., BA, BD, PhD, University of Toledo, 2801 W. Bancroft Street, Toledo, Ohio 43606, U.S.A.
Read, Professor D., BLitt, MA, PhD, Darwin College, University of Kent at Canterbury, Kent CT2 7NY.
Reader, W. J., BA, PhD, 67 Wood Vale, London N10 3DL.
Rees, Professor W., MA, DSc, DLitt, FSA, 2 Park Road, Penarth, Glam. CF6 2BD.
Reeves, Miss M. E., MA, PhD, 38 Norham Road, Oxford.
Reid, Professor L. D., MA, PhD, 200 E. Brandon Road, Columbia, Mo. 65201, U.S.A.
Reid, Professor W. S., MA, PhD, University of Guelph, Guelph, Ontario, Canada.
Renold, Miss P., MA, The Coach House, Tile Barn, Woolton Hill, Newbury, Berks. RG15 9UZ.
Reynolds, Miss S. M. G., MA, 26 Lennox Gardens, London SW1.
Richards, Rev. J. M., MA, BLitt, STL, Heythrop College, 11–13 Cavendish Square, London W1M 0AN.
*Richards, R., MA, FSA, Gawsworth Hall, Gawsworth, Macclesfield, Cheshire.
Richardson, K. E., MA, PhD, Lanchester Polytechnic, Priory Street, Coventry.
Richardson, R. C., BA, PhD, Thames Polytechnic, London SE18.
Richardson, Professor W. C., MA, PhD, Louisiana State University, Baton Rouge, Louisiana, U.S.A.
Richter, M., DrPhil, Dept of Medieval History, University College, Dublin 4, Ireland.
Rigold, S. E., MA, FSA, 2 Royal Crescent, London W11.
Riley, P. W. J., BA, PhD, The University, Manchester.
Riley-Smith, J. S. C., MA, PhD, 53 Hartington Grove, Cambridge.
Rimmer, Professor, W. G., MA, PhD, University of New South Wales, P.O. Box 1, Kensington, N.S.W. 2033, Australia.

Ritcheson, Professor C. R., DPhil, 47 Chelsea Square, London SW3 6LH.
Roach, Professor J. P. C., MA, PhD, 1 Park Crescent, Sheffield S10 2DY.
Robbins, Professor Caroline, PhD, 815 The Chetwynd, Rosemont, Pa. 19010, U.S.A.
Robbins, Professor K. G., MA, DPhil, University College of North Wales, Bangor, Gwynedd.
Roberts, J. M., MA, DPhil, Merton College, Oxford OX1 4JD.
Roberts, Professor M., MA, DPhil, FilDr, FBA, 38 Somerset Street, Grahamstown, C.P., South Africa.
Roberts, Brig. M. R., DSO, Swallowfield Park, Swallowfield, Reading, Berks. RG7 1TG.
Roberts, P. R., MA, PhD, FSA, Keynes College, The University of Kent at Canterbury, Kent CT2 7NP.
Roberts, Professor R. C., PhD, 284 Blenheim Road, Columbus, Ohio 43214, U.S.A.
Roberts, Professor R. S., PhD, University of Rhodesia, Salisbury, P.B. 167H, Rhodesia.
*Robinson, Professor Howard, MA, PhD, LLD, 75 Elmwood Place, Oberlin, Ohio, U.S.A.
Robinson, K. E., CBE, MA, DLitt, LLD, The Old Rectory, Church Westcote, Kingham, Oxford OX7 6SF.
Robinson, R. A. H., BA, PhD, School of History, The University, Birmingham B15 2TT.
Robinton, Professor Madeline R., MA, PhD, 210 Columbia Heights, Brooklyn, New York, U.S.A.
*Rodkey, F. S., AM, PhD, 152 Bradley Drive, Santa Cruz, Calif., U.S.A.
Rodney, Professor W., MA, PhD, 14 Royal Roads Military College, Victoria, B.C., Canada.
Roe, F. Gordon, FSA, 19 Vallance Road, London N22 4UD.
Rogers, A., MA, PhD, FSA, The Firs, 227 Plains Road, Mapperley, Nottingham.
Rolo, Professor P. J. V., MA, The University, Keele, Staffordshire.
Roots, Professor I. A., MA, FSA, Dept of History, University of Exeter, Exeter EX4 4QH.
ROPER, J. S., MA (*Hon. Solicitor*), Sixland, 133 Tipton Road, Woodsetton, nr. Dudley, West Midlands.
ROPER, M., MA (*Hon. Treasurer*), Public Record Office, Chancery Lane, London WC2A 1LR.
Rose, M. E., BA, DPhil, Dept of History, The University, Oxford Road, Manchester M13 9PL.
Rose, P. L., MA, D.enHist (Sorbonne), Dept of History, James Cook University, Douglas, Queensland 4811, Australia.
Roseveare, H. G., PhD, King's College, Strand, London WC2.
Roskell, Professor J. S., MA, DPhil, FBA, The University, Manchester M13 9PL.
Roskill, Captain S. W., CBE, DSC, RN(ret), Frostlake Cottage, Malting Lane, Cambridge CB3 9HF.
Ross, C. D., MA, DPhil, Wills Memorial Building, Queen's Road, Bristol.
Rothney, Professor G. O., PhD, University of Manitoba, Winnipeg R3T 2N2, Canada.
Rothrock, Professor G. A., MA, PhD, University of Alberta, Edmonton, Alberta T6A 2E1, Canada.
Rothwell, Professor H., PhD, Hill House, Knapp, Ampfield, nr Romsey, Hants.

*Rowe, Miss B. J. H., MA, BLitt, St Anne's Cottage, Winkton, Christchurch, Hants.

Rowe, W. J., DPhil, 4 Raslin Road, Irby, Wirral, Merseyside L61 3UH.

Rowland, Rev. E. C., 8 Fay Street, Frankston, Victoria 3200, Australia.

Rowse, A. L., MA, DLitt, DCL, FBA, All Souls College, Oxford.

Roy, I., MA, DPhil, Dept of History, King's College, Strand, London WC2.

Roy, Professor R. H., MA, PhD, 2841 Tudor Avenue, Victoria, B.C., Canada.

Royle, E., MA, PhD, Dept of History, The University, Heslington, York YO1 5DD.

Rubens, A., FRICS, FSA, 16 Grosvenor Place, London SW1.

Rubini, D. A., DPhil, Temple University, Philadelphia, Penn., U.S.A.

Rubinstein, Professor N., PhD, Westfield College, Hampstead, London NW3.

Ruddock, Miss A. A., PhD, FSA, Birkbeck College, Malet Street, London WC1.

Rudé, Professor G. F. E., MA, PhD, Sir George Williams University, Montreal 107, P.Q., Canada.

*RUNCIMAN, The Hon. Sir Steven, MA, DPhil, LLD, LittD, DLitt, LitD, DD, DHL, FBA, FSA, Elshiesfields, Lockerbie, Dumfriesshire.

Rupp, Professor the Rev. E. G., MA, DD, FBA, 580 Newmarket Road, Cambridge CB5 8LL.

Russell, C. S. R., MA, Bedford College, London NW1.

Russell, Mrs J. G., MA, DPhil, St Hugh's College, Oxford.

Russell, Professor P. E., MA, 23 Belsyre Court, Woodstock Road, Oxford.

Ryan, A. N., MA, University of Liverpool, 8 Abercromby Square, Liverpool 7.

Rycraft, P., BA, Dept of History, The University, Heslington, York YO1 5DD.

Ryder, A. F. C., MA, D.Phil, Dept of History, Wills Memorial Building, Queen's Road, Bristol BS8 1RJ.

Sachse, Professor W. L., PhD, Dept of History, University of Wisconsin, Madison, Wis. 53706 U.S.A.

Sainty, J. C., MA, 22 Kelso Place, London W8.

*Salmon, Professor E. T., MA, PhD, McMaster University, Hamilton, Ontario, L8S 4L9 Canada.

Salmon, Professor J. H. M., MA, MLitt, DLit, Bryn Mawr College, Bryn Mawr, Pa. 19101, U.S.A.

*Saltman, Professor A., MA, PhD, Bar Ilan University, Ramat Gan, Israel.

Samaha, Professor Joel, PhD, Dept of Criminal Justice Studies, University of Minnesota, Minneapolis, U.S.A.

Sammut, E., LLD, 4 Don Rue Street, Sliema, Malta.

Samuel, E. R., 8 Steynings Way, London N12 7LN.

Sanders, I. J., MA, DPhil, Ceri, St Davids Road, Aberystwyth.

Sanderson, Professor G. N., MA, PhD, Dept of Modern History, Royal Holloway College, Englefield Green, Surrey.

Saville, Professor J., BSc(Econ), Dept of Economic and Social History, The University, Hull HU6 7RX.

Sawyer, Professor P. H., MA, The University, Leeds LS2 9JT.

Sayers, Miss J. E., MA, BLitt, FSA, 17 Sheffield Terrace, Campden Hill, London W8.

Scammell, G. V., MA, Pembroke College, Cambridge.
Scammell, Mrs Jean, MA, Clare Hall, Cambridge.
Scarisbrick, Professor J. J., MA, PhD, 35 Kenilworth Road, Leamington Spa, Warwickshire.
Schenck, H. G., MA, DPhil, Dr Jur, University College, Oxford.
Schoeck, Professor R. J., PhD, Dept of English, University of Colorado, Boulder 80309, U.S.A.
Schofield, A. N. E. D., PhD, LittD, FSA, 15 Westergate, Corfton Road, London W5.
Schofield, R. S., MA, PhD, 27 Trumpington Street, Cambridge CB2 1QA.
Scouloudi, Miss I., MSc(Econ), FSA, 67 Victoria Road, London W8 5RH.
Seaborne, M. V. J., MA, Chester College, Cheyney Road, Chester CH1 4BJ.
Seary, Professor E. R., MA, PhD, LittD, DLitt, FSA, Memorial University of Newfoundland, St John's, Newfoundland, Canada.
Semmel, Professor Bernard, PhD, Dept of History, State University of New York at Stony Brook, Stony Brook, N.Y. 11790, U.S.A.
Serjeant, W. R., BA, 51 Derwent Road, Ipswich IP3 0QR.
Seton-Watson, C. I. W., MC, MA, Oriel College, Oxford.
Seton-Watson, Professor G. H. N., MA, FBA, Dept of Russian History, School of Slavonic Studies, London WC1.
Shackleton, R., MA, DLitt, LittD, FBA, FSA, Brasenose College, Oxford,
Shannon, R. T., MA, PhD, 84 Newmarket Road, Norwich, Norfolk.
Sharp, Mrs M., MA, PhD, 59 Southway, London NW11 6SB.
Shaw, I. P., MA, 3 Oaks Lane, Shirley, Croydon, Surrey CR0 5HP.
*Shaw, R. C., MSc, FRCS, FSA, Orry's Mount, Kirk Bride, nr Ramsey, Isle of Man.
Shead, N. F., MA, BLitt, 16 Burnside Gardens, Clarkston, Glasgow.
Shennan, Professor J. H., PhD, Glenair, Moorside Road, Brookehouse, Caton, nr Lancaster.
Sheppard, F. H. W., MA, PhD, FSA, 55 New Street, Henley-on-Thames, Oxon RG9 2BP.
Sherborne, J. W., MA, 26 Hanbury Road, Bristol BS8 2EP.
Sigsworth, Professor E. M., BA, PhD, The University, Heslington, York.
Simmons, Professor J., MA, The University, Leicester.
Simpson, G. G., MA, PhD, FSA, Taylor Building, King's College, Old Aberdeen AB9 2UB.
Sinar, Miss J. C., MA, 60 Wellington Street, Matlock, Derbyshire DE4 3GS.
Siney, Professor Marion C., MA, PhD, 2676 Mayfield Road, Cleveland Heights, Ohio 44106, U.S.A.
Singhal, Professor D. P., MA, PhD, University of Queensland, St Lucia, Brisbane, Queensland, 4067 Australia.
Skidelsky, Professor R. J. A., BA, PhD, Flat 1, 166 Cromwell Road, London SW5 0TJ.
Skinner, Q. R. D., MA, Christ's College, Cambridge.
Slack, P. A., MA, DPhil, Exeter College, Oxford OX1 3DP.
Slade, C. F., PhD, FSA, 28 Holmes Road, Reading, Berks.
Slater, A. W., MSc(Econ), 146 Castelnau, London SW13 9ET.
Slatter, Miss M. D., MA, 32 Deanfield Road, Botley, Oxford OX2 9DW.
Slavin, Professor A. J., PhD, College of Arts & Letters, University of Louisville, Louisville, Kentucky 40268, U.S.A.
Smail, R. C., MBE, MA, PhD, FSA, Sidney Sussex College, Cambridge.
*Smalley, Miss B., MA, PhD, FBA, 5c Rawlinson Road, Oxford OX2 6UE.

Smith, A. G. R., MA, PhD, 5 Cargil Avenue, Kilmacolm, Renfrewshire.
Smith, A. Hassell, BA, PhD, Inst. of East Anglian Studies, University of East Anglia, University Village, Norwich.
Smith, E. A., MA, Dept of History, Faculty of Letters, The University, Whiteknights, Reading RG6 2AA.
Smith, Professor F. B., MA, PhD, Dept of History, Australian National University, Canberra, A.C.T., 2600 Australia.
Smith, Professor Goldwin A., MA, PhD, DLitt, Wayne State University, Detroit, Michigan 48202, U.S.A.
Smith, J. Beverley, MA, University College, Aberystwyth SY23 2AX.
Smith, Professor L. Baldwin, PhD, Northwestern University, Evanston, Ill. 60201, U.S.A.
Smith, P., MA, DPhil, 81 St. Stephen's Road, West Ealing, London W13 8JA.
Smith, S., BA, PhD, Les Haies, 40 Oatlands Road, Shinfield, Reading, Berks.
Smith, W. J., MA, 5 Gravel Hill, Emmer Green, Reading, Berks.
*Smyth, Rev. Canon C. H. E., MA, 12 Manor Court, Pinehurst, Cambridge.
Snell, L. S., MA, FSA, Newman College, Bartley Green, Birmingham B32 3NT.
Snow, Professor V. F., MA, PhD, Dept of History, Syracuse University, 311 Maxwell Hall, Syracuse, New York 13210, U.S.A.
Snyder, Professor H. L., MA, PhD, 1324 Strong Avenue, Lawrence, Kansas 66044, U.S.A.
Soden, G. I., MA, DD, Buck Brigg, Hanworth, Norfolk.
Somers, Rev. H. J., JCB, MA, PhD, St Francis Xavier University, Antigonish, Nova Scotia, Canada.
Somerville, Sir Robert, KCVO, MA, FSA, 15 Foxes Dale, Blackheath, London SE3.
Sosin, Professor J. M., PhD, History Dept, University of Nebraska, Lincoln, Nebraska 68508, U.S.A.
SOUTHERN, Sir Richard (W.), MA, DLitt, LittD, DLitt, FBA, The President's Lodgings, St John's College, Oxford OX1 3JP.
Southgate, D. G., BA, DPhil, 40 Camphill Road, Broughty Ferry, Dundee, Scotland.
Speck, W. A., MA, DPhil, The University, Newcastle upon Tyne NE1 7RU.
Spencer, B. W., BA, FSA, 6 Carpenters Wood Drive, Chorleywood, Herts.
Spooner, Professor F. C., MA, PhD, The University, 23 Old Elvet, Durham DH1 3HY.
Spufford, Mrs H. Margaret, MA, PhD, 101 Horwood, The University, Keele, Staffs ST5 5BG.
Spufford, P., MA, PhD, The University, Keele, Staffs ST5 5BG.
Stanley, Professor G. F. G., MA, BLitt, DPhil, Library, Mount Allison University, Sackville, New Brunswick, Canada.
Stansky, Professor Peter, PhD, Dept of History, Stanford University, Stanford, Calif. 94305, U.S.A.
Steefel, Lawrence D., MA, PhD, 3420 Heritage Drive, Apt. 117, Edina, Mn. 55435, U.S.A.
Steele, E. D., MA, PhD, The University, Leeds LS2 9JT.
Steer, F. W., MA, DLitt, FSA, 63 Orchard Street, Chichester, Sussex.
Steinberg, J., MA, PhD, Trinity Hall, Cambridge.

Steiner, Mrs Zara S., MA, PhD, New Hall, Cambridge.
Stephens, W. B., MA, PhD, FSA, 37 Batcliffe Drive, Leeds 6.
Steven, Miss M. J. E., PhD, 3 Bonwick Place, Garran, A.C.T. 2605, Australia.
Stevenson, D., BA, PhD, Dept of History, Taylor Building, King's College, Old Aberdeen AB1 0EE.
Stewart, A. T. Q., MA, PhD, Dept of Modern History, The Queen's University, Belfast BT7 1NN.
Stitt, F. B., BA, BLitt, William Salt Library, Stafford.
Stone, E., MA, DPhil, FSA, Keble College, Oxford.
Stone, Professor L., MA, Princeton University, Princeton, N.J., 08540 U.S.A.
*Stones, Professor E. L. G., PhD, FSA, Dept. of History, The University, Glasgow G12 8QH.
Storey, Professor R. L., MA, PhD, 19 Elm Avenue, Beeston, Nottingham NG9 1BU.
Story, Professor G. M., BA, DPhil, 335 Southside Road, St John's, Newfoundland, Canada.
*Stoye, J. W., MA, DPhil, Magdalen College, Oxford.
Street, J., MA, PhD, 6 Thulborn Close, Teversham, Cambridge.
Strong, Mrs F., MA, South Cloister, Eton College, Windsor SL4 6DB.
Strong, R., BA, PhD, FSA, Victoria & Albert Museum, London SW7.
Stuart, C. H., MA, Christ Church, Oxford.
Supple, Professor B. E., BSc(Econ), PhD, Dept of Econ. and Social History, The University of Sussex, Falmer, Brighton BN1 9QQ.
Surman, Rev. C. E., MA, 352 Myton Road, Leamington Spa CV31 3NY.
Sutherland, Professor D. W., DPhil, State University of Iowa, Iowa City, Iowa 52240, U.S.A.
SUTHERLAND, Dame Lucy, DBE, MA, DLitt, LittD, DCL, FBA, 59 Park Town, Oxford.
Sutherland, N. M., MA, PhD, St John's Hall, Bedford College, London NW1.
Swanton, M. J., BA, PhD, FSA, The University, Exeter EX4 4QH.
Swart, Professor K. W., PhD, LittD, University College, Gower Street, London WC1E 6BT.
Sydenham, M. J., PhD, Carleton University, Ottawa 1, Canada.
Sylvester, Professor R. S., PhD, The Yale Edition of the works of St Thomas More, 1986 Yale Station, New Haven, Conn. U.S.A.
Syrett, Professor D., PhD, 46 Hawthorne Terrace, Leonia, N.J. 07605, U.S.A.

Talbot, C. H., PhD, BD, FSA, 47 Hazlewell Road, London SW15.
Tanner, J. I., MA, PhD, Flat One, 57 Drayton Gardens, London SW10 9RU.
Tanner, L. E., CVO, MA, DLitt, FSA, 32 Westminster Mansions, Great Smith Street, Westminster, London SW1P 3BP.
Tarling, Professor P. N., MA, PhD, LittD, University of Auckland, Private Bag, Auckland, New Zealand.
Tarn, Professor J. N., B.Arch, PhD, FRIBA, Dept of Architecture, The University, Abercromby Square, P.O. Box 147, Liverpool.
Taylor, Arnold J., CBE, MA, DLitt, FBA, FSA, Rose Cottage, Lincoln's Hill, Chiddingfold, Surrey GU8 4UN.
Taylor, Professor Arthur J., MA, The University, Leeds LS2 9JT.

Taylor, J., MA, The University, Leeds LS2 9JT.
Taylor, J. W. R., 36 Alexandra Drive, Surbiton, Surrey KT5 9AF.
Taylor, W., MA, PhD, FSAScot, 25 Bingham Terrace, Dundee.
Temple, Nora C., BA, PhD, University College, Cardiff.
Templeman, G., MA, PhD, FSA, 22 Ethelbert Road, Canterbury, Kent.
Thirsk, Mrs I. J., PhD, St Hilda's College, Oxford OX4 1DY.
Thistlethwaite, F., MA, LHD, University of East Anglia, Norwich NR4 7TJ.
Thomas Professor H. S., MA, University of Reading, Reading.
Thomas, Rev. J. A., MA, PhD, 164 Northfield Lane, Brixham, Devon TQ5 8RH.
Thomas, K. V., MA, St John's College, Oxford OX1 3JP.
Thomas, P. D. G., MA, PhD, University College, Aberystwyth SY23 2AU.
Thomas, W. E. S., MA, Christ Church, Oxford OX1 1DP.
Thomis, Professor M. I., MA, PhD, University of Queensland, St Lucia, Brisbane, 4067 Australia.
Thompson, A. F., MA, Wadham College, Oxford OX1 3PN.
Thompson, Mrs D. K. G., MA, School of History, The University, P.O. Box 363, Birmingham B15 2TT.
Thompson, E. P., MA, Warwick University, Coventry.
Thompson, Professor F. M. L., MA, DPhil, Bedford College, Regent's Park, London NW1 4NS.
Thomson, J. A. F., MA, DPhil, The University, Glasgow G12 8QQ.
*Thomson, T. R. F., MA, MD, FSA, Cricklade, Wilts.
Thorne, C., BA, School of European Studies, University of Sussex, Brighton.
Thorne, Professor S. E., MA, LLB, FSA, Harvard Law School, Cambridge 38, Mass., U.S.A.
Thornton, Professor A. P., MA, DPhil, 6 Glen Edyth Drive, Toronto, M4V 2W2, Canada.
Thorpe, Professor Lewis, BA, LèsL, PhD, Ddel'U, FIAL, FSA, FRSA, 26 Parkside, Wollaton Vale, Nottingham NG8 2NN.
*Thrupp, Professor S. L., MA, PhD, University of Michigan, Ann Arbor, Mich., 48104, U.S.A.
Thurlow, The Very Rev. A. G. G., MA, FSA, Dean of Gloucester, The Deanery, Gloucester.
Tibbutt, H. G., FSA, 12 Birchdale Avenue, Kempston, Bedford.
Tomkeieff, Mrs O. G., MA, LLB, 88 Moorside North, Newcastle upon Tyne NE4 9DU.
Toynbee, Miss M. R., MA, PhD, FSA, 22 Park Town, Oxford OX2 6SH.
Trebilcock, R. C., MA, Pembroke College, Cambridge CB2 1RF.
*Trevor-Roper, Professor H. R., MA, FBA, Oriel College, Oxford.
Trickett, Professor The Rev. A. Stanley, MA, PhD, 236 South Lake Drive, Lehigh Acres, Florida, 33936, U.S.A.
Tyacke, N. R. N., MA, DPhil, 1a Spencer Rise, London NW5.
Tyler, P., BLitt, MA, DPhil, University of Western Australia, Nedlands, Western Australia 6009.

Ugawa, Professor K., BA, MA, PhD, 1008 Ikebukuro, 2 Chome, Toshima, Tokyo 171, Japan.
Ullmann, Professor W., MA, LittD, Trinity College, Cambridge.
Underdown, Professor David, MA, BLitt, Dept of History, Brown University, Providence, Rhode Island 02912, U.S.A.

Underhill, C. H., The Lodge, Needwood, Burton-upon-Trent, Staffs DE13 9PQ.
Upton, A. F., MA, 5 West Acres, St Andrews, Fife.
Urry, W. G., PhD, FSA, St Edmund Hall, Oxford.

Vaisey, D. G., MA, FSA, 12 Hernes Road, Oxford.
Vale, M. G. A., MA, DPhil, Dept of History, The University, Heslington, York YO1 5DD.
Van Caenegem, Professor R. C., LLD, PhD, Veurestraat 18, 9821 Afsnee, Belgium.
Van Cleve, Professor T. C., MA, PhD, DLitt, Bowdoin College, Brunswick, Maine, U.S.A.
Vann, Professor Richard T., PhD, Dept of History, Wesleyan University, Middletown, Conn. 06457, U.S.A.
*Varley, Mrs J., MA, FSA, 164 Nettleham Road, Lincoln.
Vaughan, Sir (G.) Edgar, KBE, MA, 27 Birch Grove, West Acton, London W3 9SP.
Veale, Elspeth M., BA, PhD, Goldsmith's College, New Cross, London SE14 6NW.
Véliz, Professor C., BSc, PhD, Dept of Sociology, La Trobe University, Melbourne, Victoria, Australia.
Vessey, D. W. T. C., MA, PhD, 10 Uphill Grove, Mill Hill, London NW7.
Villiers, Lady de, MA, BLitt, 4 Church Street, Beckley, Oxford.
Virgoe, R., BA, PhD, University of East Anglia, School of English and American Studies, Norwich.

Waddell, Professor D. A. G., MA, DPhil, University of Stirling, Stirling FK9 4LA.
*Wagner, Sir Anthony (R.), KCVO, MA, DLitt, FSA, College of Arms, Queen Victoria Street, London EC4.
Waites, B. F., MA, FRGS, 6 Chater Road, Oakham, Rutland LE15 6RY.
Walcott, R., MA, PhD, 14 Whig Street, Dennis, Mass. 02638, U.S.A.
Waley, D. P., MA, PhD, Dept of Manuscripts, British Museum, London WC1B 3DG.
Walford, A. J., MA, PhD, FLA, 45 Parkside Drive, Watford, Herts.
Walker, Rev. Canon D. G., DPhil, FSA, University College, Swansea.
Wallace, Professor W. V., MA, New University of Ulster, Coleraine, N. Ireland.
Wallace-Hadrill, Professor J. M., MA, DLitt, FBA, All Souls College, Oxford OX1 4AL.
Wallis, Miss H. M., MA, DPhil, FSA, 96 Lord's View, St John's Wood Road, London NW8 7HG.
Wallis, P. J., MA, 27 Westfield Drive, Newcastle upon Tyne NE3 4XY.
Walne, P., MA, FSA, County Record Office, County Hall, Hertford.
Walsh, T. J., MA, MB, BCh, PhD, 5 Lower George Street, Wexford, Ireland.
Walters, (W.) E., MA, Burrator, 355 Topsham Road, Exeter.
Walvin, J., BA, MA, DPhil, Dept of History, The University, Heslington, York YO1 5DD.
Wangermann, E., MA, DPhil, The University, Leeds LS2 9JT.
*Ward, Mrs G. A., PhD, FSA, Unsted, 51 Hartswood Road, Brentwood, Essex.
Ward, Professor J. T., MA, PhD, Dept of Economic History, McCance Bldg., 16 Richmond Street, Glasgow C1 1XQ.

Ward, Professor W. R., DPhil, University of Durham, 43 North Bailey, Durham.

*Warmington, Professor E. H., MA, 48 Flower Lane, London NW7.

Warren, Professor W. L., MA, DPhil, FRSL, Dept of Modern History, The Queen's University, Belfast, N. Ireland BT7 1NN.

*Waterhouse, Professor E. K., CBE, MA, AM, FBA, Overshot, Badger Lane, Hinksey Hill, Oxford.

*Waters, Lt-Commander D. W., RN, FSA, Jolyons, Bury, nr Pulborough, West Sussex.

Watkin, Rev. Dom Aelred, OSB, MA, FSA, St. Benet's, Beccles, Suffolk NR34 9NR.

Watson, A. G., MA, BLitt, FSA, University College, Gower Street, London WC1E 6BT.

Watson, D. R., MA, BPhil, Department of Modern History, The University, Dundee.

Watson, J. S., MA, The University, College Gate, North Street, St Andrews, Fife, Scotland.

Watt, Professor D. C., MA, London School of Economics, Houghton Street, London WC2.

Watt, D. E. R., MA, DPhil, Dept of Mediaeval History, St Salvator's College, St Andrews, Fife, Scotland.

Watt, Professor J. A., BA, PhD, Dept of History, The University, Newcastle upon Tyne NE1 7RU.

Webb, J. G., MA, 11 Blount Road, Pembroke Park, Old Portsmouth, Hampshire PO1 2TD.

Webb, Professor R. K., PhD, 3307 Highland Place N.W., Washington DC 20008, U.S.A.

Webster (A.) Bruce, MA, FSA, 5 The Terrace, St Stephens, Canterbury.

Webster, C., MA, DSc, Corpus Christi College, Oxford.

Wedgwood, Dame Veronica, OM, DBE, MA, LittD, DLitt, LLD, 22 St Ann's Terrace, St John's Wood, London NW8.

Weinbaum, Professor M., PhD, 133-33 Sanford Avenue, Flushing, N.Y. 11355, U.S.A.

Weinstock, Miss M. B., MA, 26 Wey View Crescent, Broadway, Weymouth, Dorset.

Wernham, Professor R. B., MA, Marine Cottage, 63 Hill Head Road, Hill Head, Fareham, Hants.

*Weske, Mrs Dorothy B., AM, PhD, Oakwood, Sandy Spring, Maryland 20860, U.S.A.

West, Professor F. J., PhD, Dean of Social Sciences, Deakin University Interim Council, Cnr. Fenwick and Little Ryrie Streets, Geelong, Victoria 3220, Australia.

Weston, Professor Corinne C, PhD, 200 Central Park South, New York, N.Y. 10019, U.S.A.

*Whatmore, Rev. L. E., MA, St Wilfred's, South Road, Hailsham, Sussex.

Whelan, Rev. C. B., OSB, MA, Belmont Abbey, Hereford.

White, Professor B. M. I., MA, DLit, FSA, 3 Upper Duke's Drive, Eastbourne, Sussex BN20 7XT.

White, Rev. B. R., MA, DPhil, 55 St Giles', Regent's Park College, Oxford.

*Whitelock, Professor D., CBE, MA, LittD, FBA, FSA, 30 Thornton Close, Cambridge.

Whiteman, Miss E. A. O., MA, DPhil, FSA, Lady Margaret Hall, Oxford OX2 6QA.

Whiting, J. R. S., MA, DLitt, 15 Lansdown Parade, Cheltenham, Glos.
Wiener, Professor J. H., BA, PhD, City College of New York, Convent Avenue at 138th Street, N.Y. 10031, U.S.A.
Wilkie, Rev. W., MA, PhD, Dept of History, Loras College, Dubuque, Iowa 52001, U.S.A.
Wilkinson, Rev. J. T., MA, DD, Brantwood, 3 The Dingle, Farrington Lane, Knighton, Powys LD7 1LD.
Wilks, Professor M. J., MA, PhD, Dept of History, Birkbeck College, Malet Street, London WC1E 7HX.
*Willan, Professor T. S., MA, DPhil, 3 Raynham Avenue, Didsbury, Manchester M20 0BW.
Williams, D., MA, PhD, DPhil, University of Calgary, Calgary, Alberta T2N 1N4, Canada.
Williams, Sir Edgar (T.), CB, CBE, DSO, MA, Rhodes House, Oxford.
Williams, Professor Glanmor, MA, DLitt, University College, Swansea.
Williams, Glyndwr, BA, PhD, Queen Mary College, Mile End Road, London E1.
Williams, Professor G. A., MA, PhD, University of Wales, Cathay's Park, Cardiff CF1 3NS.
Williams, J. A., BSc(Econ), MA, 44 Pearson Park, Hull, E. Yorks HU5 2TG.
Williams, N. J., MA, DPhil, FSA, 57 Rotherwick Road, London NW11 7DD.
Williams, P. H., MA, DPhil, New College, Oxford OX1 3BN.
*Wilson, Professor A. McC., MA, PhD, 1 Brookside, Norwich, Vermont 05055, U.S.A.
Wilson, Professor C. H., MA, FBA, Jesus College, Cambridge.
Wilson, Professor D. M., MA, FSA, Department of Scandinavian Studies, University College, Gower Street, London WC1E 6BT.
Wilson, H. S., BA, BLitt, The University, Heslington, York YO1 5DD.
Wilson, Professor T., MA, DPhil, Dept of History, University of Adelaide, Adelaide, South Australia.
Winks, Professor R. W. E., MA, PhD, 648 Berkeley College, Yale University, New Haven, Conn. 06520, U.S.A.
Wiswall, Frank L., Jr., BA, JuD, PhD, Meadow Farm, Castine, Maine 04421, U.S.A.
Withrington, D. J., MA, MEd, Centre for Scottish Studies, University of Aberdeen, King's College, Old Aberdeen AB9 2UB.
Wolffe, B. P., MA, BLitt, DPhil, Highview, 19 Rosebarn Avenue, Exeter EX4 6DY.
*Wood, Rev. A. Skevington, PhD, Ridgeway, Curbar, Sheffield S30 1XD.
Wood, Mrs S. M., MA, BLitt, St Hugh's College, Oxford.
Woodfill, Professor W. L., PhD, University of California, Davis, Calif. 95616, U.S.A.
Wood-Legh, Miss K. L., BLitt, PhD, DLitt, 49 Owlstone Road, Cambridge.
Woods, J. A., MA, PhD, The University, Leeds LS2 9JT.
Woolf, Professor S. J., MA, DPhil, University of Essex, Wivenhoe Park, Colchester CO4 3SQ.
Woolrych, Professor A. H., BLitt, MA, Patchetts, Caton, nr Lancaster.
Worden, A. B., MA, DPhil, St Edmund Hall, Oxford OX1 4AR.
Wormald, B. H. G., MA, Peterhouse, Cambridge CB2 1RD.

Wortley, The Rev. J. T., MA, PhD, History Dept, University of Manitoba, Winnipeg, Manitoba R3T 2N2, Canada.

Wright, Professor E., MA, Institute of United States Studies, 31 Tavistock Square, London WC1H 9EZ.

Wright, L. B., PhD, 3702 Leland Street, Chevy Chase, Md. 20015, U.S.A.

Wright, Maurice, MA, PhD, Dept of Government, Dover Street, Manchester M13 9PL.

Wroughton, J. P., MA, 6 Ormonde House, Sion Hill, Bath BA1 2UN.

Yates, W. N., MA, City Record Office, The Guildhall, Portsmouth PO1 2AL.

Yost, Professor John K., MA, STB, PhD, Dept of History, University of Nebraska, Lincoln, Neb. 68508, U.S.A.

Youings, Professor Joyce A., BA, PhD, Dept of History, The University, Exeter EX4 4QH.

Young, Brigadier P., DSO, MC, MA, FSA, Bank House, Ripple, Tewkesbury, Glos. GL20 6EP.

Zagorin, Professor P., PhD, 4927 River Road, Scottsville, N.Y. 14546.

Zeldin, T., MA, DPhil, St Antony's College, Oxford OX2 6JF.

ASSOCIATES OF THE ROYAL HISTORICAL SOCIETY

Addy, J., MA, PhD, 66 Long Lane, Clayton West, Huddersfield HD8 9PR.
Anderson, Miss S. P., MA, BLitt, 17–19 Chilworth Street, London W2 3QU.
Ashton, E., MBE, FRSA, 1 King Henry Street, London N16.

Baird, Rev. E. S., BD, The Vicarage, Harrington, Workington, Cumberland.
Begley, M. R., 119 Tennyson Avenue, King's Lynn, Norfolk.
Bird, E. A., 29 King Edward Avenue, Rainham, Essex RNI3 9RH.
Brake, The Rev. G. Thompson, 19 Bethell Avenue, Ilford, Essex.
Bratt, C., 65 Moreton Road, Upton, Merseyside L49 4NR.
Brigg, Mrs M., The Hollies, Whalley Road, Wilpshire, Blackburn, Lancs.
Brocklesby, R., BA, The Elms, North Eastern Road, Thorne, nr Doncaster, York.
Bryant, W. N., MA, PhD, College of S. Mark and S. John, Derriford Road, Plymouth, Devon.
Bullivant, C. H., FSA, Sedgemoor House, Warden Road, Minehead, Somerset.
Burton, Commander R. C., RN(ret), Great Streele Oasthouse, Framfield, Sussex.
Butler, Mrs M. C., MA, 4 Castle Street, Warkworth, Morpeth, Northumberland NE65 0UW.

Cable, J. A., MA, MEd, 21 Malvern Avenue, Acomb, York YO2 5SF.
Cairns, Mrs W. N., MA, Alderton House, New Ross, Co. Wexford, Ireland.
Carter, F. E. L., CBE, MA, 8 The Leys, London N2 0HE.
Cary, R. H., BA, 23 Bath Road, London W4.
Chandra, Shri Suresh, MA, MPhil, B1/2 Wavelock Road Colony, Lucknow 226001, India.
Condon, Miss M. M., BA, 56 Bernard Shaw House, Knatchbull Road, London NW10.
Cook, Rev. E. T., 116 Westwood Park, London SE23 3QH.
Cooper, Miss J. M., MA, PhD, 203B Woodstock Road, Oxford.
Cox, A. H., Winsley, 11A Bagley Close, West Drayton, Middlesex.
Creighton-Williamson, Lt.-Col D., Foxhills, 25 Salisbury Road, Farnborough, Hants.

d'Alton, I., BA, 5 Cosin Court, Peterhouse, Cambridge.
Davies, Rev. M. R., MA, BD, MTh, The Manse, Nazareth Road, Pontyates, Llanelli, Dyfed.
Davies, P. H., BA, 64 Hill Top, Hampstead Garden Suburb, London NW11.
Dawson, Miss J. E. A., BA, 20 Beadon Road, Bromley, Kent BR2 9AT.
Dawson, Mrs S. L., 5 Sinclair Street, Nkana Kitwe, Zambia.
Dowse, Rev. I. R., Y Caplandy (The Cathedral Chaplain's House), Glanrafon, Bangor, Caerns. LL57 1LH.
Draffen of Newington, George, MBE, KLJ, MA, Meadowside, Balmullo, Leuchars, Fife KY16 0AW.

Drew, J. H., MA, FRSA, 19 Forge Road, Kenilworth, Warwickshire.
Dunster, E. R., BA, LCP, 210A Cressing Road, Braintree, Essex.

Edbury, P. W., MA, PhD, Christ Church, Oxford OX1 1DP.
Emberton, W. J., Firs Lodge, 13 Park Lane, Old Basing, Basingstoke, Hants.
Emsden, N., Strathspey, Lansdown, Bourton-on-the-Water, Cheltenham, Glos. GL54 2AR.

Fairs, G. L., MA, Thornton House, Bean Street, Hay-on-Wye, Hereford HR3 5AN.
Fawcett, Rev. T. J., BD, PhD, 4 The College, Durham DH1 3EH.
Field, C. W., FSG, The Twenty-Sixth House, Robertsbridge, Sussex TN23 5AQ.
Fitzwilliam, B. R., ACP, ThA, Rockhampton Grammar School, Archer Street, Rockhampton, Queensland 4700, Australia.
Fryer, J., BA, Greenfields, Whitemore, Nr. Congleton, Cheshire.

Gardner, W. M., Chequertree, Wittersham, nr Tenterden, Kent.
Granger, E. R., Bluefield, Blofield, Norfolk.
Greatrex, Professor J. G., MA, Dept of History, St Patrick's College, Carleton University, Colonel By Drive, Ottawa K1S 1N4, Canada.
Green, P. L., MA, 9 Faulkner Street, Gate Pa, Tauranga, New Zealand.
Griffiths, Rev. G. Ll., MA, BD, Rhiwlas, 10 Brewis Road, Rhos-on-Sea, Colwyn Bay, Denbighs.

Hall, P. T., Accrington College of Further Education, Sandy Lane, Accrington, Lancs.
Hanawalt, Mrs B. A., MA, PhD, Indiana University, Bloomington, Ind. 47401, U.S.A.
Hannah, L., MA, DPhil, Emmanuel College, Cambridge.
Harding, Rev. F. A. J., BSc(Econ), 74 Beechwood Avenue, St Albans.
Hardy, Rev. P. E., (address unknown).
Hawkes, G. I., BA, MA, PhD, Linden House, St Helens Road, Ormskirk, Lancs.
Hawtin, Miss G., BA, PhD, FSAScot, FRSAI, Honey Cottage, 5 Clifton Road, London SW19 4QX.
Heal, Mrs F., PhD, 13 Friar Road, Brighton, Sussex.
Heath, P., MA, Dept of History, The University, Hull HU6 7RX.
Henderson-Howat, Mrs A. M. D., 7 Lansdown Crescent, Edinburgh EH12 5EQ.
Hoare, E. T., 70 Addison Road, Enfield, Middx.
Hodge, Mrs G., 85 Hadlow Road, Tonbridge, Kent.
Hope, R. B., MA, MEd, PhD, 5 Partis Way, Newbridge Hill, Bath, Avon BA1 3QG.
Hopewell, S., MA, Headmaster's House, Royal Russell School, Addington, Croydon, Surrey CR9 5BX.
Hughes, R. G., 'Hafod', 92 Main Road, Smalley, Derby DE7 6DS.
Hunt, J. W., MA, 123 Park Road, Chiswick, London W4.

Jarvis, L. D., Middlesex Cottage, 86 Mill Road, Stock, Ingatestone, Essex.
Jermy, K. E., MA, 8 Thelwall New Road, Thelwall, Warrington, Cheshire WA4 2JF.

Jerram-Burrows, Mrs L. E., Parkanaur House, 88 Sutton Road, Rochford, Essex.
Johnston, F. R., MA, 20 Russell Street, Eccles, Manchester.
Johnstone, H. F. V., 96 Wimborne Road, Poole, Dorset.
Joy, E. T., MA, BSc(Econ), Cheveley Cottage, 10 High Street, Stetchworth, Newmarket, Suffolk CB8 9JJ.

Keir, Mrs G. I., BA, 25 Catton Gardens, Bath, Avon.
Kennedy, M. J., BA, Dept of Medieval History, The University, Glasgow G12 8QQ.
Kirk, J., MA, PhD, Dept of Scottish History, The University, Glasgow G12 8QQ.
Kitching, C. J., BA, PhD, 35 Brondesbury Villas, London NW6 6AH.
Knight, G. A., BA, 46 Bold Street, Pemberton, Wigan, Lancs. WN5 9E2.
Knowlson, Rev. G. C. V., St John's Vicarage, Knutsford Road, Wilmslow, Cheshire.

Laws, Captain W. F., MLitt, University of Otago, P.O. Box 56, Dunedin, New Zealand.
Lea, R. S., MA, 29 Crestway, London SW15.
Lee, Professor M. duP., PhD, Douglass College, Rutgers University, NB, NJ 08903, U.S.A.
Lewin, Mrs J., MA, 3 Sunnydale Gardens, Mill Hill, London NW7.
Lewis, J. B., MA, CertEd, FRSA, 11 Hawkesbury Road, Buckley, Clwyd CH7 3HR.
Lewis, Professor N. B., MA, PhD, 8 Westcombe Park Road, London SE3 7RB.
Loach, Mrs J., MA, Somerville College, Oxford.

McIntyre, Miss S. C., BA, Lady Margaret Hall, Oxford.
McKenna, Rev. T. J., P.O. Box 1444, Canberra City, A.C.T. 2601, Australia.
McLeod, D. H., BA, PhD, School of History, Warwick University, Coventry CV4 7AL.
Mansfield, Major A. D., 38 Churchfields, West Mersea, Essex.
Mathews, E. F. J., BSc(Econ), PhD, 2 Park Lake Road, Poole, Dorset.
Meatyard, E., BA, DipEd, Guston, Illtyd Avenue, Llantwit Major, Glam. CF6 9TG.
Meek, D. E., MA, Dept of Celtic, The University, Glasgow G12 8QQ.
Metcalf, D. M., MA, DPhil, 40 St. Margaret's Road, Oxford OX2 6LD.
Mills, H. J., BSc, MA, 71 High Street, Billingshurst, West Sussex.
Morgan, D. A. L., MA, Dept of History, University College, Gower Street, London WC1E 6BT.

Nagel, L. C. J., BA, 21 Sussex Mansions, Old Brompton Road, London SW7.
Newman, L. T., LRIC, CEng, MIGasE, AMInstF, 27 Mallow Park, Pinkneys Green, Maidenhead, Berks.
Nicholls, R. E., MA, PhD, Glenholm, Hook Road, Surbiton, Surrey.

Obelkevich, J., MA, (address unknown).
O'Day, Mrs M. R., BA, PhD, 77A St Clements Street, Oxford OX4 1AW.
Oggins, R. S., PhD, c/o Dept of History, State University of New York, Binghamton, N.Y. 13901, U.S.A.

Oldham, C. R., MA, Te Whare, Walkhampton, Yelverton, Devon PL20 6PD.

Parsons, Mrs M. A., MA, (address unknown).
Partridge, Miss F. L., BA, 17 Spencer Gardens, London SW14 7AH.
Pasmore, H. S., MB, BS, 21 Edwardes Square, London W8.
Paton, L. R., 49 Lillian Road, Barnes, London SW13.
Paulson, E., BSc(Econ), 11 Darley Avenue, Darley Dale, Matlock, Derbys.
Perry, E., FSAScot, 28 Forest Street, Hathershaw, Oldham, OL8 3ER.
Pitt, B. W. E., Flat 4, Red Roofs, Bath Road, Taplow, Maidenhead, Berks.
Priestley, E. J., MA, MPhil, 10 Kent Close, Bromborough, Wirral, Cheshire L63 0EF.

Raban, Mrs S. G., MA, PhD, Dept of History, Homerton College, Cambridge.
Rankin, Col. R. H., 3338 Gunston Road, Alexandria, Va. 22302, U.S.A.
Rendall, Miss J., BA, Alcuin College, University of York, Heslington, York YO1 5DD.
Richards, N. F., PhD, 376 Maple Avenue, St Lambert, Prov. of Quebec, Canada J4P 2S2.
Richmond, C. F., DPhil, 59 The Covert, The University, Keele, Staffs.
Rosenfield, M. C., AM, PhD, Box 395, Mattapoisett, Mass. 02739, U.S.A.

Sabben-Clare, E. E., MA, The Shambles, Yarnton Road, Cassington, Oxford OX8 1DY.
Sainsbury, F., 16 Crownfield Avenue, Newbury Park, Ilford, Essex.
Saksena, D. N., First Secretary (Education), Embassy of India, Moscow, U.S.S.R.
Scannura, C. G., 1/11 St. Dominic Street, Valletta, Malta.
Scott, The Rev. A. R., MA, BD, PhD, Ahorey Manse, Portadown, Co. Armagh, N. Ireland.
Seddon, P. R., BA, PhD, The University, Nottingham.
Sellers, J. M., MA, 9 Vere Road, Pietermaritzburg, Natal, S. Africa.
Shores, C. F., ARICS, 40 St Mary's Crescent, Hendon, London NW4 4LH.
Sibley, Major R. J., 8 Ways End, Beech Avenue, Camberley, Surrey.
Sloan, K., BEd, MPhil, 6 Netherwood Close, Fixby, Huddersfield, Yorks.
Smith, Professor C. D., MA, PhD, 416 Hall of Languages, Syracuse University, Syracuse, N.Y. 13210, U.S.A.
Smith, D. M., Borthwick Institute, St Anthony's Hall, York YO1 2PW.
Sorensen, Mrs M. O., MA, 8 Layer Gardens, London W3 9PR.
Sparkes, I. G., FLA, 124 Green Hill, High Wycombe, Bucks.
Stafford, D. S., BA, 10 Highfield Close, Wokingham, Berks.

Taylor, R. T., MA, Dept of Political Theory and Government, University College, Swansea SA2 8PP.
Thewlis, J. C., BA, The University, Hull HU6 7RX.
Thomas, Miss E. J. M., 8 Ravenscroft Road, Northfield End, Henley-on-Thames, Oxon.
Thompson, C. L. F., MA, Orchard House, Stanford Road, Orsett, nr Grays, Essex RM16 3BX.
Thompson, L. F., Orchard House, Stanford Road, Orsett, nr Grays, Essex RM16 3BX.

Thorold, M. B., 20 Silsoe House, Park Village East, London NW1 7QH.
Tomlinson, H. C., BA, Flat 2, 40 Leverton Street, London NW5.
Tracy, J. N., BA, MPhil, Phd, c/o P. Huth Esq, 6 Chaucer Court, 28 New Dover Road, Canterbury, Kent.
Tristram, B., DipEd, (address unknown).
Tuffs, J. E., 360 Monega Road, Manor Park, London E12 6TY.

Waldman, T. G., MA, 131 Riverside Drive, New York, N.Y., 10024, U.S.A.
Wall, Rev. J., BD, MA, PhD, Ashfield, 45 Middleton Lane, Middleton St George, nr Darlington, Co. Durham.
Wallis, K. W., BA, (address unknown).
Warrillow, E. J. D., MBE, FSA, Hill-Cote, Lancaster Road, Newcastle, Staffs.
Wilkinson, F. J., 40 Great James Street, Holborn, London WC1N 3HB.
Williams, A. R., MA, 5 Swanswell Drive, Granley Fields, Cheltenham, Glos.
Williams, C. L. Sinclair, ISO, Derbies, Well Street, East Malling, Kent.
Williams, G., ALA, 5 Monterey Street, Manselton, Swansea SA5 9PF.
Williams, H. (address unknown).
Williams, Miss J. M., MA, PhD, History Dept, University of Waikato, Private Bag, Hamilton, New Zealand.
Williams, P. T., FSAScot, FRSA, FFAS, Bryn Bueno, Whitford Street, Holywell, N. Wales.
Windeatt, M. C., Whitestones, Hillyfields, Winscombe, Somerset.
Windrow, M. C., 40 Zodiac Court, 165 London Road, Croydon, Surrey.
Wood, A. W., 11 Blessington Close, London SE13.
Wood, J. O., BA, MEd, Fountains, Monument Gardens, St Peter Port, Guernsey, C.I.
Woodall, R. D., BA, Bethel, 7 Wynthorpe Road, Horbury, nr Wakefield, Yorks WF4 5BB.
Woodfield, R., BD, MTh, 43 Playfield Crescent, London SE22.
Worsley, Miss A. V., BA, 17 Essex Street, Forest Gate, London E7 0HL.
Wright, J. B., BA, White Shutters, Braunston, Rutland LE15 8QT.

Zerafa, Rev. M. J., St Dominic's Priory, Valletta, Malta.

CORRESPONDING FELLOWS

Andersson, Ingvar, FilDr, Engelbrektsgatan 6A IV, Stockholm, Sweden.

Bischoff, Professor B., DLitt, 8033 Planegg C. München, Ruffini-Allee 27, Germany.

Braudel, Professor F., École Pratique des Hautes Études, 20 rue de la Baume, Paris VIIIe, France.

Cárcano, M. A., Centeno 3131, Buenos Aires, Argentina.

Coolhaas, Professor W. P., Gezichtslaan 71, Bilthoven, Holland.

Creighton, Professor D. G., MA, DLitt, LLD, Princess Street, Brooklin, Ontario, Canada.

Donoso, R., Presidente de la Sociedad Chilena de Historia y Geografía, Casilla, 1386, Santiago, Chile.

Ganshof, Professor F. L., 12 rue Jacques Jordaens, Brussels, Belgium.

Giusti Rt Rev. Mgr M., JCD, Prefect Archivio Segreto Vaticano, Vatican City, Italy.

Glamann, Professor K., DrPhil, Frederiksberg, Bredegade 13A, 2000 Copenhagen, Denmark.

Gwynn, Professor the Rev. A., SJ, MA, DLitt, Milltown Park, Dublin 6, Ireland.

Hancock, Professor Sir Keith, KBE, MA, DLitt, FBA, Australian National University, Box 4, P.O., Canberra, ACT, Australia.

Hanke, Professor L. U., PhD, University of Massachusetts, Amherst, Mass. 01002, U.S.A.

Heimpel, Professor Dr H., DrPhil, Direktor des Max Planck-Instituts für Geschichte, Gottingen, Düstere Eichenweg 28, Germany.

Inalcik, Professor Halil, PhD, The University of Ankara, Ankara, Turkey.

Kuttner, Professor S., MA, JUD, SJD LLD, Institute of Medieval Canon Law, University of California, Berkeley, Calif. 94720, U.S.A.

Langer, Professor W. L., PhD, LLD, DPhil, LHD, LittD, 1 Berkeley Street, Cambridge, Mass. 02138, U.S.A.

Michel, Henri, 32 rue Leningrad, Paris 8e, France.

Morison, Professor S. E., PhD, LittD, Harvard College Library, 417 Cambridge, Mass., U.S.A.

Peña y Cámara, J. M. de la, (address unknown).

Perkins, Professor D., MA, PhD, LLD, University of Rochester, Rochester, N.Y., U.S.A.

Renouvin, Professor P., D-ès-L, 2 Boulevard Saint Germain, Paris, France.

Rodrígues, Professor José Honório, Rua Paul Redfern, 23, ap. C.O.1, Rio de Janeiro, Gb. ZC—37, Brazil.

Sapori, Professor A., Università Commerciale Luigi Bocconi, Via Sabbatini 8, Milan, Italy.

Van Houtte, Professor J. A., PhD, FBA, Termunkveld, Groeneweg 51, Egenhoven, Heverlee, Belgium.

Verlinden, Professor C., PhD, 8 Via Omero (Valle Giulia), Rome, Italy.

Zavala, S., LLD, Montes Urales 310, Mexico 10, D.F., Mexico.

TRANSACTIONS AND PUBLICATIONS
OF THE
ROYAL HISTORICAL SOCIETY

The annual publications of the Society issued to Fellows and Subscribing Libraries include the *Transactions,* supplemented since 1897 by a continuation of the publications of the Camden Society (1838–97) as the *Camden Series,* and since 1937 by a series of *Guides and Handbooks.* The Society also began in 1937 an annual bibliography of *Writings on British History,* for the continuation of which the Institute of Historical Research accepted responsibility in 1965; it publishes, in conjunction with the American Historical Association, a series of *Bibliographies of British History*; and from time to time it issues miscellaneous publications. Additional copies of the *Transactions,* the *Camden Series,* the *Guides and Handbooks,* and the 'Miscellaneous publications' may be obtained by Fellows and Subscribing Libraries at the prices stated below. The series of annual bibliographies of *Writings on British History* and the *Bibliographies of British history* are not included among the volumes issued to subscribers, but may be obtained by them at the special prices stated below by ordering from a bookseller or from the publishers. Associates, while receiving only the *Transactions* in return for their subscription, are entitled to purchase at a reduction of 25 per cent one copy of other volumes issued to Fellows and Subscribing Libraries and one copy of each of the volumes of the *Writings on British history* and the *Bibliographies of British history* at the special price.

Copies of *Transactions, Camden Series* volumes and *Guides and Handbooks* (Main and Supplementary Series) may be obtained from D. S. Brewer Ltd., PO Box 24, Ipswich IP1 1JJ.

In the case of some of these volumes, it is possible for members to buy copies at a special price. Those who wish to take advantage of this arrangement are asked to contact the Society in the first place.

TRANSACTIONS

Additional copies of *Transactions* may be had for £5·00. (Special price to members, who should order from the Society, £3·75.)

Volumes out of print in *Transactions, Old, New and Third Series* may be obtained from Kraus-Thomson Organization Ltd.

Old series, 1872–82. Vols. I to X.
New series, 1884–1906. Vols. I to XX.
Third series, 1907–17. Vols. I to XI.
Fourth series, 1918–50. Vols. I to XXXII.
Fifth series, 1951– . Vols. I to XXVI.

MISCELLANEOUS PUBLICATIONS

Copies of the following, which are still in print, may be ordered from D. S. Brewer Ltd.

Domesday studies. 2 vols. Edited by P. E. Dove. 1886. £3·50. (Vol. 1 out of print.)

The *Domesday monachorum* of Christ Church, Canterbury. 1944. £15.
The Royal Historical Society, 1868–1968. By R. A. Humphreys. 1969. £1·25.

BIBLIOGRAPHIES ISSUED IN CONJUNCTION WITH THE AMERICAN HISTORICAL ASSOCIATION

Copies of the following cannot be supplied by the Society, but may be ordered through a bookseller. If members have difficulty in obtaining volumes at the special price, reference should be made to the Society.

Bibliography of British history: Stuart period, 1603–1714. 2nd ed. Edited by Mary F. Keeler, 1970. Oxford Univ. Press. £5. (Special price, £3·75.)

Supplement to Bibliography of British history: 1714–89. Edited by S. M. Pargellis and D. J. Medley. Edited by A. T. Milne and A. N. Newman, *in preparation.*

Bibliography of British history: 1789–1851. Edited by Lucy M. Brown and Ian R. Christie, *in preparation.*

Bibliography of British history: 1851–1914. Edited by H. J. Hanham. 1976. Oxford Univ. Press. £35. (Special price, £26·25.)

Bibliography of English History to 1485. Based on The Sources and Literature of English History from earliest times by Charles Gross. Revised and expanded by Edgar B. Graves. 1975. Oxford Univ. Press. £20. (Special price, £15.)

ANNUAL BIBLIOGRAPHIES

Copies of the following cannot be supplied by the Society, but may be ordered from a bookseller or the Institute of Historical Research.

Writings on British history, 1901–33 (5 vols. in 7); Vol. 1–3, 1968, Vol. 4, 1969, Vol. 5, 1970. London, Jonathan Cape. Vol. 1, £5·25 (special price £4·58); Vol. 2, £3·15 (special price £2·75); Vol. 3, £5·25 (special price £4·58); Vol. 4 (in two parts), £7·35 (special price £6·40); Vol. 5 (in two parts), £8·40 (special price £7·35).

Writings on British history, 1946–48. Compiled by D. J. Munro. 1973. University of London Inst. of Historical Research, £12·00. (Special price £9·00.)

GUIDES AND HANDBOOKS

Main series

1. Guide to English commercial statistics, 1696–1782. By G. N. Clark, with a catalogue of materials by Barbara M. Franks. 1938. (Out of print.)
2. Handbook of British chronology. Edited by F. M. Powicke and E. B. Fryde, 1st ed. 1939; 2nd ed. 1961. £6·00.
3. Medieval libraries of Great Britain, a list of surviving books. Edited by N. R. Ker, 1st ed. 1941; 2nd ed. 1964. £6·00.
4. Handbook of dates for students of English history. By C. R. Cheney. 1970. £2·50.
5. Guide to the national and provincial directories of England and Wales, excluding London, published before 1856. By Jane E. Norton. 1950. (Out of print.)
6. Handbook of Oriental history. Edited by C. H. Philips. 1963. £2·50.
7. Texts and calendars: an analytical guide to serial publications. Edited by E. L. C. Mullins. 1958. £6·00.

8. Anglo-Saxon charters. An annotated list and bibliography. Edited by P. H. Sawyer. 1968. £6·00.
9. A Centenary Guide to the Publications of the Royal Historical Society, 1868–1968. Edited by A. T. Milne. 1968. £2·50.

Supplementary series

1. A Guide to the Papers of British Cabinet Ministers, 1900–1951. Edited by Cameron Hazlehurst and Christine Woodland. 1974. £3·50.

Provisionally accepted for future publication:

A Handbook of British Currency. Edited by P. Grierson and C. E. Blunt.

Texts and calendars: an analytical guide to serial publications. Supplement, 1957–77. By E. L. C. Mullins.

A Guide to the Local Administrative Units of England and Wales. Edited by F. A. Youngs.

A Register of Parliamentary Poll Books, c. 1700–1870. Edited by E. L. C. Mullins.

A Guide to Bishops' Register to 1640. Edited by D. M. Smith.

A Guide to the Records and Archives of Mass Communications. Edited by Nicholas Pronay.

A Guide to the Maps of the British Isles. Edited by Helen Wallis.

The Reports of the U.S. Strategic Bombing Survey. Edited by Gordon Daniels.

THE CAMDEN SERIES

Camden Series volumes published before the *Fourth Series* are listed in A. T. Milne's *A Centenary Guide to the Publications of the Royal Historical Society.*

Additional copies of volumes in the *Camden Series* may be had for £5·50 (Special price to members £4·15.)

Volumes out of print in the *Camden Old* and *New Series* may be obtained from Johnson Reprint Co. Ltd.

FOURTH SERIES

1. Camden Miscellany, Vol. XXII: 1. Charters of the Earldom of Hereford, 1095–1201. Edited by David Walker. 2. Indentures of Retinue with John of Gaunt, Duke of Lancaster, enrolled in Chancery, 1367–99. Edited by N. B. Lewis. 3. Autobiographical memoir of Joseph Jewell, 1763–1846. Edited by A. W. Slater. 1964.
2. Documents illustrating the rule of Walter de Wenlock, Abbot of Westminster, 1283–1307. Edited by Barbara Harvey. 1965.
3. The early correspondence of Richard Wood, 1831–41. Edited by A. B. Cunningham. 1966. (Out of print.)
4. Letters from the English abbots to the chapter at Cîteaux, 1442–1521. Edited by C. H. Talbot. 1967.
5. Select writings of George Wyatt. Edited by D. M. Loades. 1968.
6. Records of the trial of Walter Langeton. Bishop of Lichfield and Coventry (1307–1312). Edited by Miss A. Beardwood. 1969.
7. Camden Miscellany, Vol. XXIII: 1. The Account Book of John Balsall of Bristol for a trading voyage to Spain, 1480. Edited by T. F. Reddaway and A. A. Ruddock. 2. A parliamentary diary of Queen Anne's reign. Edited by W. A. Speck. 3. Leicester House politics, 1750–60, from the papers of John, second Earl of Egmont. Edited

by A. N. Newman. 4. The Parliamentary diary of Nathaniel Ryder, 1764–67. Edited by P. D. G. Thomas. 1969.

8. Documents illustrating the British Conquest of Manila, 1762–63. Edited by Nicholas P. Cushner. 1971.
9. Camden Miscellany, Vol. XXIV: 1. Documents relating to the Breton succession dispute of 1341. Edited by M. Jones. 2. Documents relating to Anglo-French negotiations, 1439. Edited by C. T. Allmand. 3. John Benet's Chronicle for the years 1400 to 1462. Edited by G. L. Harriss. 1972.
10. Herefordshire Militia Assessments of 1663. Edited by M. A. Faraday. 1972.
11. The early correspondence of Jabez Bunting, 1820–29. Edited by W. R. Ward. 1972.
12. Wentworth Papers, 1597–1628. Edited by J. P. Cooper. 1973.
13. Camden Miscellany, Vol. XXV: 1. The Letters of William, Lord Paget. Edited by Barrett L. Beer and Sybil Jack. 2. The Parliamentary Diary of John Clementson, 1770–1802. Edited by P. D. G. Thomas. 3. J. B. Pentland's Report on Bolivia, 1827. Edited by J. V. Fifer. 1974.
14. Camden Miscellany, Vol. XXVI: 1. Duchy of Lancaster Ordinances, 1483. Edited by Sir Robert Somerville. 2. A Breviat of the Effectes devised for Wales. Edited by P. R. Roberts. 3. Gervase Markham, The Muster-Master. Edited by Charles L. Hamilton. 4. Lawrence Squibb, A Booke of all the Severall Officers of the Court of the Exchequer (1642). Edited by W. H. Brysom. 5. Letters of Henry St John to Charles, Earl of Orrery, 1709–11. Edited by H. T. Dickinson. 1975.
15. Sidney Ironworks Accounts, 1541–73. Edited by D. W. Crossley. 1975.
16. The Account Book of Beaulieu Abbey. Edited by S. F. Hockey. 1975.
17. A calendar of Western Circuit Assize Orders, 1629–48. Edited by J. S. Cockburn. 1976.
18. Four English Political Tracts of the later Middle Ages. Edited by J.-Ph. Genet (*in the press.*)
19. Proceedings of the Short Parliament of 1640. Edited by Esther S. Cope in collaboration with Willson H. Coates (*in preparation.*)

Provisionally accepted for future publication:

Select documents illustrating the internal crisis of 1296–98 in England. Edited by Michael Prestwich.
The *Acta* of Archbishop Hugh of Rouen (1130–64). Edited by T. Waldman.
Cartularies of Reading Abbey. Edited by B. R. Kemp.
The Letter Book of Thomas Bentham, Bishop of Coventry and Lichfield. Edited by M. Rosemary O'Day and J. A. Berlatsky.
Correspondence of Henry Cromwell, 1655–59. Edited by Clyve Jones.
Correspondence of William Camden. Edited by Richard DeMolen.
Heresy Trials in the Diocese of Norwich, 1428–31. Edited by N. P. Tanner.
George Rainsford's *Ritratto d'Ingliterra*, 1556. Edited by Peter S. Donaldson.
Early Paget Correspondence. Edited by C. J. Harrison and A. C. Jones.
The Letters of the Third Viscount Palmerston, 1804–63. Edited by Kenneth Bourne.
The Disputed Regency of the Kingdom of Jerusalem, 1264–66 and 1268. Edited by P.W. Edbury.
Edmund Ludlow's Memoir 1660–74: A Voyce from the Watch Tower. Edited by A. B. Worden.
R. R. Angerstein's English Diary, 1753–55. Edited by Torsten Berg.

STUDIES IN HISTORY

Orders for volumes should be sent, with remittance, to Swift Printers Ltd, 1–7 Albion Place, Britton St, London EC1M 5RE. All editorial enquiries should be addressed to Mrs Janet Godden, 33 Norham Rd, Oxford OX2 6SQ.

1. F. F. Foster, *The Politics of Stability: A Portrait of the Rulers of Elizabethan London*. 1977. (£6·00/$12·00).
2. Rosamond McKitterick, *The Frankish Church and the Carolingian Reform 789–895*. 1977. (£6·25/$12·50).
3. K. D. Brown, *John Burns*. 1977. (£5·85/$11·70).